£30

HUNTERS AND POACHERS

Hunters and Poachers

A Social and Cultural History of
Unlawful Hunting in England,
1485–1640

ROGER B. MANNING

CLARENDON PRESS · OXFORD
1993

Oxford University Press, Walton Street, Oxford OX2 6DP
Oxford New York Toronto
Delhi Bombay Calcutta Madras Karachi
Kuala Lumpur Singapore Hong Kong Tokyo
Nairobi Dar es Salaam Cape Town
Melbourne Auckland Madrid
and associated companies in
Berlin Ibadan

Oxford is a trade mark of Oxford University Press

Published in the United States
by Oxford University Press Inc., New York

British Library Cataloguing in Publication Data
Data available

Library of Congress Cataloging in Publication Data
Manning, Roger B. (Roger Burrow)
Hunters and poachers : a cultural and social history of unlawful
hunting in England, 1485–1840 / Roger B. Manning
p. cm.
Includes bibliographical references (p.   ) and index.
1. Poaching—England—History—16th century. 2. Poaching—
England—History—17th century. 3. England—Social conditions.
4. Poaching—Social aspects—England—History—16th century.
5. Poaching—Social aspects—England—History—17th century.
6. Game-laws—England. I. Title.
Sk36.7.M36 1993 306.4'83—dc20 92–43487
ISBN 0-19-820324-1

1 3 5 7 9 10 8 6 4 2

Printed in Great Britain
on acid-free paper by
Biddles Ltd., Guildford and King's Lynn

For Roger and Charlotte

Acknowledgements

THERE are numerous debts of gratitude which I have incurred in writing this book. Financial assistance to travel to England was provided by grants from the American Council of Learned Societies and the College of Graduate Studies at Cleveland State University. The cost of obtaining the illustrations was assisted by Dr Harry Andrist, Vice Provost and Dean of Graduate Studies at Cleveland State University. Research was carried on in the Public Record Office, Chancery Lane, the British Library, the Institute of Historical Research and the Goldsmiths Library of the University of London, and the Cleveland Public Library, and I wish to thank the archivists and librarians of those institutions. I must also acknowledge the kindness of the editors of the *Journal of Medieval and Renaissance Studies* for permission to reprint as Chapter 2 a revised version of an article which first appeared in that journal in the spring issue of 1992.

Colleagues and friends have helped in many ways. Clifford Davies, Curtis Breight, and James Stephen Taylor have offered helpful comments on various parts of this book and have rendered assistance in many other ways. Barrett Beer, Clayton Roberts, William Robison, and Joseph Biancalana have all patiently endured many hours of discussion and argument and have never failed to offer encouragement. Peter Brandon, Alan Davidson, Louis Barbato, and Donald Ramos have answered queries, offered their expertise, called sources to my attention, and otherwise rendered assistance. My students, both graduate and undergraduate, have sat through hours of tangential discussions about poaching with patience and good humour and have contributed valuable insights. I especially wish to acknowledge the kind assistance of Anne St John-Scott and Steven Miller.

Tony Morris, the history editor of the Clarendon Press, offered me unflagging encouragement, and Hilary Walford performed a heroic task of copy-editing.

Diane Monreal has done countless versions and revisions of this manuscript on the word processor with extraordinary expertise and accuracy. As always, my greatest debt of gratitude is owed to my wife, Anne Brown Manning, who never ceased to encourage me and provide me with the leisure to write this book.

R.B.M.

Cleveland, Ohio
March 1992

Contents

List of Illustrations   viii

List of Maps   ix

Abbreviations   x

Note on the Text   xii

Introduction   1
1. The Cultural and Social Context of Hunting   4
2. Poaching as a Symbolic Substitute for War   35
3. The Game Laws   57
4. The Purlieu Men and the Ancient Constitution   83
5. Hunting and Land Use in Sylvan Societies   109
6. The Structure of Poaching   135
7. Poachers and Keepers   171
8. Hunting, Poaching, and Social Privilege   196
9. Conclusion: The Persistence of the Deer-Hunting Culture   232

Glossary   237

Bibliography   239

Index   249

List of Illustrations

between pages 148 and 149

1. Facsimile of the monumental brass of James Gray, keeper of Hunsdon Park
2. Various hunting scenes in the deer park at Welbeck, Nottinghamshire
3. Nonsuch Palace, Surrey, a royal hunting lodge
4. A huntsman presenting the fewments of a hart to Queen Elizabeth
5. King James I about to take assay of a buck
6. Henry, Prince of Wales, and John, Lord Harington of Exton
7. James I and the royal court dining *al fresco* in a forest
8. A mounted hunter and two keepers of hounds with their brachs
9. Hawking scene and hunting scene

List of Maps

5.1. English forests, 1500–1640   118
5.2. English chases, 1500–1640   119

Abbreviations

Place of publication is London unless otherwise indicated.

Acts PC	*Acts of the Privy Council of England*, ed. J. R. Dasent, 46 vols. (1890–1964)
AG	attorney-general
BIHR	*Bulletin of the Institute of Historical Research*
BL	British Library
C	Chancery
Cal. CR	*Calendar of the Close Rolls*, The Deputy Keeper of the Records (1900–)
Cal. PR	*Calendar of the Patent Rolls*, The Deputy Keeper of the Records (1906–)
Cal. SP	*Calendar of State Papers*
CJCP	chief justice, Court of Common Pleas
CJKB	chief justice, Court of King's Bench
DL	Duchy of Lancaster
DNB	*Dictionary of National Biography*, 22 vols. (Oxford, 1917–)
E	Exchequer
EETS	Early English Text Society
EHR	*English Historical Review*
GEC	G[eorge] E[dward] C[ockayne] *The Complete Peerage*, ed. V. Gibbs, 13 vols. (new edn.; 1910– 40)
HMC	Historical Manuscripts Commission
JCP	justice, Court of Common Pleas
JKB	justice, Court of King's Bench
JP	justice of the peace
KR	King's Remembrancer
L&P Hen. VIII	*Letters and Papers, Foreign and Domestic, of the Reign of Henry VIII*, ed. J. S. Brewer *et al.*, 23 vols. in 38 parts (1862– 1932)
MP	member of Parliament
OED	*Oxford English Dictionary*
P&P	*Past and Present*
PRO	Public Record Office
SP	State Papers

SR	*Statutes of the Realm*, 9 vols. (1810–22)
STAC	Court of Star Chamber
VCH	*Victoria History of the Counties of England*, ed. W. Page *et al.* (1900–)

Note on the Text

In quotations from contemporary manuscripts and literary sources, spelling, punctuation, and capitalization have been modernized. However, the original spelling has been retained in the citation of titles of contemporary printed books in footnotes and bibliography.

For all dates, the year is given in new style; the day and the month in old style.

Introduction

POACHING, or unlawful hunting, is a persistent phenomenon which dates back at least to the age when the Anglo-Norman feudal monarchs attempted to assert exclusive hunting rights over vast game reserves designated as royal forests and chases. Although the forest law and the Game Laws now interest few besides historians, modern governmental and private efforts to protect wildlife, preserve endangered species, and maintain an ecological balance of flora and fauna in national parks and wildlife reserves continue to be resisted by organized gangs of poachers. As long as the market exists, a way will be found to supply the demand for venison, game, fish, ivory, animal hides, and furs which are purveyed to restaurants and shops whose patrons do not wish to know where and how such commodities were obtained. Poachers in any age are a desperate breed, and do not hesitate to resort to violence in their encounters with gamekeepers and wardens. In the period between the end of the Wars of the Roses and the beginning of the Civil Wars in mid-seventeenth-century England, many poachers positively relished such combat.

This book is intended as a companion volume to my *Village Revolts*,[1] and is concerned with many of the same issues: conflicting uses of land, the awakening of political consciousness and the forms of violence which often accompany such protests, the modes of political discourse, and the role of the Court of Star Chamber in the development of the modern law of public order. Although this study touches upon a variety of offences against the Game Laws, I shall focus primarily upon unlawful hunting in the early modern sense of the term, i.e. the unlawful taking of deer. The logistics of deer-stealing, as it came to be called in the early seventeenth century, usually required the co-operative efforts of a number of men, and one seldom encounters the solitary hunter. Because bands of hunters almost invariably numbered three or more persons, such hunting offences were technically riots. Under the Tudor monarchs, the Court of Star Chamber extended its jurisdiction over poaching affrays along with other misdemeanours which constituted breaches of public order. During the reigns of James I and Charles I, both of whom were keen hunters, the Court of Star Chamber saw a veritable flood of prosecutions for hunting offences, but the emphasis in these prosecutions shifted from the preservation of public order to the enhancement of the royal game prerogative and the preservation of

[1] R. B. Manning, *Village Revolts: Social Protest and Popular Disturbances in England, 1509–1640* (Oxford, 1988).

aristocratic hunting privileges. The statutory definition of hunting qualifications had become more socially restrictive under James I, but the memory persisted of times when the right to hunt had been more broadly conceived. This resulted in increased defiance of the Game Laws, which even lawyers admitted were based upon legal absurdities.

It is a most difficult task to give a precise definition of what constituted unlawful hunting in the view of the Court of Star Chamber and the other courts which enforced the Game Laws and what remained of the forest law during this period. Much of this book is devoted to answering that question. For the moment, suffice it to say that deer-stealing and other forms of poaching included a wide range of activities which the Game Laws rarely hint at. As one might expect, unlawful hunting comprehended the actions of legally unqualified persons who hunted to supply the commercial market with venison and game. It also masked the violent feuds of rival aristocratic and gentry factions and provided an alternative to duelling. 'General huntings' were a kind of skimmington by which the local community attempted to punish possessors of game reserves for outrageous behaviour. In the early Stuart period, crown officials sometimes attempted to depict hunting by possessors of hunting franchises as illegal, but the behaviour of such hunters was usually based upon principle, and derived from what they perceived as prescriptive rights or old royal grants of free warren. Finally, freeholders who held land within purlieus, or disafforested areas formerly belonging to the royal forests, believed that they were defending the Ancient Constitution when they resisted the efforts of the early Stuart monarchs to deny them hunting rights, which the Tudor kings had respected. Thus, there are many dimensions to the phenomenon of poaching.

At the beginning of the Tudor period, the Game Act of 1485[2] referred to the existence of outlaw bands in the Weald of Kent, Sussex, and Surrey who lived by poaching and other crimes and who were remarkably successful at escaping capture. Organized gangs of poachers continued to exist throughout the Tudor and early Stuart period, and were often led by gentlemen and not infrequently protected by corrupt magistrates. As was the case with anti-enclosure riots and the other species of agrarian protest studied in *Village Revolts*, a seemingly disproportionate number of these disturbances reveal the manipulative influence of the gentry and peerage and especially the restlessness of the small gentry, those non-armigerous gentlemen who were typically tenants on large manors and were sometimes the younger sons or brothers of the greater gentry.[3] Taken together with the poaching wars which

---

[2] 1 Hen. VII, c. 7; *SR* ii. 505.

[3] In a detailed case study of poaching in Sussex between 1500 and 1640 which I am preparing for publication, of the 444 persons who were indicted for unlawful hunting at the assizes or against whom complaints were made in the Courts of Star Chamber and Duchy of Lancaster Chamber, 3 per cent were peers, armigerous gentry, and heirs of the same, while 12

were carried on by rival factions of the peerage and gentry, this raises the question of how effective the Tudor monarchs had been in curbing the lawlessness and feudal disorders which were the legacy of the fourteenth and fifteenth centuries. Might it not be possible to view the poaching wars between rival factions of the nobility and gentry as an evolving form of bastard feudalism in its final phase?[4] My case studies of poaching wars which originated in aristocratic feuds such as the Berkeley–Dudley and Talbot–Stanhope feuds reveal that these quarrels were related to factionalism at court, which was to a certain extent encouraged by Queen Elizabeth, and suggest that she and her Privy Council did little to compose these feuds.[5]

Attempts to classify unlawful hunting as crime or as social or political protest present difficulties. In varying degrees, the many kinds of behaviour covered by the term poaching involved aspects of all of these phenomena. Of the many motives and influences which can be assigned as causes of deer-stealing, perhaps the most pervasive is what may be called, for lack of a better phrase, the deer-hunting culture. The bravado associated with hunting behaviour was displayed by gentlemen and commoners alike. I shall argue that unlawful deer-hunting was a symbolic substitute for war; following the suppression of the mid-Tudor rebellions between 1536 and 1569, it may also have become a symbolic enactment of rebellion. The symbolism and imagery of hunting are very rich; there was a covert language spoken in these rituals which was widely understood by contemporaries, although it is not always easy for us to decipher. By the same token, royal hunts, which involved the apparently gratuitous slaughter of relatively tame deer bred and confined within parks, may have dramatized the dreadful punishments which awaited traitors and rebels. Certainly, the violence which characterized many aspects of aristocratic and gentry behaviour during the Tudor and early Stuart period furnished an evil example for the commonalty, retarded the development of a civil society, and passed on an unfortunate legacy to subsequent generations.

per cent were parochial gentry and younger sons of armigerous gentry. Taken together, peers and gentry cannot have exceeded 5 per cent of the total population, yet they accounted for 15 per cent of all poachers. When one looks at the leadership of poaching gangs, the role of the gentry is even more disproportionate: Sussex poachers were led or procured by peers and armigerous gentry in 33 per cent of all cases and by small gentry in 15 per cent of the instances of unlawful hunting.

[4] J. G. Bellamy, *Bastard Feudalism and the Law* (Portland, Ore., 1989), 123–5, demonstrates the persistence of bastard feudalism well into the reign of James I. Although Professor Bellamy made use of Star Chamber records, he does not recognize that Tudor and early Stuart poaching was a form of bastard feudalism.

[5] Concerning Elizabeth's reputation for promoting factionalism, see 'The State of England Anno Dom. 1600 by Thomas Wilson', ed. F. J. Fisher, in *Camden Miscellany XVI* (Camden Soc., 3rd ser., 52; 1936), 42–3.

I

The Cultural and Social Context of Hunting

> The aristocrat has always done the same things: raced horses or com-
> peted in physical exercises, gathered at parties, the feature of which is
> usually dancing, and engaged in conversation. But before any of those,
> and consistently more important than all of them has been . . . hunting. . . .
> This is what kings and nobles have preferred to do: they have hunted.
>
> J. Ortega y Gasset, *Meditations on Hunting*, trans. H .B. Westcott
> (New York, 1972), 31

> There is a saying among hunters that he cannot be a gentlemen which
> loveth not hawking and hunting, which I have heard old woodmen
> well allow as an approved sentence among them. The like saying is that
> he cannot be a gentleman which loveth not a dog.
>
> Anon., *The Institucion of a Gentleman* (1568), fo. 45^{r-v}

T HE aristocracy of late-medieval England were above all else a warrior class.
They were bred to fight and were a dangerous and restless group when
they were not engaged in war against the king's enemies. During interludes
of peace, or when weak monarchs sat upon the throne, these magnates and
their followers repeatedly plunged England, Wales, and Ireland into civil
wars and rebellions. Between the end of the Wars of the Roses and the Civil
Wars of the seventeenth century there were fewer opportunities for military
adventure. Since aristocratic rebellion proved too dangerous for family and
household under the Tudors, peers and gentlemen sought other pursuits
which could demonstrate courage and an instant readiness to take risks and
thus perpetuate their status as a military élite.

The Tudor gentry, to a considerable extent, imitated the aristocracy in
their choice of pursuits and values. Among the pastimes which were deemed
worthy of a gentleman were duelling, hunting, gambling, and racing.[1]
Foremost among these was hunting, which in the sixteenth and early
seventeenth centuries invariably meant pursuing deer on horseback. Hunting
was a preparation for war and was regarded as the best means, short of
actual combat, for testing valour and developing the skills necessary for
mounted combat. Hunting was less dangerous than duelling, which, in any
case, was forbidden by the laws of England; it was also praised by medieval

---

[1] V. G. Kiernan, *The Duel in European History: Honour and the Reign of Aristocracy*
(Oxford, 1988), 152 *et passim.* Gambling and racing became more prevalent after the Restoration.

and Renaissance writers of manuals of courtesy for would-be gentlemen.[2] In order to buttress their shared aristocratic values, peers and gentlemen turned to the past for symbols and pursuits which reasserted the martial values of a feudal society. The fact that relatively few of them were actually descended from feudal lords and knights made them grasp all the more desperately for pursuits, such as jousting and hunting, which conferred badges of honour and chivalry.

1.1. Hunting and Aristocratic Culture

The aristocratic fondness for hunting spawned a complex deer-hunting culture in Tudor and early Stuart England. Hunting fulfilled many cultural functions: it initiated adolescents into the manly world of the hunter, assisted in the assimilation of socially inferior persons who aspired to enter the landed gentry, and, as an imitation of war, it inculcated courage and loyalty and other values which attached to the code of honour of the English aristocracy and gentry. The appeal of hunting was, of course, much more universal. But late-medieval and early modern English game legislation became more and more socially restrictive. Many persons who were excluded from hunting by the property qualifications of the parliamentary Game Laws, or who resented what came to be defined as an aristocratic privilege, continued to hunt in defiance of the law.

As the opportunities for martial glory diminished, many assuaged their boredom with an obsessive preoccupation with hunting. John Aubrey understood this when he asserted that hunting reached its peak during the peaceful years of the early Stuart period prior to 1640 and declined thereafter because the aristocrats of earlier periods of English history were busy with real wars and had less leisure.[3] By the beginning of the seventeenth century a reaction against hunting as a waste of time may be detected among the more cerebral of English aristocrats and gentlemen. This may have owed something to the bad example of the king, for James I daily demonstrated how an obsessive love of hunting could lead a king to neglect his duties.

Hunting was not only valued for its encouragement of martial skills and virtues. Contemporary writers commended it as a recreation suitable for kings and their ministers who needed a diversion from affairs of state. It was an indispensable part of hospitality in the great household, and gifts of venison and invitations to the hunt bestowed upon guests, neighbours, and friends allowed a magnate to display his power and largesse. The logistics of a large hunt could be complicated, and, in addition to the numerous

[2] Ramón Lull, *The Book of the Ordre of Chivalry*, trans. William Caxton, ed. A. T. P. Byles (EETS 168; 1926; repr. 1971), 31; Niccolò Machiavelli, *The Prince*, trans. T. G. Bergin (New York, 1947), ch. xiv; Count Baldassare Castiglione, *The Book of the Courtier*, trans. Sir Thomas Hoby (1561; repr. 1900 and New York, 1967), 54.

[3] John Aubrey, *Aubrey's Natural History of Wiltshire* (1847; repr. New York, 1969), 60.

household servants who saw to the dogs and horses and provided the catering for hunting picnics *al fresco*, tenants were also called upon to act as beaters and share in the excitement and feasting. In a sense they were tasting forbidden delights, but many lords thought that this bought the tenants' goodwill cheaply and probably reduced the temptation to poach. The more formal hunting parties of peers and magnates visibly and symbolically reinforced the social hierarchy, just as a royal hunt, which was a kind of masque performed out of doors, dramatized the power and mystique of monarchy.[4]

Most writers of books of etiquette and manuals of education of the English Renaissance agreed with their continental mentors that the type of hunting most fit for the young gentleman demanded good horsemanship, skill at arms, and physical exertion. Equestrian skills had not only a military utility; the well-mounted gentleman 'importeth a majesty and dread to inferior persons, beholding him above the common course of other men'.[5] Since wild boar were rare in England, the only beasts of the chase considered to be appropriate for hunting were the red and fallow deer. Sir Thomas Elyot thought that they should be pursued in spacious forests employing only enough hounds to dislodge the deer from their cover and to direct the hunters in their pursuit. Elyot thought that the deer should be dispatched with weapons suitable for a nobleman—the javelin, sword, or dagger—although Roger Ascham praised the longbow and allowed the use of guns.[6]

Sir Thomas Cockayne and Henry Peacham thought that hunting inured young gentlemen to the hardships of war and taught them to endure extremes of heat and cold, hunger and thirst, as well as 'continual travail [and] painful labour'.[7] Henry Peacham said that, when Lord Leonard Grey, 'our English Achilles', was lord deputy of Ireland in the late 1530s, he would cause his sons to be awakened at midnight 'in the depth of winter' and taken hunting until the next morning, when, cold and wet, they came home to a breakfast of coarse brown bread and mouldy cheese: 'and in this manner the Spartans and the Laconians dieted and brought up their children 'till they came unto man's estate'. From the point of view of military men the purpose of hunting was 'not to purchase venison and purvey for the belly, but to harden their bodies by labour against the enemy'.[8]

This represented the idealized style of hunting in the Tudor period. While

---

[4] M. Keen, *Chivalry* (New Haven, Conn., 1984), 154.

[5] Sir Thomas Elyot, *The Boke Named the Gouernour*, ed. H. H. S. Croft, 2 vols. (1883; repr. New York, 1967), i. 181–2, 186.

[6] Ibid. i. 192–6; Roger Ascham, *The Scholemaster* (1570), in *English Works*, ed. W. A. Wright (Cambridge, 1904; repr. 1970), 217; id., *Toxophilus* (1545), in ibid., pp. xii–xvii.

[7] Sir Thomas Cockayne, *A Short Treatise of Hunting, 1591*, ed. W. R. Halliday (Oxford, 1932), sig. A3ʳ⁻ᵛ; see also G[ervase] M[arkham], *Country Contentments, or the Husbandmans Recreations*, in *A Way to Wealth* (1631), 3–4.

[8] Henry Peacham, *The Compleat Gentleman* (1622; repr. Amsterdam, 1968), 182–3.

a few purists continued to do it that way, most gentlemen—both courtiers and countrymen—practised a more leisurely kind of hunting in enclosed deer parks, employing numerous dogs and hounds, beaters and nets, to trap the deer for the final slaughter. The reality was very different from the ideal. Even that old soldier, Sir Thomas Cockayne—knighted at Tournai and author of the widely read *A Short Treatise on Hunting*—valued his three Derbyshire parks, imparked and impaled in his own lifetime, nearly as much as his military exploits.[9] Only a privileged few enjoyed access to deer in the royal forests, and most gentlemen had to content themselves with finding sport in parks and warrens. Deer had become sufficiently scarce in late-medieval and early modern England for it to be deemed necessary to breed and protect deer in parks established by royal licence, enclosed with pales, hedges, and ditches, and protected by gamekeepers. Hunting had become quite artificial.

There were recognized seasons for hunting the red and fallow deer, and so country gentlemen, if they were law abiding, turned to other field sports when they could not hunt. Coursing hares with whippets or small greyhounds was quite widespread. Sir Thomas Elyot thought that it provided 'right good solace for men that be studious, or them to whom nature hath not given personage or courage apt for the wars', and was also suitable for ladies who feared that excessive exposure to the elements might spoil their complexions.[10] Gentlemen were unlikely to fish, except during Lent, when eating flesh without licence continued to be forbidden and no better sport was available; carp, pike, bream, roach, and eel were the favoured kinds of fish in inland waters. At other times of the year, outside the hunting seasons, hawking was the preferred sport. In autumn sparhawks were used to kill quail, partridge, and rail; in winter they were sent after herons, pheasant, ducks, and teal. During the summer gentlemen diverted themselves by catching larks with nets and hobbies, a small species of falcon.[11]

King James I was never fond of falconry: 'I condemn it not, but I must praise it more sparingly, because it neither resembleth the wars so neare as hunting doth in making a man hearty and skilful in riding on all grounds.'[12] Sir Thomas Elyot sneered that hawking 'measurably used' at least gave a man a 'good appetite to his supper' and kept him away from 'other daliance and disports dishonest'.[13] James Cleland, after plagiarizing James I's opinion of falconry, said that the sport was so widely pursued among the aristocracy

[9] *VCH War.*, ii. 292, quoting the inscription on Cockayne's funeral monument in Ashbourne Church, Derbyshire. He died in 1536.

[10] Elyot, *The Gouernour*, i. 195.

[11] *The English Courtier and Country-gentleman* (1586), in *Inedited Tracts*, ed. W. C. Hazlitt (1868; repr. New York, 1968), 54–5.

[12] James VI and I, *Basilikon Doron* (1599), in *The Political Works of James I*, ed. C. H. McIlwain (Cambridge, Mass., 1918), 49; [Sir Anthony Weldon], 'The Court and Character of King James', in [Sir Walter Scott (ed.)], *Secret History of the Court of James the First*, 2 vols. (Edinburgh, 1811), i. 413.   [13] Elyot, *The Gouernour*, i. 202.

that it would not do for a young man to be ignorant of the appropriate terminology and skills of hawking.[14]

There were essentially two ways by which a young gentleman from a parvenu family could gain acceptance among the gentry of the neighbourhood. He could hunt and show himself a 'thruster', or he could refuse to allow his gentility and courage to be questioned and defend his honour by accepting challenges to duels.[15] Hunting was undoubtedly the preferable alternative, since the survival rates were higher. Consequently, young hunters felt themselves constantly challenged to display feats of daring which risked life and limb. For those young men whose families did not possess hunting privileges, the act of hunting outside the law, at night, with weapons, and in the face of gamekeepers, must have further satisfied their compulsive need to prove their masculinity and martial valour.

Arthur Wilson, the historian and dramatist, in his more mature years remembered the risks which he felt obliged to take as a young man in the service of the third earl of Essex during the second decade of the seventeenth century. While hunting one summer in Cheshire, he dismounted and pursued a stag on foot with drawn sword, when he chanced to fall on a slippery bank. It was reported to him that another in the hunting party had said that Wilson had 'fallen for fear'. When challenged, that person denied that he had spoken the words and refused to accept a challenge to fight. Resuming the chase, Wilson became 'more violent in pursuit of the stag' in order to recover his reputation. Once again he encountered the same stag, which had been cornered by the dogs; the stag broke through the dogs and gored the side of Wilson's horse. Wilson jumped off his horse, stole behind the stag, and hamstrung the beast's rear legs with his sword. He then mounted the stag's back and cut its throat. When his companions rode up, they blamed his 'rashness for running such a hazard'.[16]

John Nichols recounts a similar exploit by John Selwyn, the underkeeper of the royal park of Oatlands, Surrey. Once, when Queen Elizabeth was present for a stag-hunt, Selwyn leapt from his horse to the back of a stag in the midst of the chase and, with sword drawn, 'guided him towards the Queen, and coming near her presence, plunged it into his throat, so that the animal fell dead at her feet'.[17]

Hunting had always been a dangerous sport—even when hunters did not

---

[14] James Cleland, *The Institution of a Young Noble Man*, ed. M. Molyneux, 2 vols. (Oxford, 1607; repr. New York, 1948), i. 223–4.

[15] Kiernan, *The Duel in European History*, 15; B. A. Hanawalt, 'Men's Games, King's Deer: Poaching in Medieval England', *Journal of Medieval and Renaissance Studies*, 18. 2 (1988), 175–93.

[16] 'The Life of Mr. Arthur Wilson the Historian . . . Written by Himself', in Francis Peck, *Desiderata Curiosa*, 2 vols. (1732–5), ii. xii. 10–11; *DNB, sub* Arthur Wilson (1595–1652).

[17] John Nichols, *The Progresses and Public Processions of Queen Elizabeth*, 3 vols. (1823; repr. New York, 1966), iii. 599 n. Selwyn's effigy, on his monumental brass in the parish church of Walton-on-Thames, depicts him in the act of plunging the sword into the stag's throat (reproduced in Francis Grose, *Antiquarian Repertory*, 4 vols. (2nd edn.; 1807–1809), i. 1).

take unnecessary risks. Two of William the Conqueror's sons died in hunting accidents in the New Forest: his heir, William Rufus, was killed by a stray arrow, while Richard had died earlier after colliding with a tree when in hot pursuit of a stag.[18] Arthur Wilson experienced a near-fatal accident in Needwood Forest when his horse carried him under a large branch of an oak; he saved himself by leaping backwards and landing on his feet. 'To name the saw pits and deep ditches where my horses have been forced out with ropes, and the dangerous falls I have escaped in the violence of hunting would be too tedious,' he recalled.[19]

In England or abroad, royalty and nobility took it for granted that hospitality included opportunities for hunting. Elizabeth and James I invariably entertained foreign princes with carefully staged hunts; moreover, the latter could always be counted upon to accompany his guests. James never tired of the chase, and the authors of masques performed at his court understood that they were to include frequent references to hunting.[20] On his visit to England in 1592, the duke of Württemberg was much impressed by the red deer which inhabited the numerous parks surrounding Windsor Castle and was flattered that Elizabeth had taken care to provide such 'glorious and royal sport'.[21] Hearing that the earl of Shrewsbury, president of the Council in the North, was travelling through Westmorland towards York in 1555, Lord Wharton apologized because his house at Wharton was not in a fit state of readiness to receive him, but promised the earl entertainment in the deer park there none the less.[22] When Sir William More of Loseley came to Nonsuch to discuss the Surrey County musters with John, Lord Lumley, they managed to find time to try out More's 'best dogs' against Lumley's 'slothful deer'.[23]

Perhaps because he and his ancestors were the hereditary bow-bearers of the New Forest and would therefore have been entitled to fee-deer as part of their remuneration, Sir John Oglander of Nunwell, Isle of Wight, did not possess a deer park. However, he did regard it as consistent with good hospitality to provide other kinds of field sports for the entertainment of his friends when they visited him. Under the heading 'sport for thy friends', he wrote in his commonplace book that one should 'have a small warren for some rabbits when thy friends come; build a pigeon-house and fit up a fishpond or two that at all times thou mayest have provisions at hand; [and] pale in a place to breed or keep pheasants and partridges'.[24]

[18] C. W. Hollister, 'The Strange Death of William Rufus', in *Monarchy, Magnates and Institutions in the Anglo-Norman World* (1986), 75.

[19] 'Life of Arthur Wilson', II. xii. 10–11.

[20] e.g. *Pan's Anniversary* by Ben Jonson (1624), printed in John Nichols, *The Progresses of King James I*, 4 vols. (1828; repr. New York, 1967), iv. 987–93.

[21] *England as Seen by Foreigners*, ed. W. B. Rye (1865; repr. New York, 1967), 14–15.

[22] Edmund Lodge, *Illustrations of British History*, 3 vols. (1838), i. 251.

[23] *The Loseley Manuscripts*, ed. A. J. Kempe (1835), 161.

[24] *A Royalist's Notebook: The Commonplace Book of Sir John Oglander Kt. of Nunwell*, ed. F. Banford (1936), 68, 203.

Andrew Boorde, a widely travelled physician, thought that nowhere in Christendom was venison valued so highly as in England.[25] Gifts of venison served as symbols of royal magnanimity towards ambassadors and subjects alike. In 1639 Charles I made gifts of fat venison to various foreign ambassadors and agents: three bucks each to the representatives of the king of France, the Venetian Republic, and the United Provinces, and two each to the Spanish, Swedish, Florentine, Bohemian, and Saxon ambassadors. In addition twenty-two bucks and one stag were given to the lord mayor, recorder, and aldermen of London. These animals mostly came from the royal parks of London and the Home Counties.[26] With regard to gifts of venison, the largesse of Thomas, second duke of Norfolk, was probably not much inferior to that of the king. The accounts of Richard Chamber, the ducal keeper of Framlingham Park in Suffolk, reveal that Norfolk annually bestowed upon neighbours, tenants, and servants between one hundred and two hundred deer from that park alone. Gifts of venison solidified alliances and traditional relationships. Withholding such gifts, as Norfolk did in the case of the duke of Suffolk, underscored enmities which probably stretched back to the fifteenth century when the Brandons and Howards were on different sides at the Battle of Bosworth.[27] Whereas the more traditional kind of magnanimity practised by Norfolk maintained existing influence, the largesse of Henry, eleventh Lord Berkeley, was intended to secure it. Berkeley sent yearly gifts of red and fallow venison, salmon, and lamprey pies together with gifts of money, John Smyth of Nibley tells us, to the queen, 'to judges, great officers of state, privy councillors and lawyers whereof he reaped honour and profit a hundred times more than the charge'. Such favours bestowed on the lord keeper obtained Berkeley's entry into the Gloucestershire commission of the peace, for which duties, through lack of education, he 'was not fitted'.[28] The marquis of Winchester was entitled to a 'fee-buck of the season' from the Great Park of Nonsuch Palace by virtue of his office of lord treasurer; in 1556 he chose to assign this perquisite to his 'friends, the wardens of the Company of Grocers'.[29] Gentlemen imitated peers in exchanging gifts of venison and game to reinforce social ties and obligations. Richard Cholmeley recorded receiving a 'fat doe' from

[25] Andrew Boorde, *A Dyetary of Helth*, ed. F. J. Furnivall (EETS, extra ser., 10; 1870), 274–5.

[26] J. C. Cox, *The Royal Forests of England* (1905), 77–99; C. R. Young, *The Royal Forests of Medieval England* (Philadelphia, 1979), 115.

[27] D. MacCulloch, *Suffolk and the Tudors: Politics and Religion in an English County, 1500–1600* (Oxford, 1986), 56–7; Accounts of Richard Chamber, printed in E. P. Shirley, *Some Account of English Deer Parks* (1867), 29–33, and J. Cummins, *The Hound and the Hawk: The Art of Medieval Hunting* (1988), 260–5.

[28] John Smyth of Nibley, *The Berkeley Manuscripts*, ed. Sir John Maclean, 3 vols. (Gloucester, 1883, 1885), ii. 287.

[29] *Loseley Manuscripts*, ed. Kempe, 160. See also *John Isham, Mercer and Merchant Adventurer: Two Account Books of a London Merchant in the Reign of Elizabeth I*, ed. G. D. Ramsay (Northants. Rec. Soc., 21; Northampton, 1962), p. lxxi.

a neighbour in 1614, and the next year he sent 'ten couple of rabbits' to the earl of Shrewsbury. Wardens of the London livery companies demonstrated their wealth and worshipful status by bestowing gifts of venison pasties upon even their most humble inferiors and neighbours.[30]

Hunting was widely praised as a pastime that afforded both 'pleasure and profit'.[31] Venison was considered a great delicacy among all social groups which had the means to procure it, and no feast would have been considered complete without roast venison and baked venison pasty.[32] Physicians disapproved of eating venison because it 'doth engender choleric and humours' and because the 'beast doth live in fear'. This was Boorde's professional advice, but he confessed to a fondness for venison, 'physic notwithstanding'. The by-products of venison were economically and medicinally significant: from the heart, pizzle, and horn, apothecaries derived antidotes for plague and poison, remedies for the bloody flux, cholic, gout, and the pains of childbirth in women. Deerskin was made into all sorts of clothing—most notably the buff coats worn by soldiers and hunters.[33] A well-organized, although illegal market for venison and game was taking shape by about 1600, and provided an additional incentive for poaching.

Most writers agreed that hunting afforded good exercise, although some, not wishing to be thought guilty of advocating unlawful hunting, felt constrained to point out that hunting was for great men only, 'not peasants'.[34] There were almost no lengths to which an aristocratic hunter would not go to justify his sport, but Edward, second duke of York, surely deserves to be remembered for arguing 'that hunting causeth a man to eschew the seven deadly sins'.[35]

Despite the many attempts by medieval and early modern kings and parliaments to declare that hunting was a royal and aristocratic privilege, the sport continued to appeal to popular tastes as well. To counter this

---

[30] *Memorandum Book of Richard Cholmeley of Brandsby, 1602–1623* (N. Yorks. Rec. Office, 44; Northallerton, 1988), 64, 102; I. W. Archer, *The Pursuit of Stability: Social Relations in Elizabethan London* (Cambridge, 1991), 117; see also T. B. Lennard, 'Extracts from the Household Account Book of Herstmonceux Castle, from August 1643 to December 1649', *Sussex Arch. Coll.*, 47 (1905), 125.

[31] M[arkham], *Country Contentments*, 30; *Royalist's Notebook*, ed. Banford, 204.

[32] *Early English Meals and Manners*, ed. F. J. Furnivall (EETS, os, 32; 1868), 48–9, 101, 165.

[33] Boorde, *A Dyetary of Helth*, ed. Furnivall, 274–5; *Maison Rustique, or the Countrie Farme*, trans. Richard Surflet (1600), 851; M[arkham], *Country Contentments*, 30.

[34] Boorde, *A Dyetary of Helth*, ed. Furnivall, 275; John Lyly, *Midas* (1592), iv. iii. 4, in *The Complete Works of John Lyly*, ed. R. W. Bond, 3 vols. (1902; repr. Oxford, 1967), iii. 147; M. P. Tilley, *A Collection of the Proverbs in England in the Sixteenth and Seventeenth Centuries* (Ann Arbor, Mich., 1950; repr. 1966), 334.

[35] *The Master of Game, by Edward Second Duke of York*, ed. W. A. and F. Baillie-Grohman (New York, 1909), 4–5. The belief that hunting helps a man avoid sin seems to derive from Gaston III, Comte de Foix, *La Chasse de Gaston Phebus, Comte de Foix*, ed. J. Lavalle (Paris, 1854), prologue (see M. Thiébaux, 'The Medieval Chase', *Speculum*, 42 (Apr. 1967), 260–1). It must have been on an occasion when he was not hunting that the Comte de Foix killed his own son in a fit of anger.

tendency, the writers of numerous manuals sought to make the technical terms connected with hunting and hawking as arcane as possible. From the time of William Twici, huntsman to King Edward II and the author of the first English hunting manual, the writers of such treatises taught that gentlefolk were distinguished, not only by the methods, skills, and etiquette which they employed in hunting, but also by the language which they used in their discourse. It was important to know how many points the antlers of a hart (male red deer) or a buck (male fallow deer) possessed and by what terms the hart was properly called in his first or third or fifth years (a 'calf', a 'spayard', and a 'stag').[36] *The Boke of St Albans*, the first hunting treatise printed in England, was reprinted twenty-two times between 1486 and 1615. It also provided instruction in the technical terms of heraldry. Gervase Markham's *Country Contentments* went through fourteen editions during the seventeenth century.[37]

When the Jesuits John Gerard and Robert Southwell were sent on the English mission during the reign of Elizabeth, the severe penalties enacted against seminary priests obliged them to travel in disguise. Their ability to employ the correct technical language when discussing hunting and hawking was an important part of their cover and provided an entrée into gentry circles as they went from one country house to another. Gerard recalled that, whenever he was in unfamiliar territory, he detoured around towns and villages to avoid detection; if he encountered country folk, he allayed their suspicions by pretending to look for a lost falcon. It seemed a perfectly natural thing for an English gentleman to do, since members of his class rarely undertook a journey unaccompanied by dogs or hawks.[38]

Henry, eleventh Lord Berkeley, and his retinue of 150 liveried servants usually required eight days to make the journey between London and Berkeley Castle in Gloucestershire, because he often stopped for a bit of hawking along the way. His steward, John Smyth of Nibley, disapproved of his mode of living, because Berkeley's annual expenditures were £1,500 in excess of his income and for many years he was obliged to sell off considerable parts of his patrimony to meet the deficit. Most of this sum was spent on hunting and hawking, to which he devoted three-quarters of every year.

---

[36] *The Art of Hunting, by William Twici*, ed. A. Dryden (Northampton, 1908), ll. 17–129, 164–71; *The Boke of Saint Albans by Dame Juliana Berners* (1586), facsimile edn. by W. Blades (1905), unpaginated.

[37] Cockayne, *A Short Treatise of Hunting*, ed. Halliday, pp. vi–vii; R. Hands, *English Hawking and Hunting in the Boke of St Albans* (Oxford, 1975), p. v. Ben Jonson satirizes 'the hawking and hunting languages' in *Every Man in His Humour*, i. i. Another widely used manual was *The Noble Arte of Venerie or Hunting* (1575; repr. Oxford, 1908), which was originally attributed to George Turberville (or Turbervile) and is now assigned to the authorship of George Gascoigne.

[38] John Gerard, *The Autobiography of a Hunted Priest*, trans. P. Caraman (New York, 1955), 36–7, 41–2.

He dispatched agents to buy the best hunting horses at fairs in the north of England and overseas to purchase hawks; another servant was kept in London a month or more each year to seek out the best imported 'haggard falcons', which Berkeley used for hunting waterfowl along the banks of the Severn. Because Berkeley's expenditures outran his purse, he and his wife lived part of each year with his mother in Shoe Lane, London, and at Castle Rising with his mother-in-law, the dowager duchess of Norfolk. When in London, 'he spent most of his time at cards, dice, tennis, [the] bowling-alley, and hawking and hunting near the City'. When Lord and Lady Berkeley returned each year from Castle Rising to Gloucestershire, they undertook a long 'progress of buck hunting' through the parks and forests of the Midlands, staying with friends or in their own houses along the way. Lady Berkeley was as devoted to field sports as her husband and was thought to be uncommonly proficient with the long bow. She kept merlins in her bedchamber, which sometimes spoiled her gowns with their 'mutings'.[39]

William, fifth earl of Bedford, was another peer who never travelled without his hawks, and he often took along his greyhounds, beagles, and spaniels as well. He obtained his hawks and falcons from New England, Nova Scotia, North Africa, Scotland, and Ireland. The birds usually cost £8 or £9 each in the 1660s; their food bill for a year ran to £40, and the earl's falconer received annual wages of £100. The upkeep of his hunting dogs was nearly as much as that of his hawks. Hawking was no longer fashionable after the Civil Wars, but the earl disdained shotguns for fowling and thought it important to re-establish the family tradition of hawking at the Restoration.[40]

Looking back to his youth before the Civil Wars, Anthony Ashley Cooper, earl of Shaftesbury, remembered Henry Hastings of Woodlands, Dorset, as 'an original in our age, or rather the copy of our ancient nobility— in hunting, not in warlike times'. Hastings always dressed in hunting green and lived in a house 'of the old fashion in the midst of a park well stocked with deer'. His kennels contained hounds for hunting buck, fox, hare, otter, and badger, but the dogs were more usually to be found in the house: 'the great hall [was] strewed with marrow bones; full of hawks' perches, hounds, spaniels and terriers; the upper side of the hall hung with fox-skins . . . here and there a pole-cat intermixed; guns and keepers' and hunters' poles [were] in great abundance.' Hastings, who was keeper of a walk in the New Forest, maintained open hospitality, and his neighbours, of whatever rank, were always welcome at his abundant table, which cost him very little to keep since his sports supplied everything except beef, mutton, and oysters. He

---

[39] Smyth, *Berkeley Manuscripts*, ed. Maclean, ii. 284–6, 363–4.
[40] G. S. Thomson, *Life in a Noble Household, 1641–1700* (Ann Arbor, Mich., 1959), 226–35.

lived to be 100 and, 'until past fourscore, he rode to the death of a stag as well as any'.[41]

Shaftesbury maliciously added that Henry Hastings took the same liberties with his neighbours' game as he did with their wives and daughters: 'all of his neighbours' grounds and royalties were free to him, who bestowed all of his time on these sports, but what he borrowed to caress his neighbours' wives and daughters, there being not a woman in all his walks of the degree of a yeoman's wife or under, and under the age of 40, but it was her own fault if he was not intimately acquainted with her.'[42] Peers and gentlemen were often impulsive and self-indulgent and disposed to pursue sport and adventure wherever and whenever they found it. Whether fighting duels, hunting the king's deer, or breaking into someone else's park, they showed scant regard for the king's laws or the rights of others.

Much of this was a consequence of the lawlessness which characterized the baronial wars. Following the execution of Thomas, earl of Lancaster, after the Battle of Boroughbridge in 1322, a large number of venison trespasses were perpetrated by Lancaster's followers and servants in the Forest of Pickering, which the earl had forfeited to Edward II. Some of the offenders were dispossessed forest and game officials, and their poaching forays, led by Sir John de Fauconberg and Sir Robert Capon, must have looked like incipient rebellions. Fauconberg was indicted before the king. Edward III's absence in France brought a renewed outbreak of large-scale poaching in Pickering Forest in 1339.[43] The factionalism and civil wars of the fifteenth century resulted in frequent changes of forest and game officials, as the successful contenders for the crown sought to reward their followers and punish their enemies. Ousted forest officials refused to yield their hunting privileges and perquisites of firewood and pannage, and were presented by the new officials for vert and venison trespasses. Within one year, 1466, Thomas Gresley, deputy-lieutenant of Duffield Frith, presided at the woodmote and was presented before the same court for killing a buck without a warrant—he having lost his office in the meantime. During the Wars of the Roses such men saw nothing wrong with raiding the forests of someone whom they regarded as a pseudo-king.[44]

Between 1486 and 1491 the keepers of Savernake Forest in Wiltshire repeatedly presented members of the Wroughton and Darrell families and

---

[41] Printed in John Hutchins, *The History and Antiquities of the County of Dorset*, ed. W. Shipp and J. W. Hodgson, 4 vols. (Westminster, 1861–70), iii. 154, and in W. D. Christie, *A Life of Anthony Ashley Cooper, First Earl of Shaftesbury, 1621–1683*, 2 vols. (1871), i, appendix, pp. xiv–xvii. See also J. Birrell, 'Who Poached the King's Deer? A Study in Thirteenth Century Crime', *Midland History*, 7 (1982), 11.

[42] Hutchins, *History and Antiquities of Dorset*, iii. 154.

[43] *Calendar of the Close Rolls, Edward II, 1323–1327*, 15–16; *Calendar of the Close Rolls, Edward III, 1339–1341*, 258; Cox, *Royal Forests of England*, 108–10.

[44] Ibid. 191–2.

their servants for poaching the king's deer. One member of the latter family, Sir Edward Darrell, who was described as a 'communis malefactor de venacione domini regis', was sheriff of Wiltshire on four different occasions, and much of his poaching activities corresponded with the period of his first shrievalty. Evidently, both families had supported Henry VII in the late civil wars, and the king may have excused their misdemeanours as the natural restlessness of idle soldiers. Although the Darrells and the Wroughtons had hunted the king's deer together in the 1480s, their descendants a century later, while displaying the same restless and violent characteristics, had taken to quarrelling with one another. In 1588 William Darrell, *alias* 'Wild' Darrell, complained that Thomas Wroughton was little better than a highwayman, while John Aubrey alleged that Sir John Darrell had murdered his own illegitimate child after a servant-girl gave birth to the child.[45]

William Chafin says that unlawful hunting by gentlemen 'was not deemed a disgrace', and this behaviour persisted into the early eighteenth century, when hunting in disguise was made a felony by the Black Act of 1723. Chafin gives the example of an uncle who was much addicted to the sport. The uncle, who usually drank too much at dinner, was frequently captured by keepers as he muddled through his nocturnal sports; he paid the fines and continued to commit the same offence until his 'elder brother put a stop to his career in good time'.[46] Sir John Bramston recounted how he and his schoolfellows poached pigeons and fish in their free time; his schoolmaster, 'a greatly-followed preacher . . . and a greater pretender to sanctity and religion', affected anger, but, after 'the pigeons were baked, and we ate them, and his wife commended us', the schoolmaster's anger abated and the boys continued to slaughter the pigeons in the neighbourhood.[47] Poaching was probably a common childhood experience for boys bred in the countryside, and many—gentry and commonalty alike—continued the practice as adults. John Aubrey recollected the happy times he spent as a boy catching carp in other people's ponds: 'On one occasion Squire White, the proprietor of the estate, discharged his gun . . . to deter me from this act of poaching and trespassing.'[48]

Nicholas Assheton's Puritan sympathies did not prevent him from spending much of his time hunting deer and coursing hare. Returning home after a day of hunting, he often drank until he was as 'merry as Robin Hood'. He frequently hunted the king's deer in the Forest of Bowland and thought nothing of doing so. He once hunted in the company of the chief officers of the Duchy of Lancaster; on another occasion he was caught by a keeper

---

[45] H. C. Brentnall, 'Venison Trespasses in the Reign of Henry VII', *Wilts. Arch. and Nat. Hist. Mag.*, 53 (1949), 191–212; *Aubrey's Brief Lives*, ed. O. L. Dick (repr. 1950), 245.

[46] Geo. I, c. 22; William Chafin, *A Second Edition of the Anecdotes and History of Cranbourne Chase* (1818), 72–3.

[47] *The Autobiography of Sir John Bramston* (Camden Soc., os 32; 1845), 101.

[48] Aubrey, *Natural History of Wiltshire*, 62–3.

after having killed two deer. A bribe of 5s. and a portion of the kill were sufficient to seal the keeper's lips.[49]

Not all keepers were so complacent. When, in April 1541, Thomas Fiennes, ninth Lord Dacre of the South, and his companions decided to hunt in the park of his neighbour, Nicholas Pelham, at Laughton, Sussex, a confrontation between Dacre's band and the keepers led to the slaying of one of the latter. Dacre, who was 24 at the time, and three others were indicted and condemned for murder. The three companions were executed locally, but Dacre was hanged at Tyburn, after being made to walk on foot from the Tower of London through the city and suburbs to the place of execution.[50]

A reaction against this aristocratic obsession with hunting and hawking may be discerned during the reign of Elizabeth. One writer thought that young gentlemen should be put to learning or trained in 'feats of arms', according to their aptitude, in order better to serve their princes. In neither case should they waste time hunting to excess.[51] When war with Spain became a possibility, another writer argued that hunting was wasteful and costly, because the money spent on hunting horses and hawks could be better employed in maintaining cavalry horses to supply to the prince in time of war.[52] Lord Herbert of Cherbury also thought that hunting was a waste of time for a studious man, but regarded hawking as an agreeable diversion because it consumed less time. An experienced soldier himself, he thought it very important to be skilled in horsemanship and the use of the longbow. He also valued what he learnt about fencing in France, and, being of a quarrelsome nature, he employed that skill frequently in fighting duels.[53] Francis Osborn, in giving reasons for his dislike of the chase, cited the opinion of Sir Philip Sidney, 'who said that next to hunting he liked hawking worst'.[54] Sir Hugh Cholmley also developed a respect for learning in 'riper years' and regretted the time he misspent in his youth on 'hunting, hawking, and horseraces', when he should have been applying himself to the study of the law at Gray's Inn.[55] John Barlow, a Yorkshire clergyman, associated hunting and hawking with a neglect of hospitality; the time that gentlemen wasted on such pursuits would be better spent governing their tenants and composing their neighbours' quarrels.[56] So obsessed were some

[49] *The Journal of Nicholas Assheton*, ed. F. R. Raines (Chetham Soc., 14; Manchester, 1848), 49–50, 57–67.

[50] John Stow, *Annales*, ed. Edmund Howes (1631), 582; M. A. Lower, 'The Trial and Execution of Thomas, Lord Dacre', *Sussex Arch. Coll.*, 19 (1867), 174.

[51] Anon., *The Institucion of a Gentlemen* (1568), fos. 45^{r-v}–46^{r-v}.

[52] *English Courtier*, in *Inedited Tracts*, ed. Hazlitt, 82–3.

[53] *The Autobiography of Edward, Lord Herbert of Cherbury*, ed. S. L. Lee (1866), 78–9.

[54] *The Works of Francis Osborn* (9th edn.; 1689), i. 13.

[55] *The Memoirs of Sir Hugh Cholmley* (1777; repr. 1870), 23.

[56] John Barlow, *An Exposition of the Second Epistle of the Apostle Paul to Timothy, the First Chapter* (1624), 83, quoted in J. T. Cliffe, *The Yorkshire Gentry from Reformation to the Civil War* (1969), 115.

gentlemen with field sports that hunting terminology permeated their daily speech and suggested that they had experience of little else. Samuel Butler, the author of *Hudibras*, satirized Philip, fourth earl of Pembroke, and his love of horses and dogs by depicting him as being unable to make a speech in the House of Lords without mentioning them in every other sentence.[57]

As warfare grew more technical and specialized, it became difficult to justify hunting as a form of military training. Defenders of the sport had to fall back upon the argument that it was a recreation to be enjoyed in moderation when lawfully allowed.

1.2. Popular Culture

If hunting is primarily associated with aristocratic culture, it is only because gentlemen had the leisure to enjoy it and everywhere employed the law to deny that privilege to others. This caused much resentment, because country folk relished hunting, coursing, and fishing as much as their social superiors. One of Wat Tyler's demands during the Great Revolt of 1381 was that all warrens, parks, and chases should be free 'so that throughout the realm, in . . . the woods and forests, poor as well as rich might take wild beasts and hunt the hare in the field'.[58] The widespread slaughter of deer in aristocratic parks which accompanied the riots and rebellions of 1549 and which broke out again in 1641 gave expression to this same bitterness. Hunting and fishing rights were among the first demands made by German peasants during the Peasants' War of 1524–5 and by French peasants in the early stages of the French Revolution.[59]

In actual practice hunting was never confined exclusively to those qualified by law, because peers and gentlemen invariably hunted with servants and often compelled tenants to assist them as well. The typical hunting band seems to have consisted of a dozen or so members, and consequently numerous lesser gentry, yeomen, and even husbandmen came to share with their social superiors a common set of cultural attitudes towards hunting. The preoccupation of the aristocracy with hunting therefore had a profound influence upon popular culture. This has an important bearing on the controversy over whether popular ballads, such as those about Robin Hood, were aimed at gentry or peasant audiences.

[57] Samuel Butler, *Posthumous Works*, 3 vols. (1715–19), ii. 121, 131, 161.
[58] *Chronicon Henrici Knighton*, ed. J. R. Lumby, 2 vols. (Rolls Series; 1889, 1895), ii. 137.
[59] The Articles of Memmingen of 1525, printed in G. R. Elton (ed.), *Renaissance and Reformation* (New York, 1963), 275–8; Cahiers de doléances, Parish of Longnes, no. 7; National Assembly, Decrees of 10 Aug. 1789; Petition from the Somme, 28 Dec. 1789, in J. M. Roberts (ed.), *French Revolution Documents* (New York, 1966), i. 75, 151–2, 193; Cahiers de doléances of the Third Estate of Dourdan, 29 Mar. 1789, in J. H. Stewart (ed.), *Documentary Survey of the French Revolution* (New York, 1951), 81.

The author of *The English Courtier and Country-gentleman* emphasized that 'very many' yeomen shared a common culture with gentlemen because their sons were frequently bred to be servants in the households of peers and gentlemen. Such servants presented the appearance of gentlemen dressed in their livery coats with swords and bucklers at their sides. They acquired proficiency in the use of longbows, crossbows, and guns, expertly carved and dressed all manner of food at their masters' tables, learnt how to dance, and engaged in the same sports, including running, leaping, and wrestling. They also shared the same discourse. Good servants were expected to be able to 'entertain their master with table talk, be it his pleasure to speak either of hawks, or hounds, fishing, or fowling, sowing or grassing, ditching or hedging, the dearth or cheapness of grain, or any such matters whereof gentlemen commonly speak in the country, be it either of pleasure or profit'.[60] The same writer also admitted that servants in aristocratic households were often quarrelsome and unsuited for employment on their own merits; they were retained out of a sense of obligation to friends and tenants and to preserve them from more disorderly lives, 'for well you know, it were [a] great pity to see a tall fellow to climb a gibbet'.[61]

Nicholas Breton stated that, after the harvest, hunting parties were part of the hospitality which some gentlemen landlords extended to their tenants and neighbours. The dispensing and accepting of such hospitality and the sharing of common meals and country recreations were among the ties which bound village and manorial communities together.[62] Among the labour-services owed by the customary tenants of Sutton Coldfield, Warwickshire, was the obligation to drive deer past a standing where the lord might shoot at them. They were expected to do this two days a year for each yardland owned. However, in recompense for their labour, tenants might claim the 'half part of the fee of a woodward', payable in venison.[63] The burgesses of Bishop's Castle, Shropshire, were required to drive deer three times a year or find a substitute. Their obligation was entered in the episcopal register. The citizens of Hereford customarily provided one man from each household to drive deer when the king hunted in their neighbourhood.[64]

These occasions might involve a considerable amount of ceremony. On the Feast of the Assumption (15 August) the woodmaster and eleven keepers of Needwood Chase customarily hunted and killed one buck for

[60] *English Courtier*, in *Inedited Tracts*, ed. Hazlitt, 38. See also M. E. James, *Family, Lineage and Civil Society: A Study of Society, Politics and Mentality in the Durham Region, 1500–1640* (Oxford, 1974), 32.   [61] *English Courtier*, in *Inedited Tracts*, ed. Hazlitt, 40.

[62] [Nicholas Breton], *The Court and the Country, or a Brief Discourse Dialogue-wise set down between a Courtier and a Countryman* (1618), in *Inedited Tracts*, ed. Hazlitt, 179.

[63] Thomas Blount, *Fragmenta Antiquitatis: or, Ancient Tenures of Land and Jocular Customs of Manors* (1845), 501–4.   [64] Ibid. 516–17.

themselves and another which was to be delivered to the prior of Tutbury. After the hunt, the forest and game officers of Needwood and all of their servants bore the head of the prior's buck, decorated with boughs and pieces of deer fat stuck on the horns, in procession to the priory church, blowing various hunting calls as they rode. After the prior had dined, he gave the keepers of Needwood 30*s.* to help pay for their Lady-day dinner. The prior then turned a bull loose among the minstrels. If the minstrels could catch the bull before it gored them or crossed the River Dove, they might keep it.[65]

A popular belief seems to have existed that no celebration or special occasion was complete without a bit of hunting. Lesser gentry and yeomen especially seem to have felt obliged to find some sport for their guests, whether it was lawful or not. When John Quennell of Chiddingford, Surrey, gent., stayed at the house of his friend, Thomas South of Odiham, Hampshire, yeom., while attending a baptism where Quennell was to be the godfather, several members of the christening party encouraged their greyhounds to leap over the pale of Odiham Park after the christening supper was finished. Their dogs killed five deer—more than they could carry away—and Quennell got lost in the unfamiliar park and did not emerge until the following morning, when he had to ask for directions.[66] Nicholas Hilliard, a tailor of London, went down to Kent to stay with his friend Thomas Petley, gent., while attending a wedding feast. The two of them went on a rampage in Hamsell Park, near Rotherfield, Sussex, and destroyed park pales, slaughtered several deer, and made off with Sir Thomas Waller's hounds.[67] In Lancashire, a bridegroom was lured into an unlawful hunting on the evening preceding his wedding and had the misfortune to be caught by the keepers of Myerscough Forest. One wonders if he ever made it to the altar.[68]

Gentlemen poachers, it was widely agreed, set a very bad example for lesser folk. The scene depicted by the author of *The Merry Devil of Edmonton*, in which a keeper of Enfield Chase reprimands a knight for spoiling the king's deer by darkness, would have been familiar enough to an early seventeenth-century audience. Brian, the keeper, reproves Sir Arthur Clare by asking: 'Is this a time for such as you, men of [your] place and of your gravity, to be abroad a-thieving? 'Tis a shame; And, afore God, if I had shot at you, I had served you well enough.'[69]

Joseph Hunter, the Yorkshire antiquarian, believed that a commonalty which was accustomed to poaching grew to be more assertive and was

---

[65] Ibid. 529–32.   [66] PRO STAC 8/219/19.

[67] PRO STAC 8/290/17.   [68] PRO STAC 8/23/19.

[69] Anon., *The Merry Devil of Edmonton* (1608), IV. i, in *The Shakespeare Apocrypha*, ed. C. F. Tucker Brooke (Oxford, 1908; repr. 1967), 279–80.

more likely to defend their use-rights, resist seigneurial oppression, and oppose schemes such as drainage and enclosure: 'The peasantry of a country abounding in game will be less civilized and less tractable than where there is not the same temptation to brave the hazards which attend noctural depredations. The thorough-bred poacher is a man who carries his life in his hand, and whose heart is prepared for any desperate enterprise.'[70]

There were numerous points of contact between gentlemen and commonalty by means of which aristocratic cultural attitudes concerning hunting—both lawful and unlawful—influenced popular culture. When one attempts to determine what kind of audience enjoyed the Robin Hood ballads, it is important to understand to what degree attitudes towards hunting and the methods employed in hunting differed or were shared among gentlemen and commonalty.

In a famous controversy a generation ago, Professor J. C. Holt argued that the Robin Hood ballads were aimed primarily at a gentry rather than a peasant audience—although he does admit that this audience broadened in the sixteenth century. Professor Holt based his argument upon certain assumptions which my investigations in Star Chamber proceedings concerning cases of unlawful hunting and in contemporary hunting manuals do not bear out. Professor Holt maintained that the type of hunting depicted in the Robin Hood ballads was clearly aristocratic, because it was directed only against deer in the royal forests and never against deer parks, and that Robin and his merry band hunted only with bows and never used nets or dogs.[71] In fact, gentlemen hunters in the sixteenth and seventeenth centuries raided one another's parks at least as frequently as they hunted the king's deer. They almost invariably used dogs, frequently employed nets, and killed their prey with a variety of weapons. There is no significant difference between the methods used in hunting deer employed by gentlemen and by those of inferior social rank. Although a clear aristocratic preference for deer-hunting can be detected, gentlemen did not hesitate to use greyhounds to course hare and even rabbits if no better prey were available. Nor is it correct to assume that peasants hunted only for food and gentlemen only for sport. One seldom comes across a poacher in Tudor and Stuart England who hunted unlawfully because he was hungry.[72] At the same time there were many knights and esquires holding the king's commission of the peace who poached royal deer in order to supply a growing commercial market for venison. Historians commonly assume that the social

---

[70] Joseph Hunter, *South Yorkshire: The History and Topography of the Deanery of Doncaster,* 2 vols. (1828), i. 157.

[71] J. C. Holt, 'The Origins and Audience of the Ballads of Robin Hood', *P&P,* no. 18 (Nov. 1960), 96–7. Maurice Keen, on the other hand, assumes that the tales appealed to a wider audience ('Robin Hood: Peasant or Gentleman?', *P&P,* no. 19 (Apr. 1961), 7–15).

[72] But, for an example, see Manning, *Village Revolts,* 292.

gulf between the gentry and yeomanry was a wide one. I would suggest that the frequent participation of gentry of all ranks together with yeomen in hunting fraternities argues that the deer-hunting culture narrowed that gap between gentry and commonalty.

Thus, there is good reason for believing that, during the late Middle Ages, the Robin Hood tales, together with ballads about other outlaws who had fled into the greenwood, appealed to an audience which included both gentry and commonalty. At a time when English kings were pre-occupied with foreign wars, when royal justice was often ineffectual, and official corruption was rife, there were bound to be a certain number of persons who had been dispossessed by the baronial wars, cheated of an inheritance, or injured by an officer of the law or a harsh landlord. Such men thirsted for revenge and habitually turned to violence to settle old scores. For them justice was little more than revenge, and the traditional Robin Hood ballads, where bloody vengeance was exacted on the spot from villains, must have satisfied this craving.[73] It was not actually necessary to flee to the greenwood like Robin Hood; woodland areas supplied both the cover and the opportunity to combine revenge with sport in carrying out poaching forays. Moreover, corrupt local magistrates provided a degree of immunity from prosecution which Robin's merry band never enjoyed in the ballads.

During the sixteenth century, if not earlier, the audience for the Robin Hood ballads broadened. A process occurs in which the ballads reflect actual modes of popular protest and, in turn, shape popular culture. An example of the first is the case of Robert Stafford, *alias* 'Friar Tuck', an early fifteenth-century Sussex chaplain and outlaw, who seems to have derived his nickname from the well-known follower of Robin Hood in the late-medieval versions of the ballads. Accused of numerous robberies, murders, and acts of rebellion, Stafford eluded capture for more than a decade in the Sussex Weald. He and his followers lived by hunting deer, hare, rabbits, pheasants, and partridges, terrorized the keepers of parks, chases, and warrens, and burnt their lodges. Stafford was pardoned his offences in 1429, but it appears that he and his band, although indicted, were never compelled to answer for their crimes in a court of law.[74] The preamble of a statute enacted early in the reign of Henry VII speaks as if bandits still roamed the Weald of Sussex, Surrey, and Kent, committing murders and robberies and living off gentlemen's deer parks and warrens.[75]

The Robin Hood of legend was, in turn, a potent symbol of popular protest. Thomas Bright of Carnebrooke, Yorkshire, gent., led a band of

---

[73] M. Keen, *The Outlaws of Medieval Legend* (rev. edn.; 1979), 2–7.
[74] *Cal. PR, Henry V, 1416–1422*, 84–141; *Cal. PR, Henry VI, 1429–1436*, 10; Keen, *Outlaws of Medieval Legend*, 2–7; see also R. F. Hunnisett, *The Medieval Coroner* (Cambridge, 1961), 67–8.   [75] 1 Hen. VII, c. 7; *SR* ii. 505.

poachers who raided the deer parks of William, earl of Pembroke, at Sheffield, Wadsley, and Middlewood in 1621–2. He went by the name of 'Robin Hood'; his followers, who included yeomen and artisans, were known as Robin Hood's 'merry men'; and one of his lieutenants was called 'Little John'. Among the various depredations of which they were accused, Bright's 'merry men' were alleged to have reduced one herd of 220 deer to sixty head. Witnesses testified that Bright openly boasted of his exploits and said that 'he had venison for any good fellow that came to him'. He once complained to one of Pembroke's keepers that 'you keep me not well [supplied] with venison'. Bright must have heard the Robin Hood tales recited aloud, because his inability to sign his name suggests that he was illiterate.[76]

In Staffordshire, the games played at fairs between rival parishes in order to raise money sometimes degenerated into faction fights. In one such encounter in about 1499 between the men of Walsall and the men of Wednesbury, the two rival factions were led by their parish priests. One of the priests from Wednesbury called himself 'Robin Hood', and his lieutenant took the title of 'abbot of Marham'. Some two hundred Wednesbury men were accused of committing a riot at Walsall in which they imprisoned the mayor and rescued some of their fellows who had been charged with murders committed in the previous day's fighting.[77]

By the early sixteenth century, Robin Hood had become associated with May-games in both aristocratic and popular culture. In 1515 Henry VIII celebrated May Day by riding out from Greenwich with his courtiers to Shooter's Hill, where they encountered two hundred soldiers of the royal guard clothed in green, masquerading as Robin Hood and his band of outlaws. The latter fired a couple of carefully rehearsed volleys of arrows, and then invited the king and queen and courtiers to breakfast with them on venison and wine in an arbor decorated 'with flowers and sweet herbs'.[78] Robin Hood was already a part of the May festivities of Rye in 1511, when the corporation paid for a barrel of beer to be distributed upon the occasion of Robin's 'visitation' about the town.[79] By the reign of Elizabeth, many rural parishes elected May-kings and queens, who dressed up and were known as Robin Hood and Maid Marian. They discharged duties similar to those of lords of misrule and were customarily escorted by bands of outlaws dressed in Lincoln green.[80]

---

[76] PRO STAC 8/183/45.

[77] 'Staffordshire Suits in the Court of Star Chamber, Temp. Henry VII and Henry VII', ed. W. K. Boyd, in *Collections for a History of Staffordshire* (William Salt Arch. Soc., NS 1; 1907), 80–1.

[78] Edward Hall, *Hall's Chronicle* (1809; repr. New York, 1965), 582.

[79] Graham Mayhew, *Tudor Rye* (Falmer, Sussex, 1987), 58.

[80] R. H. Hilton, 'The Origins of Robin Hood', in R. H. Hilton (ed.), *Peasants, Knights and Heretics: Studies in Medieval History* (Cambridge, 1976), 222; Peter Burke, *Popular Culture in Early Modern Europe* (New York, 1978), 180.

1.3. Methods of Hunting

Population pressure and the growing scarcity of game will always lead to more complex techniques for capturing the prey. This was especially evident in the sixteenth and early seventeenth centuries, when the methods of hunting, including those employed by kings and aristocrats, had become quite artificial.[81] The hunter puts his reputation on the line when he goes hunting, and, at all costs, he must not come back empty-handed, lest his prowess be questioned. Hunters and poachers of this period were driven to employ techniques which purists would have scorned and which a modern audience would regard as distinctly unsporting.

The red and the fallow deer were the beasts of the forest most commonly hunted in England and Wales. The red deer was the largest of the British deer. It still survived in the wild in the more remote districts such as Dartmoor, the Peak Forest, and Sherwood, but it was also bred in parks in Sussex and other more accessible places. Fallow deer were much more common, but were an exotic species, introduced at an early date into England, and more usually bred and sheltered in enclosed parks. Gervase Markham thought that they provided inferior sport to the native red deer. Many of those bred in parks must have been quite tame. Roe deer and wild boar were also classified as beasts of the forest. A fully grown roe buck stood only 26 inches high at the shoulders and bore a disconcerting resemblance to a wild goat. Once quite common in the south of England, roe deer were rarely hunted in the sixteenth century. Although much esteemed as sport on the continent, wild boar were quite scarce in Tudor and Stuart England, but still survived in Lancashire, Staffordshire, and County Durham. James I is said to have hunted a wild boar in Windsor Forest in 1617, but it must have been introduced.[82]

There were recognized legal seasons for hunting deer. Male deer were hunted from the Feast of St John the Baptist (24 June) until Holy Rood Day (14 September). Female deer might be taken between Holy Rood Day and Candlemas (2 February). As one might expect, hunting seasons were ignored by poachers.[83]

The methods employed in pursuing and killing deer varied according to the terrain and were determined by whether the hunting was done *par force* and at large in spacious forests pursuing a single animal, or within enclosed parks. The latter was the more contrived and artificial in its methods. Also,

[81] See J. Ortega y Gasset, *Meditations on Hunting*, trans. H. B. Westcott (New York, 1972), 75, 79.
[82] Cox, *Royal Forests of England*, 26–32; M[arkham], *Country Contentments*, 33.
[83] Sir Edward Coke, *The Fourth Part of the Institutes of the Laws of England: Concerning the Jurisdiction of the Courts* (5th edn.; 1671), 316; *The Art of Hunting*, ed. Dryden, 31.

1. The Cultural and Social Context

the presence of the monarch or a great peer dictated more formal etiquette of the chase and more elaborate organization and logistics.

James Cleland praised hunting on foot with running hounds because of the physical exercise it afforded—thus hardening the body for war. To dismount for the final kill evoked praise, but was rarely done after the sixteenth century. However, in 1664 the earl of Castlehaven (who was aged 50 at the time) and the earl of Arran wagered King Charles II that they could catch and kill a fat buck in St James's Park within the space of six hours— proceeding on foot and each armed only with a knife. Although their prey took to water, they drove him with stones to one side of the pond, where they dispatched him—all within two and a half hours.[84]

The style of hunting prevailing at court and among the nobility was adapted to enclosed parks and involved much ceremony. This method of hunting was known as a 'drive'; its origins go back to at least as early as the reign of Henry IV and it continued until the eve of the Great Rebellion. Lymehounds or bloodhounds flushed the deer out of the covert and greyhounds pursued them. It was the responsibility of the master of the hounds to drive the animals past a platform called a 'standing', where the hunting party stood and shot their bows at the deer as they passed. Sometimes the deer were driven into a 'hey' or temporary enclosure erected with 'toils' or nets before they were slaughtered. Standings were usually employed on royal hunts when the monarch was aged and infirm or when ladies wished to participate. Alternatively, the hunting party pursued the deer on horseback along avenues cut through parks for that purpose and the beasts were driven into nets. In the latter days of Henry VIII, when the king was at Oatlands, the deer were rounded up and held in a pen and released upon command. The king hunted vicariously, as horsemen drove the deer past the royal standing and slew them 'with darts and spears'. On one occasion Henry VIII presided over a hunt in which 240 stags and does were slaughtered with longbows and crossbows; the following day the scene was repeated using greyhounds. As a consequence of the new style of hunting, the older and more distant royal forests were neglected, and the Tudor and Stuart monarchs acquired additional royal houses and deer parks in the Thames Valley.[85]

---

[84] Cleland, *Institution of a Young Noble Man*, ed. Molyneux, i. 222–3; *Autobiography of Lord Herbert of Cherbury*, ed. Lee, 99–100; William Blundell of Crosby, *A Cavalier's Notebook*, ed. T. E. Gibson (1880), 177.

[85] Cockayne, *A Short Treatise of Hunting*, ed. Halliday, p. xv; Joseph Strutt, *The Sports and Pastimes of the People of England*, ed. J. C. Cox (1903; repr. Detroit, 1968), 11, 17–18; J. M. Gilbert, *Hunting and Hunting Reserves in Medieval Scotland* (Edinburgh, 1979), 52–5; Lodge, *Illustrations of British History*, i. 6; *Autobiography of Lord Herbert of Cherbury*, ed. Lee, 102; H. M. Colvin, D. R. Ransome, and J. Summerson (eds.), *The History of the King's Works*, 6 vols. (1962–83), iv. ii. 5, 16; *The Lisle Letters*, ed. M. St C. Byrne, 6 vols. (Chicago, 1981), vi. 177.

When the duke of Saxe-Weimar was invited to hunt with James I at Theobalds, he and the king rode to the park in a carriage and then mounted their horses. The king selected the animal which it pleased him to hunt from a herd of fallow deer. The huntsmen and the greyhounds (which were trained to follow one animal only) pursued the beast until the hounds had brought it down. The German courtier who witnessed this event thought that there was 'no particular enjoyment in this sport'.[86] James did at least hunt on horseback and sometimes killed his prey with a longbow, although he proclaimed in the *Basilikon Doron* that it was a 'thievish form of hunting to shoot with guns and bows'.[87]

Hunting with toils or nets was a very common practice in the Tudor period among all classes from kings to peasants. Elizabeth hunted in this manner at Theobalds in the 1590s, and an English courtier accompanying an embassy noted with distaste that nets were also employed at the court of the Landgrave of Hesse.[88] The author of *Maison Rustique* thought that this method of taking beasts was 'more fit for holiday men, milk sops, and cowards than for men of valour'.[89] Nets were widely used for catching conies, and, before angling became fashionable, for game-fishing. The Lancashire squire, Nicholas Assheton, did not think that it was ungentlemanly to fish with nets, and once caught sixty-five in this manner.[90] Rabbit poachers on Cannock Chase in 1618 were reported to be using a net sixty fathoms in length with which they caught a thousand rabbits. In 1538, when a large group of deer-slayers from Kent was interrogated, one of the culprits was discovered to be employing a net-maker in his household. Judging from the value placed upon nets in the inventories of fishermen (as much as 40s.), nets and toils must have represented a substantial capital investment, and their extensive use suggests the existence of a not unimportant cottage industry.[91]

Halters or snare-type traps appear to have been used only by more humble folk. This was a very cruel method of hunting, because the animal was strangled to death by hanging. This might possibly represent symbolic retribution against the king's deer, since the hunting dogs which gamekeepers confiscated from poachers were often killed in this manner. In Lincolnshire, a farmer sought revenge against Sir Henry Fiennes by trapping the latter's deer with caltrops, and slaughtered twenty animals by this

---

[86] *England as Seen by Foreigners*, ed. Rye, 153–4.
[87] *The Political Works of James I*, ed. McIlwain, 48–9.
[88] Nichols, *Progresses of Elizabeth*, iii. 245–6, 383.
[89] *Maison Rustique*, 837.
[90] *Journal of Nicholas Assheton*, ed. Raines, 25. In medieval and early modern usage a cony (from the Latin *cuniculus*) was a mature animal; juveniles were referred to as rabbits (from the medieval northern French *rabette*).
[91] PRO STAC 8/200/25; *L&P Hen. VIII*, xiii. ii, appendix 7, pp. 542–3; Mayhew, *Tudor Rye*, 160.

method.[92] Stalking horses were frequently used by hunters of all classes to advance by stealth upon herds of deer which had learnt to fear only two-footed predators. The deer might then be killed with bows fired from behind the horses.[93] In Bowland Forest in the 1520s poachers killed the royal deer by driving the beasts past crossbowmen hidden in the trees.[94] Another band of poachers in Kingswood Chase, Gloucestershire, led by Sir Richard Berkeley of Stokes, drove deer by burning the furze. In Northumberland gentlemen poachers used a long gun charged with multiple shot when they raided deer parks.[95] When Henry, prince of Wales, visited Hatfield Chase, in the West Riding of Yorkshire, in 1609, the forest officers showed him their local style of stag-hunting: when the deer 'took to water' in the meres, the hunters pursued them in boats and cut their throats. The hunters returned in triumph, and Prince Henry was described as being 'very merry and well pleased at his day's work'.[96]

One frequently hears complaints about the damage done to crops by deer wandering out of parks and forests as well as by those who hunted the animals. Sir John Carew of Carew Castle, Pembrokeshire, who possessed lands on the edge of Exmoor Forest, complained of the losses which he and his tenants suffered when poachers heedlessly pursued stray deer through four parishes, following a course of some sixteen miles and trampling and destroying corn, grass, hay, hedges, and gates. The poachers, who rode in bands of twenty to thirty, appeared to be ill disposed towards Carew and his tenants and were also accused of destroying sheep and flinging them into the river. One of the defendants, Humphrey Bowden, admitted that he was 'somewhat skilled in hunting', and said that he was hired by Sir Hugh Pollard, chief officer of Exmoor Forest, to serve as a guide, but he claimed that he hunted only at the direction of Pollard.[97]

Outside the royal court and the households of the wealthiest aristocrats, hunting by driving with beaters was too expensive and logistically complicated. Most Englishmen (and Scots, too) preferred coursing, a method of hunting in which greyhounds pursued the deer, and the hunters followed on horseback. Greyhounds were very swift dogs which hunted by sight rather than scent, and which singly or in pairs could pull the deer down and kill it. Greyhounds were used only for hunting deer and hare, and it was generally assumed that unqualified persons possessing such dogs must be engaged in unlawful hunting. Bloodhounds were especially adapted to

[92] R. W. Merriman, 'Extracts from the Records of the Wiltshire Quarter Sessions, 1603–1609', *Wilts. Arch. and Nat. Hist. Mag.*, 22 (1885), 23–4; PRO STAC 8/183/46, 27/4.
[93] PRO STAC 8/28/16.
[94] *Pleadings and Depositions in the Duchy Court of Lancaster, Time of Henry VII and Henry VIII, Edward VI, and Philip and Mary*, ed. H. Fishwick, 3 vols. (Rec. Soc. Lancs. and Ches., 32, 35, 40; Manchester, 1896, 1897, 1899), i. 125.
[95] PRO STAC 4/2/23, STAC 8/17/3.   [96] Hunter, *South Yorkshire*, i. 156.
[97] PRO STAC 8/100/11.

pursuing wounded deer or tracking poachers conveying away deer carcasses. They were also used to patrol deer parks at night in order to detect
poachers. Hunting *par force*, with scenting hounds such as harriers or brachs,
was considered to be the more honourable and valorous method. The English were very attached to their hunting dogs, and one writer thought that
their barking was 'music to content your ear . . . a heavenly noise or cry that
would make a dead man revive and run on foot to hear it'.[98]

It is arguable that there was an element of sport in the chase, or hunting
at large and *par force*; contemporary commentators make it clear that they
regard this form of hunting as the one most likely to encourage valour and
develop military prowess. Coursing and driving within parks, although
popular in court and aristocratic circles, were regarded as distinctly inferior,
and the modern observer finds it difficult to distinguish these methods of
hunting from bear- and bull-baiting and cock-fighting. Animal-baiting was
relished by monarchs on state occasions and by peasants at village fairs.
Hunters regarded all four-footed beasts as fair game, and did not scruple
even to kill pet fawns in penned enclosures.[99]

Although there was more sport in the chase than in the kill, hunters
clearly enjoyed the latter as much as the former. The large-scale slaughter
which characterized hunting by driving not only afforded pleasure but also
demonstrated power. Queen Elizabeth was, on one occasion, 'gratified' to
slit the throat of a stag, while on another occasion she demonstrated her
mercy by sparing a hart which had taken to water, and 'ransomed' his ears
instead. Young boys hunting for the first time were 'blooded' by daubing
their faces with the gore of slaughtered animals, and ladies-in-waiting, sup-
posing that it would make their skin white, smeared blood on their hands
after the breaking of the stags.[100]

One direction that the reaction against hunting took in the seventeenth
century was the encouragement of angling. Gervase Markham thought that
there were good moral grounds for promoting angling. He recommended
it as 'the sport or recreation of God's saints, of most holy fathers, and of
many worthy and reverend divines'. He anticipated Isaak Walton in arguing
that angling promoted civility, patience, and temperance, whereas far too
many other games and sports elicited blasphemy, bloodshed, and covetousness. However, the author of the *Maison Rustique, or the Countrie Farme*
thought that angling was good only for keeping servants busy on holidays

---

[98] John Caius, *Of English Dogges*, trans. Abraham Fleming (1576; repr. 1880), 3–4, 5–8, 9–
10; Gilbert, *Hunting and Hunting Reserves*, 53–61; PRO STAC 8/111/2, 100/15; *English Courtier*,
in *Inedited Tracts*, ed. Hazlitt, 54–5.

[99] Nichols, *Progresses of Elizabeth*, i. 67–8; id., *Progresses of James I*, i. 523; K. Thomas, *Man
and the Natural World: A History of the Modern Sensibility* (New York, 1983), 22–3; PRO STAC
2/3, fo. 142.

[100] Nichols, *Progresses of Elizabeth*, i. 17, 435–6; Thomas, *Man and the Natural World*, 29.

so that they might have something special to eat for their supper. Until well into the seventeenth century, most fishermen thought that it made more sense to catch fish with nets, spears, or osier baskets.[101]

1.4. Forest and Game Offices

Forest offices and keeperships of the royal game were an important means of rewarding support for the king. No systematic study of this area of patronage has ever been made for the early modern period, but it must have constituted a very large proportion of the royal bounty.[102] Whenever a royal succession signalled a change in royal policy and a realignment of factions, a certain number of courtiers and their clients in the countryside would be deprived of forest and game offices and the same regranted to the faction which currently enjoyed favour. In the medieval and Tudor periods, such offices were traditionally given to old soldiers, who were expected to be available, when summoned, for further military service. Thus, the patronage of forest and game offices helped to maintain a reserve pool of military manpower—but also contributed to the problem of retaining. The grants of forest and game offices to magnates were often extensive and, in turn, conferred upon them considerable powers of patronage. The perquisites of forest and game offices were substantial, and many gentry families depended upon them for economic survival. The higher game and forest offices anciently conferred honourable status on the holders as the many coats-of-arms bearing stag heads and other symbols of office testify. However, the fierce competition for such offices led to numerous violent and bloody encounters between different aristocratic factions and resulted in accusations and counter-accusations of unlawful hunting.

After he had won the crown, Henry VII made many grants of forest and game offices in rewarding his followers for assistance against Richard III. The keeperships of smaller royal parks in remote places such as Cornwall made suitable rewards and pensions for soldiers from the ranks. The larger and more prestigious posts, such as the keepership of the New Park in Rockingham Forest, were reserved for knights. Members of the Savage family of Worcestershire were particularly well rewarded for their loyalty: Christopher, son of Sir John Savage, was made steward, parker, and master of the game in Feckenham Forest; another son, Edward, became bailiff and parker of the lordships of Hatfield and Thorne; while Sir John Savage the younger received the offices of steward and bailiff of five manors, the parkerships of four royal parks, as well as the office of master of the game

---

[101] M[arkham], *Country Contentments*, 59 ff.; Isaak Walton, *The Compleat Angler, 1653–1676*, ed. J. Bevan (Oxford, 1983), 66–9; *Maison Rustique*, 836.
[102] See Young, *Royal Forests of Medieval England*, 164 *et passim*.

in Malvern Chase. These grants were made for life and carried with them the patronage of all lesser offices within their jurisdictions. The grander offices of lieutenant and chief forester of these various forests, parks, and chases were usually granted to peers, such as Richard, Lord Fitzhugh.[103]

When Elizabeth succeeded to the throne, she dismissed Sir Edward Waldegrave from the Privy Council for failing to support the new religious settlement and stripped him of his offices. Some of these were regranted to Sir Anthony Cooke, formerly tutor to Edward VI and the father-in-law of Sir William Cecil, with right of survivorship to his son and heir, Richard. The patent made Sir Anthony bailiff and steward of the royal manors of Havering-atte-Bower, Stanford Rivers, and Stapleford, Essex, master of the game and keeper of the woods, warrens, and parks, keeper of the manor houses, keeper of Hainault Walk, and lord warden and lieutenant of Waltham Forest. The remuneration for these offices exceeded £78 p.a., and the perquisites included housing (plus a lodge in Waltham Forest), fuel, all fallen wood, herbage and pannage, and fee-deer. Other profits derived from fines levied upon defendants in the swanimote and attachment courts; the forest gaol at Stratford Langthorne also produced a profit. The patronage rights were quite substantial: the master forestership, for example, sold for between £300 and £500. This valuable group of offices later passed into the hands of the de Vere earls of Oxford. In 1627 the trustees of the de Vere estate sold the office of lord warden and lieutenant to the earl of Lindsey for £3,500. Six years later, in 1633, the value of the office had risen to £6,642 when the earl of Lindsey granted it to his son and heir Lord Willoughby in return for paying off debts of that value.[104]

It would be an arduous task to enumerate all of the many forest and game offices, but a sampling of the evidence can indicate the dimensions of this patronage. John Norden's survey of the Forest of Windsor in 1607 revealed that this vast hunting preserve, which extended into six counties, was divided into sixteen walks and sixteen parks, each of which was presided over by a keeper. Each park was furnished with a keeper's lodge, except for Windsor Great Park, which had four lodges. These sinecures were held by courtiers or ministers of the crown, and provided fee-deer and other perquisites, which, presumably, included diet or board wages. Although the annual wages or fee of a ranger or keeper of a park might be no more than £10 or £12 p.a., the board wages alone could be worth one hundred times that amount.[105] Of course, royal game officers had to pay the wages of servants, but some of them also profited from illegal trafficking in venison which clearly exceeded the amounts which they were allowed in

[103] *Cal. PR, 1485–1494*, 7, 9, 16.
[104] *Cal. PR, 1558–1560*, 33–4, 86; W. R. Fisher, *The Forest of Essex* (1887), 114–20, 127–9.
[105] R. R. Tighe and J. E. Davis, *Annals of Windsor*, 2 vols. (London, 1858), ii. 2–3, 27–30;
G. E. Aylmer, *The King's Servants: The Civil Service of Charles I* (1961), 168–73.

fee-deer. A very incomplete list of keepers of royal houses, parks, forests, and chases from the late Elizabethan period puts the total of their annual wages at £5,268 10*s.* 4*d.* This list does not include lesser functionaries such as the master of the royal buck hounds who was paid 50*s.* p.a. and who supervised two sergeants and two yeomen prickers plus an unspecified number of grooms 'for hounds' meat'. These royal servants were paid at approximately the same rate as musicians, players, and surgeons, but appear to have ranked higher than the latter.[106]

Lodges were another valuable perquisite of forest and game offices. Although most were unpretentious, those in royal hunting preserves were more commodious, and many gentry families used them as their principal seats. The lodge assigned to Thurston Tyldesley when he was keeper of the Forest and Park of Myerscough, Lancashire, was probably typical. It was a timber structure, rebuilt in the middle of the sixteenth century and ornamented inside and out with a lavish display of carving. Myerscough Lodge contained twenty rooms, including a hall, parlour, chapel, several great chambers, and a total of thirty-two beds, which suggests a large household capable of providing entertainment for visitors. In addition there were numerous outbuildings, including a milkhouse, a brew house, and barns. During the time that John, Lord Lumley, was 'keeper, parker and governor of the Great Park of Nonsuch', he made Nonsuch his chief residence and only rarely had to share it with his royal mistress.[107]

James I's grant of the forest and park of Clarendon to William, third earl of Pembroke, is reputed to have carried with it the most complete and absolute control over a royal hunting preserve ever possessed by a subject. The grant conferred the offices of keeper, warden, lieutenant, bailiff, and bow-bearer, plus the disposal of all lesser offices, and extensive profits and perquisites. There were extensive grazing and timber rights; wood sales were worth £20 p.a.; and the rabbit warrens £200. Rentals from the six lodges produced £500 a year and other fees an additional £92. The letters patent of 1606 may have undervalued the profits, which a commonwealth survey of 1650 estimated to be worth £1,806.[108]

Forest and game offices were held by a variety of tenures. Grants for life seem to have been the most common form of tenure in the early Tudor period, but patents were sometimes renewed for the son and heir.[109] Although forest and game offices continued to be used to reward royal servants and courtiers, the tendency under Elizabeth and the early Stuarts was to make

---

[106] BL Cotton MSS, Titus B. III, fos. 175[r–v], 192–205.

[107] R. C. Shaw, *The Royal Forest of Lancaster* (Preston, Lancs., 1956), 198–9; *Cal. PR, 1558–1560*, 20.

[108] Cox, *Royal Forests of England*, 321–2.

[109] *Cal. PR, 1558–1560*, 56; Cox, *Royal Forests of England*, 17–19; E. J. Rawle, *Annals of the Ancient Royal Forest of Exmoor* (Taunton, 1893), 135–6; Fisher, *Forest of Essex*, 114–20.

grants during royal pleasure and to require purchase. Francis, Lord Norris of Rycote, had to pay £40 for his office of chief forester of Stow Wood and Shotover Forest in 1606. Presumably, the major office holders recovered their investments by selling warrants for the office of deputy or underkeeper. Royal surveys of forests frequently complained about the excessive number of underkeepers, who recovered their investments in the purchase of their offices by excessive or unlawful hunting and cutting of timber and wood, or by forging warrants for taking deer, as Lord Norris's underkeepers did.[110]

While the levels of remuneration for the principal forest and game offices were ample, underkeepers were not adequately compensated. Underkeepers were paid £6 p.a. in the Forest of Blackmore at the end of Elizabeth's reign, but the keepers and bow-bearers of several northern forests received even less. The five keepers of Bowland Forest were paid 26s. 8d. yearly and the six rangers 10s. each, while the forester of Wyresdale and Quernmore, Lancashire, received £4 10s. p.a. In 1621 Philip, Lord Stanhope, keeper of Thorneywood Chase, Nottinghamshire, complained that the growth in the size of the deer herds entrusted to his care and the prevalence of poaching made it necessary for him to increase the number of underkeepers from two to seven and their combined wages totalled £100. Stanhope appears to have been a conscientious keeper and presumably wanted honest deputies. They were better paid than most deputy keepers.[111]

Although perquisites and lodging usually went with these lesser offices, they could hardly have made up for the low wages. Consequently, what the courts and the exchequer officials called 'waste and spoil' was very widespread. In the reign of Elizabeth, James Mapperly, the keeper of Highlands Park on the edge of Needwood Forest in Staffordshire, was accused, along with his son who was an underkeeper, of removing five hundred loads of wood and timber over a four-year period and reducing an ample herd of deer to a mere ten head. The attorney-general prosecuted Richard Batten, forester of Pewsham Forest, Wiltshire, for destroying two-thirds of the deer entrusted to his care; Batten and his deputies killed so many deer that they made venison 'their ordinary meat and gave their servants no other food'. They were accused of selling the surplus and also cutting down three hundred loads of wood. When the deputy justice in eyre denounced Batten for his waste and spoil, the latter drew his sword and struck the deputy justice. Another high-ranking official prosecuted by the attorney-general during the reign of James I was Sir Richard Gifford, lieutenant of Neroche Forest, Somerset, who was accused of taking bribes to allow unlawful hunting and to remit the offences of those accused of poaching plus the usual matters of waste and spoil. Although Elizabeth would occasionally revoke grants of

---

[110] PRO STAC 8/109/16; E 134/41 and 42 Eliz., Mich. 4.
[111] Shaw, *Royal Forest of Lancaster*, 240–4, 259–62; PRO E 134/41 and 42 Eliz., Mich. 4; DL 1/24/A 29; STAC 8/259/10.

keeperships for waste and spoil, the early Stuart monarchs began a much more concerted effort to prosecute dishonest game and forest officials and to make examples of them in the Court of Star Chamber.[112]

When a game official was removed from office, it was often difficult to dislodge him. In 1577 Queen Elizabeth revoked the patent granting the keepership of Hungerford Park, Berkshire, to the earl of Pembroke, because his deputy had committed waste and spoil upon the vert and venison. The new deputy keeper complained to the Duchy Court of Lancaster that Thomas Cheyney, gent., the previous underkeeper, kept his office and lodge by force. Even when a keeper was in legal possession of his office and lodge, he needed to be prepared to defend the same. Walter Agard claimed to be the keeper of the park of Barton-under-Needwood and the escheator and coroner of the honour of Tutbury by inheritance, although he could pro-duce no other evidence for this claim except a white hunting staff decorated in the middle with silver gilt. His claim was disputed by Walter Horton, esq., who, with six retainers, broke into the park lodge and carried away the glass, casements, locks, wainscoting, floorboards, and water pumps. Horton's men proceeded next to kill the deer and cut down the 'great oaks', which stood in the park. Agard's son William sought compensation for this loss by stealing the letters patent granting Agardesley Park in Needwood Forest to a yeoman of the guard and forcibly entering into possession of the keepership himself.[113]

The fierce competition for forest and game offices led to frequent and violent disputes over the possession of forests and parks. This was espe-cially true in the north of England, where keepers and tenants of royal parks and forests had an obligation to equip themselves with horses and armour and render military service.[114] Consequently, it is likely that many of these tenants gained military experience serving on the Scottish border. In the late fifteenth and early sixteenth centuries the keeperships of parks and forests in Lancashire and Cheshire became concentrated in the hands of a few families, who held them by hereditary right—usually as deputies of the earls of Derby. Thus, Thurstan Tyldesley, the earl's receiver-general on the Isle of Man, became keeper of Myerscough Park, and his descendants retained that office into the eighteenth century. Sir Richard Sherburne of Stonyhurst was another official of the Stanley household, serving as governor of the Isle of Man and treasurer of the earl's household. Stanley patronage secured Sherburne's appointment as master forester of Bowland, bow-bearer of Bleasedale Forest, and keeper of Leagram Park. So complete was the Stanley

    [112] PRO DL 1/42/G3, 104/M9; STAC 8/7/9, 21/13.
    [113] PRO DL 1/104/M9, 196/A42, 200/A26, 200/A49; Sampson Erdeswick, *A Survey of Staf-fordshire*, ed. T. Harwood (1844), 274 n.
    [114] *Descriptive Catalogue of the Charters and Muniments in the Possession of Lord Fitzhardinge at Berkeley Castle*, ed. I. H. Jeayes (Bristol, 1892), no. 776.

monopoly on forest offices that the resulting competition among Lancashire gentry seeking keeperships heightened existing local feuds—setting Talbots and Hoghtons against Sherburnes, and Tyldesleys against Singletons.[115] Since the monarch rarely hunted in the forests of the north-west, the Stanleys and their allies got in the habit of regarding the hunting preserves as their own. In the reign of Mary, the Court of Duchy Chamber repeatedly ordered the copyholders of Bowland Forest, as the queen's tenants, to cease wearing the liveries of Sir Richard Sherburne and Sir Richard Townley. Although Sir Richard Sherburne was quick to use the royal courts to complain about the deer-stealers sent against him by his rivals, he had been known to deny royal officials access to Bowland without his permission. For a time Elizabeth regained possession of Leagram Park, which she granted to the earl of Leicester, but he, in turn, sold it back to Sherburne in 1563 for £1,618.[116]

An analysis of the deer-hunting culture reveals much about the aristocracy and gentry of Tudor and early Stuart England. In the absence of war, the rituals of hunting symbolically helped to define these social classes as a military élite. Hunting was, for many peers and gentlemen, the most time-consuming of all of their activities, and it remained an important part of country-house hospitality. A deer hunt, organized by the squire, with his servants attending and his tenants acting as beaters, provided one of those various occasions when the gentry and the commonalty gathered as a community. Like the seating arrangements in the parish church or the dispensing of justice by the justices of the peace at the quarter sessions, such ceremonial occasions were also intended to dramatize an individual's place in the social hierarchy. The ceremonies of public worship or the execution of the king's laws at the quarter sessions and the assizes had been refined over the centuries to achieve the greatest possible dramatic effect. A gathering of the aristocracy and gentry, mounted on their great hunters with dogs and beaters at their feet, or pursuing a stag through the woods and fields to the accompaniment of the music of the hounds and horns, was another spectacle that a countryman was unlikely ever to forget. Every visitor to Knole or Chatsworth or Longleat knows that the aristocracy and the greater gentry built their houses to display their power. These vast piles remain to inspire awe in the tourist, but the well-stocked deer parks, chases, and forests, which were once equally potent symbols of royal and aristocratic power and privilege, have mostly disappeared, together with deer-hunting in the old-fashioned mode.

---

[115] Shaw, *Royal Forest of Lancaster*, 84–7, 199–200; B. Coward, *The Stanleys, Lords Stanley and Earls of Derby, 1385–1672: The Origins, Wealth and Power of a Landowning Family* (Chetham Soc., 3rd ser., 30; Manchester, 1983), 85; PRO STAC 2/32/104.

[116] PRO DL 1/206/A8, 61/S1, S12, S14, S15, S16, 105/S3, 133/S7, 135/A50, DL 5/10, fos. 88–90ᵛ, 11, fo. 106ᵛ; STAC 8/15, 23/19.

The unlawful hunting of deer represented an attack upon the royal or aristocratic hunting preserve as a symbol of power, prerogative, and privilege. The Game Laws may thus be viewed as an attempt to buttress the royal prerogative and aristocratic privileges. But it was quite impossible to prevent the commonalty from poaching deer. They, too, felt the influence of the deer-hunting culture, and persisted in the belief that the law could not reserve wild beasts for the pleasure of a privileged few.

2

Poaching as a Symbolic Substitute for War

We need only recall how great a part was played by the chase in the life of a medieval man. It was the favourite sport of the nobles; in time of peace it offered a substitute for war, and was as dear to their hearts as the tournament itself.

C. Petit-Dutaillis, *Studies and Notes Supplementary to Stubbs'*
Constitutional History, trans. W. T. Waugh, 3 vols.
(Manchester, 1914), ii. 211

HUNTING was an integral part of aristocratic culture. It was the most es-teemed pastime among peers and gentlemen, and for many of them it was also the most time-consuming. Hunting, both lawful and unlawful, retained an aura of danger and adventure, and allowed a young gentleman to cut a figure by displaying feats of daring. For many it served as an adolescent rite of passage. That hunting was a rehearsal for war was a commonplace among writers of the Renaissance, who commended it the more highly because the ancients had pursued it as a pastime fit for kings and warriors. Indeed, hunting was not only a preparation for war; it was also a symbolic substitute for war at a time when, in England, the opportunities for full-scale combat were diminishing.[1]

During the early modern period the English aristocracy, like its continental counterparts, stood in danger of being overwhelmed by large infusions of new blood from inferior social groups carried upwards by wealth and fortune. V. G. Kiernan has pointed out how members of the aristocracy and gentry turned to the medieval past for symbols and pursuits which reasserted the martial values of a feudal society.[2] Just as jousting underwent

---

[1] Castiglione, *The Book of the Courtier*, 54; Lull, *The Book of the Ordre of Chivalry*, 31; Machiavelli, *The Prince*, p. xiv; Ascham, *The Scholemaster*, 217; Elyot, *The Gouernour*, i. 202 and n.; Cockayne, *A Short Treatise of Hunting*, sig. A3r−v; Peacham, *Compleat Gentleman*, 182–3. Xenophon (BC430–354), in his account of the life and education of Cyrus the elder of Persia, appears to be the source of the Renaissance maxim that hunting was a preparation for war (*Cyropaedia*, ed. and trans. W. Miller, 2 vols. (Cambridge, Mass., 1914), i. 19). Cf. also M. Thiébaux, *The Stag of Love: The Chase in Medieval Literature* (Ithaca, NY, 1974), 49. Cf. also Kiernan, *The Duel in European History*, 15, 55. For a discussion of unlawful hunting in England during this period, cf. Manning, *Village Revolts*, ch. 11. For a discussion of the concept of substitutes for war in tribal cultures, see C. Feest, *The Art of War* (1980), 11–12, 41–2.

[2] Kiernan, *The Duel in European History*, 152 *et passim*. For John Aubrey's assertion that hunting was at its peak in early Stuart times, see Aubrey, *Natural History of Wiltshire*, 60.

a resurgence in the sixteenth century and the duel emerged as a means of settling points of honour, so also rival factions of the English peerage and gentry pursued their violent feuds by means of poaching raids upon one another's deer parks. The purpose of this chapter is to describe and analyse the symbolic content of poaching in order to show its simulation of the rituals and elements of traditional land warfare.[3]

2.1. The Martial Symbolism of Hunting

The idea that hunting and war are 'symbolically interchangeable' is a familiar one to anthropologists and historians of the ancient world.[4] A medievalist has called hunting 'a surrogate for war', and, in marshalling literary evidence for a study of medieval hunting rituals, states: 'It is not inconceivable that the two activities of fighting and hunting were identified more closely at various times.'[5] Walter Burkert claims that the beginning of man as a social being derives from the need to band together and co-operate in order to hunt.[6] For Elias Canetti, the pack is a more primordial social unit than the crowd. Moreover, the hunting pack, consisting of ten to twenty people, and the war pack are closely related.[7] Both Canetti and Burkert agree that the hunting pack remained a persistent and basic unit of traditional society—as important in many ways as the family and household and certainly more so than the crowd. Indeed, Burkert assigns the hunting pack a basic role in the socialization and initiation of the boy into the world of men.

Thus man ever since the development of hunting has belonged to two overlapping social structures, the family and the *Männerbund* [hunting pack or fraternity]; his world falls into pairs of categories: indoors and out, security and adventure, women's work and men's work, love and death. At the core of this new type of male community, which is biologically analogous to a pack of wolves, are acts of killing and eating. The men must constantly move between the two realms, and their male children must one day take the difficult step from the women's world to the world of men. Fathers must accept their sons, educating them and looking after them. . . . When a boy finally enters the world of men, he does so by confronting death. . . . A man had to be courageous to take part in the hunt.[8]

---

[3] Some of the rituals and symbolic categories of traditional land warfare are derived from W. R. O'Connor, 'Early Greek Land Warfare as Symbolic Expression', *P&P*, no. 119 (Apr. 1988), 3–29. See also W. Burkert, *Homo Necans: The Anthropology of Ancient Greek Sacrificial Ritual and Myth*, trans. P. Bing (Berkeley, Calif., 1983), 47.

[4] Burkert, *Homo Necans*, 47.   [5] Thiébaux, 'The Medieval Chase', 261 and n.

[6] Burkert, *Homo Necans*, 18–19.

[7] E. Canetti, *Crowds and Power*, trans. C. Stewart (1962; repr. New York, 1978), 93.

[8] Burkert, *Homo Necans*, 18–19.

Although Burkert wrote these words about early Greek society, the belief that, in the absence of war, nothing tested a young man's courage as much as hunting, persisted into the eighteenth century. Gilbert White thought that the inclination to hunt was universal.

The temptation is irresistible; for most men are sportsmen by constitution: and there is such an inherent spirit for hunting in human nature, as scarcely any inhibitions can restrain. Hence towards the beginning of this century all this country was wild about deer-stealing. Unless he was a *hunter*, as they affected to call themselves, no young person was allowed to be possessed of manhood or gallantry.[9]

William Chafin, a late-eighteenth-century antiquarian, says that unlawful hunting by gentlemen 'was not deemed a disgrace', and this behaviour persisted into the early eighteenth century, when hunting at night or in disguise was made a felony by the Black Act of 1723. Chafin gives the example of an uncle who was much addicted to the sport. The uncle, who usually drank too much at dinner, was frequently captured by keepers as he muddled through his nocturnal sports; he paid the fines and continued to commit the same offence until his 'elder brother put a stop to his career in good time'.[10]

Just as hunting was a rehearsal for war and an adolescent rite of passage, it also came to be viewed as a more chivalrous alternative to sixteenth-century land warfare. Single combat and small skirmishes had no place in the siege warfare and massed infantry tactics of the sixteenth century. Given the highly technical and impersonal nature of warfare, military commanders necessarily placed a higher value upon the disciplined phalanxes of pikemen and musketeers than upon the valour and chivalry of mounted knights. War was stripped of glamour and adventure under such conditions, and the reaction to this manifests itself in a number of ways. Military writers of the Elizabethan period such as Sir John Smythe viewed campaigning in the Religious Wars in France and the Dutch War of Independence as chaotic, while the more idealized mode of warfare in Spenser's *Faerie Queene* took the form of individual combat.[11]

Although the major battle disappeared from European warfare during much of the sixteenth century,[12] Tudor gentlemen could still find opportunities

---

[9] Gilbert White, *The Natural History of Selborne* (1789; repr. 1965), 31–2.

[10] Chafin, *Second Edition of the Anecdotes and History of Cranbourne Chase*, pp. 72–3. See also E. P. Thompson, *Whigs and Hunters: The Origin of the Black Act* (New York, 1975), 58–62.

[11] M. West, 'Spenser's Art of War: Chivalric Allegory, Military Technology, and the Elizabethan Mock-Heroic Sensibility', *Renaissance Quarterly*, 41. 4 (1988), 654–5, 659; D. A. Jorgenson, *Shakespeare's Military World* (Berkeley, Calif. 1956), 37; C. Oman, *A History of the Art of War in the Sixteenth Century* (1937), 285–7; see also M. Vale, *Warfare and Aristocratic Culture in England, France and Burgundy at the End of the Middle Ages* (Athens, Ga., 1981), 171–4.   [12] M. Howard, *War in European History* (Oxford, 1976), 26–7.

for military service in France under Henry VIII and in the Low Countries, Ireland, and on the Scottish border during the reigns of Henry VIII's children. But James I's reign was an unusually peaceful one, and the apparent increase in gentry poaching during that period may owe something to the diminished opportunities for military service. Renaissance political theorists argued that one of the dangers faced by princes who employed their own subjects as soldiers was that such men, having acquired habits of violence and being without opportunity to win military glory and spoil, would deny the prince 'peaceful control of his state'.[13] A persistent theme which runs through Elizabethan and Jacobean literature in the writings of Shakespeare, Sir Fulke Greville, and Sir Robert Naunton is the fundamental cleavage in society between the soldier and the courtier. They inhabited two quite different worlds and held very different values. Soldiers, such as the earl of Essex and Sir John Perrot, were notoriously unable to abandon their military habits and adapt themselves to courtier society when they came home from the wars. Indeed, few men, besides Sir Philip Sidney, appear to have been able to bridge this gulf.[14] It is for this reason that even those writers who found hunting to be cruel and distasteful were inclined to excuse it as a safety-valve for the inherent human traits of aggression and violence, which might otherwise have found expression in war or rebellion.[15]

At a time when European rulers were granting numerous privileges to their aristocracies, the government of James I strictly forbade duelling[16] and restricted hunting privileges among the landed classes. Considerable numbers of non-armigerous or parochial gentry were excluded from hunting by the more stringent property qualifications of the Jacobean Game Laws.[17]

---

[13] Giovanni Botero, *The Reason of State* (1589), trans. and ed. D. P. Waley (1956), 171; see also Niccolò Machiavelli, *The Arte of War*, trans. P. Whitehorne (1560; repr. New York, 1967), 35–8; Jorgenson, *Shakespeare's Military World*, 34–5; K. M. Brown, *Bloodfeud in Scotland, 1573–1625: Violence, Justice and Politics in an Early Modern Society* (Edinburgh, 1986), 5.

[14] Jorgenson, *Shakespeare's Military World*, 216–21.

[15] J. R. Hale, 'Sixteenth-Century Explanations of War and Violence', in *Renaissance War Studies* (1983), 350–2.

[16] With the disappearance of chivalry from the battlefield in the sixteenth and early seventeenth centuries, the European aristocracies seemed to be more preoccupied with questions of honour. Elsewhere in Europe the duel seemed to be gaining ground, and a number of writers were at pains to justify it (Kiernan, *The Duel in European History*, ch. 4). The English, as prone to violence as the peoples of any other European cultures, were at the same time more legalistic than other peoples, and relished the protracted feuding that 'waging' law involved. Francis Bacon reflected the official point of view when he said that it was intolerable to have a law based upon honour and reputation for the aristocracy and divorced from religion and morality and another law for everyone else (Hale, 'Sixteenth-Century Explanations of War and Violence', 343).

[17] It is not entirely true, as Dr P. B. Munsche asserts, that the Jacobean Game Laws afforded 'sporting rights to most gentlemen and noblemen in England' (*Gentlemen and Poachers: The English Game Laws, 1671–1831* (Cambridge, 1981), 11). The Game Laws of 1603 and 1605 (1 Jac. I, c. 27; *SR* iv. 1055, and 3 Jac. I, c. 13; *SR* iv. 1088) had the effect of excluding a considerable number of small gentry who, because they held mostly copyhold land and insufficient freehold land, could not meet the property qualifications for possessing hunting weapons and dogs. See also Manning, *Village Revolts*, 286–7, 289.

Thus, when prosecuted in the Court of Star Chamber, many lesser gentry were described as being 'envious' of the deer parks of the more affluent gentry and nobility.[18] For such gentlemen, the fact that it was unlawful for them to hunt only increased the sense of adventure which surrounded the sport. Certainly, they carried chips on their shoulders regarding the denial of hunting privileges. Although gentlemen were often accompanied by servants and tenants when they went hunting, the sport remained pre-eminently an aristocratic and gentry pastime. Whatever it may have become in the eighteenth century, deer-stealing involved comparatively little warfare between gentry and peasants before 1640. Left to themselves, more humble folk preferred to take rabbits or fish.

Gentlemen deer-stealers of the pre-1640 period were not inclined to surrender meekly to gamekeepers and pay a fine, as William Chafin's uncle did. Knocking a gamekeeper on the head was half the fun of breaking into a deer park, and hunters invariably went armed and armoured for combat. This was the difference between the English gentry of the early seventeenth century and the eighteenth century. As Pareto wrote, 'Any élite which is not prepared to join in battle to defend its positions is in full decadence.'[19]

Killing and eating were highly ritualized in hunting and afford a reminder of the common sacrificial element which made hunting and warfare 'symbolically interchangeable'.[20] The ceremonies and rituals of hunting did not conclude with the kill; continuing into the early seventeenth century, hunting manuals describe the rites of 'undoing' a stag or a hart. Erasmus, in his satire of the ceremony of unlacing a buck, catches the atmosphere of religious cultism and implies that there is something distinctly unchristian in the hunters' antics:

And to this classis do they appertain that slight everything in comparison of hunting, and protest they take an unimaginable pleasure to hear the yell of the horns and the yelps of the hounds, and I believe could pick somewhat extraordinary out of their very excrement. And, then what pleasure they take to see a buck or the like unlac'd? Let ordinary fellows cut up an ox or a wether, 'twere a crime to have this done by anything less than a gentleman! who with his hat off, on his bare knees, and a cuttoe for that purpose (for every sword or knife is not allowable), with a curious superstition and certain postures, lays open the several parts in their respective order; while they that hem him in admire it with silence, as some new religious ceremony, though perhaps they have seen it an hundred times before. And if any of 'em chance to get the least peace of 't, he presently thinks himself no small gentleman. In all which they drive at nothing more than to become beasts themselves, while yet they imagine they live the life of princes.[21]

[18] PRO STAC 8/225/13, 191/6.

[19] V. Pareto, *Sociological Writings*, ed. S. E. Finer (New York, 1966), 136.

[20] Burkert, *Homo Necans*, 47.

[21] Desiderius Erasmus, *The Praise of Folly*, trans. John Wilson (1668; repr. New York, 1942), 158–9; cf. also *Sir Gawain and The Green Knight*, ed. J. A. Burrow (New Haven, Conn., 1982), 53–5, ll. 1319–71.

In an aristocratic or royal hunt, after the hunting party came upon the fallen deer, it was customary to allow a guest or the most important personage present to slit the throat of a stag or buck if it needed to be dispatched. A woodcut in Gascoigne's *The Noble Arte of Venerie or Hunting* (1575) depicts the royal huntsman handing Queen Elizabeth I a knife to open the belly of a stag.[22] Next, the hounds were coupled up, and the hunters formed lines on either side of the carcass according to rank, while the master of the game eviscerated and dismembered the carcass. The carcass was divided according to a carefully prescribed formula acknowledging the feats of the hunter or master of the hounds who had made the kill. The 'quarry' was prepared by piling the entrails neatly on the deerskin in order to reward the hounds and to reinforce the discipline to which they were subjected. The climax came when the head of the deer was severed and carried before the king or lord and the nose of the deer made to touch the ground in an obeisance which appears to have symbolized a restoration of order and the triumph of man over the natural world. While this was going on, the hunters who had horns blew the *mort*, while others hallooed and the hounds were encouraged to bay. This must have been an emotionally satisfying release, which also served to reinforce communal bonds and, on a smaller scale, to elicit a sense of fraternity. Depending upon the formality of the occasion, the hunters would march in procession homewards, bearing the parts of the deer. If the catch was abundant, portions would be bestowed on the poor, the church, and the local gentry as a demonstration of largesse. In the evening the hunting party would feast upon the catch—doubtless accompanied by much boasting about the day's exploits—and, since this was a special occasion, wine would be served instead of ale.[23] In the medieval period, even individual hunting, or stalking, when successful, was followed by a ceremonial undoing of the carcass so that the hounds might be immediately rewarded and the catch divided into more manageable portions to be hidden or carried away.[24] Observers have frequently noted that rites such as 'blooding', or the daubing of novice hunters with the blood of a dead stag, not only bespoke pagan origins, but also constituted a profanation of Christianity with its parody of baptism.[25]

The ceremonies surrounding the stag's head at the breaking of a deer

---

[22] Reproduced in H. L. Blackmore, *Hunting Weapons* (New York, 1972), 59.

[23] *The Master of Game by Edward Second Duke of York*, 194–6; *The Boke of Saint Albans by Dame Juliana Berners*, sigs. fii–iiij; Cockayne, *A Short Treatise of Hunting*, pp. vi–vii; *The Art of Hunting*, ll. 151–64; H. L. Savage, 'Hunting in the Middle Ages', *Speculum*, 8 (1933), 39; Shaw, *Royal Forest of Lancaster*, 81–2. See also Thomas, *Man and the Natural World*, 22–3; 28–9.

[24] *The Parlement of the Thre Ages*, ed. M. Y. Offord (EETS 246; 1959; repr. 1967), 2–3, ll. 65–96.

[25] J. Obelkevich, *Religion and Rural Society: South Lindsey, 1825–1875* (Oxford, 1976), 42–3. James I took delight in blooding his courtiers (D. H. Willson, *King James VI and I* (1963), 180).

appear to have been fruitful of a number of ritualized insults. When poachers wished to be particularly defiant, this symbolism was employed by displaying a stag's head impaled and in an upright position. The Northamptonshire eyre of 1272 revealed that poachers in Rockingham Forest had 'cut off the head of a buck and put it on a stake in the middle of a certain clearing . . . placing in the mouth of the aforesaid head a certain spindle; and they made the mouth gape towards the sun, in great contempt of the lord king and his foresters'.[26] The imagery is not perfectly clear, but some sort of sexual inversion and obscene gesture seems to be implied. The poachers, who were linked to an aristocratic household, also appear to be asserting that they dared to hunt in broad daylight rather than by stealth and darkness, and, having fired arrows at the keepers of the forest, were quite prepared to go on doing so.[27]

In Henrician Somerset, Sir William St Lo raided a deer park belonging to the bishop of Bath and Wells on several occasions, accompanied by as many as thirty persons. He once killed a total of thirty deer 'and in further despite did set their heads upon pales of the same park to the pernicious example and . . . great comfort and boldness of other malefactors'. St Lo may be the same person who was arrested in connection with Wyatt's Rebellion in 1554.[28] In Lancashire in 1531 gentlemen poachers defied gamekeepers who had ordered them out of the Forest of Amounderness by flinging stag heads against the keepers' lodge.[29] A gang of hunters preyed upon the deer of Sir John More, father of Sir Thomas More, at his house in North Mimms, Hertfordshire, and impaled the head of a buck upon a staff with a stick in its mouth facing towards the manor house.[30] The elder More may have aroused resentment in the neighbourhood by enclosing an illegal park.

2.2. Poaching and the Elements of Warfare

Complaints against deer-stealers in the Court of Star Chamber frequently mention banqueting and feasting by the culprits following their raids upon deer parks and forests. These simulated the feasts which traditionally followed battles. In 1622 a band of twenty or so poachers, led by Thomas Bowyer of Burnett Lodge, Leicestershire, yeom., particularly favoured the deer from a park belonging to Sir Henry Hastings of Braunston, who accused them of carrying the deer away and 'eating, spending and consuming

---

[26] *Select Pleas of the Forest*, ed. G. J. Turner (Selden Soc., 13; 1899), 38–9.
[27] Hanawalt, 'Men's Games, King's Deer', 190–1.
[28] PRO STAC 2/3, fo. 219; *The House of Commons, 1509–1558*, ed. S. T. Bindoff, 3 vols. (1982), iii. 260; *The House of Commons, 1558–1603*, ed. P. W. Hasler, 3 vols. (1981), iii. 330.
[29] Manning, *Village Revolts*, 289.
[30] PRO STAC 2/28/68.

the same deer in taverns, inns, alehouses, and in diverse other places of the said county of Leicester of evil respect and company in riotous excess [and] drunkenness'.[31] William, earl of Pembroke, lieutenant and keeper of Clarendon Park, complained that a gang of deer-stealers from Salisbury killed a buck and carried it back to town, where they feasted and banqueted in 'vaunting manner' and rejoiced 'that they had . . . killed and taken away the said buck to the great dishonour of your subject . . .'.[32] Pembroke, a great hunter himself, also was troubled by another band of poachers at his three deer parks near Sheffield. This band was led by Thomas Bright of Carnebrook, Yorkshire, gent., who styled himself 'Robin Hood'; his followers were known as his 'merry men', and one of his lieutenants was called 'Little John'. Bright's 'merry men' were alleged to have reduced one herd of 220 deer to sixty head. Witnesses testified that Bright openly boasted of his exploits and said that he 'had venison for any good fellow that came to him'. He once complained to one of Pembroke's keepers that 'you keep me not well supplied with venison'.[33] Poachers who hunted the red deer of Hatfield Chase, Yorkshire, boasted that they had accumulated so much venison that they had to salt down most of it.[34]

The venison dinners which celebrated the victories achieved in poaching raids were often the occasion for swearing oaths of loyalty and fraternal solidarity which bound together the members of hunting bands and poaching fraternities. William Cavendish, earl of Devonshire, complained that between March and December 1622 Chatsworth Park was repeatedly raided by a band of a dozen or so led by Robert Deane the younger of Beeley, Derbyshire, gent., and Philip Roulston of Wattnall, Nottinghamshire, who destroyed the park gates and hunted the deer. Devonshire stated that the poachers

did feast, riot and carouse and drink healths in very uncivil and disorderly manner, vaunting and bragging that they would have killed and slaine your subject's keepers and servants or any other that should have offered to have resisted or stayed them from killing your subject's said deer, vowing and binding themselves with many solemn oaths that whilst your said subject had any deer in his said park that they and such other good fellows their companions would not want venison, and threatening further that if they came in [for] trouble hunting in you subject's said park that they would make havock of all the deer in your subjects said park.[35]

When he was attorney-general, Sir Francis Bacon accused three members of a poaching fraternity in Kent of 'braving and rejoicing and greatly vaunting of the stolen venison and withal complotting and confederating together by oaths and other secret vows neither to reveal the same nor to

---

[31] PRO STAC 8/18/19; see also 116/18.
[32] PRO STAC 8/183/37.   [33] PRO STAC 8/183/5.
[34] PRO STAC 8/13/10; for similar boasts, see 116/19 and 32/1.   [35] PRO STAC 8/111/21.

accuse one another but to conceal the same so as it should not be manifested or discovered' . . . . The three defendants indeed refused to confess
or divulge any information.[36] The minor gentry and yeomen who took their
pleasure in Wakefield New Park were said to have organized themselves
into a 'fellowship'. They 'made great vaunts and brags that they can have
and kill so many [deer] thereof out of the said park as they think good'.
Many of them kept greyhounds, which was against the custom of the manor
of Wakefield.[37]

Hunting raids were frequently preceded or accompanied by challenges
and taunts. While patrolling the royal park of Bewdley, Worcestershire, in
June 1558, Walter Blount, an assistant to his father Sir George Blount as
keeper of the park, discovered Sir Robert Acton and his companions and
servants engaged in unlawful hunting. Acton's band assaulted Blount and
his two servants and wounded them (one of the servants was a boy). Acton
returned the same night with reinforcements to the number of twenty persons, who rode through the park and attempted to provoke Blount and
his servants into a fight by blowing their horns and shouting insults. Blount
did not answer—whether out of fear, prudence, or incapacity. Afterwards,
Acton's band went to Bewdley, where they awakened the whole town
riding through the streets boasting of their deeds.[38] In Henrician Lancashire,
Henry Kighley of Inskip, St Michael's-on-Wyre, defiantly warned the keepers
of Amounderness and Myerscough Forests that he was going to hunt deer 'in
despite of them'. In order 'to vex and weary them' with watching all night,
he boasted that he would lay the head of every deer which he killed next
to the keepers' lodge. True to his word, the keepers found the heads of a
hind and a calf next to the lodge on the morning of 20 December 1531.[39]

The hunting raid was frequently a disguised form of a challenge to a duel.
It signified that the victim was being called out to settle some point of
honour. When Sir Edward Pitt, an officer of the Court of Common Pleas,
purchased the manor of Kyre Wyre, Worcestershire, from Henry, Lord
Compton, in 1575, he acquired a deer park of five hundred acres filled with
300-year-old oaks. His neighbour, Sir Edward Foxe of Ludlow, sent a servant
with a message demanding permission to hunt in Pitt's park in words that
could only be construed as a challenge. Pitt refused, with the excuse that
most of his deer were dead of a murrain and he was not hunting himself.
Foxe knew that this was merely a pretext, and he, his wife, friends, and
servants frequently hunted in Pitt's park with great displays of defiance and,
on several occasions, laid siege to the keepers' lodge. Foxe combined these
poaching raids with extensive litigation and an attempt to have Pitt's son
arrested for highway robbery. In desperation, Pitt proposed through a

[36] PRO STAC 8/23/11; see also 37/15.
[37] PRO DL 1/149/A26–26a, DL 4/32/50.   [38] PRO STAC 4/4/54.
[39] Pleadings and Depositions in the Duchy Court of Lancaster, i. 228–9.

mediator that the dispute be settled by a duel—'in a more gentleman-like fashion'. The mediator, a neighbour named William Leighton, esq., displayed a curious ambivalence towards duelling, regarding it as the best way to settle the dispute, but withholding his consent because 'God's name be praised for it, we now live under a gracious king that governeth us in peace and . . . the law is now so proclaimed and the government so peaceable that matters were not by the sword but by the law to be decided'. Leighton was also named as a defendant by Pitt when he discovered that the former was partial to Foxe. Pitt's gamekeeper and some of Foxe's servants also exchanged challenges, but it appears that Foxe, a justice of the peace, refused to consent to any duels. One can only conclude that he preferred poaching raids as an alternative to duelling because they were legally less dangerous.[40]

The taunts hurled at gamekeepers sometimes included challenges to duels. Gervase Lee, a Nottinghamshire justice of the peace, complained that John Welcome, gent., a person of 'very quarrelsome and contentious disposition', had presumed to hunt in Sherwood Forest while the king was hunting there in 1617. Welcome's response was to call the magistrate out. Welcome frequently took deer, pheasants, and hare from Sherwood Forest and carried them to alehouses, where he had them prepared and made 'great jollity and sport' while feasting upon them. Lee was also the keeper of Norwood Park, which belonged to the archbishop of York. He was hard put to defend the deer in his charge against the bold poachers of Sherwood Forest, who regularly assaulted and beat his underkeeper, bragging 'that they came for venison and venison would have in despite of' Lee and his underkeeper.[41]

Sir Fulke Greville was faced with similar problems in Feckenham Forest, where he was master of the game, keeper, bailiff, and ranger. This gave him a considerable amount of patronage of forest and game offices. He appears to have sold the office or deputyship of master of the game to Sir Henry Bromley, who, in late November 1593, came to Greville's deputy ranger, Edmund Morgan, esq., to claim his fee-buck for the season. Morgan refused Bromley's request, because he did not have a warrant for claiming his fee-buck with him and because Bromley was accompanied by a band of twenty kinsmen, servants, and retainers and a great number of hounds, which Morgan thought was an excessive force for taking one buck. This was a great affront to Bromley, who was not to be deterred. When Morgan and his underkeepers discovered them in the forest, Bromley's hunting party, hoping to provoke the keepers into a fight, made 'terrible outcries and exclamations' and displayed their deer carcasses in front of them in order to challenge Morgan's authority. Like a faithful keeper, Morgan attempted to confiscate the venison and apprehend the poachers. They fell upon

[40] *VCH Worcs.*, iv. 282–3; PRO STAC 8/244/1.   [41] PRO STAC 8/204/5, 194/3.

Morgan, an aged man, with swords and daggers, wounded him, and took his horse away from him in order to carry the deer carcasses out of the forest.[42]

Since the hunting raid was closely related to the duel and traditional warfare, it is not surprising that victims perceived that their honour had been slighted and required satisfaction. William Shelton of Ongar Park, Essex, was much troubled with hunters raiding his park and complained on four different occasions to the Court of Star Chamber. He said that he would suffer disgrace if he allowed poachers to hunt his deer with impunity and to challenge his authority.[43] Sir Peter Leigh of Lyme Handley, Cheshire, was the master of one of those large northern households which was full of unruly servants. John Gaskell, the keeper of his deer park, together with his underkeepers and other of Leigh's servants, and tenants, made a practice of hunting deer in Macclesfield Forest. John Hallywell, one of the royal keepers of Macclesfield, complained to Leigh, but the latter failed to rebuke his servants, which only encouraged them to continue hunting. Hallywell and the other keepers of the royal forest felt humiliated, and decided to take matters into their own hands by hunting deer within Lyme Park. The keepers of Macclesfield destroyed part of Leigh's park pales and wall and drove the deer out, saying 'that they would hunt and kill your said subject's [Leigh's] deer in the said park in despite of your said subject and any thing your said subject could do'. Leigh prosecuted the royal keepers in Star Chamber, but, through mediation, he agreed to forgive the royal keepers (and presumably drop the charges) if they would make an apology admitting their wrongs. This left Leigh with his honour satisfied.[44]

Descriptions of the arms and armour worn by Tudor and early Stuart poachers indicate that they sought combat as well as venison. Hunting manuals did not specify that gentlemen hunters needed to wear or carry any equipment of war other than a hanger, dagger, and javelin, or, possibly, a longbow or crossbow. Swords and javelins were favoured by purists for killing the deer.[45] The hunting costume favoured by royalty and aristocrats who were looking only for recreation was usually distinguished by its colour—dark green—and its relative simplicity.[46] Some bills of complaint in Star Chamber state only that the defendants carried 'weapons invasive and defensive', which some historians have argued was a formulaic statement

---

[42] PRO STAC 5/G2/6, G17/26.

[43] PRO STAC 8/255/7–8, 9–10.   [44] PRO STAC 8/198/24.

[45] Elyot, *The Gouernour*, i. 192–6; *Autobiography of Lord Herbert of Cherbury*, ed. Lee, 99–100.

[46] See Robert Peake's portrait of Henry, Prince of Wales, and John, Lord Harington of Exton, in hunting attire (1604) in the Royal Collection. Also descriptions of James I in *Works of Francis Osborn*, pt. 3, pp. 444–5, and the description by Anthony Ashley Cooper, earl of Shaftesbury, of Henry Hastings of Woodland (d. 1650), printed in Hutchins, *History and Antiquities of Dorset*, iii. 154.

used to support an allegation of riot in order to gain a hearing in Star Chamber or to vex a rival with a cross suit. But many other complaints specify the kinds of weapons and armour worn by deer-stealers and make it quite clear that the weapons were actually employed.

The armour worn by one band of hunters in Corse Lawn Chase, Gloucestershire, consisting mostly of small gentry, included jacks, gauntlets, and skulls. For arms they equipped themselves with swords and bucklers, daggers, guns, dags, gabonets, forest bills, and staves, and they were accompanied by stalking horses and dogs. Although they hunted by stealth from behind stalking horses, they were not afraid to confront the keepers. When they killed a buck or two, they did openly 'march and troop' through the chase bearing their prey in triumph.[47] When Godfrey Foljambe hunted the deer of his enemy, Sir Peter Frescheville, in 1545, his men were armed with two-handed swords, bills, halberds, longbows, and crossbows, plus nets and caltrops. Disdaining to hunt surreptitiously, they employed hounds and horns.[48]

Poachers who could not afford armour of steel usually wore 'thick coats' and 'quilt caps'.[49] But in the Vale of Berkeley, where bloody poaching wars raged from the fifteenth century into the reign of James I, even husbandmen and artificers customarily wore helmets, breast plates, and quilted jacks when they hunted. Forked arrows were used for combat as well as hunting. In an encounter in Berkeley New Park between Lord Berkeley's keeper and a gang of poachers (probably procured by his rival, Sir Thomas Throgmorton), Lord Berkeley's keeper killed a poacher with a forked arrow. At the next quarter sessions the keeper was suddenly indicted for murder, while he stood in the county hall talking to John Smyth of Nibley, the antiquarian and Berkeley steward. Smyth, who was a tall man, hid the keeper under his cloak until he could get him out of the hall, and then helped him to escape out of the county.[50]

Hunting bands not only assembled wearing full arms and armour, but also performed the ceremonies of trooping and parading. Hunting horns provided music to evoke the martial spirit.[51] William Stanley, third Lord Monteagle, engaged in a most unfilial dispute with his stepmother and mother-in-law, Dame Ellen Stanley. He contended that she did not possess liberty of free warren on her dower lands on the manor of Hornby, Lancashire, and he attempted to hunt on those lands. Dame Ellen's servants and tenants demonstrated their loyalty (or manorial obligations) by assembling

---

[47] PRO STAC 8/15/27.   [48] PRO STAC 2/15, fo. 321.

[49] PRO STAC 8/198/14; see also 37/14, 224/30.

[50] PRO STAC 5/B76/35, STAC 8/80/9; Smyth, *Berkeley Manuscripts*, ii. 351.

[51] For a discussion of the metaphor of 'warfare as a musically-guided dance', see Jorgenson, *Shakespeare's Military World*, ch. 1, esp. pp. 4–5. The 'Musick of the field' was considered to be especially important for the conduct of war and the maintenance of order and morale among the ranks. Music was also the main means of communication once the battle had begun.

at the blowing of a horn on a hillside in Boltondale in order to prevent Monteagle from hunting. Monteagle sought revenge by calling out some forty of his tenants, who marched from Hornby to Boltondale, where they pulled down Dame Ellen's hedges, killed most of the deer, and trampled fields of ripe grain. One assumes that this was done in obedience to Monteagle's command to spoil and pillage his stepmother's possessions.[52]

In Henrician Staffordshire, Sir Edward Aston, the hereditary master of the game of Cannock Chase, assembled his servants and mustered several townships in order to deny Walter Devereux, Lord Ferrers, the right to hunt in Cannock Chase. Aston awakened the inhabitants with a proclamation calling upon them to assist him in preserving the king's deer and promising each a piece of venison for his labour. In order to affirm his right to hunt on Cannock Chase, Ferrers summoned his tenants to follow him. The latter probably had a manorial obligation to accompany their lord when hunting; such obligations were common in the West Midlands. Both men had been spoiling for a confrontation and each accused the other of ambushes and attempted murder.[53]

The military ceremonies employed by poachers clearly conveyed the warlike nature of their activities. On the night of 30 June 1606, a band of hunters, numbering about a dozen and led by William Hall of Milton, Wiltshire, mustered themselves in military order in the middle of Marlborough and marched off to Tottenham Park in Savernake Forest. After breaking down the gate and the park pales, they killed a buck and many other deer. The buck was paraded out of the park tied to and hanging by the feet from a long pikestaff and was borne in ceremony to the house of Thomas Powell in Marlborough. The park belonged to Edward Seymour, earl of Hertford, and the band of poachers continued to raid his deer parks in Savernake Forest for the rest of the summer. The gates of Savernake Park were kept locked and were unusually strong. The Marlborough hunters managed to get hold of a key and had a duplicate made. Equipped with guns and crossbows armed with forked arrows, they made war on the deer and keepers alike and left several of the latter seriously wounded.[54]

2.3. Poaching as Theatre

While some forms of unlawful hunting can be viewed as a game that men played or an affirmation of male prowess,[55] other forms of poaching wore

---

[52] PRO DL 1/50/S9, 65/S8.

[53] PRO STAC 2/15, fos. 50–6; Thomas Blount, *Fragmenta Antiquitatis: or, Ancient Tenures of Land and Jocular Customs of Manors* (1845), 516–17, 529–32.

[54] PRO STAC 8/255/1.

[55] Hanawalt, 'Men's Games, King's Deer', 175–93; Johan Huizinga, *Homo Ludens: A Study of the Play Element in Culture* (Boston, 1955), 64–5.

a more sinister visage. The next example will show that the symbolic content of hunting as warfare was not limited to the subculture of backwoods gentry deer-stealers. While on a royal progress in 1572, the earl of Leicester persuaded Queen Elizabeth to depart from the officially scheduled itinerary through Gloucestershire in order to visit Berkeley Castle during the absence of Henry, eleventh Lord Berkeley. While there, she and Leicester hunted Berkeley's prized red deer and 'such slaughter was made, as 27 stags were slain in the Toils in one day, and many others in that and the next [day] stolen and havocked'.[56] While it is a nice legal point as to whether the queen could commit the offence of unlawful hunting anywhere in her realm, the fact remains that 'havocking' Lord Berkeley's red deer was an act analogous to war and was so perceived.

'Havoc' is an old military term—an order given to spoil and pillage the enemy.[57] Its meaning goes considerably beyond the idea of poaching or deer-stealing. The term carries the meaning of utterly destroying the deer in a hunting preserve and implies a kind of warfare. The word is occasionally used in Star Chamber complaints to describe poachers who wantonly killed more deer than they could possibly carry away, leaving many carcasses behind to spoil.[58]

In this particular case of Elizabeth and Leicester havocking Berkeley's deer, the message intended may have been the symbolic crushing of a potential rebellion.[59] John Smyth supposed that Leicester had wished to provoke a quarrel and draw Berkeley into treason. Berkeley, who was more fond of hunting than anything else, fell into the trap and, after he heard what had happened, disparked his park in a fit of pique. Elizabeth, or someone close to her, sent an anonymous but friendly warning to Berkeley, telling him that he was treading on very dangerous ground. Smyth remembered that Thomas Burdets of Arrow, Warwickshire, had been lured into a similar trap in the eighteenth year of the reign of Edward IV after the duke of Clarence encouraged the king to hunt in Burdets's deer park. Berkeley's brother-in-law, Thomas, duke of Norfolk, had recently been executed for treason, and Elizabeth had just granted some of the Berkeley estates, which had long been disputed between the Dudley

---

[56] Smyth, *Berkeley Manuscripts*, ii. 378–9. Lord Berkeley may well have caused offence to the queen by absenting himself from the county on the occasion of a royal progress instead of offering hospitality and entertainment (L. Stone, *The Crisis of the Aristocracy, 1558–1641* (abridged edn.; New York, 1967), 208–9).

[57] *OED.*   [58] PRO STAC 8/111/21, 255/7–8, 9–10.

[59] In 1537[?] Henry VIII presided over a royal hunt in which 240 deer were slaughtered in one day and the scene was repeated the next day. M. St Clare Byrne could not help wondering if this spectacle, which one might describe as 'political theatre', did not reflect the executions of the northern rebels, which were going on at that time in the wake of the Pilgrimage of Grace (*Lisle Letters*, ed. Byrne, vi. 177). See also Hanawalt, 'Men's Games, King's Deer', 185. For an incisive discussion of Elizabeth's theatricality, see S. Greenblatt, *Renaissance Self-Fashioning from More to Shakespeare* (Chicago, 1980), 165–9.

and Berkeley families, to Leicester and his brother, Ambrose, earl of Warwick.[60]

The use of the hunting party as a cover for a military raid was an ancient subterfuge still familiar to the audiences of sixteenth-century ballads.[61] One particularly well-known ballad is 'Chevy Chase', or 'The Hunting of the Cheviot', which depicts a fictional poaching foray, undertaken by Henry Percy, earl of Northumberland, across the Scottish border into the Cheviot Hills, in which Percy vows to continue hunting for three days before return-ing. In the fictional ballad version, Earl Douglas, the chief ranger of all the parks and chases in Scotland, sends a herald to command Percy and his men to depart immediately or be prepared to forfeit their lives. Earl Percy was bound by honour to refuse, and so Douglas marched south to take up the challenge. The latter proposed a single combat between him and Percy, but their lieutenants refused to countenance this and insisted on fighting alongside their lords. The ballad and chapbook histories depict several thousand men, including Percy and Douglas, dying in the ensuing battle.[62]

'Chevy Chase' was first printed in a minstrel book in the mid-sixteenth century, but it was already old by then. 'Chevy Chase' is a variant of another popular ballad, 'The Battle of Otterburn', in which the action takes place south of the River Tweed.[63] Although the details about Earl Percy and Earl Douglas are fictional, 'Chevy Chase' is thought to reflect the spirit of border warfare as late as the middle of the sixteenth century. The fictionalized account of Earl Percy's hunting in the Cheviot Hills has been compared to the custom, described by Robert Carey, Lord Hunsdon (later earl of Monmouth), of how the Scots and the English undertook poaching forays across the border as a challenge to a contest.[64]

---

[60] Smyth, *Berkeley Manuscripts*, ii. 378–9, 288–96. For a summary of the dispute between the Berkeleys and the Lisles (and their heirs the Dudleys), which gave rise to what is supposed to be the longest lawsuit in English history, see J. H. Cooke, 'The Great Berkeley Lawsuit of the 15th and 16th Centuries', *Trans. Bristol and Glos. Arch. Soc.*, 3 (1878–9), 305–24; Sir Robert Atkyns, *The Ancient and Present State of Gloucestershire* (1768), 138–9; and GEC viii. 58 and n.

[61] It was also frequently resorted to by Attila the Hun (Thiébaux, 'The Medieval Chase', 261 n.) According to Xenophon, the young Cyrus the elder's first exposure to war came when hostile Assyrians dared to hunt in Median territory. Cyrus pursued the Assyrians and slaugh-tered them (ead., *The Stag of Love*, 49). See also Machiavelli, *The Arte of War*, 217, for an account of Hannibal's use of a similar strategem against the Romans. In anticipation of the execution of the Gunpowder Plot, Robert Catesby gathered fellow conspirators together at Ashby St Ledgers, his home in the Midlands, on 5 Nov. 1605, on the pretext of conducting a deer hunt (M. Nicholls, *Investigating Gunpowder Plot* (Manchester, 1991), 41).

[62] *The Famous and Renowned History of the Memorable but Unhappy Hunting on Chevy Chase by the River Tweed in Scotland* (1710), unpaginated.

[63] An account of the Battle of Otterburn, fought in August 1388, is found in Jean Froissart's *Chronicle*, chs. 136–43.

[64] *Bishop Percy's Folio Manuscript: Ballads and Romances*, ed. J. H. Hales and F. J. Furnivall, 3 vols. (1867–8), ii. i. 1–4; D. C. Fowler, 'Ballads', in A. R. Hartung (ed.), *A Manual of the Writings in Middle English, 1050–1500*, 9 vols. (New Haven, Conn., 1916; repr. 1980), vi. 1775; id., *A Literary History of the Popular Ballad* (Durham, NC, 1968), 12–13, 108–14; *Memoirs of Robert Cary, Earl of Monmouth*, ed. G. H. Powell (1905), 67–9.

An ambush disguised as a hunting party occurred in Nottinghamshire late in the reign of Elizabeth. Sir Charles Cavendish was keeper of a walk in Sherwood Forest, and he and his wife often used to stay at the lodge in the forest that went with the keepership. One morning, early in the summer of 1599, he rode out, accompanied by only three servants, when he spied about twenty horsemen on a hillside, which at first he took for a hunting party led by Sir John Byron, another forest official. As the hunting party galloped closer towards Cavendish, he 'perceived himself betrayed', and recognized the leader as a hated rival, Sir John Stanhope. Cavendish's horse fell upon him as he tried to turn and defend himself. Before he could draw his sword, Stanhope's men fired their pistols and Cavendish received several bullet wounds in the thigh. Yet he and two manservants and the young page who accompanied him, despite the overwhelming odds and armed only with daggers and rapiers, beat off their attackers and killed two on the spot and mortally wounded a third. Cavendish's battle trophies included two rapiers, two pistols, a sword, and a dagger, six horses, and a number of cloaks and hats—all of which he kept.[65]

This was merely one nasty episode in the feud between the Stanhopes and the Cavendishes, which was subsumed by the larger feud between Gilbert Talbot, seventh earl of Shrewsbury, and Sir Thomas Stanhope of Shelford, Nottinghamshire.[66] Although the Privy Council ordered the sheriff to take sureties from both parties to the dispute binding them to their good behaviour, it is difficult to avoid the conclusion that queen and council frequently condoned violent encounters between members of the aristocracy. The records of the Court of Star Chamber are full of such incidents which were leniently punished or which went unpunished. Although the Cavendish–Stanhope feud probably arose from competition for forest and game offices in Sherwood Forest, Sir John Stanhope was soon afterwards made keeper of Thorneywood Chase within Sherwood Forest. Despite Stanhope's reputation for being a violent and quarrelsome man, he was later raised to the peerage as Baron Stanhope of Harrington.[67]

Many poachers pursued their prey at night—often wearing vizers or blackened faces. They were usually armed and armoured and prepared to face the keepers if need be. But a number of bold hunters deliberately sought out the keepers before they commenced hunting. In Staffordshire, a gang of poachers led by the sons of John Scrimsher, esq.—both legitimate and illegitimate—made frequent forays against Knightley Park, which

---

[65] *Cal. SP, Dom., 1598–1601*, 222; *The Letters of John Chamberlain*, ed. N. McClure, 2 vols. (Philadelphia, 1939), i. 75–7. Cornelius Brown, *Lives of Nottinghamshire Worthies* (1882), 163–4.

[66] W. T. MacCaffrey, 'Talbot and Stanhope: An Episode in Elizabethan Politics', *BIHR* 33 (May 1960), 73–85, esp. 79–85. Sir Charles Cavendish was brother-in-law to Gilbert, earl of Shrewsbury.   [67] Brown, *Lives of Nottinghamshire Worthies*, 163–4.

belonged to their neighbour, Sir George Blount. This hunting band, usually comprising twenty persons, made a practice, after breaking into the park, of first attacking the keepers' lodge and terrifying the keepers into submission or flight. On one occasion a keeper protested that he would have been murdered in his bed if he had not escaped by running stark naked out of the back door of the lodge.[68] Robert Sapcotes of Ayleton, Huntingdonshire, esq., also terrorized the keepers into passivity before hunting in his neighbours' parks. Oliver Leder, one of the six clerks of Chancery under Philip and Mary, complained that Sapcotes, accompanied by fifteen men, broke down his park palings and attacked the moated keeper's lodge. Armed with crossbows and longbows, they fired several volleys at the keeper and his wife; the latter 'was put in such fear that forthwith she fell sick'. The poachers scared off the 18-year-old underkeeper, who jumped into the moat to escape a shower of arrows. The culprits then hunted at their leisure in two different deer parks belonging to Leder.[69] Brian Bellamy of Askham, Nottinghamshire, gent., raided Longwith Park, Derbyshire, belonging to William, Lord Cavendish of Hardwick, several times during the summer of 1607. On one occasion the keepers reported that the hunters were 'so desperate and well armed a company [that] in their own defence [they] were forced to flee for the safeguard of their lives'. On another occasion Bellamy fired a petronell at the keepers and forced them to yield with another cocked at their faces. They were kept prisoner until the hunters had finished and departed. Many of Cavendish's deer were hamstrung and left to die.[70]

Clearly, poaching raids of this sort went beyond sport and obtaining venison. Edward Corbet, gent., led a band of fourteen persons in a midnight attack on Allbrighton Park, Shropshire. They drove the keepers back into the lodge with volleys of arrows and kept them confined to their lodge for the duration of the hunt by showering the lodge with arrows every time a keeper showed himself. Sir John Talbot, the park owner, alleged that Corbet's men killed every deer in the park with a pack of twenty greyhounds.[71] Hunting as symbolic warfare was a tradition in some families. A large band of Lancashire gentry led by Richard Curwen of Caton hunted with impunity in the Royal Park of Quernmore in 1523–4. John Turner, underkeeper of the park, complained that the deer-stealers procured persons 'disguised in women's apparel' to lie in wait to ambush and murder him; he was so terrified that he dared not live in his lodge or discharge his office for fear of his life and he never went abroad without company. A century later, in 1602, another keeper of Quernmore Park discovered that even gifts of venison to the Curwen household did not deter them from hunting the king's deer.[72]

---

[68] PRO STAC 5/B38/18, B103/10.   [69] PRO STAC 4/6/77; see also STAC 8/178/14.
[70] PRO STAC 8/85/10.   [71] PRO STAC 2/24/234.
[72] *Pleadings and Depositions in the Duchy Court of Lancaster, Time of Henry VII and Henry VIII*, ed. Fishwick, i. 115; PRO DL 1/200/A18.

Although it was proverbial wisdom that 'the greatest deer-stealers make the best park-keepers', many keepers were wounded and not a few killed discharging their offices and defending their masters' deer. A loyal keeper would sooner die than part with his staff, the symbol of his office. Roger Garrett, gamekeeper to Richard Cholmeley, single-handedly fought off four deer-stealers who told him that he would 'lose his life or he lost his staff'. Garrett held on to his staff even after the poachers wrestled him to the ground.[73]

In a warrior society, when the conquerors have vanquished their enemies, they exult in their victory and carry away trophies and prisoners whom they enslave or hold for ransom. Similitudes may be discerned in the victory rites of hunters and poachers. After an unsuccessful attempt to repulse deer-stealers in Wyre Forest in which two underkeepers were wounded and disabled, the head keeper described Leonard Meyslie, esq., and his fellow culprits as leaving the forest 'triumphantly', carrying the deer carcasses 'as if they had thereby gotten and won a great victory and upper hand'.[74] John Norton of Norton Conyers, West Riding of Yorkshire, esq., claimed the right of free warren over his lands within the disputed lordship of Kirkby Malzeard in Craven, but Henry, first earl of Cumberland, thought that his hunting franchises superseded and extinguished everyone else's right to hunt. Norton complained that Cumberland's men assaulted his tenants while they were hunting on the former's lands, fired arrows at them and wounded a number, and carried the tenants to Skipton Castle, where they were imprisoned for two months until fines were extorted from them. Cumberland's servants continued to hunt in Norton's free warren and to intimidate Norton's tenants and servants.[75]

In a society permeated by military values, when a lord's followers were taken prisoner, he was bound in honour to attempt to rescue the prisoners. John Talbot of Bashall, Yorkshire, esq., procured a large number of his servants and tenants to hunt the king's deer in Bashall Park in Bowland Forest. Two of his men were caught by the keepers and imprisoned in the keeper's lodge. Talbot, who was a justice of the peace, assembled a large number of people the following night and then marched to the keepers' lodge and rescued the prisoners. They then hunted in Bashall Park the remainder of that night and on several subsequent occasions.[76]

An anonymous critic of young gentlemen who wasted time hunting to the neglect of their studies cited, half-jestingly, a countryman's proverb

---

[73] Tilley, *A Collection of the Proverbs in England in the Sixteenth and Seventeenth Centuries*, 148–9; Manning, *Village Revolts*, 298–9; *Memorandum Book of Richard Cholmeley of Brandsby*, 173.   [74] PRO STAC 5/B5/3.

[75] PRO STAC 2/27/143. For a discussion of the Craven riots of 1531 and 1535 and the dispute concerning the lordship of Kirkby Malzeard, West Riding of Yorks., see Manning, *Village Revolts*, 48–9.   [76] PRO DL 1/196/A25.

which said that 'he cannot be a gentleman which loveth not a dog'.[77] Englishmen were devoted to their dogs and poachers would fight fiercely to preserve their hounds from harm. Conversely, keepers and poachers regarded one another's dogs as legitimate captives or trophies of battle; one may infer that the capture of the other's hounds or the safeguarding of one's own hounds could preserve a man's honour and reputation even though other goals, such as protecting or taking deer, might not be achieved.[78] Edward Yardley of Henley-in-Arden, Worcestershire, gent., led a band of hunters in April 1608 into Lapworth Park, which belonged to Sir Thomas Holte of Dudstone, and wounded the keeper when he attempted to apprehend them. The hunters vowed 'that they would die . . . before either they or their dogs would be stayed'. Several months later another confrontation occurred in the same park between Yardley's band and the keeper, in which eight poachers battled the keeper, his wife, and the keeper's servant. One of Yardley's companions attacked the keeper with a pitchfork when the latter tried to confiscate a greyhound—'swearing great oaths that if he the said keeper laid hands on the said greyhound, he would let his puddings [down] about his heels'. The keeper, Thomas Hill, was able both to defend himself and to confiscate the greyhound. The hunters had since 'given it forth [that] if your Majesty's said subject's keeper do or shall make away the said greyhound, they or some of them would make the best blood in his body to pay for him'. The hunters had their revenge at the next market day in Henley-in-Arden, when one of Yardley's kinsmen shot the keeper's lymehound in the midst of the market. The poaching resumed on an even larger scale, and it is evident that the keeper's action in confiscating the greyhound merely escalated the conflict.[79]

William Fleetwood of Calwich, Staffordshire, was one of those lesser gentry who were more endowed with leisure than wealth. Two different complainants in Star Chamber described him as being envious of the squire-archy's deer parks. He was as much interested in picking quarrels with his neighbours as he was in raiding their parks. Hunting with bands of twelve to thirty companions, Fleetwood raided Little Park, belonging to Rowland Okeover of Okeover, esq., on numerous occasions during the summer, autumn, and winter of 1607–8, and killed a large number of deer. On the last occasion, on 26 February 1608, Fleetwood left one of his greyhounds in Okeover Little Park, so that there would be no mistaking who had killed Okeover's deer. On the next market day, Fleetwood and one hundred of his

---

[77] Anon., *Institucion of a Gentleman*, fo. 45ʳ⁻ᵛ.

[78] William, Lord Cavendish of Hardwick thought that greyhounds were not used for any purpose except hunting. He said that they were 'kept for the stealing, killing and destroying of deer being dogs that were tried and approved to be murdering dogs, and such as no deer was able to escape' (PRO STAC 8/100/15).

[79] PRO STAC 8/169/19. One of the poachers styled himself a captain and may have been recently returned from Ireland.

supporters went to Ashborne, Derbyshire, where Okeover lived, in order to demand the return of Fleetwood's greyhound. A large crowd marched to Okeover's house to rescue the greyhound, and threatened to cut off the head of Okeover's servant, William Barke, if he did not hand over the dog. The town constable, who was marching with the besieging crowd, ordered Barke, under pretence of preserving order, to give him the hound, and promised to return it when the crowd had dispersed. Instead, the constable gave the greyhound to Fleetwood, and the whole company marched off in triumph to a tavern, where they drank and boasted of their deeds for the space of four hours. Afterwards, Fleetwood and his companions went hunting once again in Okeover Little Park.[80]

Many gentlemen in Tudor and early Stuart England remained perpetual adolescents, and it is sometimes difficult to distinguish between the rites practised by hunters and children's games. The deer-stealers who frequently raided Wardour Park, Wiltshire, belonging to Lord Arundell of Wardour, on one occasion kidnapped an underkeeper to prevent him from raising the alarm. But, on another occasion, a different band of hunters, after overpowering the two keepers, merely took away their hats and staves and hid them 'where they cannot as yet be found'.[81] Gentlemen deer-stealers required symbols of their victories even where such symbols appear to be trivial and childish. Yet violent confrontations between keepers and poachers were mixed in with these more playful elements.

Hunting was many things in Tudor and early Stuart England. Certainly, it afforded sport and recreation for kings and aristocrats as it had always done and provided an opportunity to develop and display the skills and the courage necessary for war. It was also a ritualized simulation of war involving calculated and controlled levels of violence carried on between rival factions of the gentry and peerage. Symbolically, the various rites of hunters derive from the elements of traditional land warfare: challenges, taunts, boasting, swearing oaths of loyalty, wearing arms and armour, the capture and display of trophies of battle, ransom of captives, banqueting and feasting after victory, martial music and ceremonies of trooping and parading, as well as actual combat. Greyhounds might be treated as hostages and prisoners of war, while stag heads served as surrogates for the heads of the vanquished or traitors impaled upon stakes. This ritualized combat was undertaken to satisfy honour and was sometimes perceived as a more acceptable alternative to duelling under the laws of England.

Hunting was also more than a simulation of war. In a histrionic age when kings and aristocrats continued to feel the need to fashion an image, hunting

---

[80] PRO STAC 8/191/6, 225/13; see also 183/40 and 178/14. Fleetwood was still pursuing his career as a deer-stealer in 1615.   [81] PRO STAC 8/37/16, 37/15.

was also political theatre and provided an occasion to display power.[82] This was an age when both state and family were asserting themselves: the Tudor monarchs had attempted to suppress private warfare and punish rebellion very seriously; aristocratic families found the more overt forms of rebellion and civil war too dangerous and had to be more subtle and circumspect than their late-medieval predecessors in pursuing feuds or expressing political opposition. Courtiers and dramatists learnt to use plays, masques, and country-house entertainments to articulate grievances and to engage in controversy in an oblique and plausibly deniable fashion.[83] Hunting raids on deer parks and royal forests were indeed punishable as riots, but, since they were legally classified as misdemeanours, such antics remained on the safe side of the laws of treason. Yet, they spoke a covert language which was clear enough to both courtiers and backwoods small gentry.

It cannot escape the reader that the behaviour of gentlemen poachers displays at least as much bravado as action. Such displays of bravado were undoubtedly enhanced by the practice of organizing poaching raids in ale-houses. From what literary critics tell us of Elizabethan and Jacobean literature and learned culture, the symbolic rituals of gentlemen hunters appear to display a mock-heroic sensibility. Some of them must have perceived that the chivalric virtues, which they had learnt to admire from their reading, had become outmoded in sixteenth-century warfare. Thus, the attempt to act out the chivalric mode, whether in jousting, duelling, or hunting, sometimes contained an element of comedy as well as fantasy.[84]

The question must be asked why royal government tolerated such thinly disguised forms of warfare? Poaching seems to have been regarded as an excusable naughtiness in a warrior aristocracy. Between foreign wars, such restlessness was preferable to the more overt forms of violence which had characterized late-medieval England. Henry VIII had been quite prepared to exact the ultimate penalty from a peer who killed a gamekeeper while hunting in a neighbour's deer park.[85] But the encouragement of factionalism was part and parcel of Elizabeth's style of governing,[86] and she remained aware of the necessity of keeping alive the martial spirit among her nobility.[87]

---

[82] Greenblatt, *Renaissance Self-Fashioning*, 2, 162.

[83] For a discussion of the use of covert language in English celebratory drama, see L. A. Montrose, 'Celebration and Insinuation: Sir Philip Sidney and the Motives of Elizabethan Courtship', *Renaissance Drama*, ns 8 (Evanston, Ill., 1977), 3–35. That covert language was a widely accepted part of courtly discourse is testified to by George Puttenham, *The Arte of English Poesie* (1589), ed. G. D. Willcock and A. Walker (Cambridge, 1936), 299.

[84] West, 'Spenser's Art of War', 688–704.

[85] Stow, *Annales*, ed. Howes, 582; Lower, 'The Trial and Execution of Thomas, Lord Dacre', 174.

[86] 'The State of England Anno Dom. 1600 by Thomas Wilson', ed. Fisher, in *Camden Miscellany XVI*, 42–3; R. B. Manning, 'The Prosecution of Sir Michael Blount, Lieutenant of the Tower of London, 1595', *BIHR* 57 (1984), 216.

[87] Nichols, *Progresses of Elizabeth*, i. 73.

James I and Charles I took a more severe view of unlawful hunting, and the Court of Star Chamber played a highly visible role in the enforcement of the Game Laws, but stricter enforcement proved to be socially divisive.[88] Until the Civil Wars of the seventeenth century focused the attention of the peerage and gentry on more urgent matters, English monarchs were unable to prevent aristocratic poaching.

[88] Manning, *Village Revolts*, 305.

3

The Game Laws

Hunting is for kings, not peasants.

> John Lyly, *Midas* (1592), iv. iii. 4, in *The Complete Works of John Lyly*, ed. R. W. Bond, 3 vols. (1902; repr. Oxford, 1967), iii. 147

Nimrod was the first king, and he was such a bloody wretch, that he was called a hunter.

> Gerard Winstanley, *More Light Shinning in Buckingham-shire* (1649), in *The Works of Gerard Winstanley*, ed. G. H. Sabine (Ithaca, NY, 1941), 628–9

Though the forest laws are now mitigated, and by degrees grown entirely obsolete, yet from this root has sprung a *bastard slip*, known by the name of *Game Law*, now arrived to, and wantoning in its highest vigour: both founded upon the same unreasonable notion of permanent property in wild creatures; and both productive of the same tyranny to the Commons: but with this difference; that the forest law established only one mighty hunter throughout the land, *the game laws have raised a little* Nimrod *in every manor.*

> Sir William Blackstone, *Commentaries on the Laws of England* (1765–9; repr. Chicago, 1979), iv. v. 408–9

In aristocratic circles hunting was always perceived as an honourable and warlike activity. As the royal forests receded in the late Middle Ages, peers and gentlemen asserted their hunting rights, and, with royal licence, acquired extensive hunting franchises and established numerous deer parks, but were quick to deny the same privilege to others. In the fourteenth century, holders of hunting franchises usually sued poachers in the common-law courts on actions of trespass, but the Great Revolt of 1381 provided the pretext for the first Game Law enacted by Parliament in 1389–90.[1] The original assumption was that husbandmen and artificers used hunting parties as a cover for conspiracies to rise against their lords; thus, the right to hunt must be denied to those without sufficient estates as a means of preserving public order. Through the mid-Tudor period every outbreak of popular unrest brought new and more restrictive Game Laws. The Game Laws were enforced sporadically by the assizes and quarter sessions, and, beginning in the sixteenth century, complaints about game offences appear

[1] 13 Rich. II, st. 1, c. 13; *SR* ii. 65.

more frequently in the Court of Star Chamber and the Duchy Court of Lancaster.

The emphasis in game legislation and enforcement in the early seventeenth century shifted to an assertion of the royal prerogative and aristocratic privilege. There was an attempt to revive the jurisdiction of the feeble forest courts, while the attorney-general initiated an increasing number of prosecutions in Star Chamber of offences against deer in the royal forests and the deer parks belonging to court favourites. Most common lawyers found the Game Laws repugnant, believing that an individual could never claim property rights over wild beasts. The attempt by forest officials to deny freeholders their rights to hunt on their own property within the purlieus of the forests, which the latter believed were guaranteed to them by the Charter of the Forest, raised fears among lawyers and landowners that the assertion of the royal prerogative in hunting matters constituted part of a larger assault upon the Ancient Constitution.

The establishment and continuing maintenance of deer parks and rabbit warrens, combined with socially restrictive game legislation, can also be viewed as part of the seigneurial assault upon commons and wastes. Such efforts at game preservation involved enclosures and necessarily diminished common use-rights. Moreover, they went against the popular view that wild beasts and fish ought to be accessible to all. Particularly during the seventeenth and early eighteenth centuries, further enactment of game legislation and the attempt to assert possession of deer and game went hand-in-hand with the expanding doctrine of the absolute and unqualified rights of private property.

3.1. Legislation

Among the many repressive acts popularly attributed to the Normans, perhaps none aroused more resentment than the forest laws. The decrees of the Anglo-Norman kings imposed the most brutal punishments upon those who poached the king's deer or boar or who appropriated the timber, browsewood, or grass which provided cover and food for the beasts of the forest. Depending upon nothing more than the royal prerogative, the forest law established vast hunting reserves throughout England where only the king and a favoured few who possessed his licence could hunt. The royal forests, which at one time comprised a quarter of all the land in England, constituted a separate jurisdiction wholly outside the common law and alien to its concepts of justice. Although the penalties of death and mutilation ceased to be exacted for trespasses against the vert and venison under the Angevin kings, their forest and game officials continued to extort vast sums of money for the king's coffers. Baronial pressure upon King John and

Henry III compelled those monarchs in the first Magna Carta of 1215 and the Charter of the Forest of 1217 to grant important concessions which mitigated the harshness of forest law and led to extensive disafforestations of royal forest.[2]

The Game Laws were as mischievous as the forest law. They rested upon two rather dubious assumptions: that hunting, the most universal of all sports, one of the most common varieties of social intercourse, and one of the most persistent expressions of culture in every society with its rites of passage and highly emotive bonds of fraternity, could be and ought to be restricted to a privileged few. The second assumption was that deer and hare, which the common law regarded as *ferae naturae*—things of pleasure rather than profit and upon which no value could be placed in an indictment at common law—could be stolen. This legal absurdity was so apparent to lawyers that, when they drafted statutes in Parliament or framed indictments and informations in courts of law, they understood that only the circumstances in which a deer or hare was taken could be made a crime—not the act itself. Thus, the Game Laws made crimes of hunting without a sufficient estate, hunting at night or in disguise, breaking into a park, or being in possession of hunting weapons, nets, or hunting dogs. In short, between the fourteenth and eighteenth centuries, Parliament made every conceivable circumstance in which an unqualified person might hunt a crime.[3]

Animals such as deer and hare were not, strictly speaking, considered game, because they were wild beasts and belonged to no one. However, the circumstance, such as hunting at night, could turn an act into a crime. The legal principle had long existed that an act which was lawful by day could be unlawful by night. Night walking was an indictable offence both in statute law and at common law.[4] Certainly, a trespass was committed when a hunter broke the pales and entered another person's deer park, and this was actionable. Tumultuous hunting by three or more persons constituted a riot, and the Court of Star Chamber always took an interest in any breach of public order. Moreover, the process of enclosure to breed and protect young animals in parks and warrens for the landlord's sport tended to change the law regarding deer and rabbits and, in effect, partially to domesticate wild animals.[5]

The Game Laws were even more conducive to social conflict than the forest law. The forest law had provoked the outrage of all who possessed

---

[2] Young, *Royal Forests of Medieval England*, 11, 25, 107–8; Brentnall, 'Venison Trespasses in the Reign of Henry VII', 191.

[3] *The Reports of Sir John Spelman*, ed. J. H. Baker, 2 vols. (Selden Soc., 93–4; 1976, 1978), ii. 316–22; Manning, *Village Revolts*, 285; Munsche, *Gentlemen and Poachers*, 3–4.

[4] *A New Law Dictionary*, comp. Giles Jacob (9th edn.; 1772), *sub* 'nightwalkers'; 5 Edw. III, c. 14; *SR* i. 268; John Hawarde, *Les Reportes del Cases in Camera Stellata, 1593–1609*, ed. W. P. Baildon (1894), 107.   [5] Munsche, *Gentlemen and Poachers*, 3–4.

or cultivated land—lords and peasants alike. The Game Laws aligned the king and the seigneurial possessors of hunting franchises against the many who were excluded from hunting privileges. The dichotomy was not simply along class lines, because hunting qualifications were tied to annual income, possession of land, and the type of tenure by which the land was held, rather than social rank. At first, the qualification—possession of land worth 40s. per year—excluded only artificers and landless persons.[6] But the early Stuart Game Laws raised the qualifications to possession of a £40 freehold, or an £80 copyhold for those who could claim an estate for life only.[7] Since the early sixteenth century a greater fluidity in the market for small parcels of land had resulted in a situation where many small gentry were copyholders and possessed little or no freehold land.[8] Persons in this category, together with servants of aristocratic and gentry households, who were often landless gentlemen and yeomen, were the cause of a disproportionate amount of the riotous hunting in early modern England. Thus, the Game Laws, especially in the early Stuart period, not only tended to divide landlords and peasants, but also increased the frequency of confrontations over hunting privileges between peers, courtiers, and armigerous gentry on the one hand, and younger sons, gentlemen tenants, and servants on the other.

In court circles hunting was seen as a royal right and an aristocratic privilege, so justifications for narrowing hunting qualifications always existed. But it is not perfectly clear why the Game Acts of 1603 and 1605 were so restrictive as to confine hunting only to the greater gentry. The apologists of royal prerogative never tired of arguing that the heavy burden of duties which princes carried made recreation necessary for their good health and relaxation in ways that were not appropriate for lesser men. It was regarded as axiomatic that hunting was not a fit activity for men who ought to be at their trades or following a plough, because it encouraged idleness.[9] Medieval monarchs had been jealous of their hunting rights and vindictive towards those who violated them.[10] James I, whose preoccupation with hunting was notorious, frequently urged Parliament to strengthen game legislation.[11] Henry VII, another enthusiast for the chase, was both angered by the depredations of the aristocracy in the royal parks and convinced that unlawful hunting helped to breed and sustain outlaws in the forests.[12] Although it was widely

---

[6] 13 Rich. II, st. 1, c. 13; *SR* ii. 65.

[7] 1 Jac. I, c. 27; *SR* iv. 1055; 3 Jac. I, c. 13; *SR* iv. 1088.

[8] See J. Youings, *Sixteenth-Century England* (Harmondsworth, Middx., 1984), ch. 7.

[9] PRO STAC 8/5/15.

[10] See, e.g., *The Stonor Letters*, ed. C. L. Kingsford (Camden Soc., 3rd ser., 30; 1919), ii. 150.

[11] *Proceedings in Parliament, 1610*, ed. E. R. Foster, 2 vols. (New Haven, Conn., 1966), i. 51–2, ii. 62, 280–1; see also *Political Works of James I*, ed. McIlwain, 323.

[12] R. Somerville, *History of the Duchy of Lancaster*, 2 vols. (1953, 1970), i. 269; 1 Hen. VII, c. 7; *SR* ii. 505.

recognized that hunting on horseback trained and kept a man fit for war, the Star Chamber judges had become increasingly alarmed by the aristocratic and gentry feuding which often accompanied hunting in the sixteenth century.[13]

By the eighteenth century it was widely assumed that poaching led to a life of crime. Gilbert White recalled that, after the Waltham Blacks had depleted Waltham Chase of its deer, Bishop Hoadly of Winchester, when urged to restock the chase with more deer, refused to do so, saying that 'it had done enough mischief already'.[14] Removing the temptation to unlawful hunting was also used as an argument to justify disenfranchising Cranborne Chase by Act of Parliament and the destruction of its deer. William Chafin, a local antiquarian, wrote a history of the chase to argue against this, and to plead for preservation of the use-rights in Cranborne Chase which gave employment to many poor cottagers.[15] Even at the beginning of the nineteenth century, landowners were prepared to destroy the game before they would allow artificers and cottagers to hunt.

Despite the many attempts by monarchs and aristocrats to preserve beasts, fish, and fowl for their own sport, the popular belief persisted that wild animals could not be possessed and the places where they lived or swam should not be enclosed. Consequently, every popular uprising brought forth a Wat Tyler or a Gerrard Winstanley who proclaimed the principle of common access to hunting and fishing. The rebellions of 1381 and 1549 and the popular disturbances accompanying the Civil Wars of the 1640s all elicited attacks on royal and aristocratic deer parks.[16] Popular beliefs about the injustice of denying hunting rights to all persons may have derived in part from the reasoning of the common lawyers, but memories of the relative freedom to hunt which had existed prior to the first Game Law of Richard II's reign probably were more significant. Before 1389 the public had a right to hunt outside royal forests except where the land was enclosed or restricted by grant of free chase or warren—provided the hunter did not commit a trespass against someone's property. This freedom to hunt was vigorously asserted by defendants and acknowledged by the common-law courts in the fourteenth century. Moreover, the purpose of charters of free chase and

---

[13] See above, Ch. 2.

[14] White, *Natural History of Selborne*, 31–2. See also Munsche, *Gentlemen and Poachers*, 11, Thompson, *Whigs and Hunters*, 230–2, and D. Hay, 'Poaching and the Game Laws on Cannock Chase', in D. Hay, P. Linebaugh, J. G. Rule, E. P. Thompson, and C. Winslow (eds.), *Albion's Fatal Tree* (New York, 1975), 204–5.

[15] Chafin, *Second Edition of the Anecdotes and History of Cranbourne Chase*, 69.

[16] *Chronicon Henrici Knighton*, ed. Lumby, ii. 137; Gerard Winstanley, *Light Shining in Buckinghamshire* (1648), in *The Works of Gerard Winstanley*, ed. G. H. Sabine (Ithaca, NY, 1941), 612; R. B. Manning, 'Violence and Social Conflict in Mid-Tudor Rebellions', *Journal of British Studies*, 16. 2 (spring 1977), 33–4; *Journals of the House of Commons*, ii. 282, iv. 547, 595, 602, 608, v. 25. See also M. Bloch, *French Rural History: An Essay on its Basic Characteristics*, trans. J. Sondheimer (Berkeley, Calif., 1966), 182.

warren, or licences to impale deer parks, would be inexplicable if this freedom had not existed. Manorial custom and by-laws sometimes restricted the freedom of tenants to hunt, but the woodwards on the royal manor of Havering did not regard hunting in the woods outside the park and warren as unlawful.[17]

Even the more restrictive Jacobean Game Laws did little to alter popular opinion. Gervase Markham, a 'Hackney' writer on agricultural matters, argued that the husbandman was virtuous and hardworking and was entitled to recreation. For this reason it was wrong to deny him the pleasures of hunting. Markham, who had scant regard for the Game Laws, does not bother to discuss the question of who was legally qualified to hunt. He paid no attention to hunting seasons and saw nothing wrong with hunting red deer the year round.[18] An anonymous mid-seventeenth-century lawyer, who had a good grasp of forest law, maintained in a treatise which he intended for lay readers that 'if a man find a hart or deer or any other beast in his own ground out of the forest, chase or park and out of the purlieu, he may well kill and take him by what means he can devise, for he is wild of nature and it cannot be known from whence he cometh'.[19] Such advice was probably circulated widely, because defendants frequently pleaded that royal foresters could not accuse them of unlawful hunting on land which was neither forest nor purlieu.[20] Another defendant appearing in Star Chamber in 1591 maintained that he 'thinketh that by the laws of this . . . realm it is lawful for every [one of] her Majesty's subjects in his freehold or by the licence of the owner to hunt and chase in peaceable manner any wild beast being *ferae naturae* except it be a hart'.[21]

The belief that statute law could not abrogate the right to hunt was a persistent and deeply seated part of popular culture. This popular mythology was certainly well established in the Middle Ages, when poachers were numerous and drawn from all classes—including peers, clergy, royal officials, and university students as well as ordinary folk. It was all the more difficult to proceed against poachers—especially when they were organized as bands of outlaws—because they enjoyed the support and protection of numerous accomplices and the goodwill of local communities. In the many variations on the tales of Robin Hood, Robin and his merry band lived on venison in the forest. Eating venison is what many Englishmen imagined they would do if they could turn the world upside down. Consequently, Robin was a hero and an exemplar for all poachers and their

---

[17] *Select Pleas of the Forest*, ed. Turner, p. cxxxiv; *Select Cases of Trespass from the King's Courts, 1307–1399*, ed. M. S. Arnold, 2 vols. (Selden Soc.; 1985–7), ii. 268; M. K. McIntosh, *Autonomy and Community: The Royal Manor of Havering, 1200–1500* (Cambridge, 1986), 163.   [18] M[arkham], *Country Contentments*, 2–3; *DNB, sub nom.*
[19] BL Sloane MS 751, fo. 15ᵛ.   [20] PRO STAC 5/B 33/3.
[21] PRO STAC 5/P57/40; see also P56/31.

numerous well-wishers. Although labelled an outlaw, he was widely regarded as a champion of both popular and royal justice. Popular mythology
held that the two concepts of justice were not irreconcilable. Forest law was
an aberration devised by the king's evil ministers. As depicted in the *Tale
of Gamelyn*, the king's anger was directed towards his corrupt judges rather
than deer-slayers.[22]

The foreign wars, civil wars, and rebellions of the late fourteenth and
fifteenth centuries weakened the administration of forest law and led to
widespread poaching, just as these same events diminished royal authority
and subverted royal justice. As soon as Edward III had sailed to France at
the beginning of the Hundred Years War, contemporaries noticed an increase in large-scale poaching. In 1417, while Henry V was campaigning in
Normandy, Parliament complained of organized attacks on both royal and
aristocratic hunting reserves. Complaints of similar outrages carried out by
masked outlaws were uttered during the Wars of the Roses. These acts of
unlawful hunting multiplied partly because of a breakdown of royal justice.
However, they also comprehended a wide variety of conflicts, ranging from
village protests against the multiplication of enclosed rabbit warrens on
common wastes and in disafforested forests, to vicious poaching wars which
broke out between rival factions of royal forest and game officials whenever
one aristocratic faction violently displaced the previous royal incumbent
and seized the reins of government.[23]

In the first Game Law of 1389–90, Richard II's government forbade
hunting by artificers and servants for the same reason that earlier English
monarchs had condemned tournaments—because they were thought to
disguise conspiracies and breed disorder.[24] Presumably, Richard II and later
medieval monarchs thought that hunting was a safer diversion for aristocrats than jousting, but Henry VII was outraged to discover the extent to
which various prelates, peers, and officials of the Duchy of Lancaster had
plundered his hunting preserves—leaving little stock of deer for his own recreation. Henry VII also continued to view unrestricted hunting as a source
of insurrection and crime. The Game Act of 1485 was the first to make
hunting at night or in disguise a felony. However, the culprit who confessed
his crime or gave evidence against his fellow poachers was to be held guilty
of a misdemeanour rather than a felony and punished by a fine.[25]

[22] C. Petit-Dutaillis, *Studies and Notes Supplementary to Stubbs' Constitutional History*, trans.
W. T. Waugh, 3 vols. (Manchester, 1914), ii. 200–1. *The Tale of Gamelyn*, in *The Complete Works
of Geoffrey Chaucer*, ed. W. W. Skeat, 8 vols. (2nd edn.; Oxford, 1900), iv. 662–7, ll. 695–902.
[23] Petit-Dutaillis, *Studies and Notes*, ii. 245–9; F. Thompson, *Magna Carta: Its Role in the
Making of the English Constitution, 1300–1629* (Minneapolis, 1948), 384–5.
[24] 13 Rich. II, st. 1, c. 13; *SR* ii. 65; Keen, *Chivalry*, 96–7; J. R. Maddicott, *Thomas of Lancaster, 1307–1322: A Study in the Reign of Edward II* (Oxford, 1970), 99–100.
[25] Somerville, *History of the Duchy of Lancaster*, i. 269; W. S. Holdsworth, *A History of English
Law*, 13 vols. (1922–52), iv. 505–6; 1 Hen. VII, c. 7; *SR* ii. 505.

The Game Act of 1485, in its preamble, also complains that hunting by night or in disguise was especially prevalent in the Weald of Kent, Sussex, and Surrey. Other sources make it clear that poachers in the Weald were organized into outlaw bands which, earlier in the century, committed murders and robberies as well as depredations against forests, parks, warrens, and chases. These outlaws eluded capture, until, like Richard Stafford, chaplain, *alias* 'Friar Tuck', they grew too old for hiding out in the greenwood and purchased pardons. In 1486–7 twenty individuals from Kent and Sussex were bound to their good behaviour in sums varying from 40 to 100 marks following their conviction. This appears to have been the first successful effort to bring the Wealden poachers to book.[26]

Every period of popular tumult was followed by the enactment of more bloody-minded statutes. The Pilgrimage of Grace and the other smaller-scale disorders of the late 1530s resulted in new categories of felonies for hunting offences: breaking the head of a fishpond was made capital in 1539, as was hunting in disguise or at night in royal parks and forests, or taking eggs or fledglings from the nests of falcons or hawks on any of the king's manors.[27] In 1540 these same offences were made felonies wherever they might be committed.[28] The evidence is lacking to determine whether, in fact, capital penalties were exacted for these game offences, but it is unlikely that such was the case. At the beginning of the next reign, in 1547, all new felonies created during the reign of Henry VIII and certain new treasons were repealed. This included all of the capital game offences enacted in 1539 and 1540.[29] However, the widespread destruction of deer parks and game during the riots and rebellions of 1549 led to the revival for a period of three years of the capital penalty for the game offences specified in the Game Laws of 1539 and 1540. The preamble of the Edwardian Game Act of 1549–50 notes that 'in some of your Grace's parks were slain five hundred deer in a day within very few miles of your Majesty's City of London'. The authors of this statute not only wished to prevent 'the bold continuance of the like', but also to avoid 'the shame and dishonour that in other realms thereof is spoken'.[30] None of these offences was made a felony under Elizabeth I and James I. Typically, the Elizabethan approach was to make game offences misdemeanours punishable by three months' imprisonment and treble damages and to require sureties for seven years' 'good behaviour'.[31]

The medieval, early, and mid-Tudor Game Laws represent efforts to maintain public order and to discourage servants, husbandmen, and artificers from engaging in their favourite sports. Other Game Acts of the Tudor

[26] I Hen. VII, c. 7; *SR* ii. 505; *Cal. PR, 1416–1422,* 41, 84; *Cal. PR, 1429–1436,* 10; *Cal. CR, 1485–1500,* nos. 236–7.   [27] 31 Hen. VIII, cc. 2, 12; *SR* iii. 718, 731.
[28] 32 Hen. VIII, c. 11; *SR* iii. 755–6.   [29] 1 Edw. VI, c. 12; *SR* iv. 18–22.
[30] 3 & 4 Edw. VI, c. 17; *SR* iv. 18–22.   [31] 5 Eliz. c. 21; *SR* iv. 449.

period were intended to preserve game and to restrict the methods of hunting employed by qualified persons. In 1495, and again in 1580–1, qualified persons were forbidden to hunt partridges and pheasants with nets and traps except on their own freehold land, and no one might disturb the nests of hawks and swans. Indeed, certain types of English hawks and falcons were so endangered that no one might possess them except the king. Noblemen and gentlemen could keep only imported birds of prey and were required to possess certificates from customs officers proving their importation.[32] An Act of 1503–4 forbade the use of nets, hays, and stalking horses to any one not seized of a forest, park, or chase.[33] Other statutes attempted to deny the use of handguns and crossbows to persons who did not possess estates worth £100 p.a. Rarely does one hear of consideration for farmers whose crops were destroyed by hunters. The Elizabethan Game Act of 1580–1 made it unlawful to hawk or hunt with spaniels on grounds with standing corn without the consent of the owner of the corn.[34] But this and other Game Laws remain strangely silent about hunting on horseback and employing greyhounds or mastiffs in cultivated fields.

The more socially restrictive Jacobean Game Laws were enacted because the king never tired of reminding members of Parliament that 'it is not fit that clowns should have these sports'—although, at the same time, James did criticize gentlemen who hunted or hawked before the corn had been gathered in and destroyed farmers' crops.[35] The increased emphasis on the prosecution of hunting offences in Star Chamber and other equity courts certainly represented a revival of the royal prerogative in ways that the Tudor monarchs had never contemplated, and this policy was continued under Charles I.

Soon after his arrival in England, James began the practice of issuing warrants to various courtiers and other gentlemen making them responsible for the enforcement of the Game Laws and the punishment of offenders. In some cases the authority of these royal gamekeepers extended to whole counties, and they were empowered to take sureties of persons who refused to yield up hunting dogs and guns and to bind them to appear before the Privy Council.[36] Although many of the recipients of royal gamekeepers' warrants were undoubtedly justices of the peace, the whole process tended to bypass the courts of quarter session and assize, and some counties, such as Sussex, show a sharp decline in the indictments for unlawful hunting at the assizes in the reign of James I.[37] Some aristocrats were alarmed when

---

[32] 11 Hen. VII, c. 17; *SR* iii. 581; 23 Eliz. c. 10; *SR* iv. 672–3.
[33] 19 Hen. VII, c. 11; *SR* iii. 655.   [34] 23 Eliz. c. 10; *SR* iv. 672–3.
[35] *Proceedings in Parliament, 1610,* ed. Foster, i. 51–2, ii. 62, 280–1.
[36] C. and E. Kirby, 'The Stuart Game Prerogative', *EHR* 46 (1931), 239–45.
[37] *Calendar of Assize Records, Sussex Indictments, Elizabeth I* and *Sussex Indictment, James I,* ed. J. S. Cockburn (London, 1975), *passim.*

James claimed the right to hunt all of the deer and game in England, although it was not his intention to deny hunting privileges to persons of quality. But the royal gamekeepers' warrants did authorize the holders of these warrants to decide who might or might not hunt. Implicit in these broad powers was the possibility of evading the more precisely stated hunting qualifications contained in statute law. Because the broad powers contained in gamekeepers' warrants frequently conflicted with older royal grants of free chase and free warren, the exercise of the royal prerogative in hunting matters sometimes exacerbated already existing feuds in particular communities and certainly tended to broaden the social gulf between courtiers and small gentry.[38]

3.2. Enforcement

Although forest courts retained their jurisdiction over trespasses against the vert and venison of royal forests into the Tudor period, their powers of enforcement were clearly in decline. Forest law had lost its ferocity since the days of the Anglo-Norman kings, and late-medieval disafforestations had reduced the area of royal forests considerably, but Tudor judges did not doubt that the forest law and forest courts continued in force within the boundaries of royal forests.[39] Elsewhere, parliamentary statutes governed qualifications for hunting and prescribed the penalties to be imposed at quarter sessions and assizes.

The rigour with which the Game Laws were enforced varied considerably from one county to another, while the administration of forest law depended upon whether the forest administration in a particular forest had remained intact. Corrupt forest and game officers and justices of the peace weakened systems of detecting and punishing unlawful hunting, and consequently the Courts of Star Chamber and Duchy of Lancaster Chamber were increasingly called upon to deal with cases of tumultuous hunting. Charles I's dissatisfaction with this situation prompted his attempt to revive and extend forest law and forest courts.

It is difficult to generalize about the effectiveness of Tudor forest administration. In those forests where the forest administration continued to function, there were usually three types of forest courts: the Court of Justice Seat or Forest Eyre, which was presided over by the chief justice in eyre; the Swanimote, where trespasses against the vert and venison were presented by forest officers and game offences were sometimes punished; and an inferior court, variously called the Woodmote, Attachment, or

---

[38] See Manning, *Village Revolts*, 286, 301.
[39] *Reports of Sir John Spelman*, ed. Baker, i. 9; cf. also John Manwood, *A Treatise of the Laws of the Forest* (1615; repr. Amsterdam, 1976), preface, ch. 21, *et passim*.

Verderers' Court, where minor infractions against the vert of the forest were punished.[40] In the Forest of Essex, justices in eyre presided over Justice Seats at irregular intervals throughout the Tudor period and imposed very stiff fines. James I meant to go beyond pecuniary penalties when he ordered the earl of Oxford to build a gaol for the confinement of deer-hunters at Stratford Langthorne.[41] The justice in eyre was also active in punishing unlawful hunting and waste of timber in Barnewood Forest, Buckinghamshire, in the mid-Tudor period. In the reign of Edward VI, a royal proclamation commanded that all persons caught hunting in Barnewood were to appear before Protector Somerset.[42]

In some forests, such as Windsor and Rockingham, Swanimote Courts were held regularly throughout the Tudor and early Stuart periods, but in the Forest of Essex they had lapsed after 1495 and were not revived until 1630. They were then held in desultory fashion until 1640. Swanimote Courts were also rivived in Alice Holt, Wolmer, and Chute Forests, the New Forest, Whichwood, Salcey, and the Forest of Dean.[43] In Bowland Forest in the 1570s the Swanimote Court presented, but did not punish, offences against the king's deer.[44] In Sherwood Forest, in the reign of James I, the Swanimote Court imprisoned a poacher in Nottingham Castle for two weeks, but, when friends secured his release, the chief justice in eyre, Gilbert, earl of Shrewsbury, ultimately resorted to the Court of Star Chamber for more effective punishment and deterrence.[45] The Attachment Courts of Pickering Forest had ceased functioning by 1601 because of rivalries among forest and game officials.[46]

At the quarter sessions, the prosecution of poachers depended upon complaints being made by the victims or their gamekeepers. In the West Riding of Yorkshire, in the reign of Charles I, Sir Francis Wortley, bt., complained frequently about deer-stealers in the New Park at Wortley, which his grandfather had created by razing and depopulating a whole village. Wortley's gamekeepers were usually witnesses in such prosecutions. Both the unlawful hunting and the resulting prosecutions probably increased tension among the West Riding gentry. One of the culprits prosecuted by Wortley at the Doncaster Sessions was a servant from the household of a rival family, the Saviles of Dodworth; the same man was also accused of taking hares in the free warren of Elizabeth, countess of Devonshire. The West Riding justices frequently sat in judgment upon cases which resulted from their own complaints about unlawful hunting in their own parks and

---

[40] Fisher, *The Forest of Essex*, 72–6.
[41] Ibid. 93–4, 97; R. B. Pugh, *Imprisonment in Medieval England* (Cambridge, 1970), 20–1, 32, 131–2. [42] BL Cotton MSS, Titus B. II, fos. 170ᵛ–171.
[43] PRO C. 99 (Various Forest Proceedings in Chancery); Fisher, *Forest of Essex*, 80–2.
[44] Shaw, *Royal Forest of Lancaster*, 233–8.
[45] PRO STAC 8/18/18. [46] PRO DL 1/196/A43.

warrens. Sir Francis Wortley once reprimanded the sheriff, Sir Thomas Danby, for allowing one of the defendants, who had offended against Wortley, to escape. Sitting in judgment on his own complaints also allowed Wortley to make sure that he collected treble damages from those poachers who were convicted, and he could also keep such culprits in gaol until they obtained sufficient sureties to behave themselves for seven years. Gaol terms of three months were quite usual. Once the accused had made monetary satisfaction to the victim, he might be pardoned. If caught, the poacher usually discovered that it was better to confess and ask for mercy. Occasionally, the fines paid by poachers might be used to relieve the poor of the parish.[47]

Gentlemen deer-stealers were more difficult to deal with than more humble offenders. Although their hunting offences were disproportionate to their numbers, gentlemen were underrepresented in indictments for unlawful hunting in most counties where assize and quarter-sessions records survive. A large proportion of cases involving gentlemen poachers was referred to Star Chamber—especially in the reign of James I.[48] Even in Sussex, where the number of indictments for hunting offences returned against gentlemen provides a more realistic indication of the magnitude of the problem, the Privy Council reprimanded the sheriff and justices of the peace for careless enforcement of the Game Laws and for permitting their servants and friends to hunt when they did not possess the statutory qualifications.[49]

Nor were juries particularly helpful in detecting poachers. Grand juries were likely to present hunting offences only where a public nuisance was committed, such as hunters trampling corn underfoot, or where an assault was involved. Trial juries sometimes declined to convict poachers in the face of the evidence, because they refused to believe that certain acts of unlawful hunting were wrong. The effect was to nullify portions of the game code in certain localities.[50] In 1641 an East Sussex poacher bragged that local juries could not be persuaded to convict those accused of raiding the deer parks of Catholic gentry; in West Sussex the second Lord Montague, a Catholic peer, had great difficulty in obtaining convictions against those who repeatedly raided his deer parks. He was ultimately obliged to appeal to Star Chamber for justice.[51]

In Surrey and Hertfordshire, the county magistrates dealt with very few

---

[47] *West Riding Sessions Records*, ed. J. Lister, 2 vols. (Yorks. Arch. Soc., Rec. Ser., 3, 54; York, 1888, 1915), ii. 114, 186–7, 264, 320–1, 329; Fairless Barber, 'The West Riding Sessions Rolls', *Yorks. Arch. Journ.*, 5 (1887–8), 381.

[48] *Acts PC, 1601–1604*, 180–1.

[49] *Acts PC, 1621–1623*, 95; Manning, *Village Revolts*, 298.

[50] *Records of the County of Wiltshire, Being Extracts from the Quarter Sessions Great Rolls of the Seventeenth Century*, ed. B. H. Cunnington (Devizes, 1932), 31; T. A. Green, *Verdict According to Conscience: Perspectives on the English Criminal Trial Jury, 1200–1800* (Chicago, 1985; repr. 1988), 270.

[51] A. Fletcher, *A County Community in Peace and War: Sussex, 1600–1660* (1975), 29; Manning, *Village Revolts*, 294.

cases which involved gentry either as culprits or victims. Between 1608 and 1616 thirty persons—mostly yeomen, husbandmen, and artisans—were accused of unlawfully hunting conies on enclosed grounds in Surrey. Accusations of deer-stealing were referred to the assizes or Star Chamber. The victims were also all of comparable social status, except for one case in 1612 in which three husbandmen were accused of hunting rabbits in the enclosed grounds of Charles Howard, earl of Nottingham and lord admiral, at Reigate Priory.[52] The Hertfordshire justices were even more lax in punishing hunting offences.[53] But one very vindictive incident in the reign of Elizabeth stands out as an exception. In the spring of 1579 a group of villagers of Northall, Hertfordshire, attacked and destroyed a park pale owned by Ambrose Dudley, earl of Warwick. The deer park encroached upon the village common, and similar demonstrations had occurred there and at Cheshunt in 1548. As a consequence eight protesters were condemned as felons: two were hanged, two burnt in the hand, and the other four 'remained prisoners in Hertford Gaol long after'. While this incident appears to have been essentially an anti-enclosure riot, since there is no evidence that any deer were killed, it is difficult to assign it to one category or the other. It was perceived as an attack upon an aristocratic game reserve and, symbolically, an attack upon aristocratic privilege and power.[54] When the interests and prestige of a high-ranking courtier, such as the brother of Elizabeth's favourite, the earl of Leicester, were touched to the quick, the Hertfordshire justices could be galvanized into action.

By contrast, the Game Laws were strictly enforced in Middlesex. If juries in other counties effectively nullified portions of the game code by a refusal to convict in the face of the evidence, Middlesex juries sometimes carried enforcement to statutory limits by treating the hunting of deer as a felony rather than a misdemeanour, or asserting that deer could be stolen. In 1618 two persons, in separate cases, were convicted of poaching the king's deer in Hyde Park and concealing the same. Both were granted benefit of clergy and branded as felons.[55] It would appear that the defendants were prosecuted under the Game Act of 1485, which allowed the prosecution of hunting as a felony if the accused person hunted at night, or in disguise, or attempted to conceal his offence by refusal to confess to the examining magistrate.[56]

There are other cases involving hunting in royal parks where it appears

---

[52] G. Leveson-Gower, 'Note Book of a Surrey Justice', *Surrey Arch. Coll.*, 9 (1888), 195, 214.

[53] *Sessions Rolls, 1581–1698*, ed. W. J. Hardy (Hertford County Records, 1; Hertford, 1905), 32, 36, 38, 45.

[54] *VCH Herts.*, iv. 215–16; Sir Harris Nicolas, *Memoirs of the Life and Times of Sir Christopher Hatton* (1848), 113. For a discussion of the statutory authority for the prosecution of felony-riot, see Manning, *Village Revolts*, 234 n.

[55] *Middlesex Sessions Records*, ed. W. Le Hardy, 4 vols. (Middx. Rec. Soc.; 1935–41), iv. 345.

[56] 1 Hen. VII, c. 7; *SR* ii. 505.

that prosecutions for felony were brought, but the trial juries reduced the charge to one of misdemeanour. During the reigns of James I and Charles I, a number of indictments were returned against persons taking deer in Hyde Park and Theobalds Park in which a value of between £2 and £5 per head was put upon the deer killed, but the defendants were convicted of misdemeanours rather than on the charge of grand larceny. The two Hyde Park hunters confessed to the indictment, and the charge was reduced from felony to misdemeanour as authorized by the Game Act of 1485. The defendants were sentenced to three months' imprisonment each and were not to be released until they found substantial sureties for good behaviour. Recognizances of £50 to £100 were frequently demanded,[57] and, occasionally, treble damages were awarded if the victim was a private person. If the hunting was done in a royal park, a fine might be assessed for the use of the king.[58]

The strict enforcement of the Game Laws in early Stuart Middlesex is partly due to royal pressure from two monarchs who were keen hunters and were anxious to protect the royal parks from the depredations of numerous poachers who supplied the insatiable demand of the London Market for game and rabbits. Commercial poachers usually operated in gangs which were quite prepared to resort to violence to resist arrest by the Middlesex magistrates.[59]

During the Commonwealth, the parliamentary authorities continued the early Stuart practice of placing a value upon the deer killed in the Commonwealth's parks.[60] During the winter of 1642–3 Parliament, fearful of popular disorders arising from deer-stealing in the royal parks, sometimes resorted to the use of military force to suppress attacks on royal parks in the neighbourhood of the capital. Parliament sometimes ordered poachers apprehended in the royal parks and chases to be imprisoned without trial.[61]

Elsewhere, we can infer that juries almost invariably refused to convict persons charged with felonious hunting. In Lincolnshire three men accused of catching rabbits and destroying a warren during the night were charged as felons in 1556; no conviction was obtained and they were subsequently prosecuted in Star Chamber.[62] Late in the reign of Henry VIII, a similar attempt by Sir Richard Southwell, surveyor-general of the crown lands, to prosecute a poaching gang which had broken into the king's park of Wood Rising, Norfolk, for felony also miscarried and he, too, resorted to Star Chamber.[63]

---

[57] *Middlesex Sessions Records*, ed. Le Hardy, ii. 75, 147.
[58] Ibid. iii. 190–1; John Rushworth (ed.), *Historical Collections*, 8 vols. (2nd edn.; 1721–2), II. ii, appendix, p. 75.   [59] See, e.g., PRO STAC 8/29/11.
[60] *Middlesex Sessions Records*, ed. Le Hardy, iii. 190–1.
[61] *Journals of the House of Lords*, v. 597a, 609b.
[62] PRO STAC 4/5/4.   [63] PRO STAC 2/32/26.

The incarceration of unlawful hunters was one of the earliest instances in England of imprisonment for punishment as opposed to imprisonment on remand. This was a reaction against the earlier more severe punishments handed out by the Anglo-Norman kings. The practice of imprisonment for a year and a day began in Henry II's reign, and the usual place of imprisonment was in various forest prisons attached to keepers' lodges or in royal castles adjacent to parks and forests. Conviction under the parliamentary Game Laws could bring incarceration in county gaols.[64]

Medieval legislation against unlawful hunting was sometimes still enforced, as a case of 1566 shows. Lord Chandos brought an action of trespass in King's Bench against a gang of poachers for taking eleven deer out of his park. The defendants, a mixed group of gentlemen and yeomen, were found guilty and ordered to post bonds for their good behaviour. If they could not find the money for sureties, they were ordered to abjure the realm. The leader of the gang was also sentenced to serve three years in the Marshalsea Prison, a sentence prescribed by the Statute of Westminster I of 1275. A general pardon, when issued, for example, at the end of a parliament, had the effect of wiping out the penalty of banishment, but left the plaintiff free to sue for damages.[65]

Plaintiffs had the legal right to ask convicted poachers to post bonds for good behaviour, but Sir Nicholas Poyntz, the lieutenant and keeper of Kingswood Chase, Gloucestershire, tried to force persons accused of unlawful hunting to find sureties for good behaviour without bothering to obtain a conviction, and told them that, if they refused to do so, it would be assumed that they were guilty. Star Chamber depositions reveal that in one case, Alexander Neale, a weaver, had hunted in Acton Park between 1582 and 1584 in order to be revenged upon Poyntz, who was a harsh landlord. Poyntz had attempted to force Neale to post a bond for £1,000. The condition of the bond was to be that Neale would become Poyntz's 'bond slave' if he were involved in hunting again.[66] Neale refused to enter into the bond, which probably would have been invalid, because a bond must be entered into voluntarily.

Punishment for unlawful hunting also extended to dogs as well as unqualified persons. No one without a sufficient estate was allowed to keep a hunting dog which had not been 'lawed' or expediated. This meant amputating either three claws of the anterior feet or the left claws of all four feet. The rules regarding what kinds of dogs might be kept and who might keep them derived from the laws of the forest, from manorial custom, and

[64] Pugh, *Imprisonment in Medieval England*, 20–1, 32, 131–2.

[65] Sir James Dyer, *Reports of Cases in the Reigns of Henry VIII, Edward VI, Queen Mary and Queen Elizabeth*, 3 pts. in 3 vols. (1794 edn.), pt. ii, fo. 238a; *SR* i. 26–39. It is curious that Dyer specifies abjuration of the realm, since that penalty was changed to abjuration to a sanctuary by the statute of 22 Henry VIII, c. 14 (R. F. Hunnisett, 'The Last Sussex Abjurations', *Sussex Arch. Coll.*, 102 (1964), 43).   [66] PRO STAC 5/P35/26.

the Charter of the Forest of 1217.[67] Hunting dogs were widely kept not only by gentlemen but also by ordinary folk; many were in the habit of riding or walking about the countryside with unleashed dogs, which were trained to kill deer or hare and which had already been blooded—that is, they had tasted their first kill. Such people were unlikely to restrain their hounds if they went after deer. Richard Chamber, keeper of the duke of Norfolk's park at Framlingham, frequently recorded the slaughter of does and fawns by hounds. If the dogs were strays, or belonged to artificers, the parker hanged them on a tree, but, if a dog belonged to a local landowner, he needed to be more circumspect and might return the dog.[68] In Surrey, in 1613, a man was bound over to the quarter sessions on suspicion of taking sheep, but his dog was hanged without any formal judicial process.[69] The practice of executing felonious animals was quite widespread in England as well as Europe. This was done partly out of revenge, but also because the animals were, in effect, personified as servants of a household and carried the same legal responsibility for their conduct as other members of a household.[70]

Manorial courts sometimes enforced by-laws against the taking of game, and homage juries were obliged to present offences against the parliamentary Game Laws. Of the offences presented, most dealt with unqualified persons keeping hunting dogs or nets or taking hare and rabbits. It would appear that by the sixteenth century manorial courts were not expected to contend with deer hunters. In 1557 the homage jury of Rotherfield, Sussex, presented a tenant for unlawful hunting with a ferret and a net. He was fined 6*d.* Three years later the homage jury presented four men and a woman for keeping the kind of greyhounds used for catching hares. All were free tenants, but possessed incomes of less than 40*s.* a year and were therefore unqualified. They were fined 6*d.* each, but two repeat offenders, including the woman, were fined 12*d.* later in the same year.[71] In the manorial Court of Ightham, Kent, nineteen cases of rabbit-poaching were presented between 1490 and 1508. Not all of those accused paid fines, but those who did forfeited between 2*d.* and 12*d.*—mostly at the lower end of the scale. The majority of offences involved breaking a close and taking conies from the lord's demesne land or rabbit warren, but some of the defendants insisted that they had taken the rabbits in fields adjacent to the lord's demesne. Four separate accusations of unlawfully catching conies were laid

---

[67] Manwood, *Laws of the Forest*, ch. 16; Blount, *Fragmenta Antiquitatis*, 502; *SR* i (charters), 20–1.

[68] Accounts of Richard Chamber, keeper of Framlingham Park, Suffolk, printed in Shirley, *Some Account of English Deer Parks*, 29–33.

[69] Leveson-Gower, 'Note Book of a Surrey Justice', 201.

[70] E. P. Evans, *The Criminal Prosecution and Capital Punishment of Animals* (1906), 2, 10.

[71] C. Pullein, *Rotherfield: The Story of Some Wealden Manors* (Tunbridge Wells, Kent (1928?)), 72–81.

against Thomas Chipstede, tilemaker, whose rabbit-poaching career appears to have lasted from 1492 until 1506.[72] Hunting offences were rarely punished on the manor of Tyrley, Staffordshire, in the sixteenth century, but two scions of the Preston family were presented—apparently because their father was the demesne farmer and they aroused resentment by affecting gentry airs. Their offences included keeping a greyhound for coursing hare and illegal fishing.[73] Although the jurors of the Court Leet of Manchester were enjoined to present offences against the Game Laws, they never did so during the sixteenth century.[74]

How ever much the rigour with which the Game Laws were enforced might vary from county to county and from court to court, the penalties provided did very little to deter hardened deer-stealers. Complaints against poachers in the Court of Star Chamber frequently state that the defendants were 'notorious and incorrigible hunters' who had already been indicted at common law and had entered into recognizances not to hunt again.[75] Such men were full of dodges and ingenious pleas. If caught red-handed with their greyhounds in deer parks standing over the carcass of a freshly slaughtered doe, accused poachers would often say that they had been coursing hare when their hounds caught the scent of a deer and ran into the complainant's park and refused to obey their masters when whistled back. Or, poachers might plead that their dogs were pursuing vermin—animals which were not beasts of chase or warren and not protected by the Game Laws.[76] Experienced poachers picked up quite a bit of law along the way and would sometimes plead in Star Chamber that they should not be compelled to answer interrogatories for fear of self-incrimination because similar charges were pending against them in other courts or they were under indictment for the same offence and had entered into recognizances. In Essex, in 1620, a band of deer-stealers were required by the Court of Star Chamber to find sureties for their good behaviour after Sir Gamaliel Capel had twice failed to secure a conviction at the quarter sessions. Four years later, when Capel's widow Dame Jane sought to compel members of the same band to answer interrogatories in Star Chamber, the defendants

did most humbly crave the consideration of this honourable court, whether they shall be compelled to make answer to the general charge; or that upon the said charge these defendants shall have their whole lives examined whether they have

[72] E. Harrison, 'The Court Rolls and Other Records of the Manor of Ightham, pt. II', *Archaeologia Cantiana*, 49 (1937), 1–95 *passim.*

[73] F. R. Twemlow, *The Manor of Tyrley* (Collections for a History of Staffordshire, Staffs. Rec. Soc.; Stafford, 1948), 134, 140.

[74] *Court Leet Records of the Manor of Manchester in the Sixteenth Century*, ed. J. Harland, 2 vols. (Chetham Soc., 63, 65; Manchester, 1864–5), i. 29, 35, 60.

[75] PRO STAC 2/12, fos. 204–9, 2/17/173, 8/103/15.

[76] PRO STAC 8/103/15; *Select Cases of Trespass from the King's Courts, 1307–1399*, ed. Arnold, ii. 270–1.

at any time hunted upon the said grounds, whereby they may be drawn to accuse themselves and give the complainant advantage to prosecute suits against them in other courts.

The defendants went on to state that they were already bound over to appear at the Chelmsford assizes and had already been imprisoned for the same offences.[77]

In other cases, defendants claimed that they were being accused of hunting offences committed by someone else.[78] A band of 'common hunters and killers of deer' in Neroche Forest, Somerset, claimed that they were being framed for taking deer which had been killed by the keepers of the forest.[79] In Northamptonshire, villagers claimed that the duke of Lennox had prosecuted them for poaching because they were in the habit of taking a short cut through his park when walking to a neighbouring village.[80] In what appears to be part of a gentry feud in Worcestershire and Herefordshire, a couple of young gentlemen accused the keepers of Malvern Chase of entrapment when the keepers tricked them into fetching and carrying away dead deer lying in the chase and then arrested them for poaching.[81] When a group of gentlemen poachers in Suffolk were accused of breaking and entering and unlawfully hunting in Wingfield Park, they pleaded that they could not possibly have done so because the park had been disparked. They understood that the complainant needed to prove that his park was completely fenced and enclosed and replenished with deer in order to make the charges stick.[82]

It was especially difficult to bring poachers to justice when they happened to be courtiers. In 1623 Dame Elizabeth Finch, widow of Sir Moyle Finch, bt., complained that William Smith, son and heir of Sir William Smith of Hill Hall, Essex, and his younger brother, together with a number of household servants, had been in the habit of taking deer from Copped Hall Park for the previous seven years. She said that William and his brother were reputed to be 'common deer-stealers' and 'procurers' of deer-stealers, and had killed at least thirty deer. During the frequent battles with her keepers the Smith brothers had repeatedly assaulted and wounded them and left one with a paralysed hand. Lady Finch was not able to bring William Smith to justice until after he had accompanied Prince Charles and the duke of Buckingham to Spain in order to woo the Infanta. Smith was also knighted during that interval. When he was finally compelled to make answer in Star Chamber after nearly eight years of hunting escapades, Smith admitted his youthful errors and stated that he had attempted to make restitution to Lady Finch.[83]

---

[77] PRO STAC 8/108/25; see also 8/11/3.
[78] PRO STAC 8/103/15.   [79] PRO STAC 8/34/19.
[80] PRO STAC 8/34/12.   [81] PRO STAC 8/247/20.
[82] PRO STAC 8/27/14.   [83] PRO STAC 8/147/2.

3.3. *Conflicting Legal Doctrines*

The task of enforcing game legislation was made more difficult by disagreements among lawyers concerning the interpretation and application of the Game Laws to particular cases. The greatest legal thinkers, from Bracton to Coke to Blackstone, had all criticized various aspects of game legislation— whether promulgated by royal or parliamentary authority. Many early Stuart common lawyers saw the attempts to expand royal law and jurisdiction and to restrict qualifications for hunting to a privileged few as a dangerous enhancement of the royal prerogative and part of a larger constitutional conflict involving the defence of the Ancient Constitution. Consequently, lawyers were quite willing to advise clients about their hunting rights, even when that advice led their clients to contravene parliamentary statutes or to defy the Stuart game prerogative. A few lawyers, including Coke, were even willing to risk prosecution themselves by hunting in places of disputed jurisdiction.

At the same time, ancient, prescriptive rights of hunting or royal grants of free chase and warren were also capable of legal development and could work to a landowner's advantage. As the doctrine of possessive individualism, or the absolute and unqualified possession of enclosed land, free from all claims of use-rights, emerged during the seventeenth century, landowners and their lawyers began to argue that deer in enclosed places were chattels and could be stolen.

Just what constituted royal thinking about the prerogative relative to hunting privileges may be gleaned from the preambles of the informations brought by the attorney-general in Star Chamber prosecutions of poachers in the reign of James I. In 1619 Sir Henry Yelverton, AG, asserted that hunting deer was a royal recreation, whether exercised in a royal forest or an enclosed park, and was a privilege which could be enjoyed only by royal licence or grant because it was part of the royal prerogative.[84] As such this doctrine ignored those hunting rights which existed by prescription (i.e. by continual exercise from time immemorial), by ancient charter (e.g. the Charter of the Forest of 1217, which many lawyers believed gave 'purlieu men' the right to hunt in the purlieus, or disafforested areas adjacent to royal forests, subject to certain restrictions), or through parliamentary legislation (which allowed those with sufficient estates the right to hunt). The early Stuart assumption that the king could regulate hunting privileges by licence, game warrant, or proclamation was to conflict with the emerging doctrine of possessive individualism as well as certain traditional principles of the common law.

Such extravagant concepts of royal prerogative and aristocratic privilege

[84] PRO STAC 8/24/12.

could also violate traditional notions of neighbourliness. In another case, the king's cousin and gentleman of the bedchamber, Esmé Stuart, Lord d'Aubigny, claimed that the royal grant which conferred Leighton Bromswold Park, Huntingdonshire, upon him specifically limited hunting in that park to the king and the peers of England. This declaration by d'Aubigny that he was not free to extend a traditional part of aristocratic hospitality by inviting his neighbours to hunt in the park—evidently broadcast by d'Aubigny throughout the neighbourhood—provoked the retaliation of the local gentry. Twenty of them, led by Sir William Dyer, raided the park in 1622, carried off eighteen head of deer, and made a public display of their feasting and banqueting.[85]

James I frequently neglected royal business during the times when he hunted, but he moved quickly enough against deer-stealers. When Parliament proceeded too slowly in the enactment of game legislation, he resorted to proclamations. In 1604 he forbade hunting with hounds within four miles of London and Westminster; in 1610 he wrote to Sir Robert Cecil to say that he wanted deer-stealers, along with pirates and sodomites, excepted from his next general pardon, customarily issued at the end of a parliamentary session. This had not been made sufficiently explicit in the proclamation against deer-stealers issued on 9 September 1609, and he regarded their exclusion as necessary to the preservation of his honour.[86] When Sir Peter Warburton, JCP, hanged a Scottish falconer of the royal household contrary to the king's express command to reprieve him, it was rumoured that James intended to remove him. Francis Osborne thought that the king was hard on 'deer-killers' but 'indulgent to manslayers'.[87]

Although it had long been an article of popular belief, the legal doctrine that wild beasts were *ferae naturae* and belonged to no man appears to have been first articulated by Henry de Bracton (d. 1268). This attribution was made by the anonymous writer of a mid-seventeenth-century treatise on the laws of the forest.[88] While acknowledging that it was unlawful to hunt in the forest, Tudor and early Stuart lawyers still held that deer which 'have liberty to go at their pleasure' could not be stolen when they left their parks or forests. The same principle also applied to rabbits, which were considered vermin when they wandered from their warrens, and pigeons which had flown their dovecotes.[89] There was also disagreement concern-

---

[85] PRO STAC 8/43/20.

[86] *Acts PC, 1601–1604*, 511; HMC *Salisbury*, xxi. 136; *Letters of King James VI & I*, ed. G. P. V. Akrigg (Berkeley, Calif., 1984), no. 148; *Stuart Royal Proclamations*, ed. J. F. Larkin and P. L. Hughes, 2 vols. (Oxford, 1973), vol. i, no. 102.

[87] Nichols, *Progresses of James I*, iii. 192; *Works of Francis Osborn*, pt. 3. *Memoirs of Queen Elizabeth and King James*, 444–5.

[88] Henry de Bracton, *De Legibus et Consuetudinibus Angliae*, ed. G. E. Woodbine, trans. S. E. Thorne, 2 vols. (Cambridge, Mass., 1968), ii. 42–3. BL, 'Anonymous Treatise on the Laws of the Forest', Sloane MS 751, fo. 1ʳ⁻ᵛ.

[89] *Reports of Sir John Spelman*, ed. Baker, i. 64; *The Reports of Sir George Croke*, trans. Sir Harbottle Grimston (1657), 282.

ing when a person might acquire property rights over fish. Some lawyers believed that fish in their natural habitat were *ferae naturae*, but became someone's property when they had been caught and placed in a barrel. At that point someone possessed the fish and they might be stolen, and the value might be sufficient to justify indictment for grand larceny. Sir John Fyneux, CJKB, early in the reign of Henry VIII, ruled that there was no distinction between a barrel and an enclosed pond; all were in someone's possession and the fish could be stolen from them. Fyneux then muddied the legal waters by stating that a theft was committed only if the culprit took a portion of the fish in a pond; if he killed them all, that would be waste, which would allow the complainant to sue for damages, but would not permit him to seek an indictment for theft.[90]

In the seventeenth century Sir Edward Coke and Sir Matthew Hale expressed their alarm at some of the sweeping powers and drastic penalties which parliamentary game legislation had conferred upon magistrates as well as individuals possessing hunting franchises. Coke and Hale were anxious to point out some of the limitations which judicial interpretation had placed upon the enforcement of such statutes. With regard to the Game Act of 1485, Coke noted that, although the statute made hunting at night or in disguise a felony, the complainant might, if he chose, reduce the matter to a trespass only. Coke also insisted that the statute did not apply to any forest, park, or chase of the king, or to any places which were reputed to be royal forests, parks or chases, even if in point of law they were not such. Although that statute made concealing unlawful hunting by refusal to confess a felony, defendants in such cases could not be examined under oath. But Coke cautioned that, if a party charged under this statute pleaded not guilty and was convicted, then it was a matter of felony.[91]

Coke's pronouncements about forest law and parliamentary game legislation contain a certain ambiguity which can be explained by whether his legal career happened to be prospering or declining at the moment. As attorney-general in 1599, Coke prosecuted several individuals whom he described in the preamble of a Star Chamber information as 'being very dissolute, riotous and unruly persons, common nightwalkers and stealers of deer out of the forests, chases, and parks' of the queen. The preamble of a Star Chamber bill of complaint or information is, of course, comparable to the preamble of a statute; it contains propaganda and rhetoric—not legal substance. Significantly, the attorney-general was unable to put a price on the deer that the culprits 'stole'; rather, the deer-stealers were prosecuted for unlawful assembly and riot, hunting at night, and breaking a close, i.e. for the circumstances surrounding the taking of deer in an enclosed park, but not for the act of 'deer-stealing' itself.[92]

[90] *Reports of Sir John Spelman*, ed. Baker, i. 64.
[91] 1 Hen. VII, c. 7; Sir Matthew Hale, *The History of the Pleas of the Crown*, 2 vols. (1800), i. 656–7.   [92] PRO STAC 5/A12/38.

After Coke had been dismissed from judicial office, he was very much concerned to limit the jurisdiction of forest law where it conflicted with common law. He objected, for example, to the fact that forest law regarded as principal trespassers those who procured, or aided and assisted, deer hunters before or after the fact, or received stolen venison, whereas the common law would have viewed them as accessories. Coke further insisted that, if stolen venison were received outside the forest, it could not be punished by forest law. Nor would Coke recognize the validity of forest law in a particular forest unless it could be proved that the forest was enclosed by 'metes and bounds', that forest officers were still appointed, and Swanimote Courts were still held.[93]

For Blackstone, poaching was an offence defined by 'a variety of acts of parliament, which are so numerous and so confused, and the crime itself of so questionable a nature that I shall not detain the reader with many observations thereupon'.[94] The Game Laws were a 'bastard slip' of the forest law and a remnant of the 'Norman Yoke'. His publication of the *Commentaries* in the late 1760s provided the historical foundation for a challenge to the entire game code.[95]

Some lawyers indicated their contempt for the forest law by engaging in acts which brought prosecution for unlawful hunting. Sir Humphrey Browne, serjeant-at-law, was fined, required to make a humble submission in Star Chamber, and imprisoned in the Fleet Prison by command of Henry VIII for hunting in Waltham Forest, where he held land. However, this did not prevent him from being appointed a justice of the Court of Common Pleas in 1542 and serving under four monarchs until his death in 1562.[96] Sir Edward Coke was also accused of killing deer in Waltham Forest in 1609 while he was chief justice of the Court of Common Pleas. The king was reported to be 'highly offended' and determined to punish the lord chief justice in the Court of Star Chamber for offending against the proclamation against deer-stealing of 1609.[97] Considering how strongly Coke and his supporters felt about the Charter of the Forest of 1217 and the hunting rights which they believed it allowed to purlieu men, it seems more likely that he and Sir Humphrey Browne had actually hunted in the purlieus of Waltham Forest rather than in the forest itself.[98]

Lawyers were generally hostile to game legislation because it extended legal protection to 'things of pleasure'. This view was probably reinforced

[93] Coke, *Institutes*, pt. iv, pp. 317–18.

[94] Sir William Blackstone, *Commentaries on the Laws of England*, 4 vols. (1765–9; 4th edn.; 1771), iv. 175.   [95] Munsche, *Gentlemen and Poachers*, 118–19, 131.

[96] *Reports of Sir John Spelman*, ed. Baker, i. 183; Edward Foss, *The Judges of England*, 9 vols. (1848–64), v. 469–70; see also PRO STAC 2/29/147, STAC 3/3/3, STAC 4/1/46.

[97] HMC *Salisbury*, xxi. 102; *Stuart Royal Proclamations*, ed. Larkin and Hughes, vol. i, no. 102. Curiously, the actual Star Chamber case cannot be located, and Coke may never have been brought to trial.   [98] See below, Ch. 4.

by the humanist concept of the 'commonwealth'—the idea that in policy and legislation the public good should always be preferred to private commodity. This is why, for example, Parliament enacted and the crown enforced legislation against depopulating enclosures in times of disorder and dearth. Enclosed deer parks frequently encroached upon wastes and commonable woodlands, and William Harrison complained that parks were 'devourers of the people' and contributed to the decay of tillage and the shortage of able-bodied soldiers.[99] Lewis Pollard, a justice of the Court of Common Pleas in the reign of Henry VIII, thought it would be better if there were no deer parks in England because the pleasure of the great lords was inconsistent with the common profit, but he could not think of any lawful way to deprive them of their deer parks.[100] Nor did the lawyers wish to promote the idea that all things should be held in common during a time when enclosure rioting and poaching disorders were increasingly directed against aristocratic targets.[101]

The distinction between what constituted pleasure and profit in law was never easy to define, and Tudor game legislation tended to extend legal protection to things of pleasure. The Game Act of 1539,[102] which asserted that, while breeding, game was not wild and needed to be protected, made it felony to steal the eggs or fledglings of hawks and falcons; it also stated that a landowner had an equitable claim to the profits of his lands 'as well in things of high pleasure as in things commonly valuable . . . and especially of and in things of pleasure'. A decision had already been rendered in 1526 that peacocks could be stolen because they were edible and domesticated and partook of 'the same nature as hens, capons, geese, or ducks'.[103] Although Parliament had provided for capital punishment for certain hunting offences and a few judges were willing to admit that wild animals could be considered chattels under certain circumstances, the evidence of game-offence prosecutions suggests a general reluctance to allow the law to proceed to the point of exacting the death penalty. Poachers were hanged only if, like Thomas, ninth Lord Dacre of the South, they also committed murder.[104]

This did not mean that participants in a vendetta would not try to prosecute their enemies on a capital charge. In 1534 the Court of King's Bench heard a plea in the case of *R. v. Thomas Delarever, esq. et al.*, resulting from an indictment at the North Riding Quarter Sessions for 'feloniously' taking away a tame hart valued at 40s. The indictment was dismissed on the legal technicality that it was defective because it failed to specify the county in

---

[99] William Harrison, *Description of England* (1587), in Raphael Holinshed, *Holinshed's Chronicles of England, Scotland and Ireland*, ed. Sir H. Ellis, 6 vols. (1897–8), i. 343–6.
[100] *Reports of Sir John Spelman*, ed. Baker, i. 34–6.
[101] Manning, 'Violence and Social Conflict in Mid-Tudor Rebellions', 18–40.
[102] 31 Hen. VIII, c. 12; *SR* iii. 731.
[103] *Reports of Sir John Spelman*, ed. Baker, i. 36, 322.
[104] Lower, 'The Trial and Execution of Thomas, Lord Dacre', 174.

which the crime was alleged to have been committed. It appears that the decision to indict for felony had been taken by the North Riding justices out of malice and against the wishes of the complainant, the abbot of Byland. It also helped that the king's illegitimate son, Henry, duke of Richmond, interceded with Thomas Cromwell on behalf of Delarever, who served in the duke's household.[105]

Exclusive rights to hunt in a particular place could be conferred by royal grant or acquired by prescription. A royal grant of liberty of free warren made to a particular person and his heirs extinguished everyone else's right to hunt beasts of warren within the specified area. Beasts of warren included hare, rabbits, partridges, and pheasants, but not deer, which were classified as beasts of venery or of the chase—although many landowners assumed that liberty of free warren gave them title to deer on their own land, even if the deer had wandered out of a royal forest.[106] Deer could be protected while in an enclosed park, but the owner of the park was obliged to demonstrate that the park was completely enclosed and the fences, mounds, and ditches kept in good repair before he could prosecute a person for breaking and entering that park. A chase or a warren, on the other hand, need not be enclosed and the possessor of liberty of free warren needed only to demonstrate that he possessed his franchise by charter or by prescription. Although liberty of free warren was often granted to lords of manors, free warren pertained to the person and not the manor. Thus, the manor might be sold and the free warren retained by the seller. Where liberty of free warren derived from a royal grant, its limits would be known from the terms of the charter or patent. When a lord of the manor claimed free warren by prescription, his right to hunt extended not only to copyholds but also to freeholds within the manor, since prescription presumably predated the creation of freeholds out of the demesne land.[107]

The decision by the justices of the Court of King's Bench in the case of *R. v. Sherington Talbor* (1634), affirming the absolute hunting rights of those possessing liberty of free warren, was handed down over the objections of Attorney-General Noy, who was a great advocate of the king's hunting prerogatives. Noy had been busy combing the records in the Tower and the parliamentary rolls looking for precedents for raising revenue for the king.

[105] *Reports of Sir John Spelman*, ed. Baker, i. 100–1, ii. 283–4. In 1621 Anthony Kinnersley of Loxley, Staffs., asserted that the red and fallow deer in Loxley Park were 'his own proper goods and chattels'. But since he chose to prosecute the poachers who were taking his deer in Star Chamber, this was little more than rhetoric (PRO STAC 8/191/15).

[106] Cox, *Royal Forests of England*, 2–3; Manwood, *Laws of the Forest*, ch. iv; *Memorandum Book of Richard Cholmeley of Brandsby*, pp. ix, 120, 194, 199 (I owe this reference to Dr Alan Davidson).

[107] *Stroud's Judicial Dictionary*, ed. J. S. James, 5 vols. (4th edn.; 1974), v. 2981; *Select Cases of Trespass in the King's Courts, 1307–1399*, ed. Arnold, i, pp. lxxi–lxxiii; Sir Thomas Edlyne Tomlins, *The Law Dictionary*, 2 vols. (1835), ii, *sub* 'prescription'; *Reports of Sir George Croke*, 227.

Among the schemes which Noy came up with was one which proposed calling all liberties of free warren into question. He suggested £5 as the price for confirming such liberties and £10 for granting new charters of free warren. This illustrates the crass fiscal feudalism and seigneurialism which motivated much of the antiquarian research of that period.[108]

It was generally agreed that a grant of liberty of free warren never extended over the king's lands unless the terms of the grant were explicit and unequivocal. However, the king's lands were not always well surveyed and their boundaries might be uncertain, as in the case of Cannock Forest in the reign of Henry VIII. Edward Littleton, esq., the hereditary forester of Cannock, prosecuted John Wolseley, esq., for hunting in Wolseley Wood, which he stated was part of the forest. Wolseley asserted that Wolseley Wood was parcel of his manor, over which he claimed free warren by prescription, and was not part of the forest. The lord chancellor had issued a commission to sort out the conflicting claims to hunting rights and Wolseley's act of hunting was intended to assert his rights in the matter. When, as Cannock Chase, the former royal forest passed into the hands of the Pagets of Beaudesert in 1549, the new lords and their heirs took the view that their rights of free chase and free warren extended over all manors, freeholds, and copyholds within the chase and extinguished everyone else's hunting rights.[109]

Originally intended as a means of preserving public order and preventing popular unrest, the Game Laws also became a vehicle for enhancing the royal prerogative, buttressing aristocratic privilege, and asserting the dubious doctrine that a person could acquire property rights in wild beasts. Far from preserving the king's peace, the denial of hunting privileges to most of the rural population only encouraged defiance of the law and promoted social conflict. In the Tudor and early Stuart period this resulted less in conflict between lords and peasants than in feuding between rival factions of the peerage and gentry. The task of enforcing the game code was made more difficult by the opposition of many common lawyers and the frequent refusal of juries to indict or convict poachers for violating laws which they regarded as unjust. As it became more difficult to prosecute at the assizes and quarter sessions, both the crown and private complainants turned increasingly to the Court of Star Chamber to bring poachers to book. And as the Court of Star Chamber devoted more attention to upholding the royal

---

[108] Ibid.; Sir William Noy, *A Treatise of the Rights of the Crown, Declaring How the King of England May Support and Increase His Annual Revenues* (1715), 88–91; see also R. B. Manning, 'Antiquarianism and the Seigneurial Reaction: Sir Robert and Sir Thomas Cotton and their Tenants', *Historical Research*, 63 (Oct. 1990), 277–88.

[109] *Stroud's Judicial Dictionary*, v. 2981; PRO STAC 2/27/152; Hay, 'Poaching and the Game Laws on Cannock Chase', 217–18.

game prerogative and hearing cases of assault upon royal and aristocratic game preserves, that once popular court fell increasingly into disrepute.

Judicial interpretation in the early seventeenth century tended to strengthen the property rights of those possessing hunting franchises, despite the assertion by the early Stuart monarchs that hunting privileges were derived solely from the royal game prerogative and could be withdrawn at the will and pleasure of the monarch. This was perceived by landowners and lawyers alike as an attack upon the Ancient Constitution.

4

The Purlieu Men and the Ancient Constitution

The Statute of *Carta de Foresta* hath been above 30 times . . . confirmed and enacted and commanded to be put in execution, and we find no authority in law that we remember against our opinion herein; therefore we proceed and do hold that in any purlieu a man may as lawfully hunt to all intents and purposes within the purlieu within his own grounds as any other owner may do in his grounds that never were afforested at all.

Some have endeavoured to limit the purlieu man to hunting custom or prescription, but all the said Statutes were made within the time of memory against which they cannot prescribe. Some endeavour to maintain it to be by Forest law, but . . . no Forest law can stand against laws enacted by authority of Parliament.

Sir Edward Coke, *The Fourth Part of the Institutes of the Laws of England: Concerning the Jurisdiction of Courts* (5th edn.; 1671), 303

FREEHOLDERS who possessed estates worth 40s. a year within purlieus, or disafforested areas which had once been part of the vast system of medieval royal forests, were known as 'purley-men' or purlieu men. Purlieu men possessed the right to hunt on their own holdings subject to certain restrictions on the methods which might be employed in chasing deer. The hunting rights of purlieu men had been grudgingly recognized by the Angevin monarchs, but royal foresters and gamekeepers frequently sought to abridge these rights in the succeeding centuries. When set against Charles I's attempts to revive forest law and jurisdiction and to expand the royal prerogative at the expense of parliamentary legislative authority, the threat posed to the hunting and other rights of the purlieu men became a symbolic rallying-point for those who were determined to defend the notion of an Ancient Constitution. In the minds of Sir Edward Coke and others, the Ancient Constitution had existed since time immemorial, and the laws which embodied the Ancient Constitution had been restored by Magna Carta and the Carta de Foresta. Because of repeated royal attacks upon these liberties, Parliament found it necessary to re-enact the two great charters on numerous occasions.[1] Eminent lawyers, parliamentarians, and landowners were willing to risk prosecution and expensive litigation to defend these hunting rights, which they associated with the basic principles embodied in Magna Carta and the Charter of the Forest. While there is no doubt that the hunting rights of purlieu men were sometimes used as a cover for poaching, many of the conflicts between purlieu men and royal foresters and gamekeepers arose from more principled behaviour. Nowhere do we find it more difficult to distinguish between lawful and unlawful hunting than in the case of the purlieu men. The issue was all the more contentious because the origins of purlieu rights were obscure.

4.1. The Royal Prerogative and the Revival of Forest Law

Sir Edward Coke symbolically associated the rights of purlieu men with the Charter of the Forest of 1217, and designated it, along with Magna Carta, as one of the great documents of the Ancient Constitution which must be defended against the assertion of the royal prerogative by the early Stuart monarchs. Yet the Charter of the Forest makes no mention of purlieu rights, and it is difficult to derive such a connection even by inference.[2] Charles Petit-Dutaillis states that it was not the Charter of the Forest which gave purlieu men the right to hunt, but a series of legal developments independent of the Charter of the Forest and predating it, and reflecting similar practices on the edge of the royal forests in France.[3] Petit-Dutaillis appears to follow John Manwood in identifying Henry II's Assize of Woodstock of 1184, part of a series of so-called 'forest assizes', as one documentary source of purlieu rights.[4] Chapter 16 of the Assize of Woodstock forbids chasing deer at night in areas adjoining the forest—thus implying that it was legal to do so in the daytime. The problem is that no authentic copy of the Assize of Woodstock exists, and J. C. Holt regards chapter 16 as spurious. Although Professor Holt accepts the remainder of the document as accurately reflecting Henry

[1] See. J. G. A. Pocock, *The Ancient Constitution and the Feudal Law: A Study of English Historical Thought in the Seventeenth Century* (2nd edn.; Cambridge, 1987), 37–8, 44–5, 289–90; P. Christianson, 'Young John Selden and the Ancient Constitution, ca.1610–18', *Proceedings of the American Philosophical Society*, 128. 4 (1984), 286; S. D. White, *Sir Edward Coke and 'The Grievances of the Commonwealth', 1621–1628* (Chapel Hill, NY, 1979), 176. See also Sir Matthew Hale, *The History of the Common Law of England*, ed. C. M. Gray (1739 edn.; repr. Chicago, 1971), 95–6, 100.
[2] The Charter of the Forest may be found in *SR* i (Charters), 20–1, with an English translation in *English Historical Documents, 1189–1327*, ed. H. Rothwell (1975), 337–40.
[3] Petit-Dutaillis, *Studies and Notes*, ii. 234–8.
[4] Manwood, *Laws of the Forest*, ch. 20, sect. 13.

II's forest legislation, he concludes that the only authority for chapter 16 is a sixteenth-century document.[5]

It was assumed by Coke and other seventeenth-century legal writers that purlieu rights derived from the Ancient Constitution. These rights were so fundamental that they could not be altered by parliamentary statute. Thus, when the Jacobean Game Law of 1603–4[6] increased the hunting qualification for a freeholder from 40s. p.a. to £10 p.a., Coke insisted that the qualifying estate for a purlieu man remained at 40s. p.a.[7] Coke also maintained that forest law could not diminish the rights of purlieu men and that Parliament had addressed this issue by re-enacting the Charter of the Forest over thirty times.[8] As late as 1772, Giles Jacob still accepted Coke as the authority for the rights of purlieu men, and he thought Coke's legal opinion was as good as a statute or a judicial decision.[9]

Sir Edward Coke articulated his classic statement of the hunting rights of purlieu men in *The Fourth Part of the Institutes*. Although *The Fourth Part of the Institutes* was not published until 1644 (after his death), there is good reason to believe that Coke probably sketched out his summary of purlieu rights sometime after 1607 when the *Case of Forests* was discussed by a conference of royal judges assembled at the command of James I.[10] According to Coke, purlieu men might lawfully hunt deer in purlieus of the forest on their own holdings if they met the 40s. freeholder qualification. They might hunt by coursing only, using greyhounds which were exempt from the requirement that they be expediated. The purlieu man might not hunt within the forest itself, and was to call his hounds back when they entered the forest. But if his dogs refused to obey and subsequently killed a deer, he committed no offence provided he did not enter the forest 'nor meddle with deer so killed'. 'But if the dogs fasten upon the deer, before he recover the forest, and the deer drag the dogs into the forest, there the purlieu man may follow his dogs and take the deer.' For a period of forty days out of the year, purlieu men were forbidden to hunt, so that the king's rangers could rechase the royal deer into the forest. Rangers were officers distinct from foresters and royal gamekeepers, and their main duty was to rechase royal

---

[5] *Select Charters and Other Illustrations of English Constitutional History*, ed. W. Stubbs (9th edn.; Oxford, 1913), 186–7; English translation in *Sources of English Constitutional History*, ed. C. Stephenson and F. G. Marcham, 2 vols. (New York, 1972), i. 87–9; J. C. Holt, 'The Assizes of Henry II: The Texts', in D. A. Bullough and R. L. Storey (eds.), *The Study of Medieval Records: Essays in Honour of Kathleen Major* (Oxford, 1971), 100.

[6] 1 Jac. I, c. 27; *SR* iv. 1055.

[7] Coke, *Institutes*, pt. 4, p. 300. Manwood thought that the parliamentary statute altered the purlieu hunting qualification (*Laws of the Forest*, ch. 20, sect. 5), but the anonymous author of 'The Treatise on the Laws of the Forest' agreed with Coke (BL Sloane MS 751, fos. 13v–14).

[8] Coke, *Institutes*, pt. 4, pp. 304–8.

[9] *New Law Dictionary*, comp. Jacob, *sub* 'purlieu'.

[10] Sir Edward Coke, *The Twelfth Part of the Reports* (4th edn.; 1738), sigs. D2v–D3.

deer from the purlieus into the forest. Coke cited the continuing existence of the office of ranger and the oath sworn by the rangers of Pickering Forest as proof that purlieus and purlieu rights retained legal validity in the seventeenth century.[11]

Other writers amplified Coke's doctrine of purlieu rights by stating that purlieu men might not forestall royal deer by placing themselves or their dogs or physical obstacles in the way of deer attempting to seek refuge in the forest.[12] Another manuscript, cited by W. R. Fisher, which appears to refer only to Waltham Forest, states the rule that purlieu men could hunt only with their own servants, and might not hunt at night, nor on Sundays, Mondays, Wednesdays, and Saturdays.[13]

The legal doctrine of purlieu rights, as Coke understood and articulated it, can be traced and documented as far back as the mid-Tudor period. Sometime late in the reign of Henry VIII, Henry Bradshaw, AG, prosecuted Richard Sheryffe, parson of Glendon, and eleven other persons for the offence of forestalling and hunting the king's deer on the edge of Rockingham Forest, Northamptonshire, on four different occasions. The attorney-general charged that the hunters, who killed at least five deer, had been procured and unlawfully assembled by Peter Wentworth, esq.[14] That the principal defendant was none other than Peter Wentworth of Lillingstone Lovell, Oxfordshire (now Buckinghamshire), the parliamentary leader of the reign of Elizabeth, was made clear when Wentworth was prosecuted again in 1555 for unlawful hunting in Whittlewood Forest, Northamptonshire. Although the keeper of Whittlewood, John, Lord Williams,[15] alleged that Wentworth and his eleven companions had hunted within the forest, carried weapons, and had also ambushed and assaulted the underkeepers, Wentworth maintained that they had hunted only in the purlieus of the forest in peaceful manner, as it was lawful for them to do. Wentworth and his fellow defendants insisted that they carried no weapons and had hunted only with dogs. They had been prevented from exercising their purlieu rights by one of Lord Williams's underkeepers, who confiscated Michael Harcourt's dog and broke its shoulders with a crossbow. Thus provoked, Harcourt struck the underkeeper on the head with his staff. The keepers of Whittlewood Forest clearly meant to tolerate no exercise of purlieu rights. Wentworth says that, on another occasion, he and Harcourt had attempted to retrieve their greyhounds from the forest when they were confronted by

---

[11] Coke, *Institutes*, pt. 4, pp. 303–4.
[12] BL Sloane MS 751, fos 13ᵛ–14. This provision appears to have derived from the spurious sixteenth-century chapter 16 of the Assize of Woodstock of 1184 (Holt, 'The Assizes of Henry II: The Texts', 100).
[13] Fisher, *Forest of Essex*, 166–9.   [14] PRO STAC 2/24/43.
[15] Williams was 'an unpopular landlord', whose deer parks at Thame and Rycote were attacked by the Oxfordshire rebels in 1549 (*House of Commons, 1509–1558*, ed. Bindoff, iii. 620–3).

another underkeeper, who threatened to shoot their two hounds. When Wentworth reprimanded the underkeeper for his abusive language, the latter fired his crossbow at Wentworth, who ducked. The underkeeper's broad arrow missed Wentworth, but pierced the shoulder of Harcourt. The purlieu men on the edge of Whittlewood gathered behind Peter Wentworth in his defence of their hunting rights, and the fact that later hunting parties included thirty or more indicates the degree to which the conflict with the keepers had escalated. Some of the defendants in the Star Chamber trial said that they had been indicted and fined at the quarter sessions for exercising their purlieu rights.[16] Peter Wentworth's vehement defence of the hunting rights of purlieu men may well have contributed to his 'extravagant notions about the privileges and powers of Parliament'.[17]

The previous year, in 1554, Queen Mary had implicitly recognized the hunting rights of purlieu men when she issued a proclamation ordering conservation of the deer in the Forests of Whittlewood and Salcey in the Honour of Grafton. The queen made a special appeal to purlieu men: 'And further we assuredly trust, and our good opinion is such, that all gentlemen having liberty of purlieu near or adjoining to any of our said forests will so use and hunt the same in such convenient times and hours without killing unseasonable deer.'[18] While Mary Tudor was willing to take a generous view of the hunting rights of purlieu men, there was a long history, reaching back to the reign of Henry III, of royal forest and game officials ignoring the most recent perambulations of forest boundaries and attempting to assert jurisdiction over purlieu men in disafforested areas.[19] It is for this reason that purlieu men were perceived as guarding the first line of defence of the Ancient Constitution.

Purlieu men remembered that the forests of medieval England had comprised extensive areas which lay outside the jurisdiction of the common law. The arbitrary and extortionate actions of forest officials, together with harsh punishments for trespass against the vert and venison of the forest, had necessitated the frequent re-enactment of Magna Carta and the Charter of the Forest. Constant pressure was placed upon the crown both to disafforest and to mitigate the penalties of forest law. The kings of England had long resisted, not because they needed something approaching a third of England for royal sport, but because the issue touched the royal prerogative and because the royal forests produced a significant part of their revenues.[20]

During the reign of Elizabeth the judges upheld purlieu rights and the queen did not interfere with their decisions. In 1573 a famous dispute

[16] PRO STAC 4/5/49.
[17] *House of Commons, 1558–1603*, ed. Hasler, iii. 597–601.
[18] *Tudor Royal Proclamations*, ed. Hughes and Larkin, ii. 42–3, no. 411.
[19] Young, *Royal Forests of Medieval England*, 147, 157, 163.
[20] Petit-Dutaillis, *Studies and Notes*, ii. 210–11.

occurred between Arthur, Lord Grey of Wilton, and Sir John Fortescue I (1533–1607), in which Lord Grey, the royal keeper of Whaddon Chase, a former royal forest, claimed the right for his underkeepers to rechase royal deer from Fortescue's manor of Salden, Buckinghamshire, located in the purlieus of Whaddon Chase, back into the chase. Fortescue maintained that his grant of liberty of free warren over the manor of Salden extinguished the right of Lord Grey's rangers to rechase the queen's deer within his warren. This, in effect, constituted a claim to unqualified rights of private property. Fortescue complained to the Privy Council that Grey's servants were not only rechasing the royal deer, but were also breaking hedges and hunting rabbits and deer within Fortescue's warren. Assaults on the part of servants of both Lord Grey and Fortescue led to pitched battles in which three of the latter's servants were wounded and one of Grey's servants died of wounds.[21] In his answer, Lord Grey maintained his right to rechase royal deer in the purlieus, but said that he would punish his servants if he found that they had actually hunted on Fortescue's lands.[22] The dispute also led to an exchange of 'hot speeches' in the queen's presence chamber in Westminster Palace. After Fortescue's complaint to the Privy Council, Lord Grey ambushed Fortescue in Temple Bar and knocked him off his horse. The queen imprisoned Grey in the Fleet and his servants were indicted at common law for assaulting Fortescue's servants. However, the legal question of the right of the keeper of Whaddon Chase to rechase the royal deer was referred by the Privy Council to a hearing before the two chief justices and the attorney-general, and they ruled that liberties of purlieu, whether claimed by the keeper of the chase or by a purlieu man, could not be extinguished by a grant of liberty of free warren.[23] Lord Grey forfeited the favour of the queen, but the judges upheld his argument, which was the main legal issue in this case.[24]

Under James I, the Privy Council and the Court of Star Chamber, exercising the royal prerogative, displayed a clear tendency to disallow the rights of purlieu men. Considering the earlier disposition of the judges to uphold purlieu rights under Elizabeth, it seems reasonable to infer that this alteration in policy resulted from royal pressure. Quite early in the new king's reign, there was an epidemic of poaching in Waltham Forest, Essex, which John Manwood, the steward of Waltham Forest, blamed on the purlieu men: 'it seemeth the purlieu men with their adherents have consented together to destroy the forest by colour of purlieu hunting, which they have

---

[21] PRO SP 12/92/34.   [22] PRO SP 12/92/36.

[23] Dyer, *Reports*, pt. iii, fo. 327a.

[24] The editors of *The History of Parliament* for this period suggest that the rivalry was complicated by religious hostility—Fortescue having Catholic connections and Lord Grey being linked to the Puritan faction—and also spilled over into electoral contests for Buckinghamshire and Chipping Wycombe. Fortescue was later appointed chancellor of the Exchequer and chancellor of the Duchy of Lancaster (*House of Commons, 1558–1603*, ed. Hasler, ii. 148–51).

brought to pass in the Forest of Waltham; or at least they will do so in short time if their hunting be suffered as is now used.'[25] Undoubtedly, much of the destruction of deer in Waltham Forest was attributable to commercial poachers supplying the voracious London market, and the Waltham purlieu men, whether they had actually conspired with the poachers or not, were tarred with the same brush. A group of hunters from the edge of Waltham Forest were tried before Lord Chancellor Ellesmere and the judges of Star Chamber in June 1603. When the defendants were unable to document their purlieu rights, the judges disallowed their plea. They decided to submit and were convicted by their own confessions.[26] The Swanimote Court of Waltham Forest also began taking a harder line against purlieu men at the same time.[27]

Subsequently, the king's refusal to recognize the rights of purlieu men became more explicit. In November 1619 the Privy Council informed the Somerset justices that the king did not intend to tolerate the killing of deer which had strayed out of the Forest of Braden into the purlieus.[28] In January 1620 the Privy Council, displaying a clear prejudice against a group of hunters from the vicinity of Rockingham Forest 'pretending right of purlieu', ordered the attorney-general 'to examine the pretences touching the right and extent of purlieu hunting there, and to certify his opinion thereof'.[29]

Although James I ignored the rights of purlieu men, he insisted on the right of his rangers to rechase royal deer from the purlieus back into the forests. Richard Cholmeley of Brandsby, Yorkshire, a recusant gentleman who was very sensitive about his property rights, complained that the keepers of Galtres Forest ignored his liberty of free warren when rechasing deer and used their authority as royal rangers as a cover for hunting other people's deer. In April 1620 Cholmeley noted in his Memorandum Book that the king 'loves not his subjects to contest with him—notwithstanding the charters'. Cholmeley claimed to have in his possession an English translation of Magna Carta.[30] He also had some influence with the earl of Rutland, chief justice in eyre of the forests north of the Trent, and Rutland ordered the rangers of Galtres Forest to treat Cholmeley more courteously. Subsequently, the rangers asked his permission before they rechased the deer from his manor, and sometimes invited him to accompany them when they hunted.[31] Cholmeley grasped at this gesture of reconciliation; the recusant gentry were subjected to enough hostility and their deer were especially vulnerable to poachers.

A question which was implicit in the case of *Lord Grey* v. *Fortescue* about

[25] Manwood, *Laws of the Forest*, ch. 20, sect. 9.
[26] Hawarde, *Les Reportes del Cases in Camera Stellata*, ed. Baildon, 366–7 and n.
[27] Fisher, *Forest of Essex*, 169–70.
[28] *Acts PC, 1619–1621*, 69.   [29] Ibid. 113–14.
[30] *Memorandum Book of Richard Cholmeley of Brandsby*, 120, 194, 199.   [31] Ibid. 227.

the right of royal rangers to rechase the queen's deer in the purlieus of Whaddon Chase was whether Whaddon Chase was, in law, a forest. Although the judges neglected to address that question in 1573, the problem of definition was bound to arise again in connection with the legal existence of purlieus. In Bowland Chase, during the reign of Elizabeth, the officers of the master forester pursued deer outside the metes and bounds of Bowland, and the question arose whether purlieus could be said to exist, since Bowland was reputed to be a chase rather than a forest. The officials of the Duchy of Lancaster assumed that the existence of Swanimote courts and the continuing appointment of forest officials provided evidence that Bowland was a forest, and the pleadings in the Court of Duchy Chamber reveal that the lands outside Bowland were deemed purlieus. Rangers continued to rechase deer, and forestalling deer was regarded as an attachable offence.[32]

Purlieu men and inhabitants of Bowland and Leicester Forests continued to challenge this interpretation, and James I commanded the judges to confer about the question during Easter term 1607. Although the judges were hostile to a revival of forest law, they did concede that a forest was legally a forest if it was a matter of record that Attachment and Swanimote Courts and Justice Seats continued to be held, and foresters, regarders, verderers, and the like continued to be appointed. It was not sufficient to prove that the game had been preserved and protected. If a forest could not be proved to be a forest in law, then it was to be regarded as a free chase. A freehold inhabitant of a chase might lawfully cut wood upon his own holding (which could not be done in a forest without a royal licence) provided he left sufficient cover and browsewood for the royal deer, which could be hunted in a royal chase only by those possessing the king's licence or grant.[33]

Sir Edward Coke held the opinion that the king still retained the power to make new forests on his own land, but he insisted that the king could not afforest the lands of others without their consent. When Henry VIII set about to make a new forest, to be called Hampton Court Chase, he discovered that he could not do so without the consent of the freeholders and customary tenants whose lands were affected. So he concluded, through commissioners, an agreement with the freeholders and customary tenants of East Molesey, West Molesey, Walton-upon-Thames, Esher, Weybridge, and part of Cobbam, Surrey, in which forest law was imposed for the usual offences punishable in any forest or chase, but the freeholders and tenants retained their customary rights to fell wood and coppice new plantations, and to fence in their corn in order to keep the deer out. In exchange for these concessions, Henry VIII remitted a third part of the rent of every

---

[32] Shaw, *Royal Forest of Lancaster*, 213, 233–8.
[33] Coke, *Institutes*, pt. iv, p. 298; id., *Case of Forests*, in *Twelfth Part of the Reports*, sigs. D2ᵛ–D3; BL Sloane MS 751, fo. 2ʳ⁻ᵛ.

freeholder and copyholder and also reduced their entry fines by one half. The contents of this agreement were then embodied in an Act of Parliament.[34] Coke noted that Henry VIII accepted the legal limits of his power to create new forests, although he 'did stand as much upon his prerogative as any King of England ever did'.[35] In fact, the afforestation of Hampton Court Chase was never popular with the tenants, and Coke seems to have been unaware that the Privy Council, under Lord Protector Somerset, removed the deer from Hampton Court Chase to Windsor Forest in response to continuing complaints from the tenants—although preserving the legal status of Hampton Court Chase as a forest. The tenants were glad enough to pay their old rents to regain access to their common lands freed from the depredations of the deer.[36]

The attempt to revive forest law and jurisdiction may be viewed as part of the seigneurial reaction. The early Stuart monarchs, as well as lords of manors, were alert to opportunities to exploit ancient precedents for reviving feudal and seigneurial dues and courts which could yield profits.[37] Sometime after 1613, William, earl of Salisbury, with the consent of James I, revived the Court of Roundhedge, after a lapse of thirty-eight years, in order to prosecute deer-slayers and wood-stealers on Enfield Chase more effectively. Sir Fulke Greville, chancellor of the Exchequer, objected to it as 'a new devised court', but Salisbury argued that William Fleetwood, recorder of London, had convened the court regularly in his day. Following the demise of the Court of Roundhedge—presumably sometime in the 1570s—the tenants of the manor and chase of Enfield had petitioned for its revival, but Salisbury was unlikely to have been moved by any consideration of sympathy for the numerous poor people of Edmonton Hundred in which Enfield Chase lay.[38] In the 1590s Edward Parker, twelfth Lord Morley, tried to revive forest law in Hatfield Forest, Essex, one of a small number of forests still in private hands. Morley, had purchased the forest and the manor of Hatfield Broad Oak from Robert, third Lord Rich, and had attempted to revive the Swanimote Court, which he employed to deprive commoners in the forest of their use-rights. Lord Rich, who was involved in a legal dispute with

[34] This was the same act which established the Honour of Hampton Court in 1539 (31 Hen. VIII, c. 5; *SR* iii. 721). [35] Coke, *Institutes*, pt. iv, p. 301.
[36] *VCH Middx.*, ii. 323–4; *Acts PC, 1547–50*, 190–2.
[37] For a discussion of the varieties of fiscal seigneurialism, see Manning, *Village Revolts*, 4, 34–40, *et passim*, and id., 'Antiquarianism and the Seigneurial Reaction', 277–88.
[38] HMC *Salisbury*, xxii. 139; PRO DL 1/121/E5. Following the demise of the Court of Roundhedge, there was so much illegal cutting of wood and timber on Enfield Chase that the deer began feeding upon the tenants' lands. The tenants complained that the new court which replaced the old Court of Roundhedge was only interested in levying fines and not in regulating use of the chase for the benefit of all. Presumably, the manorial court had taken over the jurisdiction of the Court of Roundhedge. The understeward claimed that the old court had not served the Queen's interests because the juries making presentments to the old court had protected stealers of wood and deer.

Morley concerning title to the profits of Hatfield Fair, alleged that the Swanimote Court had not met, nor had Hatfield Forest been subject to forest law, within the 'memory of man'.[39]

The greatest threat to purlieu rights came, of course, during the reign of Charles I. At a Forest Eyre held on 21 September 1630 Charles I's forest officers proclaimed the new boundaries of the Forest of Essex, which declared most of the county of Essex a royal forest, subject to forest law, and, for all practical purposes, restored the boundaries of the Forest of Essex, which Henry III had delineated in 1301. This had the effect of cancelling all of the disafforestations promised by Magna Carta and the Charter of the Forest and subsequently purchased at considerable expense by the inhabitants of the purlieus. The significance of this declaration was not lost on the communities concerned, although no move was made to implement Charles's new policy until Sir John Finch, AG, appeared at the infamous Justice Seat held at Stratford Langthorne on 4 October 1634 and browbeat the grand jury into acceding to his demands to revive the boundaries of the fourteenth-century Forest of Essex. Here, also, the forest and game officers knelt before the chief justice of the forest south of the Trent, Henry Rich, earl of Holland, surrendered their hunting horns and had them redelivered after each forester had paid a fee of 6s. 8d., and swore an oath to protect the vert and venison of the forest within the new boundaries. Attorney-General Finch then delivered an extravagant speech justifying the new boundaries on the basis of searches undertaken in the records of the Tower of London. In response, Robert Rich, third earl of Warwick, and other Essex landowners asked for an adjournment until they were able to gather charters or other evidences out of their muniment rooms. The adjournment granted was only overnight, and the pleading of the Essex landowners was limited to a verbal response.[40] They argued that the king's forest proceedings 'were contrary to law, and to the Charter of the Liberties of the Forests and other charters and divers Acts of Parliament'.[41]

Another session of the Justice Seat was held on 8 April 1635. The court was presided over by the chief justice in eyre, the earl of Holland, and Sir John Finch, who having earned the office of chief justice of the Common Pleas by his work as attorney-general, was there to make sure that the proceedings went as rehearsed. Four attorneys representing the lords and freeholders of the county were allowed to argue their case before a jury consisting of forest officers. Many Essex landowners and householders— most of whom would have regarded themselves as purlieu men—were heavily fined for encroaching upon land which had long been disafforested

---

[39] PRO STAC 5/R18/2; GEC ix. 226.   [40] Fisher, *Forest of Essex*, 26, 37–47.
[41] Rushworth (ed.), *Historical Collections*, iii. 1056–7; G. Hammersley, 'The Revival of the Forest Laws under Charles I', *History*, 45 (1960), 85–102.

and where their ancestors had lived for generations. Many had already been fined for unlawful hunting, keeping unexpediated hounds, cutting wood without licence, and neglecting to mend their fences.[42]

The reafforestation of the purlieus of Essex was one of the grievances which members of the Long Parliament sought to have redressed. They once again reconfirmed the Charter of the Forest of 1217 and subsequent parliamentary legislation by declaring that new forests could be created only by Act of Parliament. No forest courts of any kind were to be held which had not sat during the sixty years prior to the beginning of Charles I's reign. Purlieus were not to be regarded as subject to forest jurisdiction, and the boundaries of forests were to be strictly observed as they existed in the twentieth year of the reign of James I. Nor should disafforestation adversely affect the rights of common of any tenant who had enjoyed such use-rights prior to disafforestation.[43] The rights of purlieu men were still regarded as a bulwark of the Ancient Constitution by Blackstone when, as Vinerian Professor of Law at Oxford, he published the first modern transcription of *The Great Charter and the Charter of the Forest* in 1759. It accorded well with his belief that the Game Laws were legally absurd.

4.2. *The Purlieu Men*

Purlieu men hated forest law and did battle with forest officials who tried to enforce it. Purlieu men frequently denied rangers the right to rechase deer out of the purlieus into the forest. Some tried to disafforest portions of royal forests and to enclose such land within their own parks, or attempted to assert that their grants or prescriptive rights of free warren within a forest had the effect of disafforesting that land and extinguishing forest jurisdiction. They pushed their purlieu rights well beyond the limits that sympathetic legal thinkers were prepared to allow them, and many used their purlieu hunting rights to cover large-scale poaching activities. For their part, royal keepers and rangers used their authority to rechase royal deer back into forests as a cover for pursuing private vendettas or hunting on the lands of purlieu men. Thus, the many royal forests and their borderlands were the scenes of perpetual poaching wars. In some cases, rivalries probably had their roots in the aristocratic turbulence and civil wars of the fifteenth century.

One such poaching war was played out in Sherwood Forest and Thorneywood Chase in the 1610s and 1620s. Sir John Byron (d. 1623) claimed to possess liberty of free warren in his manors of Colwick and Newstead, Nottinghamshire, by ancient prescriptive rights and asserted that his rights

---

[42] Fisher, *Forest of Essex*, 37–47.   [43] 16 Car. I, c. 16; *SR* v. 119–20.

of warren effectively extinguished forest jurisdiction. King James I had accepted Byron's hospitality when he hunted in Sherwood Forest and Thorneywood Chase in 1612 and 1614, but pointedly passed Byron by in 1616 because Byron had refused to obey the king's command to forbid his son, the younger Sir John, to enclose parkland in Newstead until it could be determined whether or not it was part of the king's forest.[44] The younger Sir John Byron lived at Colwick within Sherwood Forest and Thorneywood Chase, where he possessed a park of three hundred acres, which his hated rival, Philip, Lord Stanhope, the keeper of Thorneywood Chase, claimed was an illegal park, subject to forest jurisdiction. Surrounding the park, the younger Byron had constructed deer leaps, which enticed royal deer into the park but prevented them from getting out. The park was thus a giant trap for royal deer. When Stanhope's rangers sought to rechase the deer, Byron prosecuted them at the quarter sessions for trespass, breaking a close, and trampling the grass. The jury, which sympathized with Byron's hostility to Stanhope's rangers, found them guilty. Stanhope countered that the witnesses were perjured and the jurors suborned.[45]

The younger Sir John Byron continued to ignore the royal command not to hunt until his claim to possess liberty of free warren could be determined at law. *Quo warranto* proceedings were brought against him at the Nottinghamshire Assizes before Sir Edmund Bromley, baron of the Exchequer, and, after ancient records were exhibited proving his title, his claim to free warren was accepted. Stanhope then brought a complaint against Byron in the Court of Exchequer Chamber, where the latter's title was again upheld. Stanhope complained to the Court of Star Chamber that all the while Byron had encouraged his neighbours, supporters, and servants to hunt in the forest as well as in his park and warren. The hunters employed buckstalls and slaughtered more than a hundred deer. The deer were killed in such large numbers that they could not be consumed locally, and the surplus was sent to London and Westminster—perhaps to buy goodwill from the judges.[46]

Lord Stanhope also attempted to prosecute Byron at the Swanimote Court of Sherwood Forest, held at Nottingham Castle before Francis, earl of Rutland, who was Byron's patron. Rutland merely told Byron to cease hunting until the issue of his liberty of free warren was settled in the courts. Perhaps frustrated by his failure to get at Byron by legal means, Stanhope, a hot-tempered man, sent Byron a written challenge to a duel, accusing the latter of lying about his possession of free warren, and stating that the time had come to settle the matter by 'swords and not tongues'. Byron refused to meet Stanhope and complained to the attorney-general, who prosecuted

---

[44] *House of Commons, 1558–1603*, ed. Hasler, i. 525.
[45] PRO STAC 8/259/8.   [46] PRO STAC 8/259/9.

Stanhope for sending a challenge to a duel and for unlawful hunting in Colwick Park. Byron's hunting in Colwick Park and Warren grew more bold: he hunted frequently with bands of twenty or more and with much display and blowing of hunting horns; he defiantly boasted that he would impale the head of a large buck in front of Stanhope's lodge in Thorneywood Chase, and would continue hunting even if he encountered the king himself sitting 'on one of the hedges'.[47] Stanhope's underkeeper testified that Byron had threatened to shoot any of his men who set foot in Byron's park or warren, and the gamekeepers were too terrified to defy the squire of Colwick.[48]

Although Byron insisted that he confined his hunting to Colwick Park and Warren, he appears to have hired hunters from more distant communities to attack the deer in Thorneywood Chase and to harrass Lord Stanhope's underkeepers. The revolt of the purlieu men of Sherwood Forest and Thorneywood Chase appears to have been widespread: Sir Charles Cavendish of Welbeck, another enemy of the Stanhopes, possessed a park in his manor of Kirkby in Ashfield, Nottinghamshire, which extended into Sherwood Forest, where he also claimed liberty of free warren.[49] Besides arousing the emnity of the purlieu men by his attack on their hunting rights, Stanhope's harshness as a landlord invited attacks upon his own deer park at Horsley Park, Derbyshire and upon his fishing weirs at Shelford, Nottinghamshire. The personal animosity between Stanhope and Cavendish and the Byrons was also part of a larger feud between the earls of Shrewsbury and the Stanhope family.[50]

Sir John Thynne I of Longleat was another purlieu man, who carved a park out of Selwood Forest and trapped royal deer. Edmund Leversage, esq., the ranger of that part of Selwood which bordered on Longleat Park, complained that Thynne had constructed deer leaps which allowed the queen's deer to enter, but not to escape from, Longleat Park. To compound this offence, Thynne's gamekeepers also tracked down deer with lymehounds and drove them into Longleat Park.[51] When the ranger's men attempted to interfere with Thynne's gamekeepers, Thynne hired more hunters and sent a party of thirty men and more, fully armed, into Selwood Forest itself to assault the keepers and to spoil the deer. Here, Thynne's hired hunters were joined by reinforcements equipped with nets and greyhounds. In the ensuing battle, two of Thynne's men were wounded, captured, and identified. One of the poachers later escaped and joined his fellows at Longleat

---

[47] PRO STAC 8/70/7, 28/10, 259/7.
[48] PRO STAC 8/70/7.   [49] PRO STAC 8/14/8.
[50] PRO STAC 8/255/6; MacCaffrey, 'Talbot and Stanhope', 81. The battles of Philip, Lord Stanhope, later earl of Chesterfield, with the purlieu men of Sherwood Forest and Thorneywood Chase appear to have provided him with the necessary qualifications to command a Royalist regiment of dragoons during the Civil Wars (GEC iii. 180; *DNB, sub nom.*).
[51] *House of Commons, 1558–1603*, ed. Hasler, iii. 506–7; PRO STAC 7/15/41.

House, where they rested and had their wounds dressed before being secretly conveyed to a distant hiding place. When the forest officials sought to bring charges against Thynne's men, he used his authority as a justice of the place to discharge them.[52]

On the borders of Gillingham Forest, Richard Chafin, son of William Chafin of Zeals Clifton, Wiltshire, esq., organized the purlieu men into a 'confederacy' to defend their rights. In 1618 William, third earl of Pembroke, the warden of Gillingham Forest, prosecuted Richard Chafin and a large number of co-defendants in Star Chamber and charged them with interfering with his rangers while the latter were rechasing deer from the purlieus into the forest. Pembroke alleged that Chafin and his followers not only forestalled the deer in the purlieus, but also coursed them into the forest. The rangers followed Chafin and the others in hot pursuit to his father's house in Zeals Clifton, where they captured them with panting greyhounds 'so weary . . . with the said coursing as they were scarce able to stand'. Forest officials regarded a panting greyhound as the equivalent of a smoking gun. Pembroke further specified that Chafin's band had challenged and obstructed the rangers on numerous other occasions and so terrified the rangers that they deemed it prudent to stay out of the way of the hunters as much as possible.[53]

Richard Chafin was quite prepared to state the case for the purlieu men when he made his answer in the Star Chamber. He said that he and his companions were all gentlemen who had title to common of pasture in the lands where they hunted. They

have by all the time aforesaid . . . used to chase, hunt, kill, and take the deer there . . . freely without being questioned for offending against the said forest or the assize or liberties thereof, which from time to time in all these defendants' memory have been used without controlment [i.e. censure] or gainsaying of any of the keepers or officers of the said forest until late; and the same grounds have always been free from the assize of law of the forest, as other grounds that are not within the regard of the liberties of the forest.[54]

Richard Chafin admitted that he and his friends had hunted at the times and in the places specified in the bill of complaint, but denied the premises, namely that they had hunted unlawfully or in the forest.[55] Chafin did, however, state that a number of prominent landowners in the neighbourhood, including Lord Stourton, Lord Arundell of Wardour, Sir Thomas Thynne, Sir Edmund Ludlow, and Robert Hopton, esq., were replenishing their stock of

---

[52] PRO, STAC 5/A32/31, A51/38. Sir John Thynne I was prosecuted sometime before 1581 by Gilbert Gerrard, AG. Sir John Thynne II, his son and heir, was dropped from the commission of the peace in 1587 and was never knighted under Elizabeth, so it is possible that he continued to engage in the same activities as his father (*House of Commons, 1558–1603*, ed. Hasler, iii. 504–6).

[53] PRO STAC 8/183/44.   [54] Ibid.   [55] Ibid.

deer from the purlieus of Gillingham Forest. One may infer that one-way deer leaps were common features of aristocratic deer parks in the region.[56]

The poaching war between the purlieu men and the rangers of Gillingham Forest had been going on for at least two years when Richard Chafin was charged in Star Chamber with unlawful hunting. His father had been prosecuted for the same offence earlier, and had countered with a cross-suit against the rangers and the keepers for unlawful hunting in his liberty of free warren on the manor of Zeals Clifton. William Chafin stated that the rangers had raided his game preserve, seriously wounded two of his gamekeepers, and left them for dead. Arthur Hartgill, gent., the ranger of Gillingham and the principal defendant, insisted that Zeals Clifton was a royal manor and thus the liberty of free warren belonged to the crown. William Chafin was merely a tenant and possessed a capital messuage. The rangers had long exercised the right to rechase deer out of the purlieus until the Chafins and the other purlieu men began denying them permission to come on to their holdings. Other evidence makes it quite clear that the Chafins' servants hunted in the forest itself.[57]

The defence of purlieu rights was a growing movement, and we find purlieu men and royal rangers disputing the same issues throughout the realm. In Lancashire, William Stanley, Lord Monteagle, claimed prescriptive rights of hunting, coursing, hawking, fishing, and fowling over his lordship of Caton, including his tenants' land as well as demesne lands for which he and his ancestors had paid an annual sum of 13s. 4d. His claim to liberty of free warren and chase conflicted with the assertion by Christopher Carus, keeper of the Royal Forest and Park of Quernmore, that the lordship of Caton fell wholly within the purlieus of Quernmore Forest, where customary usage was that the royal deer could feed and graze and the rangers could rechase the royal deer without hindrance. Lord Monteagle complained that Carus failed to keep the park fences in good repair, and overcharged the park with his own cattle so that the deer were driven into the purlieus to feed and graze, where they spoiled the grass and corn belonging to Monteagle's tenants. The rangers had torn down hedges, trampled corn, and assaulted the tenants while rechasing deer. In recompense for allowing the rangers to rechase the royal deer, Monteagle was customarily allowed 'one fee-buck in summer and one fee-doe in winter . . . out of the said park', but Monteagle and his outraged tenants assembled themselves to withstand the rangers and confiscate their hounds whenever they ventured into the lordship of Caton.[58]

By the reign of James I freeholders living in purlieus had developed a more heightened awareness of their legal rights than had existed in the Tudor period. In the summer of 1606 the son of John Burton of Stockerston,

---

[56] Ibid.   [57] PRO STAC 8/92/2.   [58] PRO DL 1/100/C3, 102/S15.

Leicestershire, gent., was home on vacation from university with a friend. They were coursing deer on lands belonging to Burton's father when keepers from Leighfield Forest, Rutlandshire, accused them of poaching and attempted to confiscate the venison along with their dogs and weapons. The two students forcibly resisted and the keepers followed them to the elder Burton's house. Although John Burton the elder seemed to be less aware of purlieu rights than his son, he also stood up to the keepers, who had fetched a constable to search Burton's house. The elder Burton refused to allow the constable or the keepers to search his house because none of them was a magistrate or a sworn officer of the forest, and Burton maintained that the keepers' commission from the chief justice in eyre was 'against the law'. Later, a pursuivant dragged John Burton the elder before the chief justice in eyre of the forests south of the Trent, Charles, earl of Nottingham, who compelled Burton to make satisfaction. When John, Lord Harrington of Exton, chief forester of Leighfield, prosecuted the elder Burton in Star Chamber, the latter complained that he had not supposed that he would be compelled to answer for the same offence twice. John Burton the elder defiantly answered that the keepers of Leighfield had no right to confiscate his dogs and weapons because he did not live within the forest and was qualified by 'quality and estate' to keep dogs, crossbows, and guns, and, indeed, was required by law to have such weapons in readiness for the king's service. He persisted in believing that he was qualified by statute law to hunt and was 'moved so to believe by reason of certain records of the Tower [of London] and other ancient evidences which this defendant hath seen touching that matter'.[59]

Sir John Dormer of Dorton Park, Buckinghamshire, the verderer of Barnewood Forest, told Thomas Terringham of Nether Winchendon, Buckinghamshire, esq., that it was unlawful for purlieu men to hunt in the purlieus. Terringham was much offended by this and swore revenge upon the officious Dormer. Terringham recruited a band of hired hunters, and, together with his servants, they raided Dormer's deer park on several occasions, spoiled his deer, and assaulted Dormer's gamekeepers.[60] By contrast, the keepers of the New Forest found that they enjoyed better relations with the purlieu men if they allowed them to course deer within the forest as compensation for damage done to their crops by the king's deer.[61]

An ardent hunter could always discover new ways in which to apply the doctrine of purlieu hunting rights. When Henry Thorpe, the high constable of Northamptonshire, was accused by the attorney-general of unlawful hunting in Rockingham Forest, Thorpe answered that he was the administrator of the manor of Blatherwicke, appointed by the Court of Wards on behalf of

---

[59] PRO STAC 8/177/16.   [60] PRO STAC 8/114/13.   [61] PRO STAC 8/71/13.

the infant lord. The manor was located within the purlieus of Rockingham Forest, and he claimed that he was authorized to exercise the lord's ancient prescriptive hunting rights in order to preserve the manorial woods from damage by the deer.[62]

The purlieu men of the Somerset side of Exmoor Forest carried on a determined resistance against an attempt by the rangers of Exmoor to abridge their rights, which lasted a quarter of a century and which was unusually disruptive and divisive. In 1592 Roger Sydenham of North Quarum, Somerset, gent., the ranger of Exmoor, brought a complaint in Star Chamber against Humphrey Sydenham of Dulverton, Somerset, esq., and a number of other purlieu men, for unlawfully hunting the red deer of Exmoor. Humphrey refused to answer the subpoena and, instead, brought a counter-suit against the ranger. In order to raise money for his legal fees, Humphrey organized a church-ale to be held in Skilgate parish, where Roger was a churchwarden. This was clearly an act of defiance intended to humiliate the ranger. His objections to the unlicensed church-ale were brushed aside, and invitations were sent to seventeen adjoining parishes. Humphrey and his friends obtained three hundred or four hundred gallons of ale by breaking into a storehouse where the ale was being kept for another parish fund-raising event. Humphrey was an old soldier and a captain in the Somerset trained bands; he mustered his company at Dulverton, and marched them to Skilgate, where he commanded them to start drinking. They drank until their money was spent. He repeated this military exercise several times over a two-year period. On one occasion Humphrey's men broke up a Sunday-morning service in the parish church in order to open their church-ale; on another occasion they kidnapped a bear and paraded it through the streets of Taunton to the market-place, where they baited the bear with dogs. In this manner Humphrey Sydenham and his followers raised £60 to keep the counter-suit going.[63]

In 1611 Humphrey Sydenham was still defying the forest officials by hunting in the purlieus. He claimed that he had obtained a judgment from the earl of Nottingham, the chief justice in eyre south of the Trent, declaring that his manor of Dulverton was no part of the forest. The attorney-general prosecuted Humphrey and others for assembling their tenants as beaters and leading a hunt over a two-week period through seven parishes of Somerset, where they raided the deer parks of Richard, earl of Bath, and other rivals of their faction. Humphrey Sydenham admitted that he had crossed the earl of Bath's property, but denied that he had violated the earl's liberty of free warren because he was pursuing only red deer, which

---

[62] PRO STAC 8/27/15.

[63] Frederick Brown, 'Star Chamber Proceedings, 34th Elizabeth, 1592', *Proc. Somerset Arch. and Nat. Hist. Soc.* 29 (1883), 53–60.

were bred in his own park and which were not protected by the earl's rights of warren.[64] Other purlieu men on the edge of Exmoor used the same plea that they hunted only red deer. In 1597 one purlieu man, George Luttrell of Dunster, esq., employed the red deer which he caught for entertaining the assize justices.[65]

4.3. The Case of Cranborne Chase

Cranborne Chase was the scene of the largest and most complex dispute concerning the issue of purlieu rights. Despite the searches of many scholars, the evidence is lacking that Cranborne Chase was ever a forest; thus, it could not be disafforested under the provisions of Magna Carta and the Charter of the Forest. Yet, the medieval lords of the chase had exploited their seigneurial rights as if Cranborne Chase were a forest, and the tenants and borderers suffered much in consequence.[66] In the reign of Elizabeth, a judgment was obtained declaring that the borderers were, in law, purlieu men. In the reign of James I, Cranborne Chase, one of the largest hunting preserves in southern England, was granted to a royal favourite, William Cecil, second earl of Salisbury, with the understanding that Salisbury was to keep the chase well stocked with deer for the recreation of the king. Salisbury, an obsequious courtier, garrisoned the chase with numerous keepers and rangers in order to halt the depredations of the many hunters in the neighbourhood. The boundaries of the chase had always been ill-defined, and the more strict enforcement of Salisbury's claims regarding the boundaries of the chase led to protracted and bitter conflicts with neighbouring landowners and borderers. These disputes spilled over into three counties and persisted from 1581 until at least as late as 1632.

In the reign of James I, Cranborne Chase was estimated to contain between 700,000 and 800,000 acres—an area that was 100 miles in circumference. This vast tract of land comprised seventy-two parishes with a population of 10,000 or 12,000 inhabitants. It took in the north-east part of Dorsetshire together with the adjoining areas of Wiltshire and Hampshire, and included the towns of Salisbury, Wilton, Shaftesbury, Blandford, Wimborne, Fordingbridge, and Downton. Although the second earl of Salisbury inherited Cranborne House upon his father's death in 1612, Cranborne Chase remained in the possession of the crown until 1617, when the chase was granted to the second earl by letters patent. Salisbury appears to have assumed actual control in early 1616, when he began prosecuting alleged poachers in the Court of Star Chamber. Salisbury immediately set out to

[64] PRO STAC 8/14/1.   [65] PRO STAC 5/P29/17, P16/15.
[66] Hutchins, *History and Antiquities of Dorset*, iii. 408–9.

claim larger boundaries by beginning a suit in the Court of Exchequer against the earl of Pembroke, Lord Arundell of Wardour, and other borderers of the chase, who held land in the parish of Tollard Royal, Wiltshire, which the latter regarded as purlieu land. There were eight walks within the chase, each provided with a keeper's lodge; Salisbury began rebuilding the lodges and filling them with underkeepers to police the chase. He created much ill will by enclosing wastes and woods to provide grazing and browsewood for the deer. The tenants and borderers who had formerly exercised common rights upon these lands began uttering threats to pull down the new fences.[67]

A decision by Thomas, earl of Sussex, chief justice in eyre of the forests, in 1581 had allowed purlieu rights to the borderers of Cranborne Chase. In that year, the lieutenant of the chase, the earl of Pembroke, prosecuted John Swaine of Blandford for not permitting the keepers to rechase the deer within his manor of Tarrant Gunville, Dorset, for cutting timber and enclosing coppices without licence, for forestalling deer, and for keeping an illegal park. Swaine was able to prove to Sussex's satisfaction that he and his ancestors had maintained a park and exercised purlieu rights since time out of mind, and were entitled to do so 'by the laws of the forest and the customs of the chase'. Swaine was ordered to allow the rangers to rechase the deer into the chase, but he was also permitted to maintain his park provided it contained no one-way deer leaps.[68] In the previous year, 1580, Thomas Topp of Bridmore, Wiltshire, had prosecuted one of the keepers of Cranborne Chase on a charge of trespass for entering one of Topp's closes and trampling down the corn and grass while rechasing deer towards the chase. The court ruled in Topp's favour and awarded him damages, because the jury would not accept the argument that Cranborne Chase extended into Wiltshire.[69]

The borderers and purlieu men of Cranborne Chase had been able to obtain justice in the reign of Elizabeth, but that would change in the next reign. Both James I and Charles I were particularly fond of Cranborne Chase and continued to hunt there frequently. James I did not scruple to interfere with the course of justice in order to favour the suits of the earl of Salisbury to expand the boundaries of Cranborne Chase and thus preserve his favourite sport there. Perceiving the threat to their purlieu rights from the combined determination of King James and the earl of Salisbury, the leaders of the purlieu men in Wiltshire had obtained an order from the Court of Common Pleas confirming them in their purlieu rights. James I wrote an angry letter

---

[67] Ibid. 406, 408; Sir Richard Hoare, *The History of Modern Wiltshire*, 5 vols. (1822–43), iii. 95–9; PRO STAC 8/113/28; [T. W. W. Smart], *A Chronicle of Cranborne, being an Account of the Ancient Town, Lordship and Chase of Cranborne* (1841), 128–9; D. Hawkins, *Cranborne Chase* (1980), 43–4.

[68] Ibid. 198–9; Hutchins, *History and Antiquities of Dorset*, iii. 410.   [69] Ibid.

to the lord chief justice in June of 1616 attacking the order issued from his court and the interpretation placed upon it by the purlieu men, who continued to hunt and to offer violence to the rangers of Cranborne Chase whenever they came into the Wiltshire purlieus to rechase deer. James demanded that the lord chief justice issue another order restraining the purlieu men from these activities until the Court of Exchequer could determine the precise boundaries of the chase.[70]

Among the leaders of the revolt of the Cranborne Chase purlieu men was John Swaine of Blandford, the original leader, who was about 67 years of age in 1616. Another was Thomas, first Lord Arundell of Wardour, a Catholic peer and former soldier who had fought against the Turks in the service of the Emperor Rudolph II and was rewarded with the title of count of the Holy Roman Empire. A predecessor, Sir Matthew Arundell, had served as deputy ranger of the chase in the reign of Elizabeth, until dismissed by the earl of Pembroke—at that time lieutenant of Cranborne Chase. Also named as defendants in Salisbury's Exchequer suit and closely allied to Lord Arundell were the Gawens, another recusant family residing in Tollard Royal. Katherine Gawen and her son, Thomas, appear to have shared joint title to the manor of Norrington. Salisbury's wrath was particularly directed at Lord Arundell's two deer parks in Tollard Royal and the Gawens' claim to liberty of free warren in their manor. Other centres of organized resistance were to be found in the parishes of Ashmore, Chettle, Farnham, Fontmell Magna, Gussage St Michael, Tarrant Gunville, Tarrant Keynston, and Witchampton, Dorset, and Berwick St John and Tisbury, Wiltshire.[71]

Salisbury's Exchequer suit to expand the boundaries of Cranborne Chase was also accompanied by the prosecution for unlawful hunting of sixty-three purlieu men and tenants from eleven parishes in Dorset, Wiltshire, and Hampshire. Three lengthy bills of complaint were filed in Star Chamber between 1616 and 1618, but one defendant named in the 1616 complaint stated that Salisbury had already kept a bill of complaint against some of the defendants 'on foot these five years', so it would appear that some of the Star Chamber proceedings in this case have not survived. Salisbury was clearly waging law against the Cranborne Chase tenants and borderers and wearing them down with legal expenses. They responded with a poaching war which Salisbury described as being mounted by an organized confederacy recruited and led by persons of higher rank.[72] Although Salisbury attempted to depict the defendants as 'common hunters' or deer-stealers who sold the venison which they caught, almost all of those who can be identified were husbandmen and servants of gentlemen. A number of the

---

[70] Ibid. 380; HMC *Salisbury*, xxii. 35.

[71] *DNB*, *sub* Thomas, 1st Baron Arundell of Wardour (1560–1639); [Smart], *Chronicle of Cranborne*, 224, 270–3; Hutchins, *History and Antiquities of Dorset*, iii. 410, 414–17; PRO STAC 8/113/28, 29, 30, 31; E 124/27.   [72] PRO STAC 8/113/27.

defendants in different parishes appear to have been related one to another, and some lent assistance to confederates in other parishes. The tenants co-ordinated hunting forays to such an extent that Salisbury complained that his keepers were not able to contend with the multitudes of people opposing them and were forced 'to flee for their lives'.[73]

One particularly active group of hunters, who were repeatedly named in Salisbury's Star Chamber complaints, lived in the parish of Ashmore, Dorset. They were led by Richard Combe and his young son John and included four of their servants and a number of householders living in the parish. Salisbury accused them of killing a hundred head of deer in Ashmore and another twenty in the adjoining parishes of Fontmell Magna, Farnham, and Tollard Royal. This was more than the hunters could carry away and the carcasses which remained on the field were devoured by crows. Of the venison which they did carry away, there was such an abundance that the Ashmore hunters fed it to 'their dogs and servants'. One of the defendants was William Clark, the parish curate, who said that all of the householders were copyhold tenants of the manor of Ashmore; the deer from Cranborne Chase had spoiled their corn and grass and damaged their copses. The Ashmore copyholders considered Sir William Poulett to be the lord of the manor, but Hutchins says that there was no manor of Ashmore; it was actually part of the manor of Cranborne, which would have made it parcel of Cranborne Chase and subject to the seigneurial jurisdiction of the earl of Salisbury. The men of Ashmore denied that their parish was part of Cranborne Chase, and they defiantly claimed the right by ancient custom to keep hounds in order to course the deer which strayed on to their holdings.[74] As long as the chase was in the hands of the crown the keepers had not objected to this practice. William Clark, the curate, himself admitted that he had coursed a deer with a mastiff and a greyhound upon Easter Sunday evening after prayer. His hounds brought down the deer and he had distributed the venison among his parishioners. Clark and Richard Combe, the principal defendant, insisted that the custom of tenants coursing deer on Easter Sunday was observed throughout the Dorset parishes bordering on Cranborne Chase.[75]

Another centre of resistance to Salisbury's attempt to expand the boundaries of Cranborne Chase was located in the parishes of Witchampton and Tarrant Keynston, Dorset. This band of hunters was led by Charles Scovell, gent., and Thomas Lovell, gent., and included their sons, servants, and

---

[73] PRO STAC 8/113/31.

[74] Hutchins, *History and Antiquities of Dorset*, iii. 370; PRO STAC 8/113/30. John, Lord Poulett, was passionately fond of hunting, and probably procured the forest riot of January 1629 protesting the disafforestation of Neroche Forest, where he held the office of keeper and stood to lose his hunting rights (T. G. Barnes, *Somerset, 1625–40: A County's Government during the 'Personal Rule'* (Cambridge, Mass., 1961), 158). [75] PRO STAC 8/113/30.

neighbouring householders in Witchampton, Tarrant Keynston, Chettle, Gussage St Michael, and Farnham, Dorset. Others of their band came from as far away as the Isle of Wight, and may have been hired to help out with their expertise. Both the Witchampton and Ashmore hunters appear to have been selling venison, and it is not inconceivable that they were trying to raise a common purse to defend themselves against the earl of Salisbury. The Witchampton hunters appear to have carried on large-scale operations: Salisbury's gamekeepers claimed to have captured two nets from the hunters; one was five hundred feet in length and the other three hundred feet. In his answer, Charles Scovell complained of the damage done to local crops by deer from the chase, and he insisted that the places where he hunted were no part of the chase. He was legally qualified to keep hunting nets and he shared in the seigneurial jurisdiction of the manor of Witchampton, which carried with it liberty of free chase and warren.[76]

Also accused of unlawful hunting were Katharine Gawen and her son, Thomas, the recusant manorial lords of Norrington in Tollard Royal. The Gawens claimed free warren within their manor and had hunted on their demesne until Salisbury began to prosecute them. Salisbury was especially offended when the Gawens brought suit against Salisbury's rangers for trespass. A number of the oldest inhabitants of the parish, including former gamekeepers, testified in Exchequer depositions that the royal keepers of Cranborne Chase had customarily allowed the gentry in Tollard Royal to course deer once a year upon occasion of the manorial court. Indeed, the keepers had beat the deer out of the chase for this occasion. This was meant to provide symbolic restitution for the damage which the royal deer had done to their crops during the previous year, and the custom had helped to maintain good relations between the keepers and the borderers.[77]

The earl of Salisbury's strategy in attempting to expand the boundaries of Cranborne Chase was to pick off the large landowners first and thus deprive the lesser tenants and purlieu men of their leadership. The earl of Pembroke appears to have withdrawn from the lawsuit early on and to have made a separate peace with Salisbury. The borderers' defence against the Exchequer suit collapsed when Lord Arundell abjectly capitulated in 1618 before the Exchequer decree was handed down in 1619. Arundell not only gave up his claim to his deer parks, removed his gamekeepers, and acceded to the claim that Tollard Royal was part of Cranborne Chase; he also offered to exchange or sell lands to Salisbury and to persuade the other Tollard Royal tenants to grant Salisbury his suit to incorporate Tollard Royal into Cranborne Chase.[78]

The Tollard Royal tenants had been holding their own before Arundell's

[76] PRO STAC 8/113/27.
[77] PRO E 178/4739; STAC 8/113/27.   [78] HMC *Salisbury*, xxii. 76.

surrender. Arundell and his farmer had won a case in the Court of Common Pleas against Salisbury's keepers for trespass, and the court had awarded them damages of £20, which Salisbury never bothered to pay.[79] Another court decision had upheld the earl of Pembroke's claim to free warren and free chase in Tollard Royal. The testimony of the oldest inhabitants had made it abundantly clear that, within living memory, Tollard Royal had been regarded by both the local inhabitants and former royal gamekeepers as being purlieu land and no part of the chase. It was also established that the local gentry had hunted without interference from the royal keepers.[80] One can only guess what threats Salisbury had made against Arundell, who, as a recusant, was quite vulnerable legally. When the defendants in the Cranborne case attempted to retain a clerk in Chancery named Cole as their legal counsel, Salisbury's steward accused him of maintenance and urged his master to have Cole locked up in the Marshalsea Prison. Salisbury had also begun another suit in Chancery against the Tollard Royal defendants and used the evidence gathered from their answers in Chancery to the 'detriment' of the defendants in the Exchequer suit.[81]

The final decree in the Exchequer case was handed down on 18 November 1619 by Sir Fulke Greville, the chancellor of the Court of Exchequer Chamber. While the decree was silent on the larger borders of Cranborne Chase, it did extend the jurisdiction of the chase into the disputed lands in the parishes of Tollard Royal and Alvediston, Wiltshire, and it ordered all enclosures and deer parks obliterated so that the deer could feed unimpeded.[82] That this decree did violence to the rights of all purlieu men was immediately perceived by the inhabitants of other parishes bordering on Cranborne Chase. Very soon after the contents of the Exchequer decree of 18 November 1619 became known, the inhabitants of Tisbury, Wiltshire, presented a petition to the king requesting that he 'signify to the Court of Exchequer his royal pleasure that his name should not be used to [the] hinderance and prejudice to justice'.[83] The Tisbury petitioners requested that 'the bounds of the chase should be tried in some courts of justice, at the common law, where boundaries ought to be determined, and not in the Exchequer Chamber, which is a court of equity only'. Within a year another petition was presented to the House of Commons, claiming to represent the grievances of twenty thousand inhabitants of seventy parishes in Wiltshire, Dorset, and Hampshire and 'praying for leave to exhibit a bill reversing the decree of the Exchequer'.[84]

---

[79] Hutchins, *History and Antiquities of Dorset*, iii. 414–17.

[80] [Smart], *Chronicle of Cranborne*, 270–3, 279; PRO E 178/4739.

[81] HMC *Salisbury*, xxii. 55; PRO E 124/27; Hutchins, *History and Antiquities of Dorset*, iii. 414–17.

[82] Hoare, *History of Modern Wiltshire*, iii. 95–9; PRO E 124/27; Hutchins, *History and Antiquities of Dorset*, iii. 414–17.

[83] [Smart], *Chronicle of Cranborne*, 224.   [84] Ibid.

The Exchequer decree of 1619 did not end the resistance of the Cranborne Chase purlieu men, and Salisbury was obliged to begin another suit in the next reign in the same court against the leading landowners of the parish of Witchampton, Dorset. The leader of the resistance was John Cole the elder, who owned one of the shares of the manorial lordship of Witchampton. It seems probable that John Cole, or his son, John the Younger, was the same person as the clerk in Chancery whom Salisbury and his steward tried to intimidate in 1619 and prevent from providing legal counsel to the defendants in the earlier Exchequer case. The Witchampton purlieu men made a point of killing deer which came to feed within the parish. When presented for unlawful hunting at the Attachment Court of Cranborne Chase, they refused to answer. They carried their hunting weapons with them at all times in order to frighten the deer away and to terrify the keepers. In 1620 the attorney-general brought *quo warranto* proceedings against the lords of the manor of Witchampton in King's Bench, and, when they could not produce their charters for free warren and free chase, they were forbidden to hunt within their manor. Salisbury offered them a buck and a doe every year if they would accept such compensation 'as a courtesy and not of right' and if they would allow the deer to feed upon their lands unmolested. The Witchampton men refused to compromise and continued hunting. They were convicted of unlawful hunting and bound to their good behaviour for seven years. John Cole and his associates fought back by prosecuting Salisbury's keepers in King's Bench for trespass. They also raised a common purse and vowed that they would provide legal assistance to any gentleman or freeholder whom Salisbury prosecuted in that part of Dorset. In November 1632 the Court of Exchequer Chamber once again ruled in favour of Salisbury and ordered the people of Witchampton to allow the deer to feed upon their lands without hindrance. The Exchequer Court also ordered that the actions for trespass pending against Salisbury's keepers in King's Bench were to be stayed, and the Court told the defendants that, if they violated this Exchequer decree, they would be made to pay for Salisbury's legal expenses in undertaking the suit in the Court of Exchequer Chamber.[85]

William, earl of Salisbury, had shown himself willing to go to any length to enforce the game prerogative of the early Stuarts. He reminded the Court of Exchequer Chamber that he had been given 'especial charge' to preserve the game, and he stated that King Charles took particular delight in hunting on Cranborne Chase as had his father, King James. There is good reason to believe that this argument influenced the outcome of both the 1619 and the 1632 cases against the borderers in the Court of Exchequer Chamber.[86] Yet, when the Civil War came, he sided with Parliament. When Clarendon

---

[85] Hutchins, *History and Antiquities of Dorset*, iii. 417–19.   [86] Ibid. 380, 417–19.

remembered Salisbury in *The History of the Rebellion*, he penned the most scathing of all of his character sketches about him:

He had been admitted of the Council to King James, from which time he continued so obsequious to the Court that he never failed in overacting all that he was required to do. No act of power was proposed which he did not advance, and execute his part with the utmost vigour. No man so great a tyrant in his own country, or was less swayed by any motives of justice and honour. He was a man of no words, except for hunting and hawking, in which he knew only how to behave himself. In matters of state and counsel he always concurred in what was proposed for the king, and cancelled and repaired those transgressions by concurring in all that was proposed against him as soon as such propositions were made.[87]

In 1643 a royalist army led by Prince Maurice plundered Cranborne House. When the soldiers had departed, the tenants poured into the house and destroyed or carried away the manorial court records kept in the muniment room. Disgust for Salisbury's proceedings in the case of Cranborne Chase probably contributed to the widespread attacks upon local deer parks during the Civil War and may have led to the contempt for the parliamentary cause which was widespread in the neighbourhood.[88]

The question of the rights of purlieu men, including the right of 40s. freeholders to course deer on their own holdings within disafforested areas, or places regarded in law as purlieus, is surely one of the most neglected aspects of scholarship on the Ancient Constitution. Although medievalists generally recognize the significance of the long battle that tenants and landowners fought against the encroachments of forest jurisdiction and the extortions of royal forest and game officials, writers on early modern history and political theory—even those who have scrutinized the writings of Sir Edward Coke—have failed to recognize the constitutional and legal significance of purlieu rights in the seventeenth-century struggle to limit the royal prerogative.[89] Yet, as the epigraph to this chapter makes clear, Coke was emphatic about the importance of maintaining the hunting rights of the purlieu men as a defence against the encroachment of forest law upon areas where parliamentary legislative authority ought to prevail. Even if Coke was historically mistaken in attributing purlieu rights to the Charter of the Forest, that does not diminish the importance of purlieu hunting rights in the political discourse of the early seventeenth century, because,

---

[87] Edward [Hyde], earl of Clarendon, *The History of the Rebellion and Civil Wars in England*, 6 vols. (Oxford, 1888), ii. 542–3; GEC xi. 404–6.

[88] L. Stone, *Family and Fortune: Studies in Aristocratic Finance in the Sixteenth and Seventeenth Centuries* (Oxford, 1973), 148–9; D. Underdown, *Revel, Riot and Rebellion: Popular Politics and Culture in England, 1603–1660* (Oxford, 1985), 160.

[89] Pocock (*Ancient Constitution and Feudal Law*) and White (*Sir Edward Coke and 'The Grievances of the Commonwealth'*) never mention purlieu rights.

whatever the historical accuracy of the attribution, purlieu rights were symbolically linked to the Charter of the Forest and Magna Carta in the minds of many people, including parliamentary leaders of no less eminence than Peter Wentworth and Sir Edward Coke, as well as lesser landowners such as Richard Cholmeley of Brandsby, Richard Chafin, and John Burton of Stockerston.

The issue of purlieu rights should also interest those who study the theory of possessive individualism, since it involved questions of whether royal deer could feed upon the grass, grain, and woods of purlieu men, whether landholders had the right to fence in their lands to protect their crops from the considerable damage which could be done by deer, and, finally, whether rangers had the right to rechase deer upon the lands of purlieu men unimpeded by enclosures. As long as the prerogative courts suppressed the rights of purlieu men and regarded the game prerogative of the crown in purlieus as paramount, one cannot speak of the existence of an absolute and unqualified doctrine of private property in England.

The Tudor monarchs had respected the rights of purlieu men and understood the legal and constitutional imperatives for limiting forest jurisdiction— despite the fact that their rangers often had less respect for those rights. Although the revival of forest jurisdiction has usually been associated with the personal rule of Charles I, it is now clear that this mischievous policy had actually begun in the reign of James I with the royal attack on the rights of purlieu men. The purlieu men defiantly asserted their rights by hunting the royal deer and resisting the royal rangers and keepers while following a parallel course of litigation against forest and game officials, who trespassed upon their property, in the common-law courts. Here they could usually expect a fair hearing from judges and juries who had no reason to support the expansion of forest jurisdiction. But the prerogative and equity courts, such as Star Chamber and Exchequer Chamber, clearly were more responsive to royal pressure to protect the game prerogative, as the cases of the Waltham Forest and Cranborne Chase purlieu men demonstrate.

5

Hunting and Land Use in Sylvan Societies

By hawk and hound small profit is found.

M. P. Tilley, *A Collection of the Proverbs in England in the Sixteenth and Seventeenth Centuries* (Ann Arbor, Mich., 1950; repr. 1966), 295

The King's forests have innumerable herds of red deer and all parts have plenty of fallow deer, as every gentleman of five hundred or a thousand pounds rent by the year hath a park for them enclosed with pales of wood for two or three miles compass.

Fynes Moryson, *An Itinerary* (1617), 4 vols. (Glasgow, 1907–8), iv. 168–9

As settlements in woodland regions increased in the twelfth and thirteenth centuries and again during the sixteenth and seventeenth centuries, population pressed hard upon the resources of land. The native red and roe deer grew more scarce and the exotic fallow deer were bred in numerous enclosed parks. The carnivorous aristocracy demanded fresh meat at all seasons of the year, and their eating habits were imitated by all who could afford to do so. Other sources of semi-domesticated game, fowl, rabbits, and fish were also developed to supply their tables. Deer and game, whether wild or bred in reserves, competed with cattle and sheep in woodland and pastoral societies and often led to overgrazing and damage to crops. Sylvan regions frequently spawned rural industries, which were attracted to the cheap labour to be found amongst large concentrations of cottagers and squatters upon unenclosed common wastes or which made heavy demands upon water, timber, and wood resources. Such proto-industrial areas, with their combinations of dense populations of wage-earners and soils which were unsuited to grain production, remained chronically short of grain until improved marketing and transport systems were developed. Eventually, a technological breakthrough would occur in the West Midlands, and the Industrial Revolution would take root in these adverse conditions, but, during the Middle Ages and the early modern period, the price paid for overgrazing, overcutting of woodfuel and building materials, and, in general, the demands made upon the land by the conflicting uses of game reserves, agriculture, and industry was environmental degradation.

After describing the basic characteristics of woodland societies and economies, this chapter will examine the impact of deer parks, rabbit warrens, fishponds, and dovecotes upon the landscape and show why they were conducive to social conflict and unlawful hunting.

5.1. Conflicting Land Uses

That intrepid traveller, Fynes Moryson, thought that the English generally ate more meat than people in other countries. He also thought that English parks, 'now grown infinite in number', contained more fallow deer than all the rest of Christendom together. 'In the seasons of the year, the English eat fallow deer plentifully, as buck in summer and does in winter, which they bake in pasties, and this venison pasty is a dainty, rarely found in any other kingdom.' He also claimed that the English raised and ate more conies and doves than any other nation. Even if we allow for some exaggeration on Moryson's part, the message is clearly conveyed that the presence of venison and game on one's table was an indisputable mark of high status, and this, in turn, was a powerful stimulus to the breeding and consumption of deer and game. Moryson notes that the maintenance of deer parks was such a 'prodigal' drain upon the income of the landed gentry that some began disparking their parks in order to feed cattle and improve their incomes.[1] The taste for beef eventually began to replace that for venison, but did not displace it before 1640. The influence of the deer-hunting culture remained strong.

Stow's *Annales* asserted that there were more graziers than ploughmen in England, and maintained that a 'third of the country' was given over to feeding cattle, red and fallow deer, conies, and other animals raised for meat—including the land set aside for the hunting reserves of the nobility and gentry.[2] In the returns of depopulating enclosures for Middlesex in 1517—admittedly a county where there were rather a lot of deer parks—imparkment accounted for 47 per cent of the acreage undergoing enclosure and pasture for another 37 per cent.[3] The low weights of beef cattle before the improvements in animal husbandry were introduced may help to explain the preference for venison over beef. The accounts of the Roberts family reveal that attempts to breed or fatten cattle on the clayey and poorly drained soils of the Sussex Weald yielded oxen with average weights of only 512 lbs. and yearling bullocks and heifers weighing, on average, 276 lbs. The shortage of fodder in the Weald is also suggested by the failure to segregate cattle and sheep in their grazing grounds.[4] On Broyle Heath in

---

[1] Fynes Moryson, *An Itinerary* (1617), 4 vols. (Glasgow, 1907–8), iv. 148, 168–9, 172; W. H. P. Greswell, *The Forests and Deer Parks of the County of Somerset* (Taunton, 1905), 242.
[2] Stow, *Annales*, ed. Howes, 2.   [3] *VCH Middx.*, ii. 89.
[4] *Accounts of the Roberts Family of Boarzell, Sussex, c.1568–1582*, ed. R. Tittler (Sussex Rec. Soc., 71; Lewes, Sussex, 1977–9), pp. xix–xxi.

East Sussex, which was a royal chase, Exchequer depositions taken in 1622–3 reveal that deer from the royal park competed for the sparse grazing with non-commonable beasts such as geese, swine, and rabbits from a nearby warren, as well as cattle owned by commoners and by strangers from distant villages.[5]

Much of the land used for royal and aristocratic game reserves and deer parks was woodland pasture. This was land which was employed for both growing timber and grazing. The two uses are not very compatible, although they have been practised since prehistoric times. Deer, like cattle, cannot flourish in dense forest, but need access to grass for grazing and to underbrush for browsing. If a woodland pasture is lightly grazed, the maturing trees will eventually eliminate the underwood and the grass. If woodland pasture is overgrazed, the underwood will be destroyed and most of the trees consumed, so that replacement trees cannot grow. Thus, unless woodland pastures were imparked to exclude cattle and sheep or enclosed to form coppice woods, they degenerated into treeless commons. If they had poor soils, they deteriorated into heaths, and many woodland pastures outside royal forests disappeared during the Middle Ages. Most heaths in southern England are anthropogenic and semi-natural—that is, they have been degraded from woodland to their present condition through the intervention of man by means of timber-felling and cultivation or grazing and deliberate burning. A classic example of this process of environmental degradation is Thorpe Wood, which lay across the River Wensum from Norwich and was covered with oaks in about 1100, but through overgrazing and excessive timber-cutting had come to be known as Mousehold Heath by the early sixteenth century. Woodland on the Wealden clays was still being cleared and settled in the sixteenth century, and sylvan areas generally experienced the phenomenon of impopulation in the sixteenth and early seventeenth centuries.[6]

Muddled royal policy and wasteful management pushed the resources of the royal forests to their limits under the Tudors. In Bowland Forest the deer population was much diminished by mismanagement and the encroachment of tenants' cattle. Henry VIII had pursued a policy of increasing the royal income by raising rents, but he ran into opposition in Bowland, where the tenants threatened to leave their lands. The master forester was disliked because he refused to allow tenants to enclose their fields in order to protect their corn against the red and fallow deer. A compromise was reached whereby the number of deer was to be reduced and those remaining

---

[5] PRO E 134/20 Jac I [1622–3]/M8; T. W. Horsfield, *The History, Antiquities and Topography of the County of Sussex*, 2 vols. (Lewes, Sussex, 1835), i. 349–50.

[6] O. Rackham, *Trees and Woodlands in the British Landscape* (1976), 135–44; E. M. Yates, *A History of the Landscapes in the Parishes of South Harting and Rogate* (Chichester, 1972), 8; Manning, *Village Revolts*, 162, 170, 255.

confined to enclosed parks and the tenants were to be allowed to fence their lands against stray deer. But, in practice, the master forester leased or retained these parks at his discretion, and the deer were excluded, so that they fed upon the tenants' grain. The introduction of the tenants' cattle into the forest so increased competition for herbage and browse that a natural disaster, such as the heavy snowfall during the winter of 1570–1, could cause fearful mortality rates among deer and cattle alike. The deer of Bowland had numbered approximately two thousand during the period 1494–1523, but in 1554 the deer population had been reduced to an estimated five hundred head. A more precise official survey in 1556 revealed that their numbers had actually declined to 134 red deer and 146 fallow deer. The deer population probably recovered somewhat after this, but the harsh winter of 1570–1 caused some 329 deer to die of starvation. The toll would have been even higher, the Swanimote jury reported, had the deer not been provided with branches of holly, ash, and elder for browse.[7]

As the number of deer diminished, the human population of the forests increased. The forests and chases of Bowland, Quernmore, Wyresdale, Pendle, and a number of royal parks were all that remained of the once vast Forest of Blackburn in North Lancashire, which, in turn, had been part of the Royal Forest of Lancaster. Rossendale had also once belonged to the Forest of Blackburn; it was completely disafforested upon petition of the inhabitants. The earl of Derby, on behalf of the Duchy of Lancaster, worked out an agreement with the tenants and inhabitants, whereby they agreed to pay a 'forester fee' towards the salaries of the foresters and keepers, who had previously been in the habit of coming to the houses of forest tenants and demanding meat and drink when they were hungry. In the fifty years following the disafforestation of Rossendale its population increased fifty-fold—a rate of increase which probably takes no account of squatters. The officials of the Duchy of Lancaster sold many of the tenants illegal demesne copyholds, which they regarded as estates in fee simple until James I milked them for another composition in order to obtain a secure title to their estates.[8]

Other royal forests also witnessed conflicts between efforts to preserve the deer for royal sport and encroaching settlements. Henry VII stopped all hunting in Needwood Forest in North Staffordshire in 1492 in order to build up depleted herds, and then strictly limited hunting after 1504. A Marian survey of the deer counted nearly nine hundred head in the seven parks within the forest where the deer sought shelter. When Camden passed through Needwood in the 1520s, he noted that the local gentry helped themselves to the king's deer 'with great labour and application'. The records of the Court of Duchy Chamber contain many references to overgrazing,

---

[7] Shaw, *Royal Forest of Lancaster*, 237, 259–63; J. Porter, 'A Forest in Transition: Bowland, 1500–1650', *Trans. Hist. Soc. Lancs. and Ches.*, 125 (1975), 40–60.

[8] Cox, *Royal Forests of England*, 105–6; Manning, *Village Revolts*, 142–5.

illegal cutting of timber, fuel, and browsewood, as well as deer-stealing. In 1573 inhabitants of the forest invaded Highlands Park within Needwood, destroyed the park pales, introduced several hundred pigs into the park, and brought their children and dogs along to drive the deer out. Needwood was still a favourite hunting ground of James I and Charles I, but a commonwealth survey of 1650 recorded that the deer population had been reduced to 120 head.[9] In 1602 Duchy of Lancaster officials attempted to put a halt to large-scale wood-stealing in Enfield Chase. Seventy-eight persons from Enfield, South Mimms, and Hadley were accused of carrying away an average of twenty loads each of timber and browsewood. One of the defendants, William Wilford, gent., said that a decree of the Court of Duchy Chamber, dating from 1593–4, had granted the tenants of the manor of Enfield a reasonable yearly allowance of fuel from the chase in order to persuade them not to molest the game.[10] In 1608 James I wrote to the officials of Galtres Forest, ordering them to limit the number of horses and cattle which commoners might graze in the forest and to require inhabitants of the forest to leave hay in their meadows for the royal deer to feed upon in winter.[11] Ultimately, the response of James I and Charles I to the continued plundering of the royal forests was to disafforest many of these game preserves—especially the less accessible ones in the West and the Midlands.[12]

Probably no woodland region in England was subjected to such intensive land use as the Weald of Sussex, Surrey, and Kent in the sixteenth century. During the better part of that century it was the only location of a semi-mechanized iron industry based upon hydraulic blast furnaces and forges. Its consumption of wood for charcoal was prodigious, and the coppicing of trees for charcoal-burning did not begin until the seventeenth century. Although the Sussex ports were in decline, the Weald also exported a considerable amount of timber. The county contained an unusually large number of deer parks, and, while some of these were being disparked, new parks were also being carved out of woodland pasture and common wastes throughout the century. During the whole of the Tudor–Stuart period, enclosures for one purpose or another withdrew land from common wastes in at least 27 per cent of all the parishes in Sussex.[13] In his valuable study

[9] *VCH Staffs.*, ii. 355–6; PRO DL 1/81/A17, 160/A12, 196/A52.
[10] PRO DL 1/200/A42.   [11] PRO SP 14/31/74.
[12] For a discussion of the resistance to disafforestation and a useful bibliography, see B. Sharp, *In Contempt of All Authority: Rural Artisans and Riot in the West of England, 1586–1660* (Berkeley, Calif., 1980).
[13] P. F. Brandon, 'The Common Lands and Wastes of Sussex', Ph.D thesis (London, 1963), 127, 334–42; J. Cornwall, 'Forestry and the Timber Trade in Sussex, 1540–1640', *Sussex Notes and Queries*, xiv. 85–91; M. L. Zell, 'A Wood–Pasture Agrarian Regime: The Kentish Weald in the Sixteenth Century', *Southern History*, 7 (1985), 75–6; see also John Norden, *The Surveyors Dialogue* (1607), 214.

of land use in Sussex, Dr Peter Brandon presents convincing evidence of the rapid and extensive depletion of timber and wood resources in Sussex. Although the main colonization of the Weald occurred in the twelfth and fourteenth centuries, good timber was still available at the beginning of the sixteenth century. There are a number of indications that the depletion of wood and timber was especially severe in the sixteenth century: heaths replaced woodland and the number of rabbit warrens increased, while the declining harvest of acorns and beech mast led to a pronounced decline in swine-herding, a traditional sylvan occupation. At the same time, the conflicts between those who commoned their beasts upon the wastes and the keepers of parks and forests were another sign of increasing competition for scarce resources. The appearance of the landscape had changed from one of dense forests of oak and beech at the beginning of the fourteenth century to a more open and park-like setting at the beginning of the sixteenth century, where deer and cattle devoured the remaining undergrowth beneath a few ancient trees. Even though the iron furnaces did not operate all year round for lack of sufficient water, the difficulties of transport in the Weald meant that the wood for charcoal had to be cut within three or four miles of the furnace. In Ashdown Forest, where three furnaces operated during the sixteenth century, one-third of the estimated wood and timber was gone by 1519 and the forest utterly spent and worthless by 1632. As a consequence of clear-felling and the burning of the lops and tops of trees for agricultural use, Ashdown Forest had become a barren heath by the eighteenth century.[14]

Petworth manor illustrates, in microcosm, the varied uses to which land in the Sussex Weald was subjected. The manor contained 8,351 acres, of which 1,207 acres (or 14 per cent of the total) were given over to three parks in 1610. Another 3,794 acres (or 46 per cent) were classified as demesne land, while only 340 acres (or 4 per cent) of commons remained for the grazing needs of copyholders, who cultivated 3,010 acres of arable land. Approximately 16 per cent of the demesne was wooded, but the financial difficulties of Henry, ninth earl of Northumberland led him to cut an annual average of 1,030 cords of firewood during the period 1594–1600, in addition to the 2,000 cords allowed to the farmer of the ironworks each year. The

---

[14] Brandon, 'The Common Lands and Wastes of Sussex', 11–12, 118–19, 127; id., 'Land, Technology and Water Management in the Tillingbourne Valley, Surrey, 1560–1760', *Southern History*, 6 (1984), 92–7; *Sidney Ironworks Accounts, 1541–1573*, ed. D. W. Crossley (Camden Soc., 4th ser., 15; 1975), 5. Although the question of how much wood the Wealden iron industry consumed is controversial, Dr Brandon presents much evidence for the rapid consumption of forest resources in the sixteenth century in a part of England that was not examined by Hammersley (G. Hammersley, 'The Charcoal Iron Industry and its Fuel, 1540–1640', *Econ. Hist. Rev.*, ns 26 (1973), 593–613). See also C. E. Brent, 'Rural Employment and Population in Sussex between 1550 and 1640', *Sussex Arch. Coll.*, 114 (1976), 39.

demesne woods were not sufficiently replenished with new plantations to keep up with this rate of cutting.[15]

In order to raise more revenue to pay off his indebtedness, the ninth earl of Northumberland partially disparked some of his parks and built an iron furnace and a hammer forge. These were located on the River Rother and its tributary streams, together with seven other mills, including five corn mills, a fulling mill, and a malting mill. Three mill ponds, one of which was thirteen acres in extent, supplied water power for the ironworks. In addition, there was a small glass furnace located in the northern part of what is now Petworth Park, which was in operation after 1567. Although the Great Park was said to have been disparked for the use of the ironworks, it also continued to be used, in part, for fishponds and rabbit warrens. The deer undoubtedly disappeared, but the Great Park increased in size from 400 acres in 1557 to 804 acres in 1610, of which 691 acres were enclosed by a park pale and 351 acres were leased as arable land to the tenants. In order to compensate for the land lost to breeding deer, the eighth earl had enclosed 160 acres from the manorial common c.1578 in order to create the New Park.[16]

Disparking, overgrazing, and a paucity of mast all signify a serious shortage of fodder in woodland societies. With the growth of rural industries and the influx of population, artificers' cottages proliferated on common wastes, and heavy demands were made upon resources of pasture. The lease which the earl of Northumberland granted to the farmer of his ironworks in Petworth in 1578 allowed the farmer pasture for twelve oxen and six horses, and his workmen were permitted six pigs in addition.[17] Water meadows were highly valuable because of the amount of hay which they produced, but the 'floating' of water meadows was often interrupted by the many dams and millponds strung out along Wealden rivers and streams. In the Tillingbourne Valley of Surrey twenty-one different mill sites were used during the sixteenth and seventeenth centuries along a nine-mile stretch of river. In the eighteenth century, even denser concentrations of mills congregated along the rivers and streams of the Kentish Weald.[18] The impounding of water or its

[15] H. A. Wyndham, Lord Leconfield, *Petworth Manor in the Seventeenth Century* (1954), 45–7, 63; id., *Sutton and Duncton Manors* (1956), 2–5. There had been extensive enclosures of common waste during the sixteenth century, which had led to frequent conflicts between the lords of Petworth manor and the tenants (Manning, *Village Revolts*, 63–4, 78–9, 113, 137–8).

[16] Wyndham, *Petworth Manor in the Seventeenth Century*, 55–66, 93–103, 108–14; P. Jerrome, *Cloakbag and Common Purse: Enclosure and Copyhold in 16th Century Petworth* (Petworth, Sussex, 1979), 24–5; G. H. Kenyon, 'Petworth Town and Trades, 1610–1760, Part I', *Sussex Arch. Coll.*, 96 (1958), 73–4.

[17] M. L. Zell, 'Population and Family Structure in the Sixteenth-Century Weald', *Archaeologia Cantiana*, 100 (1984), 234; Wyndham, *Petworth Manor in the Seventeenth Century*, 93–103.

[18] Brandon, 'Land, Technology and Water Management in the Tillingbourne Valley', 76–87; R. H. Goodsall, 'Watermills on the River Len', *Archaeologia Cantiana*, 71 (1957), 106.

effusive discharge during milling operations could do considerable damage to agricultural lands and dwellings and provoked numerous attacks on dams and mill-races by outraged farmers.[19] A group of some seventeen small-holders who destroyed the mill-races at William Comber's two mills in Shermanbury, Sussex, on four different occasions in 1606 complained that he had diverted the course of the river, ruined the fishing, deprived two other mills of their water supply, and destroyed fodder and grass which the smallholders needed for their cattle. They swore that they would continue to open the dams and fill in the mill-races if Comber tried to rebuild them.[20] In Walton, Derbyshire, in the same year, Sir James Harrington destroyed a mill-race supplying water to nine mills and attacked a deer park in retaliation against Sir William Bowes for altering a water course.[21]

5.2. Deer Parks and Forests

Both forests and deer parks were intended to be used primarily as game reserves, but the former were thought to be less harmful economically and socially than the latter. Although forests were larger and occupied more land than deer parks, William Harrison believed that they were 'less devourers of the people' than parks because they contained 'much tillage and many towns'. Parks, by contrast, contained 'nothing else than either the keeper's . . . lodge or . . . the manor place of the chief lord and owner of the soil'. A further distinction that Harrison might have made is that those who dwelled within forests or in the borders and purlieus thereof usually possessed use-rights within the forest, but the enclosure of a park within pales and ditches and its severance from the common waste extinguished all such rights of usufruct and established the absolute and exclusive possession of one man. Parks might be subjected to other uses besides the breeding and preservation of deer, but Harrison was in two minds about whether deer parks ought to be regarded as a 'curse of the Lord' or of the Norman conquerors. He also blamed parks for depopulation and maintained that their continued existence deprived the early Tudor monarchs of manpower to such an extent that they were obliged to hire foreign mercenaries to fight their wars.[22]

A forest need not include wooded land, but pasture was absolutely necessary for the survival of deer. A forest was not enclosed and was defined only by its metes and bounds, within which hunting was reserved for the king and those to whom he gave licence. In the early modern period,

---

[19] PRO STAC 2/13, fos. 276–7, STAC 8/15/1.
[20] PRO STAC 8/86/12.   [21] PRO STAC 8/56/16.
[22] Harrison, *Description of England*, i. 343–6; see also *The Anglica Historia of Polydore Vergil, 1485–1537*, ed. D. Hay (Camden Soc., 3rd ser., 74; 1950), 276–7.

forests continued to be subject to forest law only if the forest administration remained intact, Swanimotes, and other courts were still held, and forest and game officials still appointed. A few forests had passed into private hands. Sussex had once possessed seven forests, but by the early seventeenth century Ashdown Forest was the only important one which still remained in crown hands. The rest were much decayed and plundered or in private possession.[23] Of the seventy-five or eighty forests which had existed in the fourteenth century, something like forty-five remained in the possession of the crown between 1500 and 1640.[24] The distinction between a forest and a chase was blurred. Chases were also defined by metes and bounds rather than fences, and could belong to the crown or be granted to a subject.[25]

The two species of deer usually hunted in English parks and forests were the red and the fallow deer. The native red deer or high deer was the larger of the two. Red deer had to be kept apart from fallow deer because of the aggressive behaviour of male red deer during the rutting season. In 1539 there were probably not more than about two thousand of them in all of the various royal game reserves in the north of England, and in southern England they were sufficiently scarce for it to be necessary to breed them in parks. Apart from Windsor Forest, herds of red deer were to be found in Ashdown Forest and in at least three parks in Sussex, in the reign of James I.[26] The smaller fallow deer was an exotic species, and had been introduced into England by the Normans. This was the species most commonly hunted in late-medieval and early modern England. Although fallow deer benefit from some woodland for cover, they feed mostly in open fields, where they compete with domestic animals for grass, mast, and heather. They are quite omnivorous given the opportunity and also browse upon the leaves and twigs of trees, orchard fruits, ferns, mosses, and tree bark from both saplings and mature trees. Fallow deer were valued not only for sport, but also because of the high quality of their venison and hides. However, they breed prolifically and will quickly outgrow their habitat if not culled.[27]

The Forest of Windsor was one of the largest game preserves in southern England. At one time it had a circumference of some 120 miles, but this had

---

[23] O. Rackham, *Ancient Woodland: Its History, Vegetation and Uses in England* (1980), 178–9; W. S. Ellis, *The Parks and Forests of Sussex* (Lewes, Sussex, 1885), 78 *et passim*.

[24] The best available map of medieval English forests is found in N. Neilson, 'The Forests', in J. F. Willard and W. A. Morris (eds.), *The English Government at Work, 1327–1336*, 2 vols. (Cambridge, Mass., 1940), i, map V; it shows seventy-one forests, but omits a number of smaller ones such as the seven Sussex forests. For the location of forests and chases extant between 1500 and 1640, see Maps 5.1 and 5.2.

[25] Harrison, *Description of England*, i. 346; Cox, *Royal Forests of England*, 2–3.

[26] Brentnall, 'Venison Trespasses in the Reign of Henry VII', 195; PRO STAC 8/5/13, 303/27, 279/26, 97/1.

[27] D. and N. Chapman, *Fallow Deer: Their History, Distribution and Biology* (Lavenham, Suffolk, 1975), 49, 127–31. C. Lever (*The Naturalized Animals of the British Isles* (London, 1977), 160) states that they were established by Roman times.

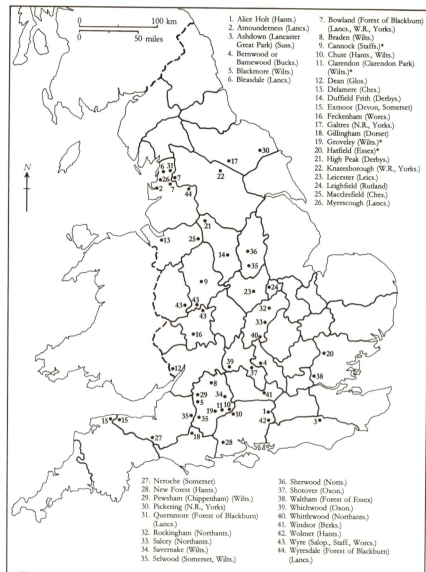

0   100 km

0   50 miles

1. Alice Holt (Hants.)
2. Amounderness (Lancs.)
3. Ashdown (Lancaster Great Park) (Suss.)
4. Bernwood or Barnewood (Bucks.)
5. Blackmore (Wilts.)
6. Bleasdale (Lancs.)
7. Bowland (Forest of Blackburn) (Lancs., W.R., Yorks.)
8. Braden (Wilts.)
9. Cannock (Staffs.)*
10. Chute (Hants., Wilts.)
11. Clarendon (Clarendon Park) (Wilts.)*
12. Dean (Glos.)
13. Delamere (Ches.)
14. Duffield Frith (Derbys.)
15. Exmoor (Devon, Somerset)
16. Feckenham (Worcs.)
17. Galtres (N.R., Yorks.)
18. Gillingham (Dorset)
19. Groveley (Wilts.)*
20. Hatfield (Essex)*
21. High Peak (Derbys.)
22. Knaresborough (W.R., Yorks.)
23. Leicester (Leics.)
24. Leighfield (Rutland)
25. Macclesfield (Ches.)
26. Myerscough (Lancs.)

N

27. Neroche (Somerset)
28. New Forest (Hants.)
29. Pewsham (Chippenham) (Wilts.)
30. Pickering (N.R., Yorks)
31. Quernmore (Forest of Blackburn) (Lancs.)
32. Rockingham (Northants.)
33. Salcey (Northants.)
34. Savernake (Wilts.)
35. Selwood (Somerset, Wilts.)
36. Sherwood (Notts.)
37. Shotover (Oxon.)
38. Waltham (Forest of Essex)
39. Whichwood (Oxon.)
40. Whittlewood (Northants.)
41. Windsor (Berks.)
42. Wolmer (Hants.)
43. Wyre (Salop., Staff., Worcs.)
44. Wyresdale (Forest of Blackburn) (Lancs.)

This list contains those game reserves which were still regarded as forests during the period 1500–1640. All were places where unlawful deer-hunting was detected and each was stocked with deer and guarded by keepers. Forest courts survived in only a few places. All were administered as royal forests except those game reserves marked with an asterisk, which passed into private hands before or during this period. Forests which were not stocked with deer and which were in private possession, such as St Leonard's in Sussex, have been omitted. Some of the game reserves customarily classified as chases (Map 5.2), such as Whaddon, Needwood, and Hampton Court, were legally regarded as forests. The distinction between forests and chases was blurred.

The sources for this list include the records of the Court of Star Chamber, the Duchy of Lancaster, and the Exchequer.

MAP 5.1. English forests, 1500–1640

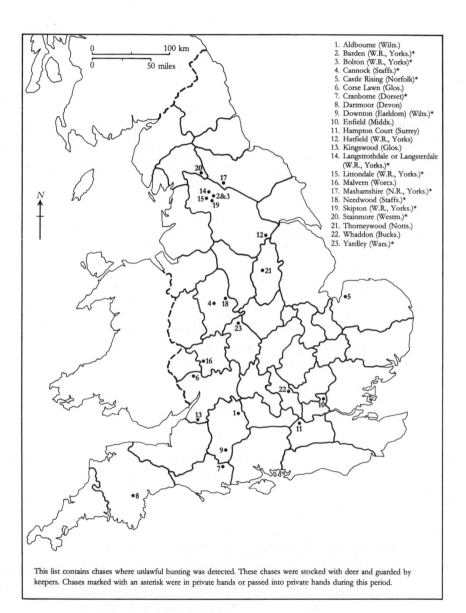

1. Aldbourne (Wilts.)
2. Barden (W.R., Yorks.)*
3. Bolton (W.R., Yorks)*
4. Cannock (Staffs.)*
5. Castle Rising (Norfolk)*
6. Corse Lawn (Glos.)
7. Cranborne (Dorset)*
8. Dartmoor (Devon)
9. Downton (Earldom) (Wilts.)*
10. Enfield (Middx.)
11. Hampton Court (Surrey)
12. Hatfield (W.R., Yorks)
13. Kingswood (Glos.)
14. Langstrothdale or Langsterdale
    (W.R., Yorks.)*
15. Littondale (W.R., Yorks.)*
16. Malvern (Worcs.)
17. Mashamshire (N.R., Yorks.)*
18. Needwood (Staffs.)*
19. Skipton (W.R., Yorks.)*
20. Stainmore (Westm.)*
21. Thorneywood (Notts.)
22. Whaddon (Bucks.)
23. Yardley (Wars.)*

This list contains chases where unlawful hunting was detected. These chases were stocked with deer and guarded by keepers. Chases marked with an asterisk were in private hands or passed into private hands during this period.

MAP 5.2. English chases, 1500–1640

gradually shrunk to $77\frac{1}{2}$ miles by 1607 when John Norden surveyed and mapped it. Originally, Windsor Forest included parts of Berkshire, Buckinghamshire, Middlesex, and a very large part of Surrey. At the time of Norden's survey, Windsor Great Park, one of sixteen within the forest, was $10\frac{1}{4}$ miles in circuit, comprised 3,650 acres, and contained 1,800 fallow deer.[28] It is possible that Henry VIII was attempting to revive part of the ancient Forest of Windsor when Hampton Court Chase, the newest forest in England, was created by Act of Parliament in 1539 as part of the Honour of Hampton Court. The chase began on the south side of the Thames and extended to Cobham and Weybridge, taking in parts of twelve parishes.[29] Nonsuch Palace was built as a hunting lodge for the king while he was seeking recreation in Hampton Court Chase; its construction necessitated razing the entire village of Cuddington, together with the manor house, parish church, and churchyard. Much of the stone employed in building Nonsuch came from the priory of Merton, recently demolished.[30] Hampton Court Chase proved very unpopular with the royal tenants, who petitioned the Privy Council several times about their losses of commons and pastures. The Privy Council concluded that the king was losing revenues through the decay of houses of husbandry, and in 1548 the lord protector and council removed the deer to Windsor Forest, tore down the pales surrounding the chase, and raised rents to the pre-enclosure level.[31]

Although the deer were removed from Hampton Court Chase, it was never disafforested, and the king retained his hunting rights there, which King Charles I attempted to reassert when he built Richmond New Park. Charles I, whom the earl of Clarendon thought 'was excessively affected to hunting and the sports of the field', began building in 1636 a great brick wall ten or twelve miles in circumference within which he intended to enclose in severalty everything between Hampton Court and Richmond. Some of the wastes and woodland already belonged to the king and he meant to offer the other landowners and tenants very generous terms for conveying their properties to him. Some of the commoners resisted the

[28] Cox, *Royal Forests of England*, 287; William Menzies, *The History of Windsor Great Park and Windsor Forest* (1864), 5; Tighe and Davis, *Annals of Windsor*, ii. 35–6; see also above, Ch. 1.4.

[29] *VCH Middx.*, ii. 322–3; 31 Hen. VIII, c. 5; *SR* iii. 721; T. E. C. Walker, 'The Chase of Hampton Court', *Surrey Arch. Coll.*, 62 (1965), 83–7. In the parish of Weybridge, Hampton Court Chase probably abutted Oatlands Park, which was enlarged by James I (Shirley, *Some Account of English Deer Parks*, 59).

[30] Colvin, Ransome, and Summerson (eds.), *History of the King's Works*, IV. ii. 179–80. Nonsuch had attached to it two parks in the time of Henry VIII: the Great Park, consisting of 911 acres, and the Little Park, containing 671 acres. The palace was built in the midst of Little Park (Shirley, *Some Account of English Deer Parks*, 59–60).

[31] *VCH Middx.*, ii. 324–5; *Acts PC, 1547–1550*, 190–2. Hampton Court Chase, which was technically a forest, was one of the very few chases surrounded by a pale. Thus, it took on the characteristics of a royal park.

king's wishes, and Charles forfeited the goodwill of the royal tenants by pressing through with the scheme—against the advice of both Archbishop Laud and Lord Treasurer Cottington. It looked 'as if the king would take away men's estates at his own pleasure', said Clarendon.

The building of the wall before people consented to part with their land or their common looked to them as if by degrees they should be shut out from both, and increased the murmur and noise of the people who were not concerned as well as them who were, and it was too near London not to be the common discourse.

Moreover, it appears that Charles did not pay for all of the lands that he took from the tenants of Mortlake. Well into the eighteenth century Richmond Park continued to be the source of much bitterness on the part of those who had lost their commons. Poachers climbed ladders, picked locks, and even breached walls in order to prey upon the royal deer.[32]

The Tudor and early Stuart monarchs expanded their hunting reserves and reasserted their hunting rights in the Thames Valley, but they often neglected less accessible reserves such as Ashdown Forest. During this period the deer gradually disappeared from Ashdown Forest as a result of poaching and environmental degradation.[33] Ironworks consumed the woods, and the local gentry encroached upon and enclosed crown lands within their own parks. Ashdown Forest belonged to the Duchy of Lancaster, and at one time thirteen thousand acres had been enclosed within a hunting reserve known as Lancaster Great Park and stocked with red and fallow deer. The neighbouring landlords in the time of Henry VIII were Sir John Gage, who was granted a lease of the duchy manor of Maresfield where much of Ashdown Forest was located, and Sir Richard Sackville, who was known as 'Sackfill' or 'Fill-sack' because of his skill in gathering church lands into his possession.[34] Sackville appears to have leased the duchy manor of Duddleswell in addition to owning the adjoining manors of Buckhurst, Sheffield, Framfield, and others. The Sackville family, whose heads in subsequent generations included Thomas, Lord Buckhurst, and the earls of Dorset, prospered through royal office-holding and held the mastership of the forest. They neglected to appoint sufficient forest and game officers, allowed the park pales to fall down, and claimed the right to kill deer straying from the forest into their manors or to pursue the same into the forest. Sackville intakes from Ashdown Forest probably added in excess of three hundred acres to their three parks in Withyham parish, bringing the total amount of Sackville parkland there to two thousand acres. Cottagers

---

[32] [Hyde], earl of Clarendon, *History of the Rebellion*, i. 132–5; P. F. Jones, *Richmond Park* (1972), 8; Thompson, *Whigs and Hunters*, 181 and plate 11.

[33] PRO DL 1/59/F21, 128/A25, DL 3/69/R12.a, 69/H2. a.a., 36/R5, DL 44/110, 860, 14; STAC 8/5/13.

[34] *DNB*, *sub* Sir Richard Sackville (d. 1566); *Collins's Peerage of England*, ed. Sir Egerton Brydges, 2 vols. (1812), ii. 107–9.

and squatters also encroached upon Ashdown Forest and consumed the woods and game.[35]

The northern forests fared no better than Ashdown. An inquisition held in 1562 revealed that in Pickering Forest, in the North Riding of Yorkshire, Sir Richard Cholmeley had felled large amounts of timber and plundered dressed stone from the ruins of Pickering Castle in order to build his house at Roxby. The red deer in Pickering had declined to 264 head since the death of Henry VIII, and six hundred fallow deer remained in Blandsby Park within the forest. In 1591 the deer herds of Pickering were so depleted that all hunting was banned for three years; by 1608 only a hundred fallow deer survived in Blandsby Park and the red deer had all but disappeared. The stone wall of Blandsby Park was in ruins and the deer ranged into the woods belonging to Sir Thomas Posthumus Hoby looking for the food which they could not find in Pickering where they had to compete with five thousand sheep. John Norden did an elaborate survey of Pickering in 1619–21 and discovered that there were only two keepers' lodges in Blandsby Park and none in Pickering. So few game and forest officials were inadequate to patrol one of the largest forests in England. There was much wood-stealing, and Norden thought that the smallholders of the neighbourhood were 'so unruly as they make their own perverse wills a law'.[36]

Bowland Forest, like many other royal forests, was transformed from a hunting reserve to a pastoral community by colonization—most of it concentrated in the sixteenth century. At first, an attempt was made to preserve the deer in two enclosed parks, Leagram and Radholme. Leagram Park once contained 1,400 acres and was surrounded by a pale six and a half miles in compass. Although this part of Bowland had once been wooded, the commissioners sent to survey Leagram Park in 1555 found that only a few dotard oaks remained and the underwood was stripped of everything except hazel and holly. By this time Leagram Park was reduced to 468 acres and the park pale, which was much decayed, could not be repaired for lack of suitable wood. Leagram Park also contained arable land at this date, but the remainder of the parkland had been so degraded that it consisted mostly of heaths and mosses. In 1556 Leagram was disparked and settlement followed. By 1678 the former park contained twenty-two households. In many parts of Bowland Forest, as the land was colonized and enclosed, stone walls had to be constructed because the soil was too poor to grow hedges.[37]

[35] Horsfield, *History of Sussex*, i. 375; C. N. Sutton, *Historical Notes of Withyham, Hartfield and Ashdown Forest, Together with the History of the Sackville Family* (Tunbridge Wells, Kent, 1902), 15–17, 369–70; *The Buckhurst Terrier*, ed. E. Straker (Sussex Rec. Soc., 39; Lewes, Sussex, 1933), 76; J. R. Daniel-Tyssen, 'The Parliamentary Surveys of the County of Sussex, 1649–1653', *Sussex Arch. Coll.*, 24 (1872), 193; E. Straker, 'Ashdown Forest and its Enclosures', *Sussex Arch. Coll.*, 80 (1940), 122–4.   [36] Cox, *Royal Forests of England*, 124.

[37] Porter, 'A Forest in Transition', 40–8, 57; *Pleadings and Depositions in the Duchy Court of Lancaster*, iii. 215–17.

The deer-park tradition had originated with the Normans, as did the system of royal forests. The Anglo-Saxons had not regarded these specialized uses of land to be necessary, but the feeding habits of fallow deer were so destructive that it was found to be desirable to confine them within enclosed parks. By the thirteenth century the deer-park tradition was well established and it became necessary to obtain a royal licence to impark land where it might possibly impinge upon a royal hunting reserve. The deer park became a familiar feature of the late-medieval and early modern landscape—as much a symbol of aristocratic privilege as the great country house. It usually consisted of woodland pasture, frequently severed from the manorial waste, and forming part of the seigneurial demesne. Typically, the park enclosure consisted of a mound and a ditch surmounted by a wooden pale, hedge, or a masonry wall, and admission was, in theory, obtained only through locked gates. Not only did smallholders lose common rights within enclosed parkland; in the late-medieval period they were frequently expected to pay 'park silver', in lieu of labour services, in order to maintain the enclosures.[38]

A deer park produced venison more efficiently than a forest. In the thirteenth century the hundred acres of the royal park of Havering-atte-Bower provided as much venison for the royal household as all the royal forests of south-western Essex combined, which contained ten times the area of Havering Park. In addition, Havering also afforded grazing to cattle. A park could be profitable and allow a variety of uses if well managed, but probably few measured up to such high standards. Young trees could be grown if coppiced, or enclosed and protected from the deer. Large timber trees did better in parks than in denser woodland and provided many of the very large special-use trees which were needed for naval construction. Launds, or open clearings in woodland, furnished grazing for animals. In short, it was necessary to segregate the various uses in a deer park, and this required fencing, which was expensive. Only large parks were suited to multiple uses. A nineteenth-century authority on parks thought that a herd of fallow deer should not exceed a density of more than one animal per acre. In fact, even the best-managed parks in the sixteenth century appear to have carried deer populations which were two and a half to three times as dense. This made it necessary to supplement the natural diet of park deer with hay. Despite supplementary feeding, Oliver Rackham calculates that the wastage of deer through starvation, disease, and other natural causes in Framlingham Park, Suffolk, in the early sixteenth century exceeded by 67 per cent the number of beasts slaughtered for venison or otherwise culled from the

---

[38] Rackham, *Trees and Woodlands in the British Landscape*, 142–8, 193; L. M. Cantor and J. S. Moore, 'The Medieval Parks of the Earls of Stafford at Madeley', *North Staffs. Journ. of Field Studies*, 3 (1963), 37; W. Hudson (ed.), 'A Series of Rolls of the Manor of Wiston', *Sussex Arch. Coll.*, 53 (1910), 156, 172.

herd. Although it is difficult to make precise comparisons concerning the potential profits which might have been made from a particular parcel of land if employed for alternative uses such as arable agriculture, it is difficult to avoid the conclusion that for most park owners deer parks were expensive status symbols.[39]

The thirteenth and fourteenth centuries had seen the great age of imparkment, but deer parks still remained numerous at the beginning of the sixteenth century. Moreover, during the next century and a half new deer parks were still being created or old ones enlarged. George Tyrell obtained a licence in 1559 to enclose a park of five hundred acres on his manor of Thornton, Buckinghamshire, together with a grant of free warren throughout the manor. At the same time he assured the queen that his park would not encroach upon the royal forest of Whaddon Chase.[40] When Henry VIII acquired Knole from Archbishop Cranmer in 1538, he spent £900 for the purchase of additional land to add to the existing four parks, which totalled 601 acres altogether. This imparkment provoked a poaching foray by several local men, who entered the royal parks in disguise and killed a number of deer. In 1544 Henry VIII ordered the Court of Augmentations to pay £5 annually to the vicar of Sevenoaks, Kent, in recompense for tithes lost through imparkment.[41] At the beginning of the sixteenth century, Sir Francis Wortley's great grandfather 'beggared' a whole village with lawsuits and, when he had cast the freeholders 'out of their inheritance', he pulled the whole village down and created Wortley New Park and built a hunting lodge in the midst of it. This infamous deed was still remembered in seventeenth-century West Yorkshire.[42]

When the earl of Leicester acquired Kenilworth Castle, it was a relatively small estate. He soon set about enlarging the grounds by adding parks, warrens, and a chase—spending a total of £60,000 on improvements. When finished, the grounds of Kenilworth were twenty miles in circuit and provided a sumptuous outdoor setting for Queen Elizabeth's visit in 1575. The mere, which Leicester constructed for fish and wildfowl, stretched over a mile westward from the castle to the 'Pleasance', a landscaped vista surrounded by water, and was large enough for a ship to sail upon. The deer park and rabbit warren were on the south side of the lake and the chase stretched forth from the northern side and was stocked with red deer. A hackney writer hired for the occasion described the chase as

---

[39] Rackham, *Trees and Woodlands in the British Landscape*, 193–5; Shirley, *Some Account of English Deer Parks*, 29–33, 233; Cantor and Moore, 'The Medieval Parks of the Earls of Stafford at Madeley', 37–58; L. M. Cantor, 'The Medieval Parks of Leicestershire', *Leics. Arch. Soc. Trans.*, 46 (1972), 14.   [40] *Cal. PR, 1558–1560*, 19–20.
[41] C. J. Phillips, *History of the Sackville Family*, 2 vols. (n.d.), ii. 395.
[42] *The Rev. Oliver Heywood, 1630–1702: His Autobiography, Diaries, Anecdote and Event Books*, ed. J. H. Turner, 4 vols. (Bingley, Yorks., 1881–5), ii. 81.

beautified with many delectable, fresh and umbrageous bowers, arbors, seats and walks that with great art, cost, and diligence were pleasantly appointed; which also the natural grace by the tall and fragrant trees and soil did so far . . . commend as Diana herself might have deigned there well enough to range for her pastime.[43]

Henry VIII was more responsive than other Tudor and Stuart monarchs to complaints concerning the damage done to their crops by deer in royal game preserves. But his responses to their petitions did not necessarily leave them better off. During the early Tudor period, when Berkeley Castle was in the hands of the crown, Berkeley New Park or Castle Park contained some five hundred or six hundred red deer. The park pales were not kept in good repair and herds of up to a hundred deer wandered at large, wasting the corn and pastures of the tenants. In consideration of a petition from the tenants filed in the Court of Star Chamber, Henry VIII in 1522 ordered the red deer of New Park to be caught and removed to Eastwood Park. But the king specified that the tenants were to pay for the cost of removal, and he cautioned the keepers not to move any female deer with calf if their removal might endanger the fawns. Once the deer had been safely transferred, the king issued further orders to enlarge the New Park and surround it with a new pale. The New Park was subsequently restocked with red deer and the tenants lost the use of the newly enclosed pastures and meadowland.[44]

Deer parks were important landmarks and Christopher Saxton's county maps published in the 1570s record their existence in every English county except Norfolk. Saxton shows a total of 817 parks in England, and we know from other sources that Norfolk possessed fifty-nine parks.[45] Altogether, evidence has been found to document the existence of 1,900 parks in medieval England, but only about half that number remained by the end of the sixteenth century.[46] The thickest concentrations of deer parks were to be found in the woodland areas of south-eastern England—especially Buckinghamshire, Hertfordshire, Essex, Sussex and Surrey—and in the West Midlands—particularly Worcestershire and Staffordshire. Essex contained 159 parks before 1535, or approximately one park to every 9.6 square miles; Hertfordshire had ninety parks, or one for every seven square miles, while

---

[43] M. Waldman, *Elizabeth and Leicester* (London, 1944), 131; T. Rowley, *The High Middle Ages, 1200–1500* (1986), map on p. 49; Robert Laneham, *A Letter: Whearin part of the entertainment untoo the Queenz Majesty, at Killingworth Castle, in Warwicksheer in this Soomerz Progress 1575 iz signified* (1575), printed in Nichols, *Progresses of Elizabeth*, i. 420–84.

[44] PRO STAC 2/26/186; *Descriptive Catalogue of the Charters and Muniments . . . at Berkeley Castle*, ed. Jeayes, nos. 689–90.

[45] H. Prince, *Parks in England* (Shallfleet Manor, IoW., 1967), frontispiece and pp. 1–2; Rackham, *Trees and Woodlands in the British Landscape*, 143; id., *Ancient Woodland*, 191.

[46] L. M. Cantor (ed.), *The English Medieval Landscape* (Philadelphia, 1982), 79–81; id., *The Changing English Countryside, 1400–1700* (1987), 108; C. G. A. Clay, *Economic Expansion and Social Change, 1500–1700*, 2 vols. (Cambridge, 1984), i. 109.

TABLE 5.1. Deer parks in Sussex

Park	No.
Ancient parks (before 1300)	51
Late-medieval parks (1300–1500)	120
Tudor parks (1500–1600)	121
Stuart parks (1600–1700)	80
Parks containing iron furnaces and/or forges (1500–1700)	29
Disparked during Tudor period	6
Disparked during Stuart period	22
Imparked or enlarged during Tudor period	4
Imparked or enlarged during Stuart period	2

Sources: PRO E 134/2 Jac. I/M8; STAC 2/27/142, 24/198, 27/142, STAC 4/8/26, STAC 5/B108/
18, M15/8, M40/15, D9/6, D29/7, N13/4, L28/24, L36/20, STAC 7/18/70, STAC 8/303/27, 255/
3, 265/25, 279/26, 111/7, 304/11, 197/1, 242/16, 84/24, 227/13, 205/8, 221/23, 40/14, 45/17,
84/21, 22; Abstracts of Star Chamber Proceedings Relating to the County of Sussex, Henry VIII
to Philip and Mary, ed. P. D. Mundy (Sussex Rec. Soc., 16; Lewes, E. Sussex, 1931), 72–3; Acts
PC, 1571–1575, 309, 1577–1578, 274–5; The Arundel Castle Archives, ed. F. W. Steer. 4 vols.
(Chichester, 1968–80), passim; Brandon, 'The Common Lands and Wastes of Sussex', 327–33;
Calendar of Assize Records, Sussex Indictments, Eliz. I, ed. Cockburn (1975), passim; H. Cleere
and D. Crossley, The Iron Industry of the Weald (Leicester, 1985), 306–67; W. S. Ellis, 'Descent
of the Manor of Hurst-Pierpoint and its Lords', Sussex Arch. Soc., 9 (1859), 65; id., Parks and
Forests of Sussex, passim; The Glynde Place Archives: A Catalogue, ed. R. F. Dell (Lewes, E.
Sussex, 1964), 244; J. J. Goring, 'Wealden Ironmasters in the Age of Elizabeth', in E. W. Ives,
R. J. Knecht, and J. J. Scarisbrick (eds.), Wealth and Power in Tudor England: Essays Presented
to S. T. Bindoff (1978), 204–27; Horsfield, History of Sussex, i. 259, 249–50; J. S. Moore, Laughton:
A Study in the Evolution of the Wealden Landscape (Leicester Univ., Dept. of Local Hist., Occas.
Papers, No. 19, 1965), 44–5; The Petworth House Archives: A Catalogue, ed. F. W. Steer and
A. McCann, 2 vols. (Chichester, 1968, 1979), ii. 64–5; Shirley, Some Account of English Deer
Parks, 64–8; Wyndham, Petworth Manor in the Seventeenth Century, 55–66; Yates, A History
of the Landscapes in the Parishes of South Harting and Rogate, passim; VCH Sussex, iv. 159,
vii. 172, 176, ix. 107–8.

Norfolk, a more remote and less heavily wooded county, possessed fifty-nine parks before 1535, or one for every thirty-five square miles.[47]

The fourteenth century was the heyday for deer parks, although they remained numerous into the Tudor period, as my tabulation and analysis of Sussex parks shows.[48] Sussex contained some 120 parks between 1300 and 1500, and the number seems to have peaked in the early sixteenth century, with a pronounced decline following in the seventeenth century. At the beginning of the sixteenth century, Sussex possessed one park for every 12 square miles. At least six parks were wholly or largely disparked in the Tudor period, and another twenty-two in the Stuart period. The profits to be made from agricultural uses during a period of sustained demographic expansion explain some of these disparkments, but most were

[47] Rackham, Ancient Woodland, 191.   [48] See Table 5.1 and list of sources.

TABLE 5.2. *Owners of deer parks in Sussex, 1400–1700*

Owner	No.	%
The crown	12	9
Peers	74	58
Temporal	(65)	
Spiritual	(9)	
Gentry	42	33

Source: As for Table 5.1.

disparked because of the presence of iron furnaces and forges. Between 1500 and 1700 twenty-nine Sussex parks contained furnaces or forges or both. As park owners found to their dismay, the preservation of deer or even the farming of fish in millponds were not compatible with industrial uses and the presence of large numbers of rural craftsmen. At the same time, there is evidence for the imparkment or enlargement of four parks in the Tudor period and two in the Stuart period. Of the 121 parks which existed in early Tudor Sussex, we have precise or estimated acreages in twenty-six cases. Sussex deer parks ranged in size from six thousand acres to twenty acres. The average size was 792 acres.

As one might expect in a county where peers were unusually thick on the ground, prelates and nobility owned 58 per cent of the deer parks existing in Sussex between 1400 and 1700. Nine parks were in the possession of the archbishop of Canterbury and the bishop of Chichester at the beginning of the sixteenth century, and ten temporal peers owned sixty-five parks between 1400 and 1700.[49] Among the more ancient noble households, the Fitzalan earls of Arundel owned eighteen parks and the Lords Abergavenny possessed eight. Of those holding more-recently created peerages, Sir Richard Sackville and his descendants, Thomas, Lord Buckhurst, and the earls of Dorset gathered into their hands nine parks, while the first and second Lords Montague possessed seven parks between their Cowdray and Battle estates. The crown retained title to twelve deer parks (9 per cent of the total number of parks), which were remnants of the seven royal forests formerly existing in Sussex. The remaining forty-two parks (or 33 per cent of the total number) were in the hands of the gentry. Many of these belonged to gentlemen who also owned ironworks: the Carylls and the Pelhams possessed

[49] Hunting and hawking were forbidden to the clergy by canon law, but allowed by English law to those who were qualified by estate (Coke, *Institutes*, pt. iv, p. 309). Peacham (*Compleat Gentleman*, 183–4) observes that many prelates had formerly possessed numerous parks, but after the Reformation 'could scarce show one of ten or twenty'. See also P. Hembry, 'Episcopal Palaces, 1535–1660', in E. W. Ives, R. J. Knecht, and J. J. Scarisbrick (eds.), *Wealth and Power in Tudor England: Essays Presented to S. T. Bindoff* (1978), 147, 153, 155.

seven parks each, the Gorings five, and the Coverts and the Gages of Firle three each.[50]

5.3. Warrens, Ponds, and Dovecotes

Andrew Boorde, sometime monk, physician, and suffragan to the bishop of Chichester, thought that deer parks, cony warrens, fishponds, and dovehouses were all necessary adjuncts to a gentleman's house. The rules of hospitality obliged a country gentleman to provide not only fresh meat or fish for his board the year round, but also recreation for his guests.[51] Although the sale of venison was illegal, conies, freshwater fish, and pigeons were all raised on a commercial basis in early modern England and could be quite profitable. However, each activity involved a competitive land use and could precipitate violent protest.

Conies were valued not only for their flesh, but also for their fur, which was used in clothing. The pelt of a rabbit fetched twice the value of its meat, and rabbit skins found a steady market at home and abroad. The pelts from silver and black conies were particularly prized and were exported to Turkey.[52] The feral rabbits which have become naturalized throughout much of the British Isles are the progeny of conies introduced into England by the Normans. Perhaps because of the diseases which periodically decimate rabbit populations, it was difficult to establish breeding colonies in England, and throughout the late-medieval and early modern periods rabbits were bred in enclosed warrens. The purpose of enclosures around cony warrens was purely symbolic—to proclaim the legal doctrine that a warren was to be regarded as a close and that, therefore, the land within was held in severalty and the rabbits were chattels and could be stolen. Obviously, hedges and fences would not contain rabbits within their warrens, nor did they deter poachers. Much ingenuity was expended upon the preservation of rabbit warrens. They were usually surrounded by earthen banks surmounted by fences or stone walls which might further be topped by hawthorn or furze branches. The mounds became undermined with burrows and had to be renewed frequently. A warrener, who perhaps leased the warren from the landowner, lived in a lodge in the midst of the warren. The lodge might be equipped with a tower from which he maintained surveillance over his charges. Outside their warrens, rabbits were intensely destructive and were popularly regarded as vermin. Rabbits competed for the same sources of food as cattle and sheep. Although a rabbit might weigh just over 2 lb., ten

---

[50] See Table 5.2.

[51] Boorde, *A Dyetary of Helth*, ed. Furnivall, 239; *DNB*, *sub* Boorde *or* Borde, Andrew (1490?–1549); *Royalist's Notebook*, ed. Banford, 68, 203.

[52] Moryson, *Itinerary*, iv. 169.

rabbits can eat as much as a sheep weighing 80 lb. However, rabbit-breeding could be carried on in sandy or barren soils such as the Breckland or heaths of the east coast, where even goats would have starved.[53]

The provisioning needs of the royal household in the medieval period stimulated rabbit-breeding throughout southeastern England. The light soils of the Petworth district in Sussex favoured rabbit-breeding, and a conygarth or cony park existed at Petworth House as early as the thirteenth century to supply the Percy board. This warren was enlarged in the 1580s. Nearby, Sir Henry Goring leased a cony warren on the north side of Sutton Common from the earl of Northumberland. In 1623 it amounted to 260 acres and caused much ill will among his neighbours.[54] Ashdown Forest contained a rabbit warren as early as the fourteenth century, which appears to have been plundered during the Civil Wars of the seventeenth century. St Leonard's Forest and Tilgate Forest had rabbit warrens, which together amounted to several thousand acres at the end of that century. On lands in Sussex which are suitable for reafforestation today, rabbit-farming was a preferred economic activity in the seventeenth century because the cost of transporting wood and timber to the London market was frequently prohibitive. The choice was an unfortunate one, because rabbit-farming caused environmental degradation. Dense populations of rabbits prevented the regeneration of native hardwood trees and encouraged the growth of bracken, which rabbits do not eat. The ferns were periodically cut or burnt to encourage the growth of grass, and so there was no opportunity for these barren heaths to revert to woodland.[55] Rabbits also competed for food with other game; hare and partridge were rarely found where rabbit populations were dense. The same was true to a lesser extent of deer, and it was also dangerous to hunt on horseback where rabbit burrows had undermined the ground.[56]

At West Dean in West Sussex there was a rabbit warren as early as 1583 which was owned by Philip, earl of Arundel. The warren was $8\frac{1}{2}$ miles in circumference. It was enclosed by mounds and ditches topped by fences, and the inner face of the banks was lined with split flints. Arundel leased the warren in 1583 to Henry Hargrave for twenty-one years for £20 p.a. payable in cash or in rabbits supplied twice a week to Arundel Castle. The value of the rabbits fluctuated from 6*d.* a couple in late spring to 9*d.* a couple in autumn and early winter. From February to May there was a closed season on rabbits because this was their most prolific breeding season. The

[53] J. Sheail, *Rabbits and their History* (Newton Abbot, Devon, 1971), 81, 83; A. M. and R. M. Tittensor, 'The Rabbit Warren at West Dean near Chichester', *Sussex Arch. Coll.*, 123 (1985), 151–3.

[54] Sheail, *Rabbits and their History*, 94; Tittensor, 'The Rabbit Warren at West Dean near Chichester', 154; Wyndham, *Sutton and Duncton Manors*, 44.

[55] Brandon, 'The Common Lands and Wastes of Sussex', 121–3; Tittensor, 'The Rabbit Warren at West Dean near Chichester', 154–5.   [56] Sheail, *Rabbits and their History*, 109.

warrener was obliged to maintain a breeding stock of at least three thousand conies, which suggests a density of three to four rabbits per acre. The
enclosure of the West Dean rabbit warren severed a considerable part of
the manorial waste of West Dean, and escaped rabbits devastated the grazing
of what remained to such an extent that by the early eighteenth century the
vegetation of this heathland could no longer sustain both the rabbits and
the tenants' sheep. During severe weather, when grass was not available,
the warrener had to cut twigs and branches to supply the rabbits with
browse.[57]

Rabbit warrens appear to have proliferated on the sandy soils of West
Sussex after the middle of the sixteenth century. In the parish of Rogate,
a warren consisting of five hundred acres was located on Durford Heath
within the banks of Downe Park, a decayed ancient deer park belonging to
the manor of Upton. Henry VIII had granted the manor of Upton together
with the site of Durford Monastery to Sir Edmund Marven, JCP, in about
1545. Possession of the rabbit warren was disputed between Marven's widow
and sons and Edmund Ford of Harting. During the 1550s members of the
two families and their servants, wearing chain mail and 'jackskulls' and
armed with swords, bucklers, and staves, repeatedly clashed with one another as each side attempted to take and retain possession of the rabbit
warren. The tenants from the manor of Upton commoned on Durford Heath
and their sheep competed with escaped rabbits for the sparse grass. They
claimed the right to catch rabbits escaped from the warren, which does not
appear to have been effectively fenced. In 1635 some of the tenants sold
their common rights and allowed part of the warren to be enclosed.[58]

In another part of Rogate parish, the Carylls of West Harting encountered
popular resistance in their attempt to carve a rabbit warren out of Harting
Combe. Harting Combe was a woodland 830 acres in extent, which, within
living memory, had been thickly covered with oaks and beeches. Its use as
a hog pasture and the presence of iron furnaces and forges had rendered
it quite treeless by 1600. Late in the sixteenth century Sir Edward Caryll had
begun enclosing part of Harting Combe for a new rabbit warren. This was
much resented by landowners and tenants in Harting and Rogate, who used
Harting Combe as their common. As Caryll's workmen 'did enfence and
enclose [the] same by day, the posts, rails, and banks were cut and thrown
down by night privily'. Caryll, who had been removed from the commission
of the peace in 1587 because he was the earl of Arundel's steward and a
Catholic, was said to be 'without [legal] remedy'.[59] By 1613 the opposition

---

[57] Tittensor, 'The Rabbit Warren at West Dean near Chichester', 159–67.

[58] PRO STAC 2/20/314, STAC 4/1/27, 4/8/26, STAC 5/F14/21; Tittensor, 'The Rabbit Warren at West Dean near Chichester', 154.

[59] VCH Sussex, iv. 21, 25; H. Cleere and D. Crossley, The Iron Industry of the Weald (Leicester, 1985), 353; Yates, History of the Landscapes in the Parishes of South Harting and Rogate, 21; PRO STAC 8/94/20; R. B. Manning, Religion and Society in Elizabethan Sussex: A Study of the Enforcement of the Elizabethan Religious Settlement (Leicester, 1969), 250–2.

to the Caryll rabbit warren had been organized by Richard Bettesworth of Rogate, gent., who possessed the manor of Fyning, and his son Peter. The Bettesworths were notorious poachers and deer-stealers and were also alleged to be receivers of stolen venison. In April 1613 the Bettesworths led some twenty of their neighbours, dressed in women's clothes, in several attacks upon the Harting Combe warren. They killed forty couple of rabbits on one occasion and returned to dig up the burrows on another. They also broke into the warrener's lodge and menaced him by thrusting pikes through the windows and doors.[60]

In 1622 Richard, earl of Dorset, possessed a very large rabbit warren north-east of Brighton, which stretched across the downs in the parishes of Meaching, Piddinghoe, and Telescombe. This was a new warren which had been started up only two years earlier. Its extent is suggested by the fact that the farmer, Peter Woodgate of Hawkhurst, Kent, gent., paid an annual rent of £146 for the lease. A large warren so close to Brighton was bound to be a temptation, and the warren was raided in August 1622 by a large gang of poachers recruited by James Dumbrell of Ovingdean, yeom., from amongst labourers and craftsmen living in Brighton. These were commercial poachers, who came equipped with dogs, ferrets, and nets, and, after disabling two of the warrener's servants, made off with 120 rabbits on one occasion and returned on other occasions to catch another seven hundred or eight hundred rabbits valued altogether at £20.[61]

Most attacks on rabbit warrens appear to have been justified by the plea that rabbit warrens encroached upon commons and devalued use-rights. The courtier, Sir John Pakington of Hampton Lovett, Worcestershire, whom Queen Elizabeth nicknamed 'Lusty' Pakington, possessed a rabbit warren on Ellesborough Hill in Buckinghamshire and a house on the adjacent manor of Aylesbury, where he stopped over on his way to and from London and Worcestershire. The tenants of the manor of Ellesborough complained that the warren encroached upon their manorial waste, which was crown land, and that Pakington had no licence for his warren. Claiming that Pakington's warrener had set mastiffs upon them when they attempted to exercise their rights of common, the Ellesborough tenants took advantage of Pakington's frequent absences and the fact that the warren was guarded by only one aged warrener, and terrorized and wounded the warrener and systematically destroyed the rabbits. On numerous occasions between June and October 1623 they invited friends from neighbouring villages to join them in plundering the warren. One of the tenants was also a warrener, and he showed them how to use ferrets and 'hare pipes' to carry out their campaign of extermination.[62]

The supply of freshwater fish never quite caught up with the demand in

---

[60] PRO STAC 8/94/20.   [61] PRO STAC 8/291/24.
[62] *DNB, sub* Sir John Pakington (1549–1625); PRO STAC 8/30/20; see also STAC 8/10/14.

Tudor and Stuart England, and the excess demand had to be satisfied with the cured products of deep-sea fishing. In order to stimulate the salt-water fisheries as a nursery of mariners, parliamentary legislation prescribed numerous meatless days. Even after the Reformation, abstinence from meat was required for a total of 153 days a year by the end of the sixteenth century.[63] Although Norden estimated the cost of constructing a fishpond at £1 for every $30\frac{1}{4}$ square yards of surface, he reckoned that fishponds could be made profitable in two or three years. Live fish were transported to London in casks from as far away as fifty miles, but even in remote parts of the realm Norden thought that local demand would be sufficient to justify the construction of fishponds—especially if the fish could be raised in millponds also employed for industrial purposes.[64]

The problem was that it was difficult to maintain fishponds, millponds, or weirs on water courses which did not impinge upon someone else's water rights or use-rights. Weirs obstructed navigation or interfered with other people's fishing rights. Large ponds permanently flooded valuable meadows or encroached upon common wastes. The enclosure of ponds was necessary to establish a claim to several fishing, and this might deny villagers access to places where they customarily watered their cattle.[65]

Millers often kept their millponds stocked with fish. William Preston, the miller of the manor of Tyrley, Staffordshire, was frequently presented at the manorial court for his transgressions. His weir interfered with other tenants' water rights, and like most millers he kept the level of the pond too high and the backpounding damaged water meadows.[66]

Disputes about fishing and water rights stirred up much conflict in local communities. Sir John Poyntz of Iron Acton, Gloucestershire, was possessed of the manor of Himschamflower, Somerset, and a grist mill. Poyntz's miller built a millpond and a mill-race across the tenement of a smallholder, Hugh Slocumbe, in an attempt to force Slocumbe to surrender his holding. This had been done without Slocumbe's permission, and the millpond flooded his water meadows and destroyed an orchard. In 1589, while Slocumbe sought relief in Chancery, he and some twenty other tenants attacked the millpond, removed a thousand fish with nets, and then broke the head of the millpond, rendering the mill inoperable. When the town constable sought to disperse them, the tenants threatened to kill him. In their defence, the tenants claimed that they were only draining Slocumbe's flooded meadows and orchard and restoring the river to its former course.[67] When John Cutler, esq., died in 1524, he bequeathed a fishpond to the Charterhouse of Henton, Somerset, because the monks ate fish instead of meat. The heir, John Cutler

[63] Clay, *Economic Expansion and Social Change*, ii. 131, 218.
[64] Norden, *Surveyor's Dialogue*, 218–20.
[65] See, e.g., PRO STAC 8/29/4; Manning, *Village Revolts*, 267–70, 302–4.
[66] Twemlow, *The Manor of Tyrley*, 132–3.   [67] PRO STAC 5/P20/4.

the younger, was so enraged by this alienation of a valuable part of the family estate that he gathered his kinsmen and allies together, destroyed the pond, and removed fish to the value of £20.[68]

Outsiders were apt to be insensitive about local property and water rights. William Corfe, a groom of the king's cellar, farmed the manorial demesne of Erdington, Warwickshire, which belonged to Francis Englefield, esq., then a ward of the crown. Thomas Ridgeley, gent., claimed to possess a lease of the fishpond from Englefield's father, which antedated the grant of the wardship. When Corfe attempted to harvest the fish from the pond in 1541, Ridgeley and some twenty servants and friends breached the dam and removed the fish themselves.[69]

Dovecotes or pigeon houses were probably the most common source of fresh meat during the winter and spring months in medieval and early modern England. Professor Cantor estimates that there may have been as many as twenty-six thousand of them in Stuart England. They were an inexpensive source of food for the landowner who possessed one, but were costly to his neighbours, whose corn the pigeons devoured. Dovecotes were usually the prerogative of the lord of the manor, and any tenant who was unwise enough to keep an unlicensed one would usually find himself presented to the court leet or suffer destruction of the nuisance. At Eardisley, Herefordshire, in 1615, neighbours tore down an offending pigeon house as well as carrying away all the fowl. During the 1520s the notorious Ellis Midmore led a poaching gang which ranged over the Weald of East Sussex for the better part of a decade destroying dovecotes, deer parks, and other enclosures which encroached upon manorial wastes.[70]

The increase in population in sixteenth-century England created new markets for agricultural products and saw an expansion of rural industries such as iron-founding which competed for natural resources and land in the same parts of the realm where medieval deer parks and royal forests and chases were most heavily concentrated. The disparkment and disafforestation of game reserves precisely coincides with this demographic and economic expansion. There is good reason for believing that the populations of red, roe, and fallow deer were all declining in Tudor England as a consequence of increasing competition for land resources in the woodland regions. It seems reasonable to conclude that, as the human population expanded and the deer populations contracted, venison and game came to be perceived as more valuable commodities. Stephen Mennell also suggests that the consumption of game by the aristocracy increased at the end of the Middle

---

[68] PRO STAC 2/32/42.   [69] PRO STAC 2/9, fo. 185, 2/10, fo. 231.
[70] Cantor, *Changing English Countryside*, 72–3; Twemlow, *Manor of Tyrley*, 132–3; PRO STAC 2/29/79, STAC 8/113/12; Manning, *Village Revolts*, 46–8.

Ages as a way for aristocrats to distinguish themselves from the inferior sort who ate butcher's meat.[71] But aristocratic and courtly tastes in eating did much to influence the tastes and aspirations of the commonalty. Thus, the attempt by the crown and aristocracy to restrict hunting privileges through the enactment of more stringent Game Laws—especially during the reign of James I—did little to stop the increasing incidence of game-poaching and the illegal sale of venison and game. In the eighteenth century, the aristocratic and popular taste for venison and game seems to have declined. This may have had something to do with the noticeable preference for beef, which became available the year around as a consequence of the widespread cultivation of tubers and other fodder crops which permitted cattle to be not only carried over but fattened during the winter months.

[71] S. Mennell, *All Manners of Food: Eating and Taste in England and France from the Middle Ages to the Present* (Oxford, 1985), 61.

6

The Structure of Poaching

Never inquire whence venison comes [*c.*1630].

M. P. Tilley, *A Collection of the Proverbs of England in the Sixteenth and Seventeenth Centuries* (Ann Arbor, Mich., 1950; repr. 1966), 696

[His Majesty] is informed that never was venison so common neither of hind nor does as this winter it has been. His Majesty expects that some order be taken for it, for he cannot endure that all his care to preserve his game is eluded in such manner, and common sale made of his does and hinds which all came out of his Majesty's grounds.

Sir Thomas Lake to Robert, earl of Salisbury (2 December 1608), HMC *Hatfield*, xx. 275

The said confederates did in unlicensed alehouses and other unlawful and blind taverns and victualling houses riotously eat and wastefully spend in banqueting and feasting some part of the flesh and venison of the said deer amongst their consorts and like rioters by space of days together and did also . . . unlawfully, to make a corrupt and ungodly game to themselves, sell and utter some of the flesh or venison of the said deer for divers great sums of money unto sundry persons . . . and did distribute and dispose of some other part thereof unto and amongst such other persons of like lewd behaviour as they liked best at their own wills and pleasures to the great revenge and damage of your said subject.

Anthony Kinnersley of Foxley, Staffs., esq. v. *John Allen the elder of Garsall, yeom.* (5 February 1621), PRO STAC 8/191/5

THE motives which led men to engage in unlawful hunting were complex. Hunting deer in all its various cultural manifestations always contained the elements of sport and adventure. This was sometimes mixed in with activities as diverse as symbolic war and illegal trading in venison and game. A considerable part of the unlawful hunting engaged in by the aristocracy and gentry reflected the perennial factionalism among courtiers or the more localized feuding within county and local communities. Some of these rivalries arose from conflicting claims to hunting rights and the competition for royal forest and game offices on the part of idle gentlemen who thought it not unreasonable that they should be paid for engaging in their favourite activity of hunting the king's deer. Except where they were themselves the victims of poachers, justices of the peace were lax in punishing unlawful hunting, because many of them hunted in derogation of other people's rights or corruptly provided protection for commercial poachers. Poaching fraternities could not survive nor could commercial poachers ply their trade for long without the protection, or at least the indulgence, of local magistrates. Finally, gentlemen poachers, and even the king's own game officers, were not adverse to turning a profit from the sale of surplus venison.

The members of village communities also aided and abetted such poaching activities or themselves destroyed deer and rabbits which escaped from their parks and warrens when such creatures damaged their crops. This was a species of social protest, but it must also have afforded a measure of diversion and sport to the participants. But poaching gangs always bred violence and lawlessness, and village communities sometimes had to fight back when members of such gangs menaced them.

6.1. Court Factionalism

Gentry feuding found an outlet in many different kinds of aggressive behaviour: through litigation in the royal courts of justice, at parliamentary elections, and through the symbolic pursuit of war in the form of hunting and poaching. The same kind of factionalism was prevalent among the aristocracy and permeated the life of the royal court, but the proprieties of courtly behaviour and the strict construction of treason legislation dictated that political dissent or protest or the vindication of aristocratic honour be carefully masked and obliquely stated. Court masques and country-house entertainments could carry subtle messages of protest,[1] but when a bolder statement was required, hunting forays provided a medium of expression which could not easily be mistaken.

Even monarchs occasionally resorted to this covert communication. When Elizabeth and Leicester invaded the deer park of Henry, eleventh Lord Berkeley, at Berkeley Castle in 1572 and havocked his deer, Elizabeth meant to tell Lord Berkeley, whose absence and failure to offer hospitality must have caused grievous offence, that the adherents of his brother-in-law, Thomas, fourth duke of Norfolk, recently executed for treason, would do well to put all thought of resistance out of their heads.[2] The presence of

---

[1] See C. Breight, 'Caressing the Great: Viscount Montague's Entertainment of Elizabeth at Cowdray, 1591', *Sussex Arch. Coll.*, 127 (1989), 147–66, for an enlightening discussion of the use of covert language in masques as a vehicle for political dissent and the vindication of aristocratic honour.

[2] This incident is discussed in Ch. 2. John Smyth of Nibley, the Berkeley steward, states that the need to fight the lawsuit in the Court of Exchequer Chamber kept Lord Berkeley in London and at court during most of that year (1572–3) and put him to great expense. It cost him £500 to obtain a pardon for intrusion upon the lands of the disputed Lisle inheritance and £1,800 in legal fees (*Berkeley Manuscripts*, ii. 288–91).

the earl of Leicester at Elizabeth's side on this occasion signified that the queen would henceforth favour Leicester's claim to the Lisle inheritance in the revival of a dispute which reached back to the fifteenth century. This event reverberated through the Vale of Berkeley and precipitated a poaching war lasting nearly fifty years between Lord Berkeley's gamekeepers and the adherents of Sir Thomas Throckmorton, Leicester's henchman in Gloucestershire.

The animosity between Berkeley and Leicester originated in the disputed division of an inheritance between William, sixth Lord Berkeley, and Thomas Talbot, Viscount Lisle, and, in the atmosphere of the Wars of the Roses, took a more violent turn. Lisle laid claim to Berkeley Castle, and, unable to obtain it by force, deceit, or litigation, challenged Berkeley to a duel. The two agreed to meet at Nibley Green in 1469, but Berkeley arranged an ambush for his rival. Lord Lisle was killed by an arrow fired by Black Will of Dean Forest and his retainers were scattered. Berkeley and his men then went to Lisle's house at Wotton and sacked it and so frightened Lisle's young widow that she miscarried. Berkeley was a very acquisitive person, but he had made so many enemies that he granted large portions of his lands to the king and others in order to buy pardons and protection. It was for this reason that the king acquired in 1488 the barony and castle of Berkeley. The grant of the lordship and castle of Berkeley had been limited to male issue and the castle reverted to Henry, eleventh Lord Berkeley, in the reign of Mary. With the return of Berkeley Castle came a tangled web of litigation which has been called the longest lawsuit in English legal history.[3]

The Dudley family had inherited the Lisle claims through the female line, and their chance to exploit these claims came under Elizabeth. Although Queen Mary had restored Berkeley Castle to the Berkeleys, the queen had also begun a lawsuit in the Court of Exchequer Chamber against Lord Henry in 1558 for intruding upon the Lisle estates in Gloucestershire, which had been forfeited to the crown by the attainder of John Dudley, duke of Northumberland. The suit was renewed by Queen Elizabeth and promoted by Sir Thomas Parry, treasurer of the queen's household and a member of the Privy Council. Lord Henry did not actively fight the suit at this time, and Parry's enmity was bought off with a favourable lease, so the suit remained dormant. The attainder of Thomas, duke of Norfolk, Lord Henry's brother-in-law, brought the suit to life again, and in 1573 the Court of Exchequer Chamber declared in favour of the queen, who then granted the lands of the Lisle inheritance to Leicester and his brother, Ambrose, earl of Warwick.[4]

[3] GEC viii. 58 and n.; Atkyns, *Ancient and Present State of Gloucestershire*, 138–9; Stone, *Family and Fortune*, 243–5.

[4] Smyth, *Berkeley Manuscripts*, ii. 288–91; Cooke, 'The Great Berkeley Lawsuit', 320–2. Stone, *Family and Fortune*, 243–5.

With great show and a multitude of people following him, Robert Dudley, earl of Leicester, made a triumphal entry into his newly restored lands in Gloucestershire. The purpose was to dramatize to the county the fact that he was now the most eminent lord and a favourite of the queen. First he went to Michaelwood Lodge and destroyed the palings of a park on Michaelwood Chase claimed by Lord Berkeley. Then he proceeded to Wotton Hill, where he played a game of stoolball, a stick-and-ball game played in the wood-pasture regions of Gloucestershire and Dorset, which has been described as a kind of 'ritualized combat'.[5] He continued on a tour of his houses, visiting Wotton and attempting to take possession by force of Slimbridge Rolls Court, held on leasehold by Arnold Ligon, a 'stout gentle-man', who successfully repulsed Leicester. During this progress Leicester designated the corrupt and contentious Sir Thomas Throckmorton of Tortworth, Gloucestershire, as his surrogate in the feud with Lord Berkeley by making Throckmorton his 'daily coach companion'.[6]

John Smyth of Nibley, the antiquarian and Berkeley steward in the latter days of Lord Henry, claims that one of the ways that Leicester went about gathering evidence for his lawsuit was to invite Berkeley to Kenilworth Castle, which was six miles from Berkeley's seat at Callowdon, and 'lodging him as a brother and fellow huntsman with him in his own bedchamber with semblance of great familarity, gave him great liberty without restraint over his deer in his parks and chase there'. Leicester clearly knew Berkeley's weaknesses, and 'fairly relating unto him how it was his greatest honour . . . to be descended from his ancient house', Leicester secured Berkeley's permis-sion to allow a herald into the Berkeley muniment room under pretext of filling in his family genealogy, but in actuality 'to draw away from this lord's evidence house some deeds and exemplifications of records'.[7] Lord Henry was extraordinarily naïve and could focus his mind on little else besides hunting. It was probably for this reason that he was known as 'Henry the Harmless'.

In order to sever the lands awarded to Leicester and Warwick by the Exchequer decree of 1573 from the remaining possessions of Berkeley, a survey of boundaries was undertaken to be based upon presentments of jurors drawn from the borough of Wotton and the manor of Wotton Foreign. The jury was packed, but even so some of the tenants could not stomach the manifest untruthfulness of the presentments and refused their assent. Their names were struck from the panel and the jury had to be

[5] Underdown, *Revel, Riot and Rebellion*, 175.

[6] Smyth, *Berkeley Manuscripts*, ii. 288–91; Cooke, 'The Great Berkeley Lawsuit', 320–2; *House of Commons, 1558–1603*, ed. Hasler, iii. 501–2; P. Williams, *The Council in the Marches of Wales under Elizabeth* (Cardiff, 1958), 307. See also S. Adams, 'The Dudley Clientele and the House of Commons, 1559–1586', *Parliamentary History*, 8. 2 (1989), 229, 238 n.

[7] Smyth, *Berkeley Manuscripts*, ii. 288–91; GEC viii. 58.

reconstituted before Leicester and Warwick got the boundaries which they wanted. The consequence was that Berkeley and his protagonists never agreed upon the division of Michaelwood Chase, and numerous clashes followed between the Berkeley and Dudley tenants concerning intercommoning rights, and between the Berkeley and Dudley gamekeepers, who charged one another with unlawful hunting.[8]

Leicester had an evil reputation for the ruthlessness with which he treated his tenants and neighbours,[9] but it must be said that not all of the blame for this quarrel can be laid at his feet. Shortly before the trial and execution of the duke of Norfolk in 1572, Leicester had proposed a marriage alliance between Berkeley's two daughters (Berkeley did not have a male heir at that time) and Leicester's nephews, Sir Philip Sidney and his brother Robert, later Lord Lisle. Katharine, Lady Berkeley, had opposed the marriage, and her refusal caused great offence to the Dudley family and forfeited any claim on the queen's sympathy.[10] John Smyth blamed the revival of the Berkeley–Lisle feud on the contentiousness and covetousness of Anne, dowager Lady Berkeley, who managed the Berkeley estates following the birth of Lord Henry shortly after his father's death in 1534. She weakened the loyalty of the Berkeley tenants, kinsmen, and allies in Gloucestershire by attempting to cancel the leases of poor tenants and entering into a violent quarrel with a gentleman of the privy chamber, Lord Henry's uncle, Sir Maurice Berkeley, concerning the inheritance of the manor of Mangotsfield.[11]

The source of contention between Lady Berkeley and her brother-in-law was whether the manor of Mangotsfield should descend to Lord Henry or pass to his uncle Sir Maurice. The matter was complicated by the fact that his father, Lord Thomas, had left two different wills. Sir Maurice had forcibly seized and retained possession of Mangotsfield mill and pond. Lady Anne sent raiding parties on three different occasions to destroy the millpond dam and remove the fish. Sir Maurice had her servants indicted and fined at the quarter sessions, and retaliated by destroying her millpond on the manor of Button and removing the fish. Lady Anne replied by bringing numerous suits against Sir Maurice and his brother-in-law, Sir Nicholas Poyntz, in the Court of Star Chamber and elsewhere. The feud escalated, and Sir Maurice and Sir Nicholas sought revenge in an attack upon her deer park at her seat at Yate. Upon this occasion they 'havocked' her deer and conspired

---

[8] Smyth, *Berkeley Manuscripts*, ii. 295–6.
[9] See, e.g., *Leicester's Commonwealth*, ed. D. C. Peck (Athens, Oh., 1985), 208 n.–209 n., 210 n., 118–21, 123; Williams, *Council in the Marches of Wales*, 237–9, 246–7; M. Waldman, *Elizabeth and Leicester* (1944), 131. Although some historians regard *Leicester's Commonwealth* as an unreliable Catholic polemic, John Smyth read it and regarded it as containing an accurate description of the Berkeley–Dudley quarrel.
[10] Cooke, 'The Great Berkeley Lawsuit', 320–2; Stone, *Family and Fortune*, 246–8.
[11] Smyth, *Berkeley Manuscripts*, ii. 414.

to set a large hayrick on fire, hoping it would spread to Lady Anne's house and consume her and her infant son. They were prevented from doing so when a rival gang of deer-slayers emerged from the haystack, where they had been hiding, for fear of being burnt alive. Sir Maurice and Sir Nicholas thought that the rival poachers were Lady Anne's men lying in wait to ambush them. Both gangs fled in terror in opposite directions. Smyth remarked that the like behaviour had not been seen 'since the lawless days of Robin Hood'.[12]

Sir Nicholas Poyntz had been forced to surrender the keepership of Berkeley New Park on an earlier occasion, and the heavy fines assessed upon him and Sir Maurice as a consequence of the judgments obtained against them by Lady Anne and Lord Henry obliged Poyntz, to sell to Lord Henry his patent for the rangership and keepership of Kingswood Chase, which offices had been held by his ancestors. Lord Henry continued to wage law against Poyntz, even though the latter was a cousin and a mesne tenant. Lord Henry finally succeeded in driving Poyntz into the arms of Leicester, who encouraged Poyntz to withhold his rent and provided him with legal counsel in resisting the Berkeleys.[13]

A dispute about the impropriated tithes of Hinton in the parish of Berkeley sharpened the animosity between Lord Henry and Sir Thomas Throckmorton. This led Sir Nicholas Poyntz into a brief alliance with Throckmorton in order to pack juries sitting on this and other related suits; the two conspirators later had a falling out with one another.[14] As both Berkeley and Throckmorton later realized, the conflict was fed by the bellicose behaviour of their respective servants and solicitors. In the years 1579 and 1580, by Smyth's account, there were thirteen bills pending in Star Chamber between Berkeley and Throckmorton and twelve suits in King's Bench and Common Pleas—not to mention other litigation in Chancery and at the assizes and quarter sessions. Much of this litigation involved charges and counter-charges of unlawful hunting arising from the failure of the Dudleys and Lord Berkeley to agree upon the division of Michaelwood Chase. At one session of the quarter sessions four separate indictments resulted in fines against forty of Berkeley's servants. The suits arising from the tithe dispute alone cost Berkeley £1,500 in legal fees plus the loss of the tithes and other lands, for he did badly in these suits. Leicester and Throckmorton possessed greater resources for packing juries and suborning witnesses than Berkeley. John Smyth was saddened by the 'dishonour' heaped on Lord Henry by these defeats, and by the damage done to friends and tenants who were left to fend for themselves and pay the legal fees and fines because Lord Henry

---

[12] PRO STAC 2/4, fos. 221–4; Smyth, *Berkeley Manuscripts*, ii. 266–70; Atkyns, *Ancient and Present State of Gloucestershire*, 139.

[13] *Descriptive Catalogue of the Charters and Muniments . . . at Berkeley Castle*, ed. Jeayes, no. 712.   [14] William, *Council in the Marches of Wales*, 209–11.

could not help them financially. These numerous suits and the epidemic of unlawful hunting also contributed to another revival of the feud between Lord Henry and the Dudleys in 1580.[15]

Between 1576 and 1596 Berkeley accused Throckmorton and eighty-eight of his kinsmen, gamekeepers, servants, tenants, and allies of unlawful hunting in numerous bills of complaint in the Court of Star Chamber. Some of them, such as Throckmorton's park keeper at Tortworth, Richard Francombe, and his sons, John and William, were prosecuted repeatedly over that twenty-year period for hunting on Michaelwood Chase and breaking into the numerous Berkeley parks. Others were incited and procured by Anne, Countess of Warwick.[16] On one occasion Throckmorton bribed the sheriff of Gloucestershire with a haunch of venison from one of Berkeley's parks in order to allow him to choose a jury.[17] Henry Parmiter of Stone, an attorney of the Court of Common Pleas, worked for the countess of Warwick by day as a solicitor and hunted on her behalf by night with a fraternity made up of nine or ten men of 'mettle and good woodmen . . . old notorious deer-stealers'.[18] They were opposed by a band of equal size raised by Berkeley's ranger of Michaelwood Chase, Anthony Hungerford. John Smyth later heard from Parmiter's own mouth how between these 'two companies many sore blows were exchanged, divers on both sides beaten to the ground and much blood drawn; which violence ceased not on either side till the fall of Smallwood by his death's wound, whereupon leaving him as dead the rest of the deer-stealers fled'.[19] For a time, Lady Warwick maintained Parmiter with financial support and legal evidence from her muniment room to buttress his defence, but when he saw that his legal practice and finances were likely to suffer, he made his peace with Berkeley and his ranger and told all. When Parmiter surrendered to Lord Berkeley with the documents provided by Lady Warwick, Berkeley was heartened enough to expand the circumference of a park in Michaelwood Chase, but Lady Warwick ordered the new park pales destroyed and began another barrage of lawsuits in 1599–1600. The earls of Leicester and Warwick had long since died, and Lady Warwick lacked the evidence to sustain the suit and the influence to manipulate justice. She decided to give up the lawsuit and pay the court costs.[20]

Besides pursuing the poaching war against Lord Berkeley, Sir Thomas Throckmorton also animated his servants and tenants of the manors of Stinchcombe and Stancombe to advance their claims to common rights

---

[15] Smyth, *Berkeley Manuscripts*, ii. 309–15; PRO STAC 5/B70/3, B81/12, B11/32, B10/14, B12/34.
[16] PRO STAC 5/B1/22, B7/24, B10/14, B14/16, B14/38, B15/31, B23/18, B24/23, B53/26, B56/24, B75/15, B81/12, STAC 7/10/29; Smyth, *Berkeley Manuscripts*, ii. 296–8.
[17] PRO STAC 5/B81/12; see also B12/34.   [18] Smyth, *Berkeley Manuscripts*, ii. 296–8.
[19] Ibid.; PRO STAC 5/B1/22.   [20] Smyth, *Berkeley Manuscripts*, ii. 296–8.

against Lord Berkeley in Cam Woods while pursuing similar tactics on Michaelwood Chase. Lord Berkeley impounded their cattle and sheep and Throckmorton complained to the Council in the Marches of Wales, of which he was a member. The council sent a commission into Gloucestershire to take depositions from the Throckmorton tenants about the extent of their rights of common, but neglected to gather evidence from the Berkeley tenants. Berkeley responded by prosecuting the Throckmorton tenants and servants for perjury and also for raiding his numerous deer parks.[21]

Lord Berkeley and Sir Thomas Throckmorton became reconciled in the last years of the reign of Elizabeth through the mediation of Throckmorton's father-in-law, Sir Richard Berkeley. Both men came to regret their lawsuits, which cost them dearly in legal fees and fines. Throckmorton recognized that his removal from the Council in the Marches of Wales in 1602 and his loss of the queen's favour were caused by his involvement in the poaching war and the other numerous quarrels and suits which he maintained. For his part, Throckmorton helped compose the quarrel between Berkeley and the Lisle–Dudley heir, Sir Robert Sidney, Viscount Lisle and later earl of Leicester, which came to an end in 1609–10. In order to pay for his legal fees, Berkeley disparked his many parks on Michaelwood Chase and cut down most of the wood and timber. He erected an iron furnace and a forge, which he leased to Throckmorton, who made little profit, although Berkeley cleared £3,000.[22] The settlement between Berkeley and Lisle in 1610 called upon Lisle, who was in financial difficulties, to yield all of the lands in litigation to Berkeley for a lump-sum payment of £7,320. Thus ended a lawsuit which had lasted 192 years.[23]

Although the feud between Berkeley and Throckmorton had been settled late in the reign of Elizabeth and the Berkeley–Lisle lawsuit brought to an end in 1610, the poaching war continued for some time thereafter. The violence perpetrated by the Berkeley and Throckmorton–Lisle protagonists had become habitual in the neighbourhood, and, according to John Smyth, the prosecutions in the Court of Star Chamber and the Council in the Marches of Wales continued seven years after Berkeley and Throckmorton had composed their quarrel. Peace came to the Vale of Berkeley only in 1614, when a Star Chamber prosecution broke up 'a compact nest of deer-stealers' consisting of about twenty-five persons. Thereafter, Lord Berkeley's 'game rested more quiet[ly] than in fifty years before they had done'.[24]

---

[21] Ibid. 340; PRO STAC 5/B75/15, B1/22, B24/23.
[22] Smyth, *Berkeley Manuscripts*, ii. 312, 378–9; Williams, *Council in the Marches of Wales*, 307. The Berkeley estates included a total of two chases and twelve parks in Berkeley Hundred alone (Atkyns, *Ancient and Present State of Gloucestershire*, 141–2). After the ironworks ceased to operate, the Berkeleys concluded enclosure agreements for Michaelwood Chase with their tenants (Manning, *Village Revolts*, 127–9).
[23] Smyth, *Berkeley Manuscripts*, ii. 331.   [24] Ibid. 314, 352–4.

The feud between the Berkeleys and the Lisle descendants affords a striking example of the failure of the Tudor monarchs to compose a long-standing quarrel reaching back to before the Wars of the Roses. While it must be admitted that the feud was never allowed to degenerate into actual civil war or aristocratic rebellion under the Tudor monarchs, the animosity was certainly fed by Elizabeth herself, reflected factionalism at court, and was sustained by continuing litigation. The symbolic drama of poaching raids was an integral part of regional culture long before the earl of Leicester appeared upon the scene in Gloucestershire and revived an ancient feud. The corrupt and vicious example of the leading landed families of the county was so pervasive that the violent and lawless habits of Gloucestershire poachers continued for some time after the principal parties to the dispute had settled their differences.

6.2. Local Feuds

The accusations of unlawful hunting which the gentry hurled at one another often originated in disputes about hunting rights and the boundaries and limits of hunting franchises and gamekeeping jurisdictions. The imparkment of lands over which the neighbourhood gentry had freely hunted and the enlargement of existing parks also caused resentment and invited retribution, as did the failure to keep park pales in good repair, for loose deer could do extensive damage to cultivated fields and competed with cattle and sheep for browsewood and herbage. These conflicts were sometimes extensions of long-standing gentry and aristocratic feuds, but threats to hunting rights were frequently perceived as matters of honour and were often causes of violent feuds.

In 1531, when Cannock Chase was still a royal forest, Walter Devereux, Lord Ferrers, claimed a prescriptive right to hunt there. Edward Aston of Tixall and Heywood, Staffordshire, who claimed to be the hereditary master of the game in Cannock Chase, proclaimed that he had a duty to protect the king's deer, and tried to prevent Ferrers from hunting by assembling his servants and the inhabitants of several towns in harness. Aston's men, each of whom was promised a piece of venison for his labour, attacked Lord Ferrers's hunting party and confiscated his greyhounds. In answer to Lord Ferrers's accusations of riot, assault, and conspiracy to commit murder, made in Star Chamber, Aston stated that Ferrers had also mustered his tenants, who 'shamefully' ambushed and tried to murder him.[25]

In Jacobean Dorset a dispute about the boundary of Holt Park led Mountjoy Blount, a ward of Henry, earl of Southampton, to accuse Sir William Uvedale

---

[25] See Ch. 5.1, 5.2.

and seven servants of unlawful hunting. The quarrel was of long standing, and Blount stated that Uvedale had been convicted of unlawful hunting previously. Blount made the extravagant claim that Holt Park was also a forest and a chase, but Uvedale maintained that he had hunted only on his own manor of Horton, which had formerly belonged to the priory of Horton before Holt Park was created.[26]

A violent feud about hunting rights broke out in the parish of Stavely, Derbyshire, in 1545 between the Fresheville and Foljambe families, and was pursued by their descendants into the reign of Elizabeth. Sir Peter Frescheville and Henry, earl of Cumberland, had jointly purchased the manor of Stavely, together with a park stocked with fallow deer. Frescheville was a soldier who had served in Scotland with the earl of Hertford, and he later bought out Cumberland's share of the manor. Frescheville was probably resented as a Protestant and an outsider; he also failed to keep the fences of his deer park in good order and his deer escaped and spoiled the grain in the arable fields in the neighbourhood—including those of the Foljambes. Godfrey Foljambe organized a hunt to kill the loose deer in Handley Wood and called upon his tenants to assist him on at least two occasions in July and August 1545. Foljambe and his tenants chased Frescheville's deer and cattle with hunting horn and hounds and drove them into nets and caltrops. Both the parish clerk and the parson, whom Fresheville employed as game-keepers, testified that Frescheville had ordered a servant to kill Foljambe if he hunted again.[27]

In 1576 Peter Frescheville, esq., son of Sir Peter, accused Godfrey Foljambe the younger, son of Sir Peter's protagonist, of procuring his servants to hunt in Handley Wood on several occasions at Christmas time. It appears that Frescheville had expanded his park into Handley Wood and infringed upon hunting rights claimed by Foljambe, who possessed a hunting lodge in Handley Wood, and excluded Foljambe's tenants from exercising common of pasture in the same place.[28]

The Foljambes had also been taking land into their parks and left themselves open to the same kind of protest. It further appears that they had been drawn into the Talbot–Stanhope feud. In the early 1590s a band of a dozen or so hunters, led by Richard Parker of Sutton, Derbyshire, attacked Foljambe's park at Walton a number of times over a period of two years; the hunters included servants from the household of Francis Leeke, esq., as well as a former servant of George Talbot, late earl of Shrewsbury. Parker and his companions admitted breaking into Walton Park and assaulting the keepers, and stated that they had already been indicted at the Derby assizes for the same offences. Their motive was revenge, because Foljambe had

[26] PRO STAC 8/47/13.
[27] PRO STAC 2/15, fos. 30–8, 321–6; *House of Commons, 1509–1558*, ed. Bindoff, ii. 154–5, 172–3.   [28] PRO STAC 5/F8/18.

procured his servants to kill many of the deer belonging to Francis Leeke, their master.[29]

Quarrels concerning forest and game offices were particularly fierce, because they involved status and honour as well as profit. Such was the case in the dispute between Henry Herbert, second earl of Pembroke, and Sir Henry Berkeley concerning the lieutenancy and stewardship of Selwood Forest, Somerset. Sir Henry Berkeley of Stoke and Bruton, Somerset, was the son of Sir Maurice Berkeley and cousin to Henry, eleventh Lord Berkeley. In addition to being keeper of the well-stocked park of Norwood, formerly belonging to the abbot of Glastonbury, Sir Henry had inherited the office of lieutenant and deputy-keeper of Selwood from his father, who had been granted that office by William, first earl of Pembroke, in 1570. The offices of lieutenant, steward, and keeper of Selwood Forest attached by hereditary right to the earl's manor of Stoke Trister.[30] Sir Henry claimed that the second earl had confirmed that grant and that he had lived in the keeper's lodge and enjoyed the profits of the office for the next twenty years without hindrance. However, in 1591 or 1592 the second earl ordered his own underkeepers to take possession of the lodge and to prevent Berkeley's men from discharging their duties. The two made numerous accusations concerning unlawful hunting against one another's keepers.[31] Berkeley replied to Pembroke's use of force by hiring reinforcements for his keepers from amongst tinkers, convicted felons, and other dissolute persons and attempted to force a confrontation at Staverdale Fair, within the forest, on 25 June 1593. Berkeley's men swelled the crowd to a thousand persons in the small forest hamlet and they trooped up and down in front of the houses where Pembroke's underkeepers dwelled in an effort to provoke a fight. Finally they broke into one of the houses, overturned the furniture, and jostled the inhabitants. A number of Berkeley's men were bound over to the quarter sessions for their assaults. Subsequently, at the Bridgwater sessions, which were presided over by Sir John Popham, CJKB, Berkeley and his confederates on the Somerset bench got up very early in the morning and released Berkeley's servants before the other justices had assembled. When the lord chief justice arrived and attempted to reopen the proceedings, Berkeley launched into a tirade against the chief witness, Pembroke's head keeper, and called him a 'whore hunter and baggage companion'.[32]

Berkeley continued to hire 'desperate persons' to help him regain control of Selwood, and Pembroke complained that Berkeley led 'troops and

---

[29] PRO STAC 5/F17/15; *House of Commons, 1558–1603*, ed. Hasler, ii. 144–5; MacCaffrey, 'Talbot and Stanhope', 73–85. See also PRO STAC 3/5/60, and R. B. Manning, 'Patterns of Violence in Early Tudor Enclosure Riots', *Albion*, 6. 2 (1974), 122–3.

[30] *House of Commons, 1558–1603*, ed. Hasler, i. 430–1; *VCH Somerset*, ii. 304 n., 567–8; PRO STAC 5/B61/15, B87/34, P6/36.

[31] PRO STAC 5/B61/15, P6/36.   [32] PRO STAC 5/P6/36, P1/2.

companies' of friends and followers into the forest to hunt the king's deer at his pleasure. In November 1597 Berkeley regained possession of the keeper's lodge in Brewscombe Walk, which he used as a base for destroying the deer or driving them into the purlieus where his own lands were located. Although Berkeley's claim to possession of the keeper's lodge was declared invalid by the Court of King's Bench, Pembroke was unable to regain possession. In 1600 the attorney-general, Sir Edward Coke, intervened in the case with a Star Chamber prosecution and accused Berkeley of deer-stealing and harbouring felons, including a highwayman, John Symmes, who was supposed to be awaiting execution in Somerset Gaol. When Pembroke's keepers attempted to reassert their jurisdiction and confiscated a buck from Berkeley's men, the latter threatened to muster the whole town of Bruton to recover the same. Friends dissuaded him from pursuing the quarrel himself, so he sent his son and half a dozen friends and supporters to recover the buck, so that he 'might not endure the soil and disgrace to have a deer taken from his men' by Pembroke's keepers. Berkeley's men attacked the house where Pembroke's keepers lived, recovered the buck, and beat them and 'left them for dead'. Witnesses who tried to halt the fighting stated that Berkeley's son and supporters declared 'that they would not be taken or bound by any law, but would keep themselves out of reach of the same'. The buck was thrown over the back of a horse, and the hunters marched in 'triumphing, warlike and rebellious manner' back to Bruton.[33]

Although the reason why Pembroke attempted to eject Berkeley from the keepership of Selwood Forest is not explicitly stated, it seems reasonable to infer that it was because of the latter's notoriously corrupt and lawless behaviour. Berkeley's keepers killed deer on a grand scale and they enticed forest dwellers into hunting and then extorted fines from them for unlawful hunting.[34] Berkeley harboured felons and obstructed justice, and was, through Pembroke's influence, dismissed as deputy-lieutenant—although subsequently reinstated by the Privy Council.[35] In 1591 Berkeley brought an action of libel against a soldier in the regiment, which he had raised during the time of the threatened Spanish invasion, for saying that Berkeley had made a profit of £40 by overcharging his men for their uniform coats. The libel was spread by word-of-mouth and in writing all over the country and did much damage to Berkeley's reputation. Even on this occasion, Berkeley did not scruple to hand out bribes in an attempt to suborn witnesses, according to the testimony of the vicar of Ashill.[36] It appears that only Berkeley's death in 1601 put an end to his disreputable activities.

Although Sir Henry Berkeley's title to the keeper's lodge had been declared

---

[33] PRO STAC 5/A48/7.   [34] PRO STAC 5/B66/33, B87/16.
[35] *House of Commons, 1558–1603*, ed. Hasler, i. 430–1.
[36] PRO STAC 5/B87/38, B83/28.

invalid, his son and heir Sir Maurice was referred to as the lieutenant and keeper of Selwood in 1605. It appears that Sir Maurice regained the patronage of the Pembrokes when the 'generous and open-handed' William, third earl, succeeded to the title in 1601. The same outlaws whom Sir Henry had employed to slaughter the royal deer in Selwood—including the notorious John Symmes *alias* Jenkin Symmes, condemned highwayman now pardoned, but bound to his good behaviour—continued in the service of Sir Maurice Berkeley. In 1605 Sir Carew Raleigh, the lieutenant of Gillingham Forest, complained that Symmes and a number of Sir Maurice's underkeepers, together with Sir Maurice's brother, had havocked the deer in Gillingham Forest.[37] At the same time, deer-stealing and lawlessness had become so widespread on the Somerset–Wiltshire–Dorset border that Sir Maurice was hard pressed to defend the deer in Selwood against the depredations of rival bands of hunters—including those made up of persons claiming to be purlieu men.[38] John Symmes was still in Berkeley's service in 1622 when he was accused of raiding Lord Stourton's park. Twenty of Lord Stourton's friends, servants, and keepers revenged themselves by spoiling the deer in Selwood Forest. Symmes was a close prisoner in the custody of the Court of Star Chamber in 1622, but he continued in Berkeley's employ at least as late as 1625.[39] In that year, the keeper of Lady Rachael Hopton's park was accused by Sir Maurice Berkeley of unlawful hunting. His answer to the Star Chamber complaint makes it clear that Berkeley and Symmes were working their old extortion racket again. They had invited Lady Rachael's keeper, Hugh Fry, to hunt in Selwood in exchange for a grant of the same courtesy in Lady Rachael's park. When Fry hunted in Selwood, he was prosecuted for poaching and presumably fined.[40]

In Elizabethan Lancashire numerous gentry competed for a limited number of forest and game offices. These were dispensed under the patronage of the Duchy of Lancaster and the earls of Derby, and they tended to be concentrated in a few hands. Sir Richard Sherburne enjoyed the favour of the earl of Derby as the master forester of Bowland Forest, but he was unable to get along with Sir Richard Houghton, the bow-bearer and master of the game of the same forest. Whenever Houghton issued warrants allowing friends and guests to hunt in Bowland, Sherburne's servants would confiscate their weapons and dogs. Houghton's underkeepers frequently accused Sherburne's men of unlawful hunting in return.[41] Sherburne's relations with John Calvert, master of the game of Wyresdale Forest, were also bad. In 1585 Sherburne stated that Calvert had allowed the deer in Wyresdale to become so depleted that he had to bring his new hounds into Bowland in order to 'flesh' them, and had also invited many gentlemen to join him

---

[37] *Aubrey's Brief Lives*, ed. Dick, 145; PRO STAC 8/246/21, 47/4.
[38] PRO STAC 8/47/3.   [39] PRO STAC 8/73/13.
[40] PRO STAC 8/47/4.   [41] PRO DL 1/199/S15, 105/S3, 149/A16.

in chasing a large stag which had escaped from Bowland. Sherburne also accused Calvert of confiscating one of his hounds when his rangers attempted to rechase deer from Wyresdale back into Bowland. Calvert's men cut the dog's ears off and let it loose again as a warning to the men of Bowland.[42] The Talbots and Braddills were also rivals of the Sherburnes and frequently hunted in Bowland without permission—taking numerous guests with them as they did so. In 1590 the attorney-general of the Duchy of Lancaster declared that the deer in duchy parks were to be reserved for royal recreation and fee-deer for duchy officials only. In a remote place like Bowland Forest, which the queen was unlikely ever to visit, this meant that the deer were reserved for the Sherburnes and the occasional visiting duchy official. Consequently, the many local gentry families who were envious of the few who possessed forest and game offices felt free to continue hunting in the various constituent parts of the Forest of Lancaster.[43]

6.3. Official Corruption

The woodland societies where illegal deer-hunting flourished provided the breeding grounds for an alarming degree of lawlessness. Aristocratic and gentry feuds were an inescapable part of the social and political scene of Tudor and early Stuart England, but conflicts concerning hunting rights and franchises and the competition for forest and game offices afforded the occasions for particularly nasty and violent encounters. The increasing legal complexity and social restrictiveness of the Game Laws—especially following the accession of James I—undoubtedly made the task of enforcing those laws more difficult. It was not always an easy matter to distinguish lawful from unlawful hunting; defendants and lawyers could employ compelling legal arguments to defeat prosecution and persuade sympathetic juries to acquit. Yet, when all is said, it remains clear that large-scale, sustained poaching could flourish only where corrupt magistrates protected poachers or were prepared to look the other way.

Early in the reign of Henry VIII, Cuthbert Tunstall, later bishop of London and Durham, complained to the Duchy Court of Lancaster that John Claghton and his servants had repeatedly hunted deer, killed rabbits, and assaulted the keepers in Fairthwaite Park, Lancashire, which belonged to his nephew and ward, Marmaduke Tunstall. The defendants were indicted at the Lancashire sessions and bound over to appear before the chancellor of the duchy in the Court of Duchy Chamber, but Lawrence Starkey, the undersheriff, refused to apprehend the defendants and confine them to prison as ordered. Claghton continued at large, hunting and hawking as a

[42] PRO DL 1/133/S7.   [43] PRO DL 1/135/A50, 149/A11.

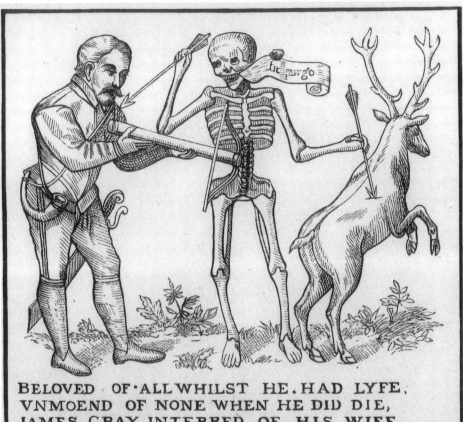

BELOVED OF·ALL WHILST HE.HAD LYFE,
VNMOEND OF NONE WHEN HE DID DIE,
JAMES GRAY, INTERRED OF HIS WIFE,
NEER TO HIS DEAHS SIGNE BRASSE DOH IYE,
YEARES THIRTIE FYVE, IN GOOD RENOWNNE
PARKE AND HOVSE KEPER IN THIS TOWNE,
OBHT 12 DIE DECEMBRIS A° DNI 1591
ÆTATIS SVE 69 ·

1. Facsimile of the monumental brass of James Gray, keeper of Hunsdon Park, in the Church of Hunsdon, Hertfordshire, (reproduced in E. P. Shirley, *Some Account of English Deer Parks* (1867), facing p. 55; Bodleian Library)

2. Engraving depicting various hunting scenes in the deer park at Welbeck, Nottinghamshire (from William Cavendish, duke of Newcastle (1592–1676), *New Method and Extraordinary Invention* (1657), a famous treatise on horsemanship; Bodleian Library)

3. Scene of Nonsuch Palace, Surrey, a royal hunting lodge, showing in the fore-ground mounted hunters and hounds pursuing a buck (early seventeenth-century oil painting, Flemish School; Fitzwilliam Museum, Cambridge)

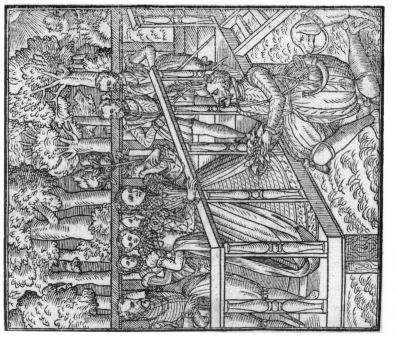

5. Woodcut depicting King James I about to take assay of a buck (from *The Noble Art* [*sic*] *of Venerie or Hunting* (1611), 133; Bodleian Library).

4. Woodcut of a huntsman presenting the fewments of a hart to Queen Elizabeth, who receives the report positioned on a 'standing' (from *The Noble Arte of Venerie or Hunting* (1575), 95, originally attributed to George Turberville (or Turbervile), but now accepted as having been written by George Gascoigne)

6. Oil portrait of Henry, Prince of Wales, and John, Lord Harington of Exton,
dressed in green hunting costumes by Robert Peake (1604, Royal Collection);
Prince Henry is drawing his sword in preparation for slitting the belly of a stag

7. Woodcut depicting James I and the royal court dining *al fresco* in a forest (from
The Noble Art of Venerie or Hunting (1611), 91; Bodleian Library). This illustration
first appeared in *The Noble Arte of Venerie or Hunting* (1575). In the 1611 edition,
the image of James I has been superimposed on that of Queen Elizabeth.

8. Woodcut depicting a mounted hunter and two keepers of hounds with their brachs, a type of scenting hound or mastif, pursuing their prey (from *The Noble Art of Venerie or Hunting* (1611), 35; Bodleian Library)

9. Long cushion cover, showing hawking scene on the left and hunting scene on the right with a mounted hunter blowing a horn accompanied by a hound pursuing a buck (English, about 1575–1600; Victorian and Albert Museum, English renaissance, Primary Galleries, T. 79–1946)

companion to Edward Stanley, esq.[44] In Henrician Cheshire magistrates can also be found acting in concert to defeat attempts to punish unlawful hunting. Sir William Brereton wrote to Thomas Cromwell in 1538 that George Mullington had confessed to killing the king's deer in Delamere Forest and had given evidence against his accomplices. Brereton had issued a warrant to arrest Mullington and imprison him in Chester Castle, 'but he was rescued by Dame Julian, wife to . . . Sir Piers Dutton, who keeps him there without punishment'. Brereton was unable to persuade the sheriff to arrest Mullington, and reported that the sheriff had made a false return on the arrest warrant.[45]

Sir Henry Bainton, JP and deputy justice in eyre of the forests under Charles, earl of Nottingham, was the very model of a poaching magistrate. In 1606 Richard Batten, the deputy-warden of Chippenham (also known as Pewsham) Forest in Wiltshire, accused Bainton of extensive unlawful hunting and illegal cutting of timber valued at £300. While serving as sheriff, Bainton had caused the stones marking the boundaries of the forest to be dug up and removed so that subsequent sheriffs could not certify to the Exchequer what the actual boundaries were. He built some twenty illegal cottages upon the waste in the forest, which he rented to persons who spoiled the game and engaged in wood-stealing. Bainton had also enclosed a portion of the forest waste and constructed an illegal park enclosed by a pale one mile in circumference and built one-way deer leaps leading from the forest into his park. Bainton and his friends also forestalled deer and drove them into the park. Within a period of two years, Batten specified six occasions on which Bainton or his servants and kinsmen, in bands as large as fifteen, had hunted within the forest. Bainton hid some of his accomplices to keep them from testifying against him and had one of them beaten when he did give evidence.[46]

Another Wiltshire magistrate, Sir Henry Moody, frequently hunted within the Forest of Braden. He claimed to be a purlieu man and exploited his hunting rights for all they were worth, but refused to allow the rangers to rechase the royal deer, claiming liberty of free warren and absolute possession of deer on his lands and those of his tenants. Moody's prosecution for unlawful hunting by the attorney-general in 1620 may have resulted from a quarrel between him and George Ivy concerning precedence on the commission of the peace, but the Star Chamber judges found enough evidence against Moody to convict him and fine him £300.[47]

Deer-stealing flourished in the vicinity of Hatfield Chase, Yorkshire,

---

[44] *Pleadings and Depositions in the Duchy Court of Lancaster*, ii. 237–9.

[45] *L&P, Hen. VIII*, XIII. i, no. 17; for a Yorkshire example of the rescue of a poacher by his master, see above, Ch. 2.

[46] PRO STAC 8/47/19; *House of Commons, 1558–1603*, ed. Hasler, i. 411.

[47] PRO STAC 8/28/15; A. Wall, 'Faction in Local Politics, 1580–1620: Struggles for Supremacy in Wiltshire', *Wilts. Arch. Mag.*, 72–3 (1980), 131–2.

because of the corruption of the keepers and local magistrates. John Estofte of Estofte, Yorkshire, who was on the commission of the peace of both Yorkshire and Lincolnshire, hired poor men to supply him with venison and deerskins for the market between 1614 and 1617. The attorney-general accused him of using his official position to shield his confederates instead of committing them to prison. This he did by taking inadequate bonds from poor men who had nothing to lose by disappearing, or by refusing to arrest those whom he hired to do his work.[48] In 1618 Sir Robert Swift was accused of abusing his office of bow-bearer of Hatfield Chase for the previous eighteen years by killing the king's deer and misappropriating the hay intended to carry the deer through the winter. He had allowed the keeper's lodge to fall into ruin and so had to remove himself to Doncaster, where he stirred up many quarrels. He once raised a force of one hundred persons, who committed a riot at an inn and then paraded through the streets with drawn swords to the mayor's house and menaced and insulted him. Although Swift had been dropped from the commission of the peace, he continued to sit at the quarter sessions and usurped the authority of a justice. A violent quarrel with Thomas Mountenay about possession of a pew in Doncaster Church led Mountenay to complain about Swift's corrupt and violent behaviour, but in his answer Swift stated that he never knew Mountenay or his father 'to be without provision of red deer and other venison . . . ready dressed in their houses'.[49]

In the honour of Ampthill, astride the Bedfordshire–Buckinghamshire border, a cluster of seven royal deer parks stocked with red and fallow deer and a variety of game constituted a strong temptation to the local inhabitants. The park pales were very rotten and many had been blown down by windstorms. Those that remained were pulled down by the numerous poachers who swarmed into the parks and devastated the deer and game. One gang which the attorney-general singled out consisted of nineteen persons from the villages of Whaddon, Buckinghamshire, and Shillington, Ridgemont, and Husborne Crawley, Bedfordshire. All of them were servants, tenants, or dependents of George Russell of Ridgemont, esq., a Bedfordshire justice of the peace who sustained and protected them, hindered prosecution by the park keepers, and obstructed examination by the other justices of the peace. The defendants, who bound themselves together by secret oaths never to give evidence against one another, openly boasted about their steadfast loyalty and solidarity and threatened anyone who might be thinking about testifying with murder and mayhem. The park keepers were beaten and terrorized into keeping out of the way. Between 1614 and 1619 the attorney-general estimated that Russell's gang, which ranged over a four-county area, carried away 327 red and fallow deer. Other losses

---

[48] PRO STAC 8/27/5.   [49] PRO STAC 8/217/18.

included a thousand hare, fourteen hundred rabbits, five thousand pheasants, a thousand partridges, and two hundred herons—most of which were sold on the market.[50]

Sir William Throckmorton of Tortworth, bt., the son and heir of the eleventh Lord Berkeley's old protagonist, was, perhaps, one of the most corrupt magistrates in England. He was a justice of the peace and the chief ranger of Corse Lawn Chase, which appears to have possessed the status of a forest. His legacy, like that of his father, who had been the keeper of the chase, was a sordid one, and Corse Lawn remained a nest of vipers even after Sir William ceased to be the chief ranger. Sometime between 1613 and 1617 Sir Francis Bacon, AG, prosecuted Sir William Throckmorton in Star Chamber for killing at least eighty deer. Throckmorton, who had sold the family seat of Tortworth in 1608, was in serious financial troubles, and he purveyed venison to innkeepers, used it to secure loans from moneylenders, and paid his tailors' bills with it. Some of it ended up on the London Market. Throckmorton also sold unauthorized licences to hunt on Corse Lawn Chase. In his duties as a justice of the peace, Throckmorton was not content to take bribes in order to show favour to defendants. He also falsely accused innocent persons of unlawful hunting in order to extort more money. Attorney-General Bacon charged that Throckmorton had falsely accused Thomas Good, a 10-year-old boy, of burglary. When the boy's father refused to pay the bribe which he demanded, Throckmorton ordered his servants to strip the boy naked and whip him. A violent and abusive man, Throckmorton, on various occasions, stabbed Walter Longe, his deputy-keeper, wounded a messenger because a message from his brother-in-law displeased him, and verbally abused and physically assaulted a fellow justice of the peace, who insisted upon sustaining a true bill against a defendant from whom Throckmorton had taken a bribe. Many other assaults against the young and the old were alleged against him.[51]

When Sir Thomas Throckmorton died in 1607, his son inherited the office of keeper of Corse Lawn Chase and appears to have sold the office of chief ranger to Sir Richard Tracy of Hosfield, bt., 'a man daring to attempt any unlawful act or enterprise whatsoever'. With the help of nine or ten confederates 'of great kindred and alliance in the country and of great revenue and power', Tracy killed deer valued at £600 over a period of some five years in a reserve which was normally stocked with about a thousand deer. Not content with systematically slaughtering the deer in Corse Lawn Chase, Tracy and his hunting companions, operating in bands of up to twenty persons, ranged as far away as Woodstock in Oxfordshire—another royal hunting preserve twelve miles distant from Corse Lawn Chase. Tracy had such an abundance of venison that he fed it to his servants the year round,

---

[50] PRO STAC 8/24/12.   [51] PRO STAC 8/23/15.

sold it to alehouses, and used it to pay off debts to moneylenders and attorneys practising in church courts. Tracy also attempted to induce persons living on the edge of Corse Lawn Chase to hunt on the chase, and then extorted money from them to avoid prosecution for unlawful hunting. He was alleged to have collected £100 in bribes in this manner. He also enticed young boys to fish upon the common waste of his manor of Hasfield, and then imprisoned them 'in a dark and loathsome place and kept them without meat or drink by the space of three days together' until their parents or friends 'did redeem and ransome them with a good sum of money to the value of twenty pounds at the least'.[52] The complaint against Tracy in Star Chamber was brought by William Longe, gent., who had been the much-abused deputy of Sir William Throckmorton when he held the office of chief ranger. Longe stated that he had already brought Tracy's misdeeds to the attention of the Council in the Marches of Wales and the chief justice in eyre for the forests south of Trent, but Tracy had so far escaped unpunished.[53]

Probably most keepers of royal parks and forests took more venison then they were allowed as official perquisites, and they needed to replenish their game preserves from time to time. William Alcock, keeper of the royal park of Grindon, Staffordshire, did his restocking from a park belonging to Robert Meverell of Throwley. It appears that Alcock had been supplying venison to some of the neighbouring magistrates and gentry when Meverell insisted on making a Star Chamber matter out of it. Meverell's attempt to rechase his deer back into his own park was repulsed by hunters procured by Sir George and Dame Grace Manners. When a Star Chamber commission was issued to examine witnesses at Bakewell, George Parker, one of the defendants, and Sir George Fulwood, a JP, suborned witnesses to give false testimony. When the clerk refused to write down the perjured evidence, they denied him a seat and took down the depositions themselves.[54]

6.4. Local Communities

Deer parks often encroached on common wastes and woodland pasture, and, while most deer parks had first been impaled in the late-medieval period, popular memories of seigneurial assaults on the commons persisted and periodically erupted in anti-enclosure riots. The fences of deer parks were frequently in a state of disrepair, and escaped deer damaged crops

---

[52] Although only sheriffs were to have custody of felons, the law was less clear concerning the custody of those charged with lesser offences. The only remedy was to bring an action for false or unjust imprisonment (Pugh, *Imprisonment in Medieval England*, 52, 216–17).
[53] PRO STAC 8/195/29.   [54] PRO STAC 8/216/25.

and competed with cattle for browse and fodder. It was virtually impossible to confine rabbits to their warrens until the invention of wire fences, and, while they did not range as far as deer, they did more intensive damage. Villages which retained open or common fields were, of course, especially vulnerable. If a person's property was located within a free chase, he was not allowed to enclose his cultivated fields. The inhabitants of village and manorial communities might take collective action against deer and conies themselves, or they might invite or allow experienced hunters to come in and do the job for them. But the presence of hardened poachers in a community could cut both ways; their violent and lawless habits sometimes made it necessary for villagers to defend themselves against the poachers.

There is a remarkable example of a kind of skimmington or charivari directed against a park owner in late Henrician Nottinghamshire, in which both the local community and the county community participated. George Wastnes of Heydon, esq., had carved a new park out of a wooded common waste claimed by John Hercy, esq., and his tenants on the manor of Grove. The park was not fully enclosed by pales and ditches and was probably unlicensed. All of the many witnesses agreed that loose deer from Heydon Park had damaged tenants' crops and the manorial woods. The punishment of Wastnes, in the form of two large hunts in 1543 and 1544, must have involved considerable preparation. On the first occasion, the hunt lasted for eight days and, on the second, the sheriff of Nottinghamshire and eighty members of the county gentry participated. The inhabitants of seven villages also joined in, led by the bailiff of Gamston and a parson armed with a bow. The schoolmaster of Gamston led thirty of his scholars acting as beaters, who, with sixty hounds, helped drive Wastnes's deer into a battery of eight buckstalls. There was much drinking before and after the hunt, and the whole business had a festive air about it. Afterwards, venison was distributed among the villagers.[55]

Such disputes were complex; they touched upon popular grievances and were fuelled by aristocratic and gentry feuds. In 1609, after the High Peak Forest of Derbyshire had been disafforested and its lands sold off, numerous cottages were erected in the former forest and the population grew very rapidly. The royal tenants and borderers, who had formerly possessed common of pasture within the forest, were outraged and organized themselves into 'several troops and companies'; in a number of riots in May and June of 1609 and again in 1610 they assaulted the farmer of the new owners, drove off his cattle, attacked the gamekeepers, and exterminated the deer. The leaders of this protest were stirred up by Lord Cavendish of Chatsworth, and their animosity was directed at Gilbert, earl of Shrewsbury, the master

---

[55] PRO STAC 2/21/24, 23/52, 28/117, 118; *House of Commons, 1509–1558*, ed. Bindoff, ii. 345–6.

of the game of the Peak Forest and the chief justice in eyre north of the Trent.[56]

Smallholders sought to protect crops in unfenced fields in various ways. In Neroche Forest, Somerset, Thomas Wilmont, a husbandman whose holding lay within the purlieus of the forest, hired a small boy, William Roswell, to drive off any deer or cattle which wandered into his corn. When Wilmont went out to fetch the boy home, the former was attacked and badly wounded by the rangers of Neroche. The rangers charged that Wilmont and three companions were armed and equipped with crossbows and greyhounds and had killed a deer, and they caused Wilmont to be prosecuted in Star Chamber. Wilmont answered that this was a tactic to extort an unjust composition from him and to compel him to drop his suit at common law against the rangers for injuring him.[57]

Many tenants kepts dogs to guard their cultivated fields. One witness deposed that in Lincolnshire the smallholders of Barnetby-le-Wold, who maintained open fields, allowed greyhounds to roam in their corn to prevent damage by deer escaping from Retleby Park. The owner of the park, William Tyrwhitt, insisted that the loose hounds were often accompanied by townspeople, who between 1618 and 1620 killed forty of his deer. Tyrwhitt pastured cattle in Retleby Park, and his deer had to look elsewhere to feed themselves.[58] In addition to the prohibition in forest law against unexpediated hunting dogs, manorial custom usually forbade the possession of hounds by unqualified persons, but such prohibitions were widely evaded. In the barony of Kendal in Westmorland in 1614, a defendant accused of coursing a hare in Holme Park said that his greyhounds were trained to pursue foxes, which were vermin, and not deer or hare. Since his indictment, he could no longer hunt foxes with dogs, and he and his neighbours now had no way to protect their sheep against such predators which were common in the neighbourhood.[59]

The Lords Berkeley maintained a huge rabbit warren at Tetbury, Gloucestershire, which was a perennial nuisance and a source of friction between the Berkeleys and their tenants. The manor of Tetbury belonged to the Berkeleys between 1502 and 1633, when it was sold to trustees of the parish of Tetbury. Tetbury was a market town and supported thirteen taverns in 1594. The manor was usually reserved for one of the Berkeley sons, and the heads of the family never lived there. As early as the reign of Philip and Mary, the tenants complained that the rabbits from the warren and other game had consumed corn growing over an area of one hundred acres. At that time, the two sons of John Gastrell, gent., together with friends and servants, attempted to destroy a large number of conies on their father's

---

[56] PRO STAC 8/11/14, 15.   [57] PRO STAC 8/157/29.
[58] PRO STAC 8/29/2.   [59] PRO STAC 8/21/16.

land adjoining the warren, when they were attacked by six or seven warreners.[60] The Star Chamber records reveal that there were further attacks on Tetbury Warren in 1566 and 1576.[61] John Smyth of Nibley states that between 1583 and 1608 there was a long series of lawsuits, mostly in King's Bench, but partly in Chancery, between Thomas Estcourt of Tetbury, a bencher of Grey's Inn, and John Savage, Lord Berkeley's farmer, arising out of disputes with the tenants. There was not only the continuing problem of the rabbit warren; Savage was also accused of overcharging the manorial waste with the seigneurial flock.[62] After 1579 the attacks on Tetbury Warren were led by various members of the Webb family, three of whom were in the service of Henry, eleventh Lord Berkeley's enemy, Sir Thomas Throckmorton. Further raids, led by the Webbs against Tetbury Warren, were made in 1596 and 1618. In 1596 the Webbs and another thirty or so defendants in a Star Chamber prosecution were also accused of attacking Berkeley New Park in Michaelwood Chase. It is clear that Throckmorton exploited the discontent of the Tetbury tenants to further his own quarrel with Lord Berkeley.[63] Henry, Lord Berkeley, was regarded as one of the most benevolent landlords in England, yet there is abundant evidence that he invariably put his interests before those of his tenants.[64]

Complaints concerning rabbit warrens become more frequent after the middle of the sixteenth century, and undoubtedly reflect a rapidly expanding market for rabbit fur and flesh. After enduring the decay of three hundred acres of arable as a consequence of a new cony warren, the tenants of the manor of Warminster, Wiltshire, were on the verge of abandoning tillage. Instead they destroyed the rabbits by digging trenches across the warren and turning ferrets loose to drive them into nets. Between 15 and 24 December 1550 the tenants killed one hundred couple of conies. The decision was probably not unconnected with the desire to enjoy rabbit pie for their Christmas festivities! Lord Mordaunt, the lord of the manor, brought in a Welshman to start a second warren, and the first warrener brought suit against both the tenants and the Welsh warrener.[65]

Philip, Lord Stanhope, hereditary keeper of Thorneywood Chase, Nottinghamshire, was both a harsh landlord and an extortionate game officer, who aroused much resentment in his tenants and neighbours. In 1615 Stanhope prosecuted a number of smallholders for coursing a buck in Thorneywood Chase and driving it towards a gap in a hedge set with ropes and snares on the enclosed grounds of John Walker, one of the defendants. This caused the buck to be hanged, which may have been a symbolic form of punishment, since the defendants claimed that deer from the chase had

[60] *VCH Glos.* xi. 265; PRO STAC 4/4/61.   [61] PRO STAC 5/B13/37, B53/15.
[62] Smyth, *Berkeley Manuscripts*, ii. 348–9.   [63] PRO STAC 5/B15/30, B53/26, 8/28/12.
[64] Stone, *Crisis of the Aristocracy*, 144; Manning, *Village Revolts*, 127–9.
[65] PRO STAC 3/1/64.

done much damage to their corn. The buck was killed and carried away to John Walker's house, where it was divided and shared. Two of the defendants, it turns out, were also woodwards of Sherwood Forest. In their answer the defendants described Stanhope's harsh and arbitrary treatment of them: they had been arrested without warrant, denied bail, and imprisoned in Nottingham Castle for seven weeks before being released. Then they were tried and acquitted of the charge of unlawful hunting by a jury in the Swanimote Court of Sherwood Forest, the earl of Rutland presiding. Stanhope's underkeepers later served them with a process from the Court of Star Chamber. Asked if they would not prefer to compound with Stanhope rather than spend their money defending themselves before the Court of Star Chamber in London, the defendants, who were poor men, claimed that they paid compositions to Stanhope of between 7s. and 10s. each, yet found that they still had to travel to London and answer Stanhope's complaint. The defendants bitterly lamented that Stanhope was a quarrelsome and malicious person, who would not even permit people to walk through the chase, and frequently tormented his neighbours with litigation. They also charged that, despite Stanhope's boast about preserving and increasing the number of deer in Thorneywood Chase, there was none who was so great a destroyer of the king's deer there as Stanhope himself—despite a recent royal proclamation that forest and game officers were to forbear taking their fee-deer. They added that Stanhope also despoiled the woods by cutting copses reserved for the crown, and allowed his keepers to graze their cattle in the chase—thus forcing the deer to range over a wider area in search of herbage.[66]

In order to protect his deer against poachers, Stanhope hired more keepers and claimed that he had increased the size of the herd from four hundred head in his father's time to sixteen hundred head. However, since the fodder and browse in the chase were inadequate to feed that number of deer, Stanhope compelled his tenants to furnish hay from their own stocks of fodder and to allow the deer to feed upon their meadows and cornfields. Stanhope's tenants rebelled against this and threatened to abandon their tenancies unless Stanhope granted them rent abatements, Although Stanhope insisted that he had reduced their rents, it was not enough to allay the discontent of his tenants. It appears that the tenants, beginning in June 1620, invited a band of hunters from Nottingham—a mixed group consisting mostly of artisans with one gentlemen—to come and remove some of the deer. This the Nottingham hunters did with a vengeance—hunting on at least three occasions over the next seven months. During one raid they killed thirty deer and wounded another thirty.[67]

There were a number of unpopular landlords in the West Riding of

---

[66] PRO STAC 8/259/11.   [67] PRO STAC 8/259/10.

Yorkshire whose behaviour offended neighbours and tenants and elicited community punishment. One such person was Christopher Danby. His cruelty towards his wife and tenants and his riotous living outraged his kinsmen, neighbours, and servants. Danby, who resided at Leighton Hall, Mashamshire, was a well-connected recusant squire. A cousin of Sir Thomas Wentworth, later earl of Strafford, he married Frances Parker, daughter of William, Lord Morley and Monteagle, who had an income of £1,000 p.a. She left her husband within one month of marriage. Subsequently, a reconciliation took place, but the marriage was a troubled one and Monteagle refused to settle the marriage portion on Danby until he had granted his wife a jointure of one-third of his lands. Danby's brother-in-law described him as 'unthriftily disposed' and given to 'riot and ill-company whereby he did grow very dissolute'. He also evicted tenants and tore down the cottage of an old man who had squatted on his land. His servants, offended because he beat his wife, prepared to stage a riding of the stang, a kind of skimmington, but were headed off by the intervention of a Danby relative. Another kinsman with the same name, Christopher Danby, stirred up the neighbourhood against the squire of Leighton Hall, and eventually succeeded in having him declared an outlaw and a bankrupt.[68]

Others were prepared to inflict the punishment which Danby's servants were dissuaded from carrying out. Between 1607 and 1622, two years before Danby's death, several bands of deer-stealers repeatedly raided Danby's chase of Mashamshire, killed his deer, and assaulted his keepers. One gang was led by Philip Shaw of Nidderdale, yeom., a professional poacher who frequently hunted in the various game reserves of the earl of Cumberland and who was often procured to do so by Sir John York of Gowthwaite. In 1622 another poaching gang, led by Peter Craven, yeom., and made up largely of his kinsmen, invaded Leighton Hall while Danby was away, and demanded venison, menaced the servants, and uttered threats against Danby. All of these incursions by the various bands of West Riding deer-stealers were accompanied by much boasting concerning their exploits, and appear to have been conceived as elaborate skimmingtons.[69]

Francis Clifford, fourth earl of Cumberland, was by far the most powerful landowner in the West Riding of Yorkshire. He possessed several very large free chases, which extended, so he claimed, over other peoples' manorial wastes, demesnes, and arable fields, and he assumed that his hunting rights extinguished everyone else's right to hunt. In 1608 Cumberland complained against George Clapham, esq., lord of the manor of Beamsley, and accused him of procuring his servants and tenants and hiring two poaching gangs led by Philip Shaw and John Tennant of Chapelhouse to kill Cumberland's

---

[68] C. Whone, 'Christopher Danby of Masham and Farnley', *Thorseby Society*, 37 (1936–42), 1–28.   [69] PRO STAC 8/102/5, 6, 116/16, 17, 18.

deer. Cumberland alleged eleven acts of unlawful hunting in the chases of Littondale and Barden and Skipton in Craven, resulting in the loss of eighteen deer over a two-year period. He further stated that Clapham and Tennant were receivers of stolen venison. Cumberland's lands at Bolton Priory and the manor of Beamsley were separated by the River Wharfe, which Cumberland's deer could easily cross when the water was low. Cumberland and his ancestors had made small effort to confine their deer, and the deer had extensively damaged the crops in Beamsley ever since the time of Clapham's grandfather. Clapham was in the habit of hiring four or five extra servants to watch over the corn when it was ripening, and he furnished them with greyhounds. The servants and hounds frequently pursued the deer across the river into Cumberland's lands. Cumberland usually imprisoned Clapham's servants and refused to release them until Clapham had made a submission. When Clapham complained about the presence of Cumberland's deer, the latter would muster all of his tenants in Bolton, and, without asking permission, would send them across the river with his gamekeepers to trample through the fields of grain belonging to Clapham and the Beamsley tenants in order to rechase the deer back to Bolton Priory. The dispute had been smouldering for several generations and Clapham always forcibly resisted the invasion of the Bolton men as his grandfather had done before him.[70]

Francis, earl of Cumberland, possessed another hunting reserve in Westmorland on the Scottish border where James I had once hunted. The reserve consisted of Uglebeard or Onglebeard Chase, which Cumberland claimed was a forest, and Whinfell Park. The park was not properly fenced and Cumberland's servants overstocked the park and chase with sheep and cattle, which competed with the deer for the meagre grass. The deer and livestock spilled over into neighbouring pastures and common wastes in search of grazing, and the gentry and smallholders of the neighbourhood had impounded the deer and livestock for trespassing and required Cumberland's keepers to pay fines for their release. One witness testified that on one occasion he had seen as many as thirty of Cumberland's deer, feeding in a field of ripe grain belonging to Lancelot Hough, gent. Cumberland said that he made a practice of inviting the local gentry to hunt in Uglebeard Chase in order to diminish their temptation to poach his deer, but this appears to have been no more than an abortive attempt to buy some support in the neighbourhood. In retaliation, between 1618 and 1622, the local gentry hunted Cumberland's deer virtually to extinction and did not hesitate to kill his sheep as well. Although the conflict divided the local community, no one in the neighbourhood could be found to testify on Cumberland's behalf except his servants and keepers, while much evidence

[70] PRO STAC 8/107/16.

was offered concerning the damage done by Cumberland's deer and live-stock. The case dragged on in Star Chamber from 1623 until 1626.[71]

Another unpopular West Riding landlord, whose deer were frequently attacked, was Sir Francis Wortley, bt. He was the owner of New Park, Wortley, which his grandfather had imparked after razing a whole village. He tried as hard as any magistrate to make the charges stick against those who hunted in Wortley Park by presiding over the trials himself and making sure that his keepers were present at the quarter sessions to give evidence. Between 1637 and 1642 forty-two indictments were returned against thirty-seven persons who had hunted in his park and killed seventy-three deer (five were repeat offenders). The poachers came from West Yorkshire and Derbyshire and included a priest, a gentleman, a tailor, and a joiner; the remainder were yeomen, husbandmen, and labourers. Of the thirty-seven persons indicted, five were imprisoned, but nineteen evaded arrest or escaped from custody. On one occasion, the sheriff—whether from sympathy or negligence—allowed one of the prisoners to escape.[72]

Smallholders who wished to punish owners of game reserves for allowing their deer to damage crops frequently called upon poaching bands to do their work. It is very clear that there were gangs of deer-stealers in Yorkshire, the Midlands, and in southern and south-western England which made a living from illegal hunting. They behaved like outlaws and sometimes terrorized whole villages. One such gang was led by John Latham, gent., and Michael Walshe, gent., both of Abberly, Worcestershire, and consisted of about twenty members. They did not limit themselves to raiding deer parks belonging to the king and other landowners; they also attacked and assaulted the servants and families of landowners in the neighbourhood. In one instance, in 1607, the Latham gang assaulted Sir John Folyot in his park at Great Whitley, ambushed Folyot's servant, Richard Barber, on the Worcester Road, and invaded the house of John Griffith in Abberly and beat his wife so badly that she was said to be unlikely to live.[73] In Somerset, in 1546, a group of men claiming to be soldiers on their way to the wars stopped to do some hunting in John Rodney's park. Rodney's tenants informed against the soldiers, who later attacked them with crossbows. The constable mustered the whole village, but the soldiers barricaded themselves in a house and fought off the the villagers, leaving two of them badly wounded.[74] The warden of Neroche Forest, Sir Richard Gifford, mustered 'a great company of people' in the spring of 1613 to drive off some deer-stealers led by John Welche of Fivehead, Somerset, gent., after the under-keepers had failed to expel them from the forest. The poachers prevailed

---

[71] PRO STAC 8/101/1.

[72] *West Riding Sessions Records*, i. 38–9, 76–7, 186–7, 264; Barber, 'The West Riding Sessions Rolls', 381.

[73] PRO STAC 8/141/7.   [74] PRO STAC 2/29/98.

and hunted at their pleasure for the remainder of the summer and into the following autumn and winter.[75]

6.5. Poaching Fraternities

Hunting and coursing deer required co-operation and were usually pursued as a social activity. One very seldom encounters the solitary hunter, and it seems only natural that hunters formed themselves into permanent bands displaying fraternal loyalty and solidarity. Hunting, on either side of the law, was a dangerous activity, and hunters, whether pursuing a feud or engaging in commercial poaching, undoubtedly preferred to seek their sport and adventure in the company of those whom they knew and trusted.

Certain characteristics and rituals distinguished the poaching fraternity. One was permanence: these bands held together over a period of time—perhaps five or six or even ten years. The hunters swore oaths of loyalty and secrecy to one another. The oath of secrecy was a promise not to testify against one another—sometimes reinforced with an exchange of bonds. The oath did not bind them to refrain from talking about their exploits, because there was little point in hunting if hunters could not boast about their brave deeds. Indeed, hunting forays mounted by such poaching fraternities often began in taverns and alehouses with much drinking and ended in the same places with feasting and banqueting upon their stolen venison, accompanied by 'braving, rejoicing and great vaunting' of their feats of daring.[76] Taverns and alehouses were also the places where venison and game were usually traded. Keepers testifying against poachers sometimes remarked upon the laughing and jovial behaviour of such gangs and their insistence upon engaging the keepers in teasing games intended to demonstrate the impotence of the keepers.[77] While many poachers did testify against their comrades—especially those who were very young and, perhaps, hunting for the first time—a substantial number of such bands held together and stubbornly refused to answer or confess when examined under oath in Star Chamber proceedings. But, on other occasions, brave hunters could not resist bragging that they had killed so many deer that they could not carry all of the carcasses away; or that they still had so much venison that they fed it to their dogs and servants, baked numerous venison pasties, and then had to salt down the remainder.[78]

Bold hunters did not hesitate to poach in such places as Windsor Forest and its numerous parks as well as the other royal deer parks up and down

[75] PRO STAC 8/157/28.
[76] PRO STAC 8/23/11, 224/30, 183/4; see also P. Clark, *The English Alehouse: A Social History, 1200–1830* (1983), 232.
[77] PRO STAC 8/37/15, 16, 15/27.   [78] PRO STAC 8/13/110, 32/1, 224/30.

the Thames Valley. One band, led by Thomas Habergill of Windsor, gent., hunted in Windsor Forest as well as Windsor Great Park and the Little Park over a period of five years until finally brought to book in 1622. Armed and equipped with longbows, crossbows, guns, long pikes, and greyhounds, they were one of a number of gangs who plundered the red and fallow deer in the sixteen royal parks at Windsor.[79] In the North Riding of Yorkshire another band led by Thomas Worsley of Sutton, gent., consisted of at least twenty-four members, whose principal occupation was said to be hunting deer in Galtres Forest—whether in season or not. Despite their boasting and open defiance of the keepers, they held together for at least five years until prosecuted in 1624. Worsley's band was one of several companies hunting in Galtres Forest over extended periods of time; the keepers were simply overwhelmed and unable to protect the king's deer— especially since some of the lesser forest officials had secretly confederated with the deer-stealers.[80] The same was true in Hatfield Chase, where the very highest officials and justices of the peace were in league with poaching gangs.[81]

The poaching band that hunted in the New Forest in the 1620s was unusually large. Fifty-five members are specified by name in four separate bills of complaint filed in Star Chamber by the rangers and keepers in 1622 and 1623. Like all poaching fraternities, the membership showed democratic tendencies; eight were gentlemen and the remainder were a mixed bag of yeomen, husbandmen, servants, and craftsmen. The most likely leaders of the band were William Jenkins of Owen, gent., and his three sons. The core of the membership appear to have resided in the purlieus of Burley Walk of the New Forest; at least twenty-one of the poachers lived in seven households or were kinsmen. Three or four of them came from Dorset and Wiltshire across the Hampshire border. Again, they showed the usual characteristics of meeting both publicly in alehouses and secretly in private dwellings to feast upon venison and to boast of their exploits. They havocked the deer, killing ninety upon one occasion, and did not forget to engage the keepers in combat. Their trophies were so numerous that they removed only the haunches of the venison and left the remainder of the carcasses to rot upon the field. The gang sustained their poaching activities and repulsed keepers sent to arrest them and confiscate their dogs for five or six years before the law caught up with them.[82]

In Cornwall there was a poaching gang which held together for thirteen years under the leadership of Lyttleton Trenance of Lanhydrock, esq. Trenance was about 30 years of age in 1606, when Sir Reynold Mohun of Boconnoc complained to the Court of Star Chamber that Trenance had led

---

[79] PRO STAC 8/29/7, 182/26, 13/3, 22/20. [80] PRO STAC 8/32/1.
[81] PRO STAC 8/17/12. [82] PRO STAC 8/224/30, 31, 32, 47/17.

his poaching band in a number of raids upon Boconnoc Park. The deer-stealers were all servants and followers of Trenance, 'Trained and bred up by him for [the] managing of such lewd actions and enterprises whereof the country hath had of late too great experience'. The Trenance gang began with about six members, but soon grew to twenty, of whom at least eight members, including his brother, rode with him for ten or eleven years. In 1609 Trenance conspired with John Clarke, keeper of St Winnow Park, and his two underkeepers to hunt deer belonging to Thomas Lower, esq. After his herd of fallow deer had dwindled from 300 to 240, Lower dismissed Clarke and his two underkeepers; at the time of his discharge, Clarke had been in Lower's service for ten years. In revenge for their dismissal, the three gamekeepers joined Trenance's band and, together, they havocked the deer in St Winnow park. Other small gentry and yeomen in the neighbourhood joined with Trenance to seek revenge because Lower had impounded their cattle. In his answer, Trenance stated that he had begun enclosing his own park and that Lower had reneged on a promise to give him some prime bucks for his herd. The Trenance gang did not consider the score to be settled, and Trenance and his brother Thomas and Lower's former keepers were still raiding St Winnow Park in November 1619.[83]

That poaching fraternities could hold together for so long suggests that they enjoyed the support of local communities or the protection of magistrates. This was especially true of the purlieu men of Cranborne Chase in their resistance to the second earl of Salisbury's attempts to expand the boundaries of the chase. One group of hunters who participated in the resistance to Salisbury's keepers in 1617 was the Lovell gang.[84] The members of this band lived in the purlieus on the Dorset side of Cranborne Chase, and, although they entered into an alliance with other purlieu men to oppose the odious earl of Salisbury, it is clear that they were experienced, professional poachers long before James I granted title to Cranborne Chase to Salisbury. The Lovells, consisting of Thomas of Dean, Dorset, gent., his son George of Rawson, Dorset, and Thomas's brother George, had been raiding Chitterwood Walk since 1611, but the family's connection with unlawful hunting dates back to at least 1577, when an ancestor was accused of unlawful hunting in Alice Holt Forest.[85]

The Lovell gang used tactics which effectively discouraged resistance by the keepers of the chase. They employed, or were allied with, former keepers, and they retained the services of William Comber, styled 'Captain Comber', who appears to have been a veteran of the Irish Wars. Their strategy was to fire guns in one part of the chase in order to lure the keepers away from the places where their confederates were hunting in a more quiet manner.

---

[83] PRO STAC 8/198/14, 203/7, 207/14.
[84] See Ch. 4.3.   [85] PRO STAC 8/11/2, 113/27; DL 1/146/14.

Their favourite time for hunting in Cranborne Chase was Sunday morning, when other people were in church. If the keepers were foolish enough to intervene, the Lovells, who always went about well armed, would threaten them with guns. Thomas Lovell frequently hid poachers in his house in Dean, but when the authorities bore down upon them, he would spirit them away to Ireland, where Capt. Comber had friends who would shelter them.[86]

Members of poaching gangs eluded capture in various ways. Hunting at night, wearing masks, or blackening faces were all common methods of disguise.[87] Safe houses were frequently employed by poaching bands as places to hide themselves or to keep dogs, weapons, and nets. One group of merchants and townsmen from Gloucester kept a safe house near the Forest of Braden in Wiltshire, where they had hoped that they might hunt without being recognized.[88] But many bold hunters scorned such methods and preferred to terrorize the keepers into impotence.[89] In Jacobean Worcestershire, the members of a poaching gang which hunted in Malvern Chase were not only disdainful of the fines which were assessed against them, but boasted of their exploits. They were sustained by Francis Rosse of Great Malvern, who was described as 'being a person of great wealth and one that beareth much sway in that part of the said country by his store of money and ability'.[90]

6.6. Commercial Poaching

Hunting could not be confined within lawful limits as long as the market for venison and game remained strong and the profits high. Parliamentary statutes and royal proclamations repeatedly attempted to stop this illicit trade,[91] but commercial poaching remained a profitable venture throughout much of England and especially in London and Middlesex. Although the Game Laws were more strictly enforced in Middlesex than elsewhere, London and its suburbs sustained a thriving trade in venison, hare, and wildfowl as well as deerskins and other by-products. The sale of conies and rabbit skins from commercial warrens was legal, but it is evident that many rabbits sold on the open market had been stolen. The London market in illicit venison and game was well organized and drew upon much of southern England, although enterprising individuals were prepared to supply the demand from local sources such as the numerous parks, warrens, and ponds in Middlesex

---

[86] PRO STAC 8/11/2.   [87] PRO STAC 8/37/14.   [88] PRO STAC 8/180/14.
[89] PRO STAC 8/237/18.   [90] PRO STAC 8/247/22.
[91] 32 Hen. VIII, c. 8 (*SR* iii. 753) prohibited the sale of partridges and pheasants; 1 Jac. I, c. 27 (*SR* iv. 1055) forbade selling venison and hare as well as all wildfowl regarded as game.

and the Thames Valley—including those belonging to the crown. Commercial poaching had been carried on in the Tudor period, but it became a major problem only at the beginning of the seventeenth century.[92]

A skilled and successful poacher could earn as much in one night as a husbandman or artisan could make in a month or more. In Melksham, Wiltshire, in 1628 Philip Taylor deposed that he heard two poachers boast that between them they had earned four gold crowns (20s.) for the previous night's work. Using only a crossbow armed with a forked arrow, they had brought down a buck. Possessing so much pocket money undoubtedly had some disadvantages, because Taylor said that on his way home from the alehouse that same night he had found one of the poachers 'much overcome with drink' and asleep under a hedge. Presumably, the poacher missed a night's work.[93] In Windsor Forest, Sir Richard Norton, the keeper of Lynchford Walk, traded in illegal venison through his subordinates. He gave his underkeeper and another servant 16s. 8d. for killing a stag and promised them further payment for delivering the animal to the buyer.[94] A Nottinghamshire justice accused John Welcome, gent., of poaching deer, pheasants, and hares and selling them in alehouses in order to obtain the money 'to maintain his lewd and loathsome drinking and troublesome course of life'.[95] When George, third earl of Cumberland, came of age in the late 1570s he prosecuted a band of hunters led by Reynold Anderson, which had destroyed most of the deer in Stainmore Chase, Westmorland, during his minority. Cumberland maintained that the Anderson gang sold venison 'into foreign parts for great sums of money, making thereof their whole trade of living' and were 'otherwise altogether destitute of all honest trade'.[96]

Most of those who engaged in commercial poaching probably did so on a part-time or seasonal basis. A legitimate occupation helped provide cover for their activities, and there were plenty of opportunities for craftsmen to turn a profit. Peter May, a weaver of Cranbrook, Kent, traded in venison which he killed in Sissinghurst Park with a crossbow. When the weaving trade was slow, he used his servants to carve up the deer carcasses, and to transport and deliver venison. He also fed his servants on the leftover heads and necks. May employed a glover in Goudhurst to tan deerskins, which he later traded for cloth. He used the occasion of hay-making to scout the deer in Sissinghurst Park, and then hunted two or three times a week at night with companions. May left instructions with his servants that, if the keeper of Sissinghurst were to come looking for evidence while he was away, one servant was to engage the parker in conversation while the other dashed out of the back door to hide May's crossbow under a hedge. May had

---

[92] Manning, *Village Revolts*, 295–6.
[93] *Records of the County of Wiltshire*, ed. Cunnington, 87.
[94] PRO STAC 8/13/3.   [95] PRO STAC 8/204/5.   [96] PRO STAC 5/C67/29.

threatened to kill anyone who gave evidence against him. Eventually, May was indicted for unlawful possession of a crossbow, but his hunting companions assaulted the constable who held him in custody and rescued him.[97]

A ready market could be found for venison, game, deerskins, and the like in many parts of England. In 1604 Sir Francis Leeke of Sutton-in-the Dale, Derbyshire, accused John Stubbing, a glover by trade, of being one of a band of poachers who frequently raided his deer park on Sundays and holydays. Stubbing bought deerskins from other poachers and tanned them himself. He boiled the meat and sold it to customers in Chesterfield.[98] Nicholas Poole, a glover of Hampton, Middlesex, obtained his deerskins and rabbit pelts directly from the parks and warrens of Hampton Court Palace. It was a dangerous occupation and Poole and his companions were captured in 1624 after a pitched battle with the authorities. The Game Laws were strictly enforced in Middlesex, and a magistrate committed Poole to Newgate Prison for a month without bail before he was prosecuted in Star Chamber by the attorney-general.[99] Commercial poaching provided alternative employment during trade slumps for clothiers such as Richard Wallis of Exford, Somerset, and his companions. When Edmund Leversage of Wallis prosecuted them in 1619 for removing some five hundred conies from his warren over a period of seven years, he also accused Wallis's gang of hunting deer in the forests of Selwood and Blackmore as far back as 1607. Wallis also traded in venison and conies.[100] William Earl of Crudwell, Wiltshire, described as a 'high constable', led a large gang which specialized in raiding cony warrens in Gloucestershire. They attacked the warren of George, twelfth Lord Berkeley, in Tetbury in January, February, and August of 1619. They broke into at least seven other warrens during the same period and rarely carried away fewer than eighty to a hundred couple of conies, which they sold to alehouse keepers. Rabbit poachers were seldom prosecuted by the attorney-general, but the boldness of the Earl gang and the attack upon the warren of a peer evidently required that they be made exemplary.[101] By 1638, Yorkshire magistrates were rigorously enforcing the Game Act of 1603 against commercial poachers. William Warwick, yeom., and Henry Pauperman, yeom., both of Knaresborough, were convicted at the quarter sessions of selling forty-four partridges in a single day. They were ordered to be committed to the county gaol, according to the statute, for three months, unless they could pay 20s. for every partridge caught to the overseers of the poor in the parish where the partridges were taken.[102]

It is evident that many Englishmen not only did not enquire whence their venison came, but did not want to know. Gentry households frequently

---

[97] *Kentish Sources, vi. Crime and Punishment*, ed. E. Melling (Maidstone, Kent, 1969), 39–40. [98] PRO STAC 8/205/11.
[99] PRO STAC 8/29/11. [100] PRO STAC 8/199/11.
[101] PRO STAC 8/24/3. [102] *West Riding Sessions Records*, ed. Lister, ii. 42–3.

made purchases of venison which were illegal. The household accounts of the Roberts family of Sussex record purchases of venison on two occasions without specifying where it originated. In one instance it was brought by one Saxbee, who usually delivered their meat.[103] When John Isham, who had been chosen warden of the Mercers' company at the young age of 42, procured thirty-three fat bucks for the Mercers' annual feast in 1567 from his gentry friends, his fellow mercers could not help but think that the transaction was 'most strange'.[104] Lady Cholmeley was described as being a receiver of stolen venison after she accepted venison from a small-gentry poaching gang operating in Cheshire in 1621. She could hardly have been ignorant of where the venison came from, since the deer-stealers, who were led by John Stanley and members of the Manwaring family, were notorious in the county. They had been attacking Sir Rowland Egerton's deer park for the previous seven years and had nearly destroyed all of the deer and pales on their most recent raid.[105] Dame Isabel Foster, a widow living in the borders of Hatfield Chase, Yorkshire, was accused in 1615 of being not only a receiver of stolen venison but also a procurer of unlawful hunting in the chase.[106] Sir Fulke Greville, the ranger of the royal park of Wedgnocke, which was attached to Warwick Castle, claimed that the deer-stealers who raided his park in 1610 knew that they could always sell venison to Sir Clement Throckmorton, whose house was located nearby in Haseley. Indeed, some of the deer-stealers were servants in Throckmorton's household.[107] Richard Batten, the forester of Pewsham Forest, Wiltshire, traded in venison to such an extent that Sir Edward Coke, AG, accused him of destroying two-thirds of the deer entrusted to his care. He fed his servants on venison as 'their ordinary meat' and he used part of the surplus to buy grain. Batten gave gifts of venison to friends and relatives 'to the intent to receive like pleasures and other good turns from them'. Among the recipients of his largesse were 'old Lady Longe [now] deceased' and his widowed mother.[108]

James I was dismayed by the amount of venison for sale in London, and he believed that London magistrates did not do nearly enough to halt this illicit trade.[109] The Privy Council frequently ordered the lord mayor of London to halt the sale of game, which was openly hawked by butchers and poulterers in London and the suburbs.[110] The poachers who supplied the

---

[103] *Accounts of the Roberts Family of Boarzell, Sussex*, ed. Tittler 70, 91.
[104] *John Isham, Mercer and Merchant Adventurer*, ed. Ramsay, 171.
[105] PRO STAC 8/140/4.   [106] PRO STAC 8/20/17.
[107] PRO STAC 8/158/26; Sir William Dugdale, *The Antiquities of Yorkshire*, 2. vols. (1730), i. 272.
[108] PRO STAC 8/7/9.   [109] HMC *Salisbury*, xx. 275.
[110] *Acts PC, 1599–1600*, 238–9; see also *Acts PC, 1600–1601*, 278–9 and *Acts PC, 1595–1596*, 322–3.

metropolitan market gathered in taverns such as the Bull's Head in Cheapside. Some of the commercial poachers who gathered at the Bull's Head had connections with poachers in Edmonton, including Thomas Wray, a servant in Edmonton Parsonage. After hunting in Enfield Chase, they arranged to hide out in safe houses if pursued by the keepers.[111] Many tavern keepers were receivers of stolen venison and eagerly vied for the wares of commercial poachers. Richard Humble was a successful vintner and the proprietor of a tavern in Southwark. He also owned land in Hornchurch within Waltham Forest. He took the initiative in obtaining supplies of red and fallow venison by organizing and leading forays into Waltham Forest and the royal park of Havering-atte-Bower. His hunting associates included his son Peter, Augustine Simpson, a surgeon of London, John Hynde, brick-layer, and Robert Savage, baker.[112] John Stock and Thomas Cratch, 'innholders' of St George's Southwark, obtained their venison from St James's Park.[113]

Butchers and those in the victualling trade were in the best position to dispose of illicit venison; once cut up it was not readily distinguishable from beef or mutton. James Atkin of Chigwell lived on the edge of Waltham Forest and hired a butcher to shoot deer from behind his backyard fence with a crossbow. The butcher then broke up the deer carcasses in Atkin's kitchen.[114] Butchers and victuallers sometimes belonged to poaching gangs which were prepared to defend one another. When a constable came to arrest a fellow hunter, William Fanner of Field Lane, butcher, William Swyer, victualler, and Francis Mason, victualler, both of Clerkenwell, assaulted the constable and attempted to rescue their comrade. All were accused of steal-ing deer from Hyde Park.[115]

A considerable part of the venison sold in London appears to have come from the grounds of Windsor Castle. John Taylor had been a brewer in Millford Lane, Middlesex, before he moved to Berkshire, where he rented a house called Tille Place within Windsor Forest near Windsor Castle. Taylor, his wife Sarah, and his servants killed red and fallow deer for four years before they were detected. Wishing to increase his kill Taylor hired a highly skilled deerstalker, whom he hid in his house and 'by his assistance destroyed multitudes of your majesty's deer'. They were especially active when the keepers of Windsor Forest 'necessarily attended your majesty in other places'. Taylor fed his family and servants on venison, gave some away to friends, and disposed of the remainder in London. Escaping detection for so long, Taylor grew 'impudent' and began hunting more boldly with firearms.

---

[111] HMC *Salisbury*, ii. 189–90.   [112] PRO STAC 8/211/21.
[113] *Middlesex Sessions Records*, ed. Le Hardy, ii. 90.   [114] Fisher, *The Forest of Essex*, 216.
[115] *Middlesex Sessions Records*, ed. Le Hardy, iii. 25–6; see also *Middlesex County Records*, ed. Jeaffreson, i. 269.

Eventually, someone informed and he was convicted and fined in Star Chamber in 1616.[116] Another supplier of venison for the London market was Richard Hanbury of Datchet, Buckinghamshire, gent. He and his servants usually hunted in Ditton and Windsor Great Parks and sometimes worked with other poachers living in Datchet and Windsor. The venison was carved up in Hanbury's house, packed in hampers, and sent by water to Peter Callow, tailor, who lived in the parish of St Martin's-in-the Fields. The details of Hanbury's activities over the previous three years were revealed when a young servant broke down and confessed to the authorities while being examined at the King's Arms in Windsor in 1608.[117] Richard Rither of St Clement Danes, gent., was another person suspected of purveying the king's deer. He appeared at the Middlesex Sessions in 1617, but was discharged for lack of evidence.[118]

When John Smyth of Nibley looked back upon the poaching war which had raged for nearly fifty years between Henry, Lord Berkeley, and the Dudley clientele in Gloucestershire led by Sir Thomas Throckmorton, he noted that the raids upon Lord Berkeley's parks and chases had been perpetrated variously by a 'compact nest of deer-stealers' or by men of 'mettle and good woodmen . . . old notorious deer-stealers'.[119] On an earlier occasion, when describing the feuding and the poaching raids which the dowager Lady Berkeley and her brother-in-law, Sir Maurice Berkeley, mounted against one another, Smyth remarked that such behaviour had not been seen 'since the lawless days of Robin Hood'.[120] In these words Smyth acknowledged the ability of outlaw poaching gangs to hold together over extended periods of time and wreak havoc over wide areas with surprisingly little deterrence from either the central government or local magistrates. The Berkeley–Dudley feud is, admittedly, an extreme example—one in which the queen herself played an active partisan role. The Elizabethan Court of Star Chamber and the Privy Council failed to curb this feud, although dozens of complaints were filed in Star Chamber over a twenty-year period. The poaching war did not come to an end until 1614. The Berkeley–Dudley quarrel was the final episode in a feud that reached back to before the Wars of the Roses; it was resolved not through the intervention of royal justice, but rather by the wealth and longevity of the Berkeleys. The Dudley brothers, Leicester and Warwick, failed to outlive Henry, eleventh Lord Berkeley, and Warwick's widow lacked the financial resources to carry on the litigation against the Berkeleys and sued for peace. The quarrel between Berkeley and Throckmorton was composed by the good offices of a relative of both

---

[116] PRO STAC 8/22/20; T. G. Barnes, 'Fines in the High Court of Star Chamber, 1596–1641' (typescript in PRO Round Room), 34.
[117] PRO STAC 8/182/26.   [118] *Middlesex Sessions Records*, ed. Le Hardy, iv. 107.
[119] Smyth, *Berkeley Manuscripts*, ii. 296–8, 331.   [120] Ibid. 266–70.

men. Only when financial support was withdrawn from the belligerents was the Court of Star Chamber able to suppress the last of the poaching gangs in the Vale of Berkeley.

John Smyth perceived the historical significance of poaching gangs surviving through the Tudor period. It was well known that the early Tudor monarchs had attempted to crush outlaw gangs and quasi-feudal disorder. But whether Elizabeth did so as consistently and effectively as her father and grandfather is a question which needs to be re-examined more critically. Moreover, such poaching bands became widespread in many parts of England during the reign of James I and often could escape punishment for five or ten years at a time. Evidence of their existence derives largely from the proceedings of the Court of Star Chamber, which began taking a greater interest in poaching offences in the reign of James I. What we do not know for certain is whether this represents an increase in detection and reporting or an increase in gang-poaching over the previous reign. I suspect that it was both.

The original Game Laws of the late-medieval and early Tudor periods were framed to impose a greater degree of social regulation upon the lower orders because hunting and other field sports were thought to provide cover for treasonous conspiracies among artificers. The Jacobean Game Law of 1603 was drafted in such sweeping terms that it disqualified many small gentry. The intention of this law may have been to break up those poaching gangs which were led by the gentry. This led to new and troublesome problems of law enforcement, which the justices of the peace could not deal with in an even-handed manner because they were all too often personally involved in such illicit matters themselves. Most allegations of the unlawful hunting of deer discussed in this and the preceding chapters arose from the factionalism which flourished in Tudor and early Stuart England, conflicts originating in overlapping hunting franchises and jurisdictions and competition for forest and game offices among the aristocracy and gentry. Other causes included the assertion of the royal prerogative against purlieu rights, the widespread market demand for venison and game, and the envy of small gentry excluded from hunting by the Jacobean Game Laws. The gentry were engaged in all of these species of poaching—usually on an organized basis.

Although the poaching of wildfowl, rabbits, hares, and fish was widespread, these forms of unlawful hunting and fishing were largely confined to persons beneath the rank of gentleman and appear to have involved much less organization and violence than the activities of gentry-led gangs of deer-stealers. Comparatively few of the attacks upon deer parks and chases came from smallholders protesting damage done to their crops by loose deer, and, even when we do come upon such cases, the hand of the aristocracy and gentry is never far removed. The violence perpetrated by deer-stealers and poaching gangs can be explained by the extent to which martial values still permeated the deer-hunting culture of the aristocracy and the gentry. The transition from a quasi-feudal and lineage society based upon honour and kinship to a civil society based upon respect for the law had still not been completed before 1640.[121]

---

[121] For a discussion of the distinction between lineage and civil society, see James, *Family, Lineage and Civil Society*, 26–7, 32, 183–4, 186, 191–2.

7

Poachers and Keepers

The greatest deer-stealers make the best park-keepers.

M. P. Tilley, *A Collection of the Proverbs in England in the Sixteenth and Seventeenth Centuries* (Ann Arbor, Mich. 1950; repr. 1966), 148–9

In a traditional rural society, hunting, coursing, fowling, hawking, and fishing provided occasions for social intercourse and expressed feelings of fraternal and communal solidarity. Such field sports are universal in rural societies, and, in early modern England, were so interwoven with gentry and popular life that the attempt to declare them to be aristocratic privileges or part of the royal prerogative was bound to present serious problems of law enforcement. Attempts to delineate overlapping hunting franchises, conflicting land uses, and customary use-rights were also likely to sharpen feuding and faction-fighting, which were very much a part of the fabric of rural life. For those concerned with the preservation of public order and good household government, unlawful hunting had come to be associated with popular and aristocratic rebellion, and it was becoming axiomatic that poaching, when engaged in by adolescents, constituted a kind of behaviour which was habit-forming and could lead to a life of crime. Thus, poaching was looked upon in much the same way as our own age views the phenomenon of juvenile delinquency. Patriarchal authority and household discipline were undermined by the temptations presented to sons and servants to engage in unlawful hunting, and such acts were frequently perceived as expressions of youthful rebellion. Indeed, households full of unruly servants, idle sons, discontented younger brothers, as well as fathers and masters who encouraged or winked at such behaviour, spawned the disorders associated with unlawful hunting and contributed to the violence which pervaded these cultures. Many poachers who fell afoul of the law were youthful delinquents and first-time offenders. For some, one brush with the law, followed by the intervention of angry fathers, older brothers, or masters was sufficient to deter them from future mischief, but other poachers displayed the hardened attitude of the habitual offender who glibly invented alibis, employed artful dodges, and specious pleas to counter every accusation of offending against the Game Laws.

In such circumstances, poachers were distinguished from gamekeepers by degree rather than by kind. Only a gamekeeper who had served his apprenticeship in the 'mystery' of illicit hunting would be sufficiently acquainted with the tricks and dodges of the professional poacher to discharge his office effectively. Some gamekeepers were reformed poachers and displayed loyalty to their masters and great courage in repulsing poachers, but others continued to conspire with their old friends among the poaching fraternity.

7.1. Gentlemen and Clergy

Poaching was a habit that many gentlemen acquired in adolescence, and some of them never grew out of adolescence nor that species of delinquency. Most usually began in a small way—trapping pigeons, catching rabbits or hares with snares, or taking fish from other people's ponds. Poachers who went after this sort of game quietly were seldom caught, and this must have appealed to their youthful sense of adventure. Eventually, they would tire of such children's games, and, like Thomas Leigh of High Leigh, Cheshire, gent., would express their rebelliousness by seeking entrée into the adult world of deer-stealing. This Leigh found at 'one Hugh Johnson's house, being an alehouse in Norton'. Young Leigh frequently sought adventure in the company of Brian Burton, Richard Okell, and William Shuttleworth, who appear to have been of the same age. Young Leigh was usually accompanied by his servant, Randle Ashley, aged 34, who appears to have functioned as a kind of ineffectual baby-sitter. According to Ashley's deposition, his young master and his companions had tired of coursing hare, and Leigh sent another servant back to High Leigh to fetch a 'pied dog' for hunting deer. Ashley deposed that he warned his master that deer were out of season and that it would be difficult to carry a deer home without being observed. Burton and Okell said that they knew of several parks and other places where they might hunt with little chance of detection. They decided upon Hatton Park as 'the fittest and safest from all dangers [of discovery]'. Ashley confessed that he told the boys that he would obtain a horse to carry any deer they might kill to a safe hiding place. They planned their raid upon Hatton Park for midnight that evening and young Okell provided a brace of greyhounds with which they killed one deer.[1]

Another band of youthful poachers was led by Thomas Garling of King's Lynn, gent. His hunting companions included his younger brothers Edward and William—the latter a Cambridge undergraduate 17 years of age—and others to the number of ten. According to their answer to a prosecution in Star Chamber, they had been coursing hare in the marshes near King's Lynn when one of their greyhounds caught the scent of a deer and pursued it on

---

[1] PRO DL 4/42/65. The date was 42 Eliz.

to the property of Sir Arthur Capel of South Wootton. The Garling brothers stated that they were able to call back their hound, but Anne, dowager countess of Arundel, insisted in a Star Chamber complaint that the Garling gang frequently and habitually hunted in Castle Rising Chase with dogs, stalking horses, guns, and crossbows. On the night of 28 March 1613 the Garling brothers and their companions killed six deer and continued hunting through the next day, when they killed two more. When a keeper tried to stop them, the young deer-stealers fired at him with a gun charged with hailshot and wounded him in eight places.[2]

William and Thomas Smith were introduced to deer-stealing by their father, Sir William Smith of Theydon Mount, Essex, and frequently hunted in the company of their father's servants. Sir William was a purlieu man and he claimed that he had never exceeded his legal hunting rights and had always admonished his sons never to pursue deer into Waltham Forest. But Sir Thomas Coventry, AG, painted a very different picture when he prosecuted the Smiths in Star Chamber in November 1622. The attorney-general stated that the defendants, together with their servants and friends from Theydon Garnon, had ranged through the Forest of Waltham and the royal park of Havering-atte-Bower for the previous ten years killing the red and fallow deer in order to provision their household with venison. On at least three occasions the royal keepers had been fired upon or had sustained wounds trying to protect the king's deer from the Smith gang. Like many experienced deer-stealers, Sir William was willing to concede small portions of the accusation in an attempt to plead guilty to lesser charges. He admits, for example, that his son Thomas, another rowdy Cambridge undergraduate aged 17, had happened upon a dead deer lying by the side of the road while passing through Waltham Forest. Thomas had picked up the deer carcass and brought it home, but the father claimed that the deer had been dead for so long that it was unfit to eat. The story becomes somewhat less credible when we learn that this had happened more than once. Moreover, Thomas Burton, a hunting companion of young Thomas Smith, confessed that he had killed one of the deer which the Cambridge student had carried home. Another ploy which the Smiths frequently used was to spirit the dead deer out of the forest in the family coach. Sir William Smith's other son, William the younger, was also reputed to be a 'common deer-stealer' for many years. The younger Sir William subsequently abandoned his poaching ways after he became a courtier.[3]

Gamekeepers frequently complained about how difficult it was to deal with juvenile poachers. In 1529 Richard Egerton of Ridley, Cheshire, reported that his keeper had discovered Hugh Calverly, son of George Calverly of Lea, hiding in Ridley Park with his hound and a dead deer. The boy

---

[2] PRO STAC 8/46/14.   [3] PRO STAC 8/29/14, 147/2; see also above, Ch. 3.2.

defiantly refused to yield the deer and there was an angry exchange of words as the keeper took the deer from him forcibly. Hugh Calverley departed in great fury uttering threats against the keepers. Within a few days young Calverley returned with a number of his father's servants and ambushed two of Egerton's keepers as they returned home from church. One of them was seriously wounded.[4] When Edmund Garrett, the earl of Pembroke's underkeeper, discovered two sons and a servant of Francis Perkins of Battington, Wiltshire, esq., hunting in Groveley Forest in 1609, he told them that he was going to report them to the ranger. The Perkins brothers revenged themselves by posting copies of a scurrilous libel against Garrett around the village, organizing another poaching raid in the forest and, finally, ambushing and wounding the underkeeper.[5]

In 1622 a gang of deer-stealers composed of young gentlemen and yeomen led by Thomas Whaley of Scriveton gained access to Norwood Park, Nottinghamshire, by bribing the underkeepers, who included the younger brother of Gervase Lee, esq., the park keeper, to unlock the gates. When one of the hunters heard that Lee was going to prosecute them in Star Chamber and would likely exaggerate their offences, he wrote to Philip, Lord Stanhope, who leased the park from Tobie Matthew, archbishop of York, explaining what had actually happened and asking Stanhope to intercede on their behalf with the archbishop. The archbishop signified his desire to drop the charges after Stanhope had reprimanded the hunters for 'their boldness past' and advised them 'to be better neighbours' to the archbishop's game. Stanhope reproved Lee for undertaking the Star Chamber prosecution without first consulting with him, and demanded that Lee surrender the keepership of Norwood Park immediately.[6]

It was characteristic of youthful hunters that they were willing to resort to desperate measures to escape detection. After several night-time raids on Clarendon Park, Wiltshire, during the summer of 1612, a poaching gang led by Leonard and John Muggeridge lost their hounds to the park keepers. Fearing that their dogs could be used to discover their identity, the Muggeridge brothers and their fellow hunters broke into the keeper's lodge in Clarendon Park in order to rescue their hounds. They went from room to room breaking down doors until they found their dogs in a chamber on the second floor, and then carried them to the Muggeridge house some twenty miles distant.[7]

That Sir Alexander Culpeper II (1581–1639) had become a hardened deer-stealer by the time he was 24 years of age is hardly surprising when one considers his family background. He was the son and heir of Sir Alexander Culpeper I (d. 1599) of Bedgebury in the parish of Goudhurst, Kent, who

---

[4] PRO STAC 2/14, fo. 41.   [5] PRO STAC 8/152/11.
[6] PRO STAC 8/194/3.   [7] PRO STAC 8/183/40.

had himself been indicted for poaching at the Sussex assizes in 1582. The Culpepers were recusants, and were allied to the Lords Dacre by marriage and to the Viscounts Montague by religion and a partnership in the iron-founding business.[8] Unlawful hunting was pervasive in the Culpeper family and the younger Sir Alexander's kinsmen, Nicholas Culpeper of Wakehurst, Sussex, and Alexander Culpeper of Cowhurst, Kent, had all been prosecuted for raiding their neighbours' deer parks.[9] The younger Culpeper's casual attitude regarding the deer in other people's parks is made clear by an answer that his fellow hunter, Thomas Stillyon of Mayfield, Sussex, gent., gave to the Court of Star Chamber in 1605: Stillyon and Culpeper were passing by a deer park which belonged to Culpeper's kinsman, Sir Thomas Waller of Gromebridge, Kent, when Culpeper said that he did not think that Waller would object to their coursing a deer since his father had once made a gift of some deer to Waller. Clearly Waller and Culpeper held different concepts of hospitality. Culpeper's greyhound killed a deer and Waller objected enough to prosecute him and his companion. The attorney-general had compelled Culpeper and Stillyon to appear before Star Chamber just the previous year for being part of a large gang which had, on several occasions, killed deer in Ashdown Forest and assaulted the keepers. In 1606 Sir Thomas Baker complained that Culpeper was the leader of a poaching gang based upon Thomas Lake's alehouse in Cranbrook which had broken into Sissinghurst Park, the property of Baker's ward, Henry Baker, esq., and had resisted arrest by Baker, who was sheriff of Kent at the time. Culpeper was not at all intimidated by having to make answer in Star Chamber, and demanded that Baker prove that his ward was under age and that he had title to the park. In the same year, the attorney-general once again accused Culpeper, Stillyon, and another member of their gang of several more attacks upon Ashdown Forest as well as assaults upon the gamekeepers.[10]

When gangs of gentry-led poachers enjoyed aristocratic protection, they grew very bold. In Sutton, Derbyshire, in 1610, Thomas Langford's band numbered some twenty or so hunters, including servants from the household of Lord Cavendish, and operated out of the alehouse kept by William Roberts, a constable. In what was clearly an episode in the continuing Talbot–Stanhope feud, one of Lord Cavendish's servants, James Hallom, was accused of bringing in outside deer-stealers to reinforce raids upon the deer park of Sir Francis Leeke at Sutton-in-the-Dale. The hunters boasted that their dogs were 'so well fleshed with bucks in Sir Francis Leeke's park'

[8] *Calendar of Assize Records, Kent Indictments, Eliz. I*, ed. Cockburn, no. 1859; *Calendar of Assize Records, Sussex Indictments, Eliz. I*, ed. Cockburn, no. 934; C. Buckingham, 'The Troubles of Sir Alexander Culpeper of Goudhurst', *Cantium*, 2 (1970), 5–8.

[9] *Calendar of Assize Records, Sussex Indictments, Eliz. I*, ed. Cockburn, no. 310; F. W. Attree, 'The Sussex Colepepers, Pt. II', *Sussex Arch. Col.*, 47 (1905), 80, 85; PRO STAC 8/200/11.

[10] PRO STAC 8/294/6, 5/13, 53/4.

that they would no longer course hares. In a series of three raids during the summer of 1620 Langford's gang killed sixteen deer and boasted that they were going to pull down Leeke's house. The fact that Leeke was a justice of the peace and a deputy-lieutenant offered him no protection against having his house unthatched.[11]

Some gentry poaching gangs were more casually organized, and were sometimes made up of persons who frequented a particular alehouse. Edward Yardley of Henley-in-Arden, Warwickshire, often made contacts at an alehouse adjacent to Lapworth Park, where, on one occasion, he arranged to meet one Captain Hawes and Thomas Hill, the keeper of Lapworth Park, who had agreed to let them course their greyhounds in the park. What Hill did not agree to was allowing Yardley and Hawes actually to kill deer. When this happened, he feared discovery by his master. Another keeper came upon the dead fawn and confiscated the hounds. Yardley demanded the return of his hounds, which had been sequestered in the keeper's lodge. When Yardley tried to retrieve his hounds, Hill, his wife, and two servants attacked Yardley and ran him through the hand with a pike staff. Yardley still managed to escape with his dogs.[12]

In Wiltshire, a poaching gang composed of small gentry living in the borders of Downtown Chase (also known as Earldom Chase), so terrified the keepers of William, third earl of Pembroke, that for a period of four years between 1612 and 1616 they dared not confront the deer-stealers. Not only did these bold hunters help themselves to Pembroke's deer with impunity; they also refused to allow Pembroke's keepers to hunt in the chase. Pembroke finally brought a complaint in Star Chamber in 1616 against Samuel Lynch, gent., and Cuthbert Clifford, gent. The former answered that he and his companions had hunted only foxes (although one might question how useful greyhounds were for that purpose!). He did admit that on one occasion, while coursing a fox, his greyhound had pursued a deer into the New Forest, although he had never commanded the hound to do so.[13]

Gamekeepers frequently had good reason to be suspicious of gentlemen who lived near hunting reserves. The royal keepers of Waltham Forest suspected that Sir Francis Calton, who lived in the midst of the forest, was a 'common hunter of deer'. In order to escape their suspicions, he removed his residence to a cottage on the edge of Havering Park, which was described as 'a very mean house', altogether unbecoming his 'rank, quality and yearly revenue', but 'yet most fitting and opportune for the close and secret killing of deer'. The suspicions of the keeper of Havering Park were very much increased when the deer began to disappear in large numbers, and a close

---

[11] PRO STAC 8/200/1; see also above, Ch. 6.2. Another attack upon Pontefract Park, where George, earl of Shrewsbury, was keeper, early in the reign of Elizabeth, could also be connected with the Talbot–Stanhope feud (PRO DL 1/70/A13).
[12] PRO STAC 8/169/19; see also above, Ch. 2.3.   [13] PRO STAC 8/183/39.

surveillance of Calton revealed that he was frequently to be found in the park 'at unseasonable times and in very suspicious manner', so the keeper warned Calton to stay out of the park. Calton then attempted to purchase a lease of the herbage of a part of the park for his horses and cattle so that he would have an excuse for entering the park, but this was denied him as a suspected deer-stealer. Calton sought revenge against the keeper by posting eclogues defaming the keeper throughout the village of Havering—including one on the gate of the king's house at Havering-atte-Bower. The keeper never did catch Calton in the act of deer-stealing and instead prosecuted him for seditious libel.[14]

It was not unheard of for Tudor and early Stuart women to engage in poaching, but more usually they acted as inciters and abetters. Margaret York of Laverstock, Wiltshire, who lived on the western edge of Clarendon Park (just north-east of Salisbury) during the reign of Henry VIII, became involved in a fierce quarrel with the royal keepers of the park. The ranger stated that her house and lands were located within the forest of Paunsett, and she claimed that a portion of those lands had been wrongfully enclosed within Clarendon Park. In order to dispute the king's claim to her land, Margaret not only encouraged her own servants to hunt within Clarendon Park and forcibly to resist the keepers; she also issued an open invitation to all the gentry of the neighbourhood, telling them that they would not lack 'meat, drink, lodging nor good cheer' as long as they hunted in Clarendon Park.[15]

Clerics were forbidden to hunt or to hawk by Roman canon law because the weapons and mode of exercise employed were thought to be 'military', but this prohibition was widely evaded in pre-Reformation England. Indeed, many bishoprics and monastic houses were well endowed with deer parks—the bishop of Norwich alone possessing no fewer than thirteen parks. Sir Edward Coke assumed that canon law was null and void in England after the Reformation, and stated that 'by the common law of the land they may for their recreation, to make them fitter for the performance, duty, or office, use the recreation of hunting'. Of course, Coke assumed that only those clergy qualified by income or enfranchised by royal grant could lawfully hunt. Most of the deer parks belonging to bishops or monastic houses had long since been snatched away by the crown or greedy courtiers, and only a few of the upper clergy continued to hunt.[16]

In the sixteenth and seventeenth centuries one could still find parish clergy who hunted—on both sides of the law. Josias Calton, described as a 'parson', might have argued that he did not hunt in the strictest sense of

[14] PRO STAC 8/181/5.

[15] PRO STAC 2/11, fo. 31; see also STAC 8/190/15 for a poaching gang which included several women.

[16] Coke, *Institutes*, pt. 4, p. 309; Peacham, *Compleat Gentleman*, 183–4.

the word, but only coursed deer with his greyhound in Enfield Old Park. This he did in May 1578, in the company of half a dozen farmers, servants, and labourers who lived in Edmonton, Middlesex.[17] Jeffrey Wybarre or Wibergh, vicar of Long Preston, was the leader of a poaching gang in Craven in the West Riding of Yorkshire in 1595. Richard Topcliffe, the rackmaster of the Tower of London, acting as steward of the lands and parks confiscated from Richard Norton, esq., who had been attainted for treason, complained that Wybarre's band had ranged throughout the parks and chases of Craven and frequently assaulted gamekeepers, but Wybarre pleaded that the hunting reserves in question belonged to the earl of Cumberland and he maintained that he had hunted with the permission of the earl. His gang numbered at least eight members and included a female deer-stealer named 'Agnes Bland, the daughter of Mother Bland of Hebden . . . a very loose and dissolute woman by the procurement of . . . her said father and mother Bland'.[18] Hugh Bampton, rector of Hatch Beauchamp, Somerset, was described in 1622 as having 'for divers years . . . been a secret and common killer and destroyer of deer'. The deputy-keeper of Neroche Forest charged that Bampton derived 'more delight and pleasure in feeding himself with the said deer than in the vigilant feeding of the flock committed to his charge'.[19]

7.2. *Servants*

It was axiomatic that servants who hunted unlawfully were spawned by disorderly aristocratic and gentry households.[20] Thus, when servants were apprehended for poaching, their masters might be held accountable, or at least reprimanded for their failure to govern their households. Richard Kingswell the elder of Liss, Hampshire, gent., was summoned before the Privy Council in 1609 to explain why he allowed his servants to hunt in Wolmer Forest. He pleaded that his servants had removed his greyhounds from their kennel without his knowledge and had killed a stag belonging to the king. One servant subsequently confessed his misdemeanours and was committed to Bridewell, where he was whipped, and Kingswell was discharged. But, two days later, Kingswell and his son, Richard Kingswell the younger, were themselves accused of killing deer in Wolmer Forest and the elder Kingswell was once more called before the Council table. The matter was turned over to Viscount Haddington, the lieutenant of Wolmer Forest, and the prosecution was dropped when Kingswell agreed to pay £6 13s. 4d. for the dead deer plus legal costs. In 1618 the Kingswells were

---

[17] HMC *Salisbury*, ii. 174.   [18] PRO STAC 7/6/29.
[19] PRO STAC 8/243/3.   [20] *English Courtier*, in *Inedited Tracts*, ed. Hazlitt, 40.

again prosecuted for killing numerous deer in Wolmer Forest. The evidence against the Kingswells revealed that they were associated with a large poaching gang which operated in West Sussex and eastern Hampshire.[21] Unlawful hunting by gangs of small gentry and their servants was widespread in Sussex, and, in 1621, the Privy Council, responding to a complaint from the king, reprimanded the sheriff and the entire commission of the peace in Sussex for permitting their servants and other unqualified persons to hunt and for conniving at their doing so.[22]

The household of Edward Parker, Lord Morley was especially disorderly. On his Lancashire estates, which he acquired by right of his marriage to the daughter and heir of William, Lord Monteagle, some of his household servants conspired and banded together with the servants of other gentry households to raid his own deer park at Hornby Castle and do battle with his park keepers.[23] On his Essex estates, Morley's unruly servants spent their days drinking at alehouses, quarrelling with one another, and slaughtering their master's deer in Hatfield Forest. One faction of his servants was said to have recruited hunting companions from among persons who included a 'conjurer' and 'a fugitive and vagrant person'.[24] The plea of George Clapham of Beamsley, esq., that his servants hunted in the chases of Francis, earl of Cumberland, without his permission was unconvincing, since he was one of those West Riding gentry who waged a poaching war against Cumberland in retaliation for the latter's assertion of absolute and unqualified hunting rights throughout the Craven district. Moreover, it was well known that Clapham helped his servants to eat the venison which they brought home. Clapham probably would have hunted with them himself, had he not been 80 years of age.[25]

Households where serving men banded together to form poaching gangs were common in the north of England. Peter Middleton, who leased Derwentwater Park, Cumberland, complained in 1535 that the deer in his charge were being decimated by a poaching gang which consisted entirely of serving men.[26] In 1582 Sir Richard Sherburne, steward and master forester of Bowland, also reported raids on the king's deer by gangs of servants from gentry households.[27] On the other hand, some servants were exploited to such an extent that the prospect of a little poaching on the side must have presented a strong temptation. After working as a butler during the day, Thomas Wright's master, John Dutton of Dutton, Cheshire, esq., required him to sit up all night in Dutton Park watching for poachers. Little wonder that Wright fell in with a gang of poachers who included a kinsman, William Wright. When prosecuted in Star Chamber in 1607, the other

---

[21] PRO STAC 8/190/15.   [22] *Acts PC, 1621–1623*, 95.
[23] PRO STAC 5/M26/15, undated, temp. Eliz. I.   [24] PRO STAC 8/58/5, 23 July 1605.
[25] PRO STAC 8/107/16, 26 Apr. 1608; see also above, Ch. 6.4.
[26] PRO STAC 2/27/154.   [27] PRO DL 1/27/S26.

poachers offered the excuse that, when travelling on the road through Dutton Park, their greyhound, 'by chance', coursed and killed a doe, which they carried off to a nearby house.[28]

Idle servants were capable of all sorts of nefarious tricks. Two professional poachers prosecuted by Gervase, Lord Clifton, in 1610 told of being enticed into hunting at Leighton Bromswold Park, Huntingdonshire, by two of Clifton's servants. One of the deer-stealers, Roger Tuder or Tedder, said that one Swayneman, a bricklayer who also acted as one of Clifton's gamekeepers, came to Tuder and said that his master had commanded him to kill a buck to be presented to the undersheriff. Since Swayneman was not a skilled hunter—so he claimed—he asked Tuder to help him, which the latter agreed to do. They arranged to meet that same evening and Tuder brought along his colleague, Richard Grace. When they started hunting, the first deer that they pursued was wounded and escaped, so they killed another deer in the park. But Henry Hollingsworth, another of Clifton's gamekeepers, persuaded Tuder and Grace to hide that deer to share among themselves, and they resumed pursuit of the wounded deer and brought it down. They also swore oaths to keep the theft of the other deer a secret. But Swayneman and Hollingsworth played a double game and immediately rallied Lord Clifton's other servants, who ambushed Tuder and Grace while spiriting away the buck which they had agreed to share.[29]

Poaching by members of disorderly households perpetuated the legacy of lawless and violent behaviour. But even respectable households could be turned upside down by the involvement of servants, sons, or younger brothers in unlawful hunting. In 1620 William, earl of Pembroke, the lieutenant and principal keeper of Gillingham Forest, complained against a group of 'very turbulent and disordered persons' who dwelt in the forest and its purlieus, and specialized in hunting and forestalling the king's deer. Among the many persons named as defendants were Francis Weekes, his younger brother Seymour, and his servant, Arthur Gough. In his answer, Francis Weekes confessed that his younger brother and Gough had taken his greyhounds without his knowledge and had killed a buck in the forest. Seymour and the servant returned home in the early hours of the morning with the keepers and their bloodhounds pursuing them. Francis Weekes was very angry with his brother and his manservant, but, because of the lateness of the hour, he sent his brother to bed 'without further conference'. When Francis returned to bed himself, he could not sleep because he was 'very much troubled in mind'. Although he was himself innocent, he feared that he would incur the displeasure of the earl. When the earl's keepers finally arrived at his door, Francis Weekes decided to tell all. He surrendered his greyhound—the other having already been taken up by the

[28] PRO STAC 8/123/10.   [29] PRO STAC 8/98/4.

keepers—and he turned his servant Gough over to the keepers, who carried him before a justice of the peace for punishment. Gough was committed to prison in Allington, Wiltshire, 'a very loathsome place', for nine days. Francis Weekes then discharged Gough, but the keepers entreated him to take Gough back into his service because they thought that he was unlikely to commit the same offence again.[30]

Although unruly servants in gentry and aristocratic households were careless in their observance of the Game Laws, they were usually more careful about their masters' hounds. In 1610 Sir Maurice Berkeley, lieutenant of the Forest of Frome Selwood, accused Emmanuel Hole of belonging to a poaching gang which had hunted in Staverdale Walk on several occasions. Hole denied the accusation and claimed that Henry Bainton, the ranger, had confiscated a greyhound belonging to his master with which Hole had been coursing conies in a rabbit warren located in Penn Purlieu, a parcel of land on his master's estate. Hole's master, William Chafin of Zeals Clifton, Wiltshire, esq., was a leading proponent of purlieu rights, and, since the keepers of the forest had already killed four or five hounds belonging to Chafin, Hole was determined to retrieve the dog. Hole and Richard Willoughby of Silton, Dorset, gent., a fellow defendant in the Star Chamber case, went to the keeper's lodge to look for Chafin's hound. When they arrived, they told the keeper's wife that they wished to buy drink and were invited into the lodge. Hole spied the missing hound, which he released and led away—but not before being assaulted by the keeper's wife.[31]

Servants from gentry and aristocratic households were immersed in hunting culture. Like their masters, when travelling, they often broke their journeys with a bit of sport. John Bishop, servant to John Drew of Vize Green, Wiltshire, gent., was accused of unlawful hunting at the Wiltshire quarter sessions in 1609. In his confession, Bishop told of how he had been sent on an errand one morning in May when he spotted a young deer in Rowde Marsh. He was heading towards a nearby friend's house to borrow a dog when he came upon a stray greyhound. Apparently, Bishop and the stray hound agreed that it was a nice morning to course a deer. The stray dog and the errant servant killed the deer, which Bishop carried on his shoulders to his house. He then placed the deer on a horse and conveyed it to his master's house—evidently expecting to be rewarded.[32]

William Dymer served in the household of John Alleyn of Horsham, Sussex, master of the queen's barges. In August 1591 his master gave Dymer a horse and sent him into Essex to bring back another horse and a couple of maidservants from the household of relatives of Mistress Alleyn living in Colchester and Aveley. While travelling to Essex, Dymer stopped at the

[30] PRO STAC 8/183/42.   [31] PRO STAC 8/47/3; see also above, Ch. 4.4.
[32] *Records of the County of Wiltshire*, ed. Cunnington, 28.

Green Dragon in Lambeth, where he encountered a couple of confidence men who had a supply of very special fish hooks. He sat for some time drinking with the two tricksters while they regaled him with stories of how many fish their marvellous hooks had caught and he purchased a couple before resuming his journey. He had not yet reached Aveley when he was arrested in a grove in Waltham Forest where the royal keepers took note of his fishing tackle. Dymer insisted that he was only grazing his horse while waiting for a stranger whom he had met at another tavern in Ilford. This person had promised to show Dymer the way to Aveley.[33] We do not know whether Dymer ever completed his journey, but, clearly, he needed direction.

7.3. *Smallholders and Artisans*

A legend had developed in Warwickshire during the seventeenth century which held that William Shakespeare, in his youth, had poached deer in Sir Thomas Lucy's park at Charlecote. Nicholas Rowe, an early editor of Shakespeare, assembled some of these legends and anecdotes at the end of the seventeenth century. In 1709 Rowe wrote that Shakespeare

had, by a misfortune common enough to young fellows, fallen into ill company; and amongst them some that made a frequent practice of deer-stealing engaged him with them more than once in robbing a park that belonged to Sir Thomas Lucy of Charlecote, near Stratford. For this he was prosecuted by that gentleman, as he thought somewhat too severely; and in order to revenge that ill usage, he made a ballad upon him. And 'though this, probably the first essay of his poetry, be lost, yet it is said to have been very bitter; that redoubled the prosecution against him to that degree that he was obliged to leave his business and family in Warwickshire for some time and shelter himself in London.[34]

---

[33] PRO SP 42/15, fo. 127[r–v].

[34] Nicholas Rowe, *Some Account of the Life of Mr. William Shakespeare* (1709; repr. 1948), p. v. While this story has the ring of truth and warrants comparison to accounts of deer-stealing followed by seditious libel taken from Star Chamber proceedings discussed earlier in this chapter, the fact remains that there is no contemporaneous documentary evidence for this story. Another problem with this anecdote is that Sir Thomas Lucy I, who died in 1600, did not possess a deer park in Warwickshire, but only a rabbit warren. Shakespeare left Stratford some time after 1585. However, Lucy most likely possessed liberty of free warren over his estate, where deer were known to inhabit the woods. One must also remember that it is not easy to document the existence of deer parks, and that the absence of a licence to enclose a park from the patent rolls does not constitute proof that one did not exist. A person possessing seigneurial jurisdiction was required to obtain a licence to enclose a park only where it was necessary to demonstrate that the park would not impinge upon a royal game reserve or royal hunting rights. A park did exist at Charlecote after 1618, when Sir Thomas Lucy III (1585–1640) was licensed to impale one (M. Eccles, *Shakespeare in Warwickshire* (Madison, Wisc., 1961), 72–5). I owe the above references to the courtesy of Dr Louis Barbato.

The first mention of Shakespeare's poaching is by Richard Davies (d. 1708), rector of Saperton, Gloucestershire. Davies wrote that the young Shakespeare was

much given to all unluckiness in stealing venison and rabbits, particularly from Sir [blank] Lucy, who had him oft whipped and sometimes imprisoned, and at last made him fly his native country to his great advancement. But his revenge was so great that he [Lucy] is his Justice Clodpate, and calls him a great man, and that in allusion to his name, bore lice ['lowses' in the original] rampant for his arms.[35]

That these stories of Shakespeare's youth may or may not be true is not of much importance. What is significant is what the survival of these legends and anecdotes tells us about seventeenth-century popular culture: that poaching was a usual rite of passage for the youth who wanted to assert his manhood or lay claim to genteel status. It is something that might have been expected of an Elizabethan or Jacobean poet and dramatist whose language was so virile and who displayed a technical mastery of hunting terms.

Poaching was becoming a national pastime in Tudor and early Stuart England. Poachers came from a wide variety of backgrounds. Those from the landed and propertied classes—peers, gentlemen, merchants,[36] and yeomanry—organized themselves into poaching fraternities, which not only perpetuated lawless and violent behaviour, but also manifested levelling tendencies. When smallholders, servants, adolescents, women[37] or masterless men belonged to poaching bands, this suggested an even more dangerous threat to patriarchal authority and opened up the prospect of a world turned upside down.

It was commonly assumed that youthful poaching led to a life of crime. It also surprised no one that hardened criminals were sometimes employed for poaching activities. When Sir Maurice Berkeley was pursuing a dispute with Sir Carew Raleigh, lieutenant of Gillingham Forest, he hired desperate men out of Wales, a common recruiting ground for bully boys, to fight Raleigh's underkeepers and to slaughter the deer in Gillingham. One such person was John or Jenkin Symmes, a convicted highwayman whom Berkeley employed as an underkeeper in Selwood Forest. Symmes had somehow obtained a pardon, but he was still bound to his good behaviour. Symmes's brother William and his sons, John and Henry, who were also underkeepers in Selwood, were of the same ilk.[38] When William Pitt and his neighbours

---

[35] *The Reader's Encyclopedia of Shakespeare*, ed. O. J. Campbell and E. R. Quinn (New York, 1966), 178, 478–9. Davis is referring, of course, to Justice Shallow in *The Merry Wives of Windsor*, Act I, Sc. i, whose coat of arms bore twelve white luces, or pike, which was, in actual fact, the coat of arms borne by Sir Thomas Lucy of Charlecote.

[36] PRO DL 1/54/D5; STAC 8/290/17, 180/14.

[37] For more examples of female poachers, see PRO DL 1/203/H23; STAC 8/215/1.

[38] PRO STAC 8/98/16, 246/21, 80/4, 73/13, 47/4.

wished to protest Sir Herbert Croft's enclosure of a new park in Hereford-shire, they found willing accomplices in Radnorshire who came to Croft Park in September and October 1613 to help the Herefordshire men slaughter the deer and level the pales.[39]

When popular disorders such as enclosure disputes and poaching were generated by court factionalism and aristocratic feuding, they frequently spread over wide areas and persisted for a long time. The fall of Essex in 1601 produced these kinds of reverberations in Wales. Sir Robert Mansell was a quarrelsome naval officer who had once killed a man in a duel. His arrest of the earl of Essex's followers earned him high favour with the Cecils, but also stirred up enmity between his followers and the late earl's sympathizers, which still lingered on as late as 1615. In that year poachers came from all over Pembrokeshire and Carmarthenshire to make war upon the deer in Mansell's park at Laugharne Castle, formerly one of Essex's seats in Wales which Mansell had obtained by reversion.[40]

Many defendants in unlawful hunting cases in Star Chamber refused to make answer to the bills of complaint. Such persons were frequently members of poaching fraternities who had sworn one another to secrecy. But hardened and experienced poachers knew all of the dodges and tricks and liked to display bravado. The gang of hunters who raided Thomas Baskerville's park at Netherwood, Herefordshire, in the winter and spring of 1620 killed over eighty deer. They had forged a warrant to show to Baskerville's keepers. When the latter indicated that they intended to report these depredations to Baskerville, who was away in London at the time, the hunters threatened to murder the keepers. When Baskerville brought a suit against them in Star Chamber, the culprits pleaded that Baskerville was disabled from bringing suits at law because he was himself outlawed.[41] In 1601 the keepers of Needwood Forest came upon two deer-stealers in the act of plying their trade. One of them, with the improbable name of Henry Toogood, escaped; the other, George Blacknoll, was captured and carried to the keeper's lodge, whence he escaped, leaving behind his crossbow. Blacknoll then had the audacity to demand the return of his weapon, and a friend brought an action in the Honour Court of Tutbury on his behalf to recover the crossbow. The attorney-general of the Duchy of Lancaster was of the opinion that the return of the crossbow would undermine the keepers' authority and set a bad precedent.[42]

When Thomas Isaac of Tillingham, Essex, was charged in about 1542 with keeping a hawk without a licence from the Privy Council, he provided a long list of reasons why the statute of 32 Hen. VIII did not apply in his case. He stated that the proclamation enforcing that statute had been

---

[39] PRO STAC 8/98/16, 108/12.   [40] PRO STAC 8/215/2.
[41] PRO STAC 8/8/13.   [42] PRO DL 1/196/A12.

published in only four market towns in Essex. He could not possibly have heard the proclamation, because at the time of publication he was upon a ship sailing from Winchelsea to Bradwell-upon-Sea. While on the ship, which was on a return voyage from Denmark, he had purchased a goshawk from a sailor who had acquired it from Denmark. Therefore, he could not be prosecuted under the statute, which specified that a licence was needed only for a 'hawk of the realm', and it could not be presumed that a hawk imported into the country belonged to the king.[43]

John Smyth of Nibley noted that poachers commonly gave false testimony when prosecuted because 'it was held a rule and no offence with deer-stealers to forswear the fact and outbrave the keepers'.[44] At the height of the poaching wars in the Vale of Berkeley, Henry, Lord Berkeley, noted that the deer-stealers, many of whom were his own tenants, were regarded as being so dangerous that his keepers deemed it prudent not to apprehend them. When Berkeley prosecuted a group of a dozen of his tenants in 1592, most denied their guilt and were quick to provide answers. One defendant insisted that he was a 'husbandman and followed his trade of husbandry without losing of his time in any such disport of hunting'.[45] Poachers were so thick upon the ground that rival gangs of hunters frequently stumbled upon one another at night or engaged in territorial disputes. One such encounter between two rival gangs, dressed in jacks and breastplates and armed with pistols and crossbows, occurred in Berkeley New Park on the night of 7 August 1601. When they encountered one another, the first gang challenged the second gang, who answered, 'Here are good fellows!', which was apparently the wrong password. The leader of the second gang killed a hound belonging to the leader of the rival poachers, who exclaimed: 'Villain! Hast thou killed my dog? I will kill or be killed before I go hence!' Before the affray was over, two men had been shot dead with pistols. The poachers included weavers, smallholders, servants, and a warrener. When Lord Berkeley had them summoned before the Court of Star Chamber to make answer, they were full of legal quibbles: one defendant boldly stated that the bill of complaint had been drawn up in a defective manner, and another, while admitting that he owned a greyhound, insisted that it was the kind that was only used for coursing hare.[46]

A common ploy used by poachers in answering complaints was to blame their misdeeds upon their dogs. This had the effect of personifying their dogs and attributing to them the ability to distinguish right from wrong. In 1609, with the connivance of an underkeeper of Blackmore Forest in Wiltshire, six men made plans to 'flesh' a young greyhound in Spy Park. The hound, which was on a leash, 'Chanced to break loose and ran after

[43] PRO STAC 2/23/248; *Tudor Royal Proclamations*, ed. Hughes and Larkin, vol. i, no. 211; 32 Hen. VIII, c. 11; *SR* iii. 755. [44] Smyth, *Berkeley Manuscripts*, iii. 352–3. [45] PRO STAC 5/B1/23. [46] PRO STAC 5/B76/35.

a deer and coursed him out of the park . . . and having run him about the distance of a furlong from the park . . . the dog pulled the deer down'. The deer was not seriously injured and some of the defendants had wanted to let it go, but the majority decided to kill the deer and remove the evidence. The greyhound proved to be a fast learner and was so eager to course another deer that the poachers resolved to go into Bowdon Park, where the dog pulled down another deer.[47] In 1595 Thomas Eyre of Benefield, North-amptonshire, husbandm, and a companion entered Sir Thomas Tresham's park at Lyvedon with a brace of greyhounds, 'intending only to have a course at some prickett or barren doe'. Eyre insisted that his hounds did not kill or wound any animal. Tresham's keepers pursued Eyre and his friend, and, in the ensuing mêlée, the keepers were wounded. Eyre had difficulty seeing where he had done wrong, but submitted and threw himself on the mercy of the court.[48] When Sir Henry Berkeley of Bruton, Somerset, pro-secuted several tenants of the manor in about 1589 for allowing their dogs to kill a deer which had escaped from Norwood Park, one of the tenants disclaimed any responsibility by saying that he had 'rebuked' the dog but was unable to recall him.[49]

Keepers frequently punished dogs for their masters' misdeeds, and this invariably led to acts of revenge. In Nottinghamshire, in 1545, the very unpopular George Wastnes prosecuted Thomas Frith for allowing his hounds to break into Heydon Park and pursue a deer. In punishment for the deed, his keepers hanged Frith's dogs from the park palings. Frith insisted that his dogs were actually pursuing a fox in Thomas Hercy's wood and not in Heydon Park. Frith attempted to save his dogs by pulling down the pales which they were hanging from, and this led to a fight between Frith and Wastnes's keepers.[50]

A similar incident occurred in the barony of Kendal, Westmorland, in 1614. Thomas Lucas of Burton, yeom., claimed that the tenants needed hunting dogs to protect their sheep from foxes, which were vermin and not game. The keeper of Holme Park, Tristram Lucas, thought that greyhounds were singularly ill-suited for hunting foxes, and he tried to 'chastize' the hounds, which provoked the wrath of Thomas Lucas and some forty of his companions, who mounted a raid on Holme Parke with 'twenty or thirty couple of greyhounds' and destroyed fifty deer. On another occasion the hunters ambushed Tristram Lucas's servant, Robert Frank, and threatened to murder him 'for beating the hounds and dogs of the said Thomas Lucas'. The latter drew his dagger on Frank and viciously stabbed him several times and did 'most maliciously, furiously and barbarously vow and protest that the same dogs he had beaten should eat and devour him'.[51] The hunters

---

[47] Merriman, 'Extracts from the Records of the Wiltshire Quarter Sessions', 26.
[48] PRO STAC 7/15/35.   [49] PRO STAC 5/B76/1.
[50] PRO STAC 2/23/22; see also above, Ch. 6.4.   [51] PRO STAC 8/21/16.

continued to havoc the deer in Holme Park and feasted upon their illicit venison in an alehouse in Barton. Thomas Lucas was indicted for his offences at the Westmorland Quarter Sessions, and he threatened to fight the keepers with cross-suits and counter-suits and reduce them to beggary. Thomas Lucas then forged a number of legal documents and bonds purporting to show that Frank owed money to him, and began an action of debt against Frank at the Assizes. A few months before the issue was to be tried, Thomas Lucas told Frank that he would drop his action for debt against Frank if he would withdraw his testimony against Lucas on the charges of assault and mayhem. Frank refused and Lucas proceeded with his action for debt and won. Lucas had already sought his revenge against the head keeper, Tristram Lucas, a few months earlier by stealing Tristram's lymehound and training it to hunt deer in Holme Park. Thomas Lucas then hanged the lymehound within sight of Tristram's lodge in Holme Park.[52]

By personifying the hounds and visiting acts of vengeance upon the dumb animals, poachers and keepers displayed a notable lack of moral responsibility that is characteristic of the deer-hunting culture among both gentry and commonalty. The confession of a Salisbury clothier, who was examined by members of the city's commission of the peace, reveals some of this moral ambivalence and naïvety. Thomas Ray stated that he and Barnaby Legate, carpenter, had met at a farmhouse outside Salisbury on the night of 2 June 1606. Legate then persuaded Ray and two other companions from Salisbury to go with him into Clarendon Park at about ten or eleven p.m. Ray insisted that he did not know what he was being drawn into until the other two arrived leading greyhounds. He claimed that he departed when he realized what they were up to, but instead of going home he went to a place near Clarendon Park where he could watch and determine if, indeed, they were going hunting there. On the way to Clarendon Park, Ray once more bumped into Legate and the other two hunters and they again invited him to accompany them. Ray 'answered and said he would not for forty pounds assent thereunto for fear of offending my lord, meaning . . . the earl of Pembroke [who had brought a complaint in Star Chamber against the four deer-stealers]'. Unable to entice Ray into the park, the other three asked Ray if he would watch their horses until they returned. Ray says that he remained three-quarters of an hour until they returned with the carcass of a buck. He then went home to bed without offering them any further help. But about two or three o'clock in the morning the three hunters knocked at Ray's door and dragged the buck into his house and left it there until they returned about three hours later, when they broke up the carcass. One quarter was dressed and cooked in Ray's house by a servant of Stephen Bowman, gent., one of the four deer-stealers. Maintaining his innocence

---

[52] Ibid.

beyond the limits of credibility, Ray deposed that he ate no part of the venison cooked in his house—even when it was offered to him—and never consented to go hunting. Ray also added that William Smith, the fourth deer-stealer, was a servant of Edward Estcourte, esq., one of the magistrates who took down his deposition, and that the two greyhounds and the horse used to carry home the deer carcass also belonged to Estcourte.[53]

The Game Laws, especially the Acts of 1485 and 1563, encouraged confession by poachers who had been apprehended or could be compelled to appear in court. The first statute reduced certain acts of unlawful hunting from felony to misdemeanour if the accused confessed his misdeeds, while the second Act allowed the complainant to release the culprit on his own recognizance following confessions.[54] Younger poachers were more likely to confess than seasoned hunters. In 1606 Henry, Lord Berkeley, attempted to break up a gang of deer-stealers composed of clothworkers living in the village of Nibley, Gloucestershire. None of the older men volunteered much information, but Nicholas Tyndall, an apprentice to John Nolme, weaver, told how his master had ordered him, against his will, to assist them in preparations for hunting in Michaelwood Chase and to rise out of his bed in the middle of the night to accompany the older men on their poaching expedition.[55] In Wiltshire, in 1605, Edith Blacker, maidservant to Edward Burden, a weaver of Donhead St Mary, testified how her master always kept on hand a large supply of carp which he had removed from neighbourhood ponds. He stored the fish in casks in his milkhouse and chamber and his wife baked them in great pies, which they ate behind locked doors. She added that Burden had also tried to bribe another witness to testify that the fish were mackerel rather than carp.[56]

Indebtedness was sometimes given as a motive for poaching. A band of more than two dozen metalworkers raided Sir Thomas Holte's deer parks and cony warrens in Aston, Warwickshire, in July 1607 after he demanded forfeiture of a bond offered by one of the defendants to guarantee payment for a ton of bar iron. One of the defendants was unable to answer Holte's complaint because he had been 'since executed for felony'.[57] John Bretland, a butcher of Chesterfield, Derbyshire, said that he accompanied a large band of artisans who had raided the deer park of William, Lord Cavendish, at Langwith in 1611 because he was indebted to Henry Thornley, who had told Bretland that he might discharge part of his debt by procuring some venison for Thornley to bestow upon a friend as a gift. Bretland, who had some experience in these matters, was expected to organize the raid and

---

[53] Merriman, 'Extracts from the Records of the Wiltshire Quarter Sessions', 25; PRO STAC 8/183/37.

[54] I Hen. VII, c. 7, and 5 Eliz. I, c. 21; Manning, *Village Revolts*, 300; see also above, Ch. 3.1.

[55] PRO STAC 8/80/9.

[56] Merriman, 'Extracts from the Records of the Wiltshire Quarter Sessions', 27–8.

[57] PRO STAC 8/163/7/7; see also 8/169/20.

obtain hunting dogs. Thornley came along, but refused to enter the deer park himself and left the actual hunting up to Bretland and his friends.[58]

Many kinds of public gatherings could quickly turn into poaching affrays. In Kent, in June 1609, a group of smallholders and artisans playing games suddenly invaded the earl of Salisbury's deer park at Canterbury 'under colour of playing at football or other such unlawful game or exercise'. The players spoiled the deer, tore down a great part of the park pales, and assaulted and wounded the keeper when he ordered them to depart.[59] In 1616 Anne, dowager Lady Howard of Effingham, decided to dispark Bletchingley Park in Surrey, which she held as part of her jointure. She sold or gave the herd of forty fallow deer to the king, who sent keepers in November to catch the deer in toils and convey them to a nearby royal park. Before the day arrived to begin disparking, a rumour had spread through Surrey that there was to be a general and public hunting. A crowd of forty persons with their dogs descended upon Bletchingley on 20 November and began coursing and killing the deer and returned again the next day. The royal keepers were in the process of gathering up deer, and many of their nets were destroyed and the park fences levelled before order could be restored.[60]

7.4. Keepers

A keeper's life was not a happy one. The underkeepers who patrolled their masters' game reserves were constantly exposed to danger, because poaching gangs were often determined to engage them in combat. The fact that they were obliged to watch over forests and parks at night did not allow them to lie in bed during the daylight hours and leave their game reserves unguarded. Keepers had many duties besides repulsing or apprehending deer-stealers. Their other duties included cutting browse and spreading hay for their charges and keeping the fences in good repair. It was in the nature of things that they would never be welcomed into local communities. Many keepers and their families and servants must have led lonely lives living in isolated lodges in the midst of their parks and forests.

The status of gamekeepers varied widely. The head keepers of royal forests and parks, perhaps bearing the title of lieutenant or bow-bearer or master of the game, were peers or gentlemen, usually held other offices in the royal household as well, and would not have spent all their time in the country. Sir Edward Rogers, the keeper of the royal park of Pulton, Gloucestershire, was also an esquire of the body to Henry VIII, captain of

---

[58] PRO STAC 8/106/1. [59] PRO STAC 8/16/2. [60] PRO STAC 8/183/29.

the guard, vice chamberlain of the household, a privy councillor, and a member of Parliament. When he was in the country, he shared the dangers of the underkeepers and led them in repelling attacks by dangerous gangs of poachers. Perhaps, for a soldier, beating off deer-stealers raiding a park was the Tudor equivalent of going on manœuvres.[61]

In gentlemen's households, such as that of Richard Egerton of Ridley, Cheshire, in 1528, the servants sometimes did double duty as game-keepers.[62] Other gamekeepers worked as artisans and lent a hand guarding against poachers in their spare time.[63] William Turville's chaplain was expected to act as his bow-bearer when Turville hunted on his Leicestershire estate during the time of Henry VIII. Since Turville was engaged in a dispute with the marquis of Dorset concerning the precise location of the boundary between their respective deer parks, the duties of Turville's chaplain and bow-bearer included accompanying his master on poaching forays into Dorset's park and repelling raids by Dorset's keepers.[64]

Although Tudor domestic architecture reflected the relatively more peaceful conditions of that era, keepers' lodges often continued to be moated and equipped with heavy shutters to deflect arrows and pikes. Poachers sometimes practised psychological warfare against keepers by depriving them of sleep, performing acts of defiance such as flinging stags' heads against the doors of their lodges, or terrorizing keepers into impotence before commencing their raids upon the deer.[65] John Turner, the underkeeper of Quernmore Park during the 1520s, described how a gang of Lancashire gentry deer-stealers, led by Richard Curwen of Caton, procured persons 'disguised in women's apparel' to lie in wait to ambush and murder him. Turner was so terrified that he dared not discharge his duties as keeper or live in the keeper's lodge, and he never left home except in the company of others.[66]

Some of the poaching raids of the early Tudor period differed little from the random violence which accompanied the baronial wars of the fifteenth century. On the manor of Allbrighton, Shropshire, Edward Corbet led a gang of deer-stealers in an attack upon Sir John Talbot's deer park. The fourteen hunters outnumbered the keepers and drove them back into the lodge and kept them confined and covered there, showering the keepers with arrows every time they tried to sally forth from the lodge. The hunters brought twenty greyhounds with them and completely destroyed the deer in the park.[67] In Yorkshire, during the reign of Edward VI, Matthew Philip,

---

[61] PRO STAC 4/3/66, dated 1555; *House of Commons, 1509–1558*, ed. Bindoff, iii. 206–7; *DNB, sub* Sir Edward Rogers (1498?–1567?).

[62] PRO STAC 2/14, fo. 43; see also STAC 8/123/10.

[63] PRO STAC 8/98/4.	[64] PRO STAC 2/26/169, 377.

[65] PRO STAC 4/6/77; *Pleadings and Depositions in the Duchy Court of Lancaster*, i. 228–9.

[66] Ibid.	[67] PRO STAC 2/24/234.

yeom., led a band of sixty deer-stealers, who completely overwhelmed the keepers of the West Park of Middleham, a crown estate. The deer-stealers operated quite openly and did not trouble to hide their identity from the keepers, who knew better than to try to defend the deer against the hunters. Nor did the keepers dare to risk searching the houses of suspected deer-stealers, because, as the keepers complained to the Star Chamber, the poachers had threatened to 'lay the brains of your said suppliants . . . upon their shoulders if they would enterprise any further in the fetching home' of the deer.[68] As late as 1608 William, Lord Cavendish, stated that, on several occasions, Brian Bellamy of Askham, Nottinghamshire, gent., led his servants and others in an attack on Langwith Park, Derbyshire. After being wounded, Cavendish's keepers were not equal to 'so desperate and well-armed a company' and 'in their own defence were forced to flee for the safeguard of their lives'.[69]

Keepers routinely sustained wounds in the discharge of their duties. After lying in wait for poachers to recover a dead deer which they had hidden in Neroche Forest, Somerset, Anthony Pitts, an underkeeper, was so seriously wounded that it was thought that he was unlikely to recover or to be able to discharge his duties 'to the ruin of his wife and children'.[70] His assailants were bound over to the assizes, but were discharged when they proved that Pitts was a notorious deer-stealer himself. Edward Herbert, an underkeeper in the park of Edward, earl of Bedford, at Melchbourne, Bedfordshire, was fired upon in 1605 by Duchy of Lancaster officials in a dispute concerning the location of the boundary between the earl's deer park and the duchy woods. Herbert 'did long languish in great peril of death, having many pieces of his skull for furtherance of his cure taken out of his head by surgeons to the utter disabling of him from being a man of strength and ability'.[71] Sir George Blount's two underkeepers in Wyre Forest were both disabled in 1569 by poachers who had fired forked arrows at them. After they took to their beds to recover from their wounds, Blount, an aged man, watched helplessly while the deer-stealers plundered the forest.[72] When Sir Thomas Holte's gamekeeper tracked a band of deer-stealers to a house in the parish of Aston, Warwickshire, in 1610, they attacked him with a long pitchfork and left him bleeding from the 'mouth, head, and ears'. No one dared to arrest the leader of the gang, who habitually went about armed with a gun.[73]

When one considers the number of gamekeepers who were former poachers, it seems remarkable how little sympathy the two groups displayed towards one another, or how little consideration gamekeepers showed for each other. Such was the brutalizing influence of the deer-hunting culture.

[68] PRO STAC 3/3/2. [69] PRO STAC 8/85/10. [70] PRO STAC 8/34/19.
[71] PRO STAC 8/48/11. [72] PRO STAC 5/B5/3, B38/18 [73] PRO STAC 8/169/20.

Anthony Daston, gent., claimed to possess the right of free warren for rabbits on his holding, although he was only a tenant of Sudeley Manor, Gloucestershire. This was disputed by the keepers of Sudeley Park and the warrener of the rabbit warren adjacent to Sudeley Park. On the night of 9 December 1547, the latter, together with nine park keepers and other servants of Sir John Briggs, broke into Daston's rabbit warren, carried away all of the rabbits, and assaulted Daston's warrener, who later died of his wounds. When Daston charged the keepers with murder, they threatened to burn his house down. Daston fled to London to complain to Star Chamber, and the keepers of Sudeley occupied his house and warren.[74]

The unhappy lives of keepers aroused little sympathy, because they gave as good as they got in their dealings with poachers and neighbours, and the methods which they employed were often of dubious legality. In 1615 the keepers of Malvern Chase were accused of practising extortion and entrapment upon their victims, accepting bribes, and demanding excessive sureties from poachers before releasing them from gaol. One youthful poacher, John Wrenford, lamented how the Malvern keepers had bound his feet and those of his companion beneath the bellies of their horses, after which they were humiliated by being paraded through a market town. Young Wrenford was then offered the choice of going to gaol or sending for his father to act as his surety. Wrenford's father also had to find another person to act as a surety before he was released. Each surety was in the amount of £40 and bound Wrenford and his father to appear in Star Chamber upon twenty days' notice. Wrenford's hunting companion got off scot free after paying a bribe.[75]

In Elizabethan Wiltshire a state of war existed between the keepers of Aldbourne Chase and the inhabitants of Ogbourne St George. Thomas Waldron, the keeper of the chase, accused Vincent Goddard, the farmer of the royal manor of Ogbourne St George and a man 'of wealth and some credit in the same county', of procuring his brother, his son, and his servants to destroy the deer within the chase and the conies within a warren leased by Waldron. The keepers caught the alleged deer-stealers in the act of erecting their nets. When the keepers attempted to confiscate the nets, Goddard's men assaulted the keepers, 'who were driven to flight'. During the combat, one of Goddard's servants was slain, and Goddard obtained the indictment of four keepers for wilful murder on the argument that the nets had been pitched outside the chase. As a consequence, two of the keepers were condemned as felons and a third remained under indictment. Waldron secured a reprieve for the two condemned underkeepers from a justice of assize when he admitted to the judge that the boundaries of the chase were imprecisely marked.[76]

Goddard's men were sufficiently emboldened to continue hunting in

[74] PRO STAC 3/5/21.   [75] PRO STAC 8/247/20.   [76] PRO DL 1/43/W3.

Aldbourne Chase. On one occasion they confiscated a lymehound from one of Waldron's underkeepers. On another occasion, an underkeeper and his hound invaded Goddard's house in a search for venison, and Goddard's son James drove the hound out of the house and cut the bowstring of the underkeeper. Goddard insisted that he took rabbits and deer only on his own land.[77] By 1585, William Young had replaced Goddard as the farmer of Ogbourne St George, but little had changed for the keepers. The dispute concerning the metes and bounds of Aldbourne Chase continued as late as 1636, and the keepers accused members of the new farmer's family and household of poaching. They and the inhabitants of Ogbourne continued to do battle with the keepers of Aldbourne Chase.[78]

Considering their background, it is not surprising that gamekeepers sometimes suffered relapses. In 1611 Anthony Kinnersley of Loxley, Staffordshire, accused Ralph Wall, his warrener, of betraying his trust and destroying all the rabbits in Kinnersley's warren over a two-year period. Wall tried to blame the deed on a group of schoolboys.[79] In 1618 William Jacob, an underkeeper to Lord Zouch, was a prisoner in the Marshalsea for killing his master's deer in Odiham Park.[80] The rangers and keepers of Bowland Forest killed deer without warrants on a large scale. In 1570 the Court of Duchy Chamber learnt that Roger Sherburne, the bow-bearer of the forest and a kinsman of the master forester, Sir Richard Sherburne, was part of a conspiracy to keep knowledge of the depredations of his rangers and keepers from the master forester.[81] Richard Cholmeley thought that the keepers of Galtres Forest were so closely allied with the deer-stealers of the North Riding as to be almost indistinguishable.[82] In 1585 John Rigmaiden, who had been master forester of the Forest of Wyresdale and Quernmore since 1556, was removed 'for great disorders in office' as well as destruction of the deer. Lawrence Parkinson, the keeper of Wyresdale, testified to a special Duchy of Lancaster commission that Rigmaiden had unlawfully killed 227 deer over a period of twenty-six years, of which eighty-seven were killed out of season.[83] Sir Henry Bainton, the deputy justice in eyre of the forests, in 1614 accused Thomas Lansier or Landseer, the head keeper of Spy Park in Wiltshire, together with Lansier's son and two underkeepers, of being in league with a band of local deer-stealers. Because of the special trust which he had placed in his head keeper, Bainton thought that Lansier should be charged with the crime of embezzlement.[84]

---

[77] PRO DL 1/109/A16, DL 4/21/48.

[78] PRO DL 1/128/A30, DL 4/27/71, DL 1/119/A21, 135/A60, 187/A40, 124/A47; Rushworth (ed.), *Historical Collections*, II. ii, appendix, p. 74.   [79] PRO STAC 8/192/5.

[80] *Acts PC, 1617–1619*, 316.   [81] Shaw, *Royal Forest of Lancaster*, 234.

[82] *Memorandum Book of Richard Cholmeley of Brandsby*, 173.

[83] PRO DL 44/381; *Pleadings and Depositions in the Duchy Court of Lancaster*, iii. 214–15.

[84] PRO STAC 8/69/10. Bainton was himself a poaching magistrate; see above, Ch. 6.3.

Having examined the lives of poachers and keepers and the answers which the former gave when examined by magistrates concerning their alleged misdeeds, it is difficult to avoid the conclusion that habitual poaching fostered a lack of moral responsibility—even where poaching was engaged in to protest the extinction of common rights by the imparkment or expansion of deer parks and rabbit warrens, or where it was done to prevent damage to crops by loose deer or rabbits.[85] It was a commonplace that hunting promoted idleness among those who ought to have been following their ploughs or working at their trades. Unlawful hunting was widely perceived as being inimical to good household government, because it led young men and servants into the company of those who lived outside the law and beyond the reach of religion. Unlawful hunting also fostered disrespect for established hierarchies and patriarchal authority, since it was widely perceived that poaching bands displayed levelling tendencies. When the legal doctrine of possessive individualism emerged in the seventeenth century, poaching was recognized as posing a threat to private property, and the Game Laws shifted the emphasis of hunting qualifications from social status to economic status.

Popular disorder continued to pose a challenge to the emerging absolutist state in early modern England as elsewhere in Europe. Of all the species of disorder in England, probably only the Civil Wars of the seventeenth century were more injurious to royal government and aristocratic privilege than the phenomenon of large-scale, organized poaching. This was especially true of deer-stealing by the gentry and servants of aristocratic and gentry households, because their influence was widespread and their example particularly corrupting.[86] Since these poaching disorders were not infrequently linked with aristocratic feuding, there existed the potential danger that such conflicts could lead to a revival of baronial power if not punished.

We have already noticed that there was an epidemic of unlawful hunting beginning early in the reign of James I and probably continuing down until the eve of the Civil Wars. Whether poaching was sustained at the same level during the period 1625–40 cannot be verified easily because of the destruction of Star Chamber Proceedings for the reign of Charles I as well as the disappearance of the entire series of Star Chamber Entry Books of Decrees and Orders.

Hunting disorders were, of course, a legacy of the fifteenth century, but their resurgence early in the seventeenth century seems to be attributable to the absence of opportunities for military adventure overseas and the continuing problem of gentry violence at home.[87] The violent behaviour of

---

[85] See White, *Natural History of Selborne*, 31.

[86] See J. A. Sharpe, *Crime in Early Modern England, 1550–1700* (1984), 129–30.

[87] K. M. Brown, 'Gentlemen and Thugs in 17th-Century Britain', *History Today*, 40 (Oct. 1990), 27–32; Sharpe, *Crime in Early Modern England*, 96–9.

the gentry certainly owes much to the persistence of martial values among a large segment of the aristocracy and gentry and to the pervasive influence of a deer-hunting culture, which helped to perpetuate a taste for blood-letting and martial endeavours and to popularize the notion that a young man could not be possessed of manhood unless he was a hunter. Adolescent poaching must have been very widespread and probably constituted a common experience for country-bred boys, but the most destructive aspect of the deer-hunting culture was the prevalence of gentry-led deer-stealing.

8

Hunting, Poaching, and Social Privilege

I have passed much time in seeing the royal sports of hunting and hawking, where the manners were such as made me devise the beasts were pursuing the sober creation, and not man in quest of exercise or food.

Sir John Harington from Theobalds (1606) to Secretary Barlow, in
Nugae Antiquae, ed. Thomas Park, 2 vols. (1804), i. 352

One man might with more safety have killed another, than a rascal deer; but if a stag had been known to have miscarried and the author fled, a proclamation with the description of the party had been presently penned by the attorney-general, and the penalty of his majesty's high displeasure (by which was understood the Star Chamber) threatened against all that did abet, comfort, or relieve him. Thus satyrical, or if you please, tragical was this sylvan prince against deer-slayers and indulgent to man-slayers.

Memoirs on Queen Elizabeth and King James, in *The Works of Francis Osborn* (9th edn., 1689), pp. 444–5

ROYAL indulgence in hunting was justified as a necessary recreation to help the monarch bear the cares and burdens of government. This same line of reasoning was also used to justify hunting by the king's ministers in an age of conciliar monarchy. Hunting as a rehearsal for war continued to be the rationale for encouraging the traditional sport of pursuing deer upon horseback among the nobility and the armigerous gentry, and Renaissance writers of manuals of education for courtiers and gentlemen reiterated this ancient argument for conferring hunting privileges upon a military élite. Yet the hunting methods employed by the king and the nobility between *c.* 1500 and 1640 displayed an artificiality which belied their supposed simulation of martial endeavours. Royal deer hunts constituted a theatrical display which dramatized the royal mystique and sought to perpetuate the image of the monarch as a descendant of warrior kings of medieval England, but, in fact, they had become a metaphor for military power featuring a tableau of the king destroying his enemies with the deer standing in as surrogates. However, the Tudor monarchs hunted in relative moderation and their field sports evoked only admiring comments. Clearly, a new sensibility was developing by the beginning of the seventeenth century—perhaps because

James I's obsessive fondness for blood sports stood in stark contrast to his pacific foreign policy. The unseemly behaviour and drunken orgies which accompanied the Jacobean royal hunts were perceived as a foul perversion, and the sordid tone of Jacobean court life together with the king's neglect of his duties did not fail to elicit criticism from among persons of an aesthetic or morally sensitive disposition.

As the human population of England and Wales increased and the deer population diminished, the king and those who possessed hunting franchises became less indulgent towards unlawful hunting by social inferiors. The popular disorders spawned by the deer-hunting culture were attacked on several levels. From the late fourteenth century to the middle of the sixteenth century the Game Laws had stressed the preservation of public order. With the accession of James I the emphasis shifted more to the revival of the royal prerogative in hunting and forest matters and the preservation and enhancement of the hunting privileges of the crown and aristocracy. The royal attack upon purlieu rights and the revival of forest law aroused widespread resistance among property owners who found themselves deprived of ancient hunting rights. The exclusive hunting rights claimed by peers, such as the earls of Cumberland in the Craven district of West Yorkshire, provoked long and bitter poaching wars. Although the Courts of Star Chamber and Duchy of Lancaster Chamber had taken an interest in unlawful hunting involving breaches of public order throughout the sixteenth century, the reign of James I saw a veritable flood of Star Chamber prosecutions of organized bands of poachers, and the evidence which has survived the parliamentary destruction of Star Chamber records for the reign of Charles I suggests that this trend continued down until 1640.[1] From the pulpit, clergymen increasingly depicted hunting and hawking as idleness in aristocrats as well as artificers. Hunting as mere sport became less defensible because of the cruelty which it inflicted upon animals.[2] Some writers of courtesy manuals thought that rounds of visits by young gentlemen, with their hounds and servants, from country house to country house, promoted a community solidarity which helped to avoid the 'danger of discontents and quarrels', but the author of *Cyvile and Uncyvile Life* saw it as an abuse of hospitality. The more fastidious of the landed gentry abhorred these all-too-frequent incursions of 'gentlemen's houses, with man and horse, hawk and dog, 'til the poor master of the house hath all his linen foul, all his provisions eaten'.[3]

---

[1] See Rushworth (ed.), *Historical Collections, passim*, and *Reports of Cases in the Courts of Star Chamber and High Commission*, ed. S. R. Gardiner (Camden Soc., NS 39; 1886). Some of the Caroline prosecutions for unlawful hunting are discussed in Manning, *Village Revolts*, ch. 11.   [2] Thomas, *Man and the Natural World*, 162–5.
[3] F. Heal, *Hospitality in Early Modern England* (Oxford, 1990), 13–14, 22, 61.

8.1. The Tudor and Early Stuart Monarchs

Little is known of Henry VII's hunting activities beyond the fact that he was determined to protect his deer and to punish those who destroyed them or violated his parks and forests.[4] He hunted daily and was conscious of the need to project the image of a warrior-king who led his soldiers into battle, and so hunting must have served, in the medieval manner, to hone his military skills and to afford recreation. Henry VIII was a natural athlete, skilled in horsemanship and archery. Hearing that the Emperor Maximilian, whom he both admired and envied, was a skilled hunter, Henry determined also to excel in that sport. Richard Pace, the king's secretary, told Wolsey in 1520 that 'the king rises daily, except on holy days, at four or five o'clock, and hunts 'til nine or ten at night. He spares no pains to convert the sport of hunting into martyrdom.'[5] A foreign ambassador reported that 'he is very fond of hunting and never takes his diversion without eight or ten horses which he causes to be stationed beforehand along the line of country he means to take, and when one is tired he mounts another and before he gets home they are all exhausted'.[6]

These descriptions of the energy which Henry VIII expended upon the chase suggest that, in his younger days, the king hunted *par force* and at large, but from sometime in the mid-1530s the style of hunting appears to have changed to the method of driving the deer past standings from which the king and his courtiers fired at the deer with crossbows.[7] Certainly, drives past standings were being conducted by 1537, and after about 1535 there was a great flurry of building activity as new palaces and hunting lodges, together with deer parks and standings, were erected or reconstructed in the Thames Valley and the Home Counties, where the terrain was better suited to this style of hunting.[8] Because Henry did not range as far in his travels as his ancestors had, a number of the older royal forests and royal residences were neglected. The more outlying parks and forests remained important only in so far as they generated revenues for the crown, furnished patronage for courtiers and royal servants, supplied venison for the royal table and largesse, or bred replacements for herds in the Thames Valley deer parks.[9]

---

[4] See, e.g., 1 Hen. VII, c. 7; *SR* ii. 505.

[5] Blackmore, *Hunting Weapons*, p. xx; *L&P Hen. VIII*, III. i. 450.

[6] Quoted in A. F. Pollard, *Henry VIII* (1902; repr. 1951), 31.

[7] See Ch. 1.3. A standing might be nothing more than a raised timber platform with balustrades, as depicted in George Gascoigne, *Noble Art of Venerie*, or it might be a more elaborate multi-storey structure, enclosed and unglazed at the upper levels, such as the so-called Queen Elizabeth's Hunting Lodge, which survives at Chingford in Epping Forest, Essex. This structure was probably erected *c*.1542–3, soon after Henry VIII impaled a new park there (Colvin, Ransome, and Summerson (eds.), *History of the King's Works*, IV. ii. 16).

[8] *Lisle Letters*, ed. Byrne, vi. 177; Colvin, Ransome, and Summerson (eds.), *History of the King's Works*, IV. ii. 5; J. Guy, *Tudor England* (Oxford, 1990), 99.

[9] McIntosh, *Autonomy and Community*, 16–18; see also above, Ch. 5.

Some idea of the new arrangements for coursing deer with greyhounds may be gained from a contemporary description of the construction and furnishing of the new royal park at the More in Hertfordshire in 1535. Within the enclosed area all trees were removed so as to provide 'a great plain laund for the king's course'. Several timber structures were erected on masonry piers to provide shelter for the deer in inclement weather and accommodation for the keepers. Two standings were built within the park from which the king and his court could view the proceedings.[10] The new park might more accurately be described as a deer-pit, since the activities carried on within it resembled nothing so much as an arena for baiting bulls or bears.

The increase in the king's building activities in the 1530s was financed by Thomas Cromwell's reorganization of the royal finances and the opportunities for plundering the wealth of the church which followed Cromwell's survey of clerical incomes in the *Valor Ecclesiasticus*—undertaken for purposes of taxation and the expropriation of ecclesiastical wealth.[11] The change in the royal mode of recreation from the vigorous pursuit of deer on horseback to more sedentary sports such as hawking, cock-fighting, and slaughtering deer as they were driven past standings appears to reflect Henry's declining health and increasing corpulence. These bloody sports were also a kind of political theatre and may have contained lessons for those who participated in rebellions against the crown between 1536 and 1541.[12] Apart from the new parks and hunting lodges, this required the construction of other facilities such as kennels for greyhounds, 'hawk mews', bear-pits, cock-pits, and bridges upon the Woolwich Marshes so that the king might cross streams without fording.[13]

In addition to acquiring the vast piles of Hampton Court Palace and York Palace or Whitehall from Cardinal Wolsey, Henry VIII also made extensive alterations to the older palaces at Greenwich and Eltham, built new royal residences at Bridewell and New Hall, near Chelmsford. As his mobility lessened, Henry asserted absolute and exclusive rights of hunting and hawking along the routes which lay between the various royal palaces and hunting lodges. In 1545, the area bounded by St Giles-in-the-Fields, Islington, Highgate, Hornesey Park, Hampstead Heath, Willesdon, Acton, and the north bank of the Thames down to Westminster was closed off. The vast hunting reserve of Hampton Court Chase, extending from Richmond to Hampton Court Palace and served by the hunting lodges of Nonsuch and Oatlands, has already been mentioned. In April 1545 all hunting was prohibited between London and Kingston-upon-Thames in order to protect

---

[10] Colvin, Ransome, and Summerson (eds.), *History of the King's Works*, iv. ii. 168.
[11] D. Starkey (ed.) *The English Court from the Wars of the Roses to the Civil War* (1987), 96–7; Guy, *Tudor England*, 146–7.　　　　　　　　　　　　　　　[12] See Ch. 2.3.
[13] Colvin, Ransome, and Summerson (eds.) *History of the King's Works*, iv. ii. 106.

any deer which might have strayed from Hampton Court Chase or Combe Park. In addition, deer parks were also provided for the amusement of the royal bastard, Henry, duke of Richmond, such as the one in Bedhampton, Hampshire. Altogether, Henry VIII built thirty new palaces and hunting lodges after 1535, and, by the time of his death in 1547, he owned a total of fifty residences. Between 1539 and the end of the reign, the king spent £500,000 on the construction of palaces and hunting lodges, exclusive of the furnishings.[14]

Elizabeth, like her father, hunted on horseback in her youth—always with an eye to theatrical effect. Her favourite hunting lodge appears to have been Hatfield, where she kept a large stable of hunters. Hatfield Great Park, in those days, extended all the way to Theobalds and Enfield Chase and afforded a large unimpeded hunting reserve. In April 1557 it was recorded that the young Princess Elizabeth set out from Hatfield to hunt the hart in Enfield Chase. She was accompanied by twelve ladies-in-waiting dressed in white satin and twenty mounted yeomen clothed in green. 'At entering the chase . . . she was met by fifty archers in scarlet boots and yellow caps, armed with gilded bows, one of whom presented her with a silver-headed arrow, winged with peacock's feathers'. Sir Thomas Pope had planned these tableaux, and the role assigned to Elizabeth was to dispatch the hart by cutting its throat.[15]

In Tudor England, royal hunting parties took on many of the forms of the court masque. Everything was rehearsed and nothing left to chance—including the role that the deer were meant to play. Nowhere is this better illustrated than in George Gascoigne's *The Noble Art of Venerie*. While Gascoigne contrasted the artificiality of court life with the natural setting of the hunt, he none the less incorporated many of the stylized dramatic devices of the court masque into his manual of deer-hunting. For example, the royal butler and cook, in laying out an elaborate picnic in a shaded sylvan bower, are made 'captains' in the battle against hunger and command and deploy battalions of hams, sausages, and cold roast fowl in order to vanquish that gnawing enemy from the field—thus emulating the masque's struggle between two opposing forces. Gascoigne had devised a masque for the queen's entertainment at Kenilworth in 1575, and, perhaps, knowing

---

[14] See Ch. 2; *Tudor Royal Proclamations*, ed. Hughes and Larkin, vol. i, nos. 254, 347; Walker, 'The Chase of Hampton Court', 87; PRO STAC 2/13, fo. 104; Guy, *Tudor England*, 79, 184. In 1604 the solicitor-general was ordered to draw up a proclamation prohibiting all hunting within four miles of London and Westminster (*Acts PC, 1601–1604*, 511). Simon Thurley lists and provides a map of the location of sixty-two royal houses, palaces, and hunting lodges during the reign of Henry VIII ('Palaces for a Nouveau Riche King', *History Today*, 41 (June 1991), 12).

[15] *VCH Herts.*, i. 346; Nichols, *Progresses of Elizabeth*, i. 17. Administering a *coup de grâce* in this manner appears to have been a traditional prerogative of the queen (see also Tighe and Davis, *Annals of Windsor*, i. 632–3).

how devoted Elizabeth and her courtiers were to both hunting and masques, he could not resist combining the two in his free translation of Jacques du Foulloux's *La Venerie*. The connection between hunting and masques was not all that fanciful, for both required music, dance-like movements, a stage-like setting, and well-co-ordinated direction.[16]

By 1575, when Elizabeth was in her late forties, she still hunted the hart on horseback on important occasions, such as her visit to the earl of Leicester at Kenilworth. But, on the same progress through the West Midlands, she took a position upon a standing in Hallow Park, near Worcester, and fired at the deer with a crossbow as they were driven past her. Elizabeth showed a distinct preference for tamed landscapes in her amusements; on her progress through the Weald (the 'Wild' as Lord Burghley called it) of Kent and Sussex in 1573, she found the 'dangerous rocks and valleys' more dismal and forbidding than the High Peak of Derbyshire—although she only skirted the edge of the Weald. When she next returned to Sussex in August of 1591, Elizabeth visited Lord Montague at Cowdray. Now in her late fifties, the queen was content with more sedate forms of field sports. During the morning's entertainment, Elizabeth was escorted, on horseback, into a deer park, where she dismounted and sat in a bower while musicians played. Some thirty deer were rounded up and placed in a paddock while Elizabeth and her ladies-in-waiting picked off the beasts with crossbows. The queen killed three or four deer on this occasion. That evening, after dinner, Elizabeth ascended to the turret or banqueting tower of Cowdray, and watched while greyhounds coursed and killed sixteen bucks on the lawn below. The entertainment had been devised by Henry Browne, Lord Montague's third son and ranger of Windsor Forest.[17]

When Queen Elizabeth undertook a royal progress through her realm, she did so in order that she might be seen by her subjects. The pleasures of the hunt or her own amusement were of secondary consideration to spreading the cult of Gloriana and enhancing the royal *mystique*. Thus, hunting at the Elizabethan court had become merely another pretext for lavish theatrical displays which made the queen's subjects admire her all the more.[18]

For James I, on the other hand, a royal progress was first and foremost a hunting holiday. Moreover, James was careless about his appearance and disliked having his subjects watch while he was 'at his sports'.[19] Francis Osborne claimed to have seen James setting out on a royal progress dressed

[16] C. and R. Prouty, 'George Gascoigne, *The Noble Arte of Venerie*, and Queen Elizabeth at Kenilworth', in J. G. McManaway, G. E. Dawson, and E. E. Willoughby (eds.), *John Quincy Adams Memorial Studies* (Washington, 1948), 639–65.

[17] Nichols, *Progresses of Elizabeth*, i. 334, 420–84, 541, iii. 91; Ellis, *Parks and Forests of Sussex*, 99. For a description of the contrived landscape of Kenilworth, see above, Ch. 5.2.

[18] J. Neale, *Queen Elizabeth I: A Biography* (1934; repr. New York, 1957), 208 *et passim*, esp. p. 211.   [19] *Royalist's Notebook*, ed. Banford, 195.

in a hunting costume of green, with 'a horn instead of a sword at his side'.[20]
Roger Coke said that his father remembered that the king drank heavily of
strong wine while hunting and was so affected thereby that he grew careless about his posture and demeanour and slumped in the saddle with his
hat awry.[21]

The king maintained that he needed to hunt frequently in order to preserve his health. He was angered by those who interrupted his field sports
with requests for favours or urged matters of state upon him, and especially
by subjects who gawked at him in his parks and chases.

If they came to him in troops, as they usually did to Queen Elizabeth, he would
passionately swear and ask the English nobles what they would have. They would
answer, they came out of love to see him. Then he would cry out in Scottish, 'God's
wounds! I will pull down my breeches and they shall also see my arse!'[22]

At first, James was willing to allow his subjects to approach him as he was
coming to and from his hunting, but, in 1609, he resorted to stricter measures; he created the office of marshal of the field, and charged that officer
to prevent anyone approaching him while he was hunting who was not a
royal companion.[23]

Under the Tudor monarchs excessive hunting only very rarely occasioned
comments, and these were always stated obliquely.[24] It is indicative of an
erosion of respect for the monarch and, perhaps, a heightened sensibility
about the more unseemly aspects of hunting, that criticism of James's
preoccupation with the chase and the consequent neglect of his duties
became more candid and more frequent. Archbishop Hutton told Cecil that
he wished to see 'less wasting of the treasure of the realm and more moderation in the lawful exercise of hunting, both that poor men's corn may be
less spoiled and other his Majesty's subjects more spared'.[25] His secretaries
frequently complained of delays in getting James's signature on official
papers because the king 'kept long his bed, having hunted hard yesterday
and the day before'.[26] John Chamberlain reported in 1624 that the French
ambassador, having sought an interview with the king at Woodstock while
the latter was on progress, came away feeling frustrated because James had
'dealt seriously with him about hunting and such trifles, but trifled with him

---

[20] *Works of Francis Osborn*, 444–5.

[21] Roger Coke, 'Detection of the Court and State of England during the last four Reigns', in
[Sir Walter Scott (ed.)], *Secret History of the Court of James the First*, 2 vols. (Edinburgh, 1811),
ii. 3 n.–4 n.   [22] *Royalist's Notebook*, ed. Banford, 196.

[23] Nichols, *Progresses of James I*, ii. 214.

[24] D. Starkey, *The Reign of Henry VIII: Personalities and Politics* (New York, 1986), 11–15;
Neale, *Queen Elizabeth I*, 80.

[25] Matthew Hutton, abp. of York, to Sir Robert Cecil, Viscount Cranborne, 19 Dec. 1604,
HMC *Laing*, i. 99–100.

[26] Sir Thomas Lake to Sir Robert Cecil, earl of Salisbury, 6 July 1608, HMC *Salisbury*, xx. 205.

about the main business'.[27] On this occasion, the king's attention was focused on matters other than the negotiations in Paris for the forthcoming
marriage of Prince Charles and Henrietta Maria. There was, wrote Chamberlain, 'great sport at Woodstock at the hunting of "Cropear", a noted and
notorious stag, whose death was solemnized with so much joy and triumph
as if it had been some great conquest, there wanting nothing but bells and
bonfires'.[28]

No contemporary observer was quite so outspoken as Sir John Harington,
Queen Elizabeth's godchild, who remembered the decorum that the late
queen had insisted upon at her court. Harington's account of James's entertainment of the king of Denmark at Theobalds in 1606 leaves the impres-
sion that neither of the two monarchs, nor their courts, achieved sobriety
for several days. The evenings were given over to masques in which the
actors stumbled about and vomited, and the days were taken up with hunting
and more drinking. As the epigraph of this chapter indicates, Harington
thought that the hunting world had been turned upside down with 'the
beasts pursuing the sober creation'. Harington did not bother to hide his
disgust.[29]

James's deportment is not surprising in a man who was always 'very
merry' when attending cock fights and bull- and bear-baitings.[30] Towards the
end of his life 'he could not ride fast' and 'had little pleasure in the chase'.
Sir John Oglander remarked that 'his delight was to come at the death of the
deer and to hear the commendations of the hounds'.[31] Although James
professed a distaste for hunting deer with guns, in fact he did so himself.
Nicholas Assheton provides an eye-witness account of how the king made
a mess of killing a deer while hunting in Lancashire. He fired at a stag and
missed the first time and broke its leg with the second shot. Lord Compton
had to fire again to put the animal out of its misery.[32]

Despite the fact that James condemned the practice in others,[33] farmers
often had to endure damage to their crops when royal hunting parties rode
across their fields. One day in 1604 the king's favourite hound Jowler
disappeared, but was found the next day with a note attached to his collar:
'Good Mr Jowler, we pray you speak to the king (for he hears you every day,
and so doth he not us) that it will please his majesty to go to London, for
else the country will be undone'.[34] On another occasion, after spending

---

[27] John Chamberlain to Sir Dudley Carleton, 21 Sept. 1624, Nichols, *Progresses of James I*,
iv. 1001.   [28] Ibid. 1003.
[29] Sir John Harington, in *Nugae Antiquae*, ed. Thomas Park, 2 vols. (1804) i. 352; Nichols,
Progresses of James I, ii. 72–4.
[30] Ibid. i. 67–8, 528, iii. 264–5.   [31] *Royalist's Notebook*, ed. Banford, 195.
[32] James VI and I, *Basilikon Doron*, in *Political Works of James I*, ed. McIlwain, 48–9;
Journal of Nicholas Assheton, ed. Raines, 40.
[33] See Ch. 3.1.; *Proceedings in Parliament, 1610*, ed. Foster, i. 52.
[34] Lodge, *Illustrations of British History*, iii. 245.

the day hunting in some cornfields near Thetford, James was much offended when an angry farmer threatened to sue him for trespass.[35]

The atmosphere of blood sports, indulged in without restraint, could not
but affect the tone of court life and the perceptions of that courtly culture
among those of more tender conscience and sensibilities. This is well
illustrated by the case of George Abbot, archbishop of Canterbury. The
archbishop had been invited by Edward, Lord Zouch, to hunt in Bramshill
Park, Hampshire, in 1621. Archbishop Abbot accidently killed a keeper with
a barbed arrow, just as the man ran into a herd trying to arrange the deer
so as to afford the hunting party a better target. The king pitied the archbishop, saying 'It might have been my chance or thine.' Abbot was much
distraught and spent the rest of his life atoning for the accident, but many
of the clergy regarded him as 'a man of blood', and John Williams, bishop
elect of Lincoln, refused to be consecrated at his hands. Archbishop Abbot
was suspended from the exercise of his duties while a royal commission
looked into the matter. Ultimately the king granted him a pardon for the
accidental killing, but the incident was not forgotten, and the Laudians
laboured to remove him from office in the next reign.[36]

If the king was of a mind to hunt in a particular part of the realm, the
landowner in that county who held one of James's game warrants,[37] was
required to stay all hunting until the king arrived on progress. James and his
queen, Anne of Denmark, visited Oliver, Lord St John, lord-lieutenant of
Bedfordshire, on several occasions at Bletsoe, near Bedford. In 1607 Lord
St John incurred the king's high displeasure, as Sir Robert Cecil informed
him, for allegedly allowing his servants and followers to hunt after being
informed that the king intended to pursue the stag in those parts of Bedfordshire. Lord St John was much taken aback by the reprimand and protested his innocence. Later, St John learnt from Cecil that the deer had
actually been killed by a rival, Sir Thomas Tyrringham of Henwick Hall,
Bedfordshire.[38] Earlier, in 1605, Tyrringham, who was the keeper of a Duchy
of Lancaster game reserve in Bedfordshire, had been prosecuted in Star
Chamber for slaying a 'moted stag', which the earl of Bedford had been
preserving for the king's sport.[39] When a notable deer was marked for the
king's recreation, some bold hunters might take such notice as a challenge.
Sir Francis Leigh of East Wickham, Kent, complained in Star Chamber in
1617 that Francis Goodyear, of Newgate Street, Hertfordshire, gent., and

---

[35] Nichols, *Progresses of Elizabeth*, ii. 275, see also i. 496 n.

[36] Thomas Fuller, *The Church History of Britain*, 3 vols. (1837), iii. 286–8; Thomas Rymer, *Foedera, Conventiones, Literae et Cujuscunque Generis Acta Publica*, 17 vols. (The Hague, 1761), VIII. iii. 219–20; P. Crawford, ' "Charles Stuart, That Man of Blood" ', *Journal of British Studies*, 16. 2 (1977), 43; *DNB, sub* George Abbot (1562–1633) and John Williams (1582–1650).

[37] See Kirby, 'The Stuart Game Prerogative', 242; see above, Ch. 3.1.

[38] GEC, xi. 336 n.; Nichols, *Progresses of James I*, i. 518, 523, ii. 203; HMC *Salisbury*, xvi. 209, xix. 191, 194, 200.   [39] PRO STAC 8/48/11.

Lambert Cook of North Gray, Kent, gent., had killed a 'fair, large, bold and crop-eared buck of especial note, which your said subject did especially reserve for your majesty's own disport, and which your majesty was determined to have hunted' in East Wickham Park.[40]

As Archbishop Hutton had lamented as early as 1604, the king's preoccupation with field sports cost him much treasure and goodwill among his subjects. In 1612 the clerk of the Pells Office estimated that it cost £57,847 3s. 1d. to pay for the king's hunting expenses for a six-month period. This included the repairs and maintenance for fourteen deer parks in the Thames Valley region, the expenditures for toils and tents by the Revels Office plus the salary for the master of the Revels, and £3,776 13s. 4d. extraordinary expenses for the purchase of lands to be annexed to Theobalds Park.[41] The list must have been put together hurriedly, because it is incomplete. It omits the sixteen parks in Windsor Forest, as well as those in the London area, such as St James's, Marylebone, and Hyde Parks, and it mentions only one park in Essex. No account is taken of any of the royal forests except Whichwood, nor of the many parks and forests and chases which belonged to the Duchy of Lancaster. It would be difficult to estimate the total cost of the king's hunting and other 'sports', but it must have been a considerable sum. For example, in 1618 the treasurer of the chamber paid the master of the toils £159 13s. 4s. for capturing 479 deer running at large in Blackmore Forest and confining them to a new park within the forest.[42]

The expansion of Theobalds Park provides a dramatic and detailed case-study of James's carelessness about expenditure and his contempt for the goodwill of his subjects. Theobalds was a large and stately house built by Lord Burghley for the entertainment of Queen Elizabeth and intended as a bequest for his younger son, Sir Robert Cecil. When he first hunted there in 1607, James was much taken with the house and its gallery lined with stags' heads, and he persuaded Cecil to exchange Theobalds for Hatfield Palace. It was to become James's favourite hunting lodge. The king's enlargement of Theobalds Park, however, aroused resentment and provoked violent protest in the neighbourhood.[43]

It was actually the Cecils who began the enlargement of Theobalds Park. John Stileman, Sir Robert Cecil's head keeper, had told his master in 1597 about the resistance which he had encountered from neighbouring landowners, who disputed the extent of Cecil's hunting rights. They defied and intimidated Cecil's keepers and had so reduced the deer herd that Stileman did not know where to find a buck to send as a gift to the queen. Some of the gentlemen of the neighbourhood were Duchy of Lancaster officials

[40] PRO STAC 8/198/18.
[41] BL Cotton MSS, Titus B. IV, fos. 371–3ᵛ.   [42] *Acts PC, 1617–1619*, 338.
[43] *VCH Herts.*, i. 347; J. Summerson, 'The Building of Theobalds, 1564–1585', *Archaeologia*, 97 (1959), 107–26.

living in Edmonton Hundred; they and their ancestors had been poaching the king's deer in Enfield Chase since the time of Edward VI.[44] Cecil's expansion of Theobalds Park also extinguished certain use-rights in the neighbourhood of Hatfield, and, upon his death, prompted the following popular epitaph:

> Here lies thrown for the worms to eat,
> Little 'bossive' Robin that was so great.
> Not Robin Goodfellow, nor Robin Hood,
> But Robin th'encloser of Hatfield Wood.[45]

The next expansion of Theobalds Park got underway in 1608 when James annexed some 320 acres, chiefly from Cheshunt Park. Negotiations began with local landowners for the purchase of additional land, and in February 1612 payments totaling £11,070 13s. 6d. were authorized. Apparently, it was easier to secure the co-operation of the larger landowners such as Sir Robert Wroth and Sir Thomas Dacre than some of the smaller freeholders who refused the king's offer—even when above market value. The chancellor of the Exchequer, Sir Fulke Greville, was in charge of the negotiations for the purchase of land and the surrender of common rights. The king thought that he was proceeding too slowly, but Greville cautioned 'how easily this light sea of busy people is raised up with every wind'. When the surveyors appeared on their commons, Greville found that the people 'began to mutiny and threaten those who had any hand in that service'.[46]

As early as 1605, James had complained about the hordes of squatters and new tenants who were encroaching upon Enfield Chase. In 1611, 120 acres were detached from Enfield Chase to be added to Theobalds Park, but there was much murmuring among the commoners of Enfield Chase that the area to be enclosed was actually three hundred or four hundred acres. The consent of the tenants of Enfield, Edmonton, Hadley, and South Mimms to an enclosure agreement was arranged by commissioners, who offered a cash settlement and allowed the tenants to accompany the surveyors in marking off the actual boundaries in order to assure them that such rumours exaggerated the amount of land to be imparked. Subsequently, part of the money authorized for purchasing land was diverted into a charitable trust for relief of the poor.[47] The imparkment commissioners also encountered popular disturbances among the villagers of Cheshunt, who distrusted the king and feared that he meant to take their commons in Waltham Marsh

---

[44] HMC *Salisbury*, vii. 321–2.

[45] 'Historical Memoirs on the Reigns of Elizabeth and King James, by Francis Osborne', in [Sir Walter Scott (ed.)], *Secret History of the Court of James the First*, i. 235. The word 'bossive' appears to refer to Cecil's hump-backed deformity.

[46] *VCH Herts.*, ii. 448–9; PRO SP 14/66/77, 91/43, 44, 50.

[47] HMC *Salisbury*, xvii. 473; Manning, *Village Revolts*, 42–3, 68–9, 174; PRO SP 14/66/77, 91/43.

away from them.[48] Greville thought 'the king will find that he pays like a king for his pleasure'.[49] As soon as workmen began to erect the new fences around Theobalds Park, the inhabitants of the surrounding villages proceeded to tear them down and make off with the palings.[50] Many commoners, and squatters also, felt aggrieved about the depletion of wood fuel on Enfield Chase and the other commons that were swallowed up by Theobalds Park, and in 1618 a project was devised to set the poor to work in the Enfield parish workhouse to reduce the problem of wood-stealing. By 1620 the decision had been reached to enclose the 2,500 acres of the enlarged Theobalds Park within a brick wall ten miles in circumference.[51] The project was so enormous that the master bricklayers were granted a commission to impress bricklayers and labourers and to requisition horses and carts for transporting materials.[52]

In 1623 anti-enclosure rioters levelled part of the wall or fence which had been built around Cheshunt Common. During the next year, workmen were once again busy repairing some of the coping of the wall where the rioters had clambered over it. The workmanship was not, perhaps, of the best quality, because in 1637–8—only fifteen years after it was built—eighty-seven buttresses had to be added to keep the wall from collapsing. However, the wall lasted longer than the Stuart monarchy.[53]

King Charles I was very much his father's son in matters of hunting. Sir Simonds D'Ewes remembered observing the young Prince Charles hunting on the estate of Sir William Eliot in Bushbridge, Surrey. Charles took unnecessary chances when hunting, and Eliot felt it necessary to admonish him after he had leaped 'on horseback over a most dangerous hedge and ditch'. Afterwards, D'Ewes thought Charles displayed an unnatural curiosity in examining every part of the carcass of the dead stag.[54]

Customarily, the heir to the throne, when he had reached a certain age, established his own household and was assigned royal deer parks for his amusement. Prince Charles took the responsibility for preserving the deer in his game reserves very seriously. One of Charles's parks was attached to the manor of Berkhamstead, Hertfordshire, which was parcel of the Duchy of Cornwall. Berkhampstead Park had recently been enlarged by imparking three hundred acres of Berkhamstead Frith, thus, at one fell swoop,

---

[48] PRO SP 14/92/23.
[49] *VCH Herts.*, iii. 448–9. The cost of expanding Theobalds Park was listed as one of the reasons why the king needed to take out a loan of £120,000 from city merchants in 1617 (ibid.)
[50] *Acts PC, 1617–1619*, 100–1; PRO SP 14/91/50.
[51] HMC *Salisbury*, xxii. 76, 152; *VCH Herts.*, iii. 448–9.
[52] Rymer, *Foedera*, viii. iii. 201.
[53] PRO SP 14/153/5, 6, 7; Colvin, Ransome, and Summerson (eds.), *History of the King's Works*, iv. ii. 275–8.
[54] [Hyde], earl of Clarendon, *History of the Rebellion*, i. 132–5; Sir Simonds D'Ewes, *Diary*, quoted in Nichols, *Progresses of James I*, iv. 1003–4; see also above, Ch. 5.2.

enclosing one-quarter of a waste that many smallholders depended upon for grazing their beasts. In July 1620 some two hundred anti-enclosure rioters assembled, armed with guns, bows, and arrows, and chopped the park palings into small pieces. In their answers to the attorney-general's information against them, some of the tenants of Little Gaddesden mentioned that they had suffered long imprisonment for their participation in the riots at Berkhamstead Park. Several of them admitted that they had assented to the enclosure agreement, but, as in the case of the enlargement of Theobalds Park, it is unlikely that they were offered many alternatives to Prince Charles's plan to impark their commons.[55] If the imparkment of a new chase or park and the extinction of ancient use-rights added to the number of paupers, Charles's solution was to order that a parish workhouse be erected at the expense of the local community so that poachers and fence-levellers would leave his game and park pales alone. In February 1619, taking note of the fact that his father had ordered the magistrates of the hundred of Broadwater, Hertfordshire, to erect a workhouse for setting the poor to work on 'manu-factures', with the cost of £60 to be assessed upon the town of Hatfield, Prince Charles suggested to William, second earl of Salisbury and lord-lieutenant of Hertfordshire, that he and the justices of peace might erect a similar house of correction in the hundred of Dacorum in order to set the poor of Berkhamstead and Little Gaddesden to work.[56]

Charles vigorously defended his hunting reserves against poachers while he was heir to the throne, and, upon ascending that throne, he supple-mented his father's game legislation and expanded the royal prerogative in forest and game matters. The Court of Star Chamber played an especially important role in defending the king's hunting and game prerogatives, and certainly went well beyond the statutory limits of the Game Laws in enforc-ing his game prerogative.[57] Yet the king was prepared to pardon the most egregiously violent of deer-slayers, such as Sir Thomas Lunsford, if they expressed a willingness to assist him against his parliamentary enemies.[58]

James I and Charles I had made the royal hunting reserves a symbol of royal tyranny. Just as during the disorders of 1549 and 1569 parks and enclosures were singled out as targets for popular vengeance, as early as September 1641 popular attacks against Windsor Forest were reported. The earlier attacks on deer parks were motivated by anti-aristocratic sentiment, but the Windsor Forest Riots of 1641 display a distinct anti-monarchical bias. The king's revival of forest law had provoked a statute enacted by the Long Parliament in 1641 for the 'Certainty of Forests (16 Car. I, c. 16)', which

---

[55] PRO STAC 8/32/16.   [56] HMC *Salisbury*, xxii. 83.

[57] PRO STAC 8/33/15; *Stuart Royal Proclamations*, ed. Larkin and Hughes, vol. ii, nos. 188, 192; Rushworth (ed.), *Historical Collections*, ii. ii. 3, 8, 12, 43, 74–5; see also above, Ch. 4.3.

[58] Rushworth (ed.), *Historical Collections*, ii. ii. 47–8; *DNB, sub* Henry, Sir Herbert and Sir Thomas Lunsford; Manning, *Village Revolts*, 291.

was intended to restore the forests to their pre-Jacobean boundaries. The presence of parliamentary commissioners in Surrey, who were sent to survey the Forest of Windsor, led to new popular tumults.[59] It was thought necessary to adjourn the meetings of the commissioners and to take the precaution of publishing a declaration that their proceedings were in no way meant to prejudice the king's rights to the vert and venison of his forests. Because of the difficulty of repressing popular tumults, it was decided not to resume meetings of the parliamentary commissioners.[60] By April 1642 the riots and tumultuous poaching had spread into the Berkshire part of Windsor Forest, and Windsor Great Park had been invaded. These riots and the large-scale slaughter of deer continued until 1644. By 1643 the soldiers brought in to protect Windsor Castle and Windsor Forest had joined in the plunder, cutting timber, attacking and sometimes killing the park keepers, and slaughtering whole herds of deer. The House of Lords had now taken over the function, formerly exercised by the Court of Star Chamber, which had been abolished in 1641, of punishing those who killed the king's deer.[61]

8.2. Anti-Aristocratic Sentiment

In Tudor England, outside the years of popular rebellion and widespread rioting, it was unusual for members of the commonalty to attack the deer parks of the temporal nobility unless the peers were Catholic recusants.[62] Where such raids did occur, they were almost invariably manifestations of aristocratic feuding and were usually led by gentlemen.[63] Beginning in the reign of James I, poaching raids on aristocratic deer parks, which symbolized the special privileges possessed by peers, increased in frequency. Whether we should regard this phenomenon as part of the 'crisis of the aristocracy' described by Professor Lawrence Stone,[64] or a reaction to the more restrictive Jacobean Game Laws, or a distortion of historical perception caused by the greater emphasis that the Court of Star Chamber placed on the vigorous enforcement of game legislation is difficult to say. But the evidence does suggest that popular resentment of aristocratic hunting privileges and the continued existence of numerous deer parks was widespread and was articulated in more generalized terms. That large-scale, organized poaching increasingly focused upon aristocratic game reserves during the relatively peaceful years from 1603 to 1641 was portentous for the English aristocracy.

[59] *Journals of the House of Commons*, ii. 282. In 1548–9 the presence of commissioners to enquire into depopulating enclosures in certain localities had helped to precipitate anti-enclosure rioters (Manning, 'Violence and Social Conflict in Mid-Tudor Rebellions', 28).

[60] *Journals of the House of Lords*, iv. 473a, 503b–504a, 506b, 547a–b, 595b, 608a.

[61] Ibid. v. 25a, 35a, 199b, 719a, vi. 21a, 39b, 77a, vii. 7, 281.

[62] Manning, *Village Revolts*, 292–4; see also below, Ch. 8.3.

[63] See Ch. 6.1, 6.2.   [64] Stone, *Crisis of the Aristocracy*.

When Sir Francis Bacon, as attorney-general, prosecuted Edward Lowe of Alderwater, gent., and a gang of deer-stealers in 1615 for hunting in the park of Gilbert, earl of Shrewsbury, at Sherland, Derbyshire, he accused them of 'grudging that your majesty's nobles and statesmen should have any privileges or immunities more than they'.[65] There were many reasons why poachers of various social ranks would want to attack the deer parks of aristocrats or courtiers who enjoyed royal game warrants and extensive hunting franchises, but the attorney-general pinpointed a major cause of such raids—the envy of the small gentry and yeomanry. Lowe, the principal defendant, had compelled a number of his neighbours to join him in attacks on Sherland and other deer parks in Derbyshire. Those who assisted him were rewarded with a venison dinner at Lowe's house, prepared by his wife Jane. Those who informed against him, such as the miller John Browne, might expect to be ambushed and badly beaten.[66]

Popular attacks on aristocratic deer parks had frequently occurred during outbreaks of rebellion. Unpopular landlords were especially vulnerable. During the Oxfordshire Rebellion of 1549, the rebels attacked Sir John Williams's parks at Thame and Rycote, disparked the same, and 'killed all the deer'.[67] During the Suffolk Rising of 1569, which followed a depression in the cloth trade, agricultural labourers and clothworkers spoiled aristocratic and royal parks, which encroached upon prime agricultural land. The rioters also did violence to the keepers of aristocratic and royal parks, although attacks against persons rather than property was unusual behaviour in anti-enclosure rioters. 'Their intent', an informant told Sir James Crofts, 'was plainly to have spoiled all the gentlemen and wealthy personages that they might overtake, beginning with Sir Ambrose Germayne.'[68]

What had changed by 1615, according to Sir Francis Bacon, was that attacks on aristocratic deer parks were 'nowadays grown to be so common that there are few shires wherein the baser sort of people, whom God hath called to live by their honest labour, will not stick to presume to do the like'. Bacon remarked that raids by various poaching gangs on the earl of Shrewsbury's deer parks in Derbyshire and the Hallamshire district of Yorkshire had become especially troublesome, and he noted that the poachers intended not merely to obtain venison, but also to havoc the earl's deer.[69]

This is not to say that aristocratic game reserves were immune from

---

[65] PRO STAC 8/20/32. For other examples of the small gentry's envy of the hunting privileges of the aristocracy and seigneurial gentry, cf. PRO STAC 8/225/13, 191/6.

[66] PRO STAC 8/20/32.

[67] 'Two London Chronicles from the Collections of John Stow', ed. C. L. Kingsford, in *Camden Miscellany XII* (Camden Soc.; 1910), 18; B. Beer, *Rebellion and Riot: Popular Disorder in England during the Reign of Edward VI* (Kent, Oh., 1982), 149.

[68] *Cal. SP*, Spanish, 1568–1579, 179–80; MacCulloch, *Suffolk and the Tudors*, 310–11.

[69] PRO STAC 8/20/32.

poaching prior to the reign of James I. The well-stocked deer parks of the aristocracy naturally exerted a certain degree of temptation, but in southern England this species of deer-stealing was infrequent and done on a very small scale.[70] In the north of England and in parts of the Midlands there were still a lot of restless gentry and yeomen trained and experienced in the use of arms who found fewer opportunities for employment in military enterprises or aristocratic retinues. The earls of Derby, for example, whose estates spread across much of north-western England, had many neighbours holding their lands by tenant-right tenures to which military obligations were still attached. In 1553 the park of Edward, earl of Derby, at Broughton, Lancashire, was raided by a gang of deer-stealers from Cumberland.[71] In 1601 a band of Lancashire gentry led by Richard Molyneux of Hawkesley attacked the park of William, earl of Derby, at Knowsley.[72] In the latter part of the reign of Elizabeth, William Probert of Pentglass, gent., led his tenants into Wisewood Chase in Monmouthshire, where they assaulted the keepers of Henry, earl of Pembroke, spoiled his red deer, and pulled up hedges in an attempt to reclaim their rights of common.[73] But before 1603 there are far more examples of temporal peers attacking gentry deer parks than vice versa.

In the early Tudor period, a gentleman who took on a peer in a dispute over hunting franchises or offices was apt to find himself engaged in a very unequal contest. Sometime early in the reign of Henry VIII, Sir William Turvile had a falling out with Thomas Grey, marquess of Dorset, over Turvile's claim to be master of the game in a couple of parks in Leicestershire belonging to Dorset. Turvile had acquired the offices, worth 40*s*. p.a. and a fee-buck from each park, from Dorset's father, and Dorset had withheld these profits from him. Dorset's method of dealing with Turvile's impertinence was to break down the gates of Turvile's park and kill his deer. Turvile sought advice from a cousin named John Beaumont, who was a barrister and a justice of the peace. Beaumont advised Turvile to seek an indictment for riot against the marquess at the Loughborough Sessions, but Dorset replied by hauling Turvile before the Court of Star Chamber on charges of *scandalum magnatum*, maintenance, and champerty. The last offence arose out of Beaumont's actions as his cousin's legal counsel at the Loughborough Sessions, where he stood behind Turvile while the latter was pleading and urged Turvile to accuse Dorset of 'stealing' and 'retaining of the justices of the peace'.[74]

---

[70] For the instances occurring in Essex during the reign of Elizabeth, see *Calendar of Assize Records, Essex Indictments, Eliz. I*, ed. Cockburn, nos. 430, 854; F. G. Emmison, *Elizabethan Life: Disorder: Mainly from Essex Sessions and Assize Records* (Chelmsford, 1970), 238–41.
[71] *Pleadings and Depositions in the Duchy Court of Lancaster*, iii. 128.
[72] PRO DL 1/197/D4.   [73] PRO STAC 5/P38/29.
[74] PRO STAC 2/31/165. The marquess of Dorset was chief justice in eyre of the forests south of the Trent from 1523 until his death in 1530 (GEC iv. 419–20).

One suspects that it was not respect for the peerage that deterred organized attacks by deer-stealers, because hunters frequently spoiled the game reserves of spiritual peers during the Tudor period. To cite only one example, the bishop of Hereford's deer park at Prestbury, Gloucestershire, was subjected to large-scale attacks by neighbouring gentry on at least three different occasions between 1516 and 1528.[75] Rather, the more plausible explanation of why attacks on aristocratic deer parks were infrequent before 1603 is that during the Tudor period temporal peers still had sufficient retainers, wealth, and power to revenge themselves upon such attackers. In the early Stuart period, aristocratic households functioned with much-reduced household staffs and had to watch expenditures. The rules of courtly behaviour increasingly discouraged such crude violence, and peers were more likely to turn to the Court of Star Chamber to bring deer-stealers to book.

Poaching raids on aristocratic game reserves proliferated during the reign of James I. In 1610 a poaching gang composed of yeomen revenged themselves upon Dudley, third Lord North, for complaints which he had made against them in Star Chamber on an earlier occasion. Cloaked and visored, they broke into North's deer park at Sketchworth, Cambridgeshire, while most of his keepers were at church, and destroyed thirty deer. They then waited in ambush for the keepers as they returned from church and assaulted them.[76] The ancient deer park at Sudeley Castle, Gloucestershire, which belonged to Gray Brydges, fifth Lord Chandos, known as 'king of the Cotswolds', was hunted by a gang of gentlemen deer-stealers on three different occasions in 1611–12. The defendants refused to confess anything in Star Chamber and were probably hardened poachers.[77] Sir William Lane of Horton, Northamptonshire, a justice of the peace, invited friends from as far away as Huntingdonshire, Cambridgeshire, and Buckinghamshire to 'kill and spoil' the deer of William, Lord Compton, in Yardley Chase and Yardley Park. Lane was 'not willing to show himself publicly' against Lord Compton, but his hunting guests 'did in vaunting manner give out [that] they would kill as many of your subject's deer as they pleased and that they would beat, kill, and wound as many of your subject's servants as should resist them'. Lord Compton complained that Lane had been hiring poaching gangs to plunder his game reserves for years, and had used his office as a magistrate to prevent prosecution of these offences and had also attempted to bribe Compton's servants to prevent their giving evidence.[78] Thomas, Lord Gerard, a very harsh landlord, saw his deer park in Aston, Lancashire, subjected to repeated attacks in 1615–16. He alleged that the defendants, who consisted

---

[75] *Diocese of Hereford: Extracts from the Cathedral Registers, AD 1275–1535*, ed. E. N. Dew (Cantilupe Soc.; 1932), 143; PRO STAC 2/22/328, 32/50. For other examples of poaching raids directed against other spiritual peers, see STAC 2/16, fos. 74–6, STAC 8/155/13.

[76] PRO STAC 8/120/10; *DNB*, *sub* Dudley, 3rd Lord North.

[77] PRO STAC 8/84/17; *House of Commons, 1558–1603*, ed. Hasler, i. 508–9.

[78] PRO STAC 8/105/13; John Bridges, *The History and Antiquities of Northamptonshire*, ed. Peter Whaller, 2 vols. (Oxford, 1791), i. 394.

of yeomen and artisans from the neighbourhood, had slaughtered a total of a hundred deer on at least twenty-seven different occasions over a period of nearly two years, and had pulled down the walls and pales of his park.[79] What is especially striking in these cases is that persons beneath the rank of gentleman had become emboldened to hunt in aristocratic game reserves without gentry leadership and were mounting large-scale attacks.

The most notable assault upon the hunting privileges of the nobility occurred in the Craven district of the West Riding of Yorkshire, where, between 1581 and 1625, tenants and neighbours waged a poaching war against the third and fourth earls of Cumberland. Henry, first earl of Cumberland, had acquired vast holdings of land during the last days of northern feudalism, but he and his successors never succeeded in winning the loyalty or affections of their mesne or knight-service tenants. The succeeding earls of Cumberland continued to lay claim to absolute and exclusive hunting franchises throughout their extensive honours, fees, and lands, which would admit of no one else's right to hunt. This was but little tempered by the granting of game and forest offices or licences to hunt to their gentry tenants and neighbours, whose loyalties in many instances still attached to the collapsed Percy or Dacre interests. The Tudor earls of Cumberland were remarkably unsuccessful in their exercise of good lordship, and the decay of the military obligations of their mesne tenancies in the years following the Pilgrimage of Grace of 1536–7 undermined any justification which might be advanced for their extravagant claims to hunting rights over the lands of their mesne and smallhold tenants.[80]

Henry, eleventh Lord Clifford, created earl of Cumberland in 1525, was an experienced soldier who saw extensive service on the border leading his tenants against the Scots. Although reputed to be a harsh landlord, he kept his tenants loyal to the king during the Northern Rebellions of 1536–7—but just barely. Many of his smallhold tenants never forgave his failure to support the Pilgrimage, but Henry VIII rewarded him in 1542 with a partial gift of most of the estates of the dissolved priory of Bolton in Craven. Earl Henry had already purchased lands formerly held by the late priory of Marton in 1540, and the sixth earl of Northumberland had granted him the Percy fee in Craven, consisting of four manors, in 1529. Together with the Clifford fee in Craven, these vast estates made the earls of Cumberland the largest landowners in the West Riding.[81] Henry, the second earl (d. 1570), succeeded in 1542, and withdrew from court in 1547. A Catholic sympathizer, he favoured Mary, queen of Scots, during the Northern Rebellion of 1569.

---

[79] PRO STAC 8/157/24; Manning, *Village Revolts*, 114–16, 139–40.

[80] The interpretation of the career of Henry, 1st earl of Cumberland, remains controversial. The most important authorities are M. E. James, 'The First Earl of Cumberland (1493–1542) and the Decline of Northern Feudalism', *Northern History*, 1 (1966), 43–69, and R. W. Hoyle, 'The First Earl of Cumberland: A Reputation Reassessed', *Northern History*, 22 (1986), 63–94.

[81] Ibid. 75, 80–1, 94; H. Miller, *Henry VIII and the English Nobility* (Oxford,1986), 249.

Although he still accepted homage at military courts from his knight-service tenants in Craven and Westmorland as late as 1568, the second earl was never a border magnate and his control over his mesne tenants was rapidly disintegrating.[82]

George Clifford, the third earl of Cumberland (1558–1605), who succeeded in 1570, was a courtier who had been raised in the south under Puritan influence. He valued his West Riding estates only for 'the hunting and chasing that barren country yieldeth'.[83] A naval commander during the Armada and a privateer, he found sacking Puerto Rico more to his liking than governing his tenants, who knew him only as an absentee landlord. His extravagance forced him to sell off or mortgage his patrimony and borrow from his tenants. In order to cancel his indebtedness, Earl George, early in the seventeenth century, offered long leases to his mesne and smallhold tenants which, in effect, converted tenancies-at-will to something approximating estates of inheritance, which was very beneficial to his tenants.[84] The cause of the extensive poaching wars on his Craven estates arose from the fact that he and the fourth earl retained their extensive hunting franchises, including liberty of free chase and free warren, over lands which many tenants came to regard as their own. The earls of Cumberland claimed the same hunting franchises over the lands of most of the gentry throughout Craven. Even in the days of the first earl, his practice of sending his game officers on to the holdings of his mesne tenants and neighbours to survey the deer or to hunt had caused much friction.[85] The third and fourth earls were careless about confining their deer to parks and consequently much damage was done to their neighbours' corn and pastures. They also lacked the manpower to patrol their extensive hunting reserves in the West Riding, Westmorland, and Cumberland.[86]

It is significant that the Craven poaching wars first broke out in the Chases of Bolton and Langstrothdale. These were areas where tenant loyalty to the earls of Cumberland was weak, and their power never quite filled the void left by the granting of the Percy fee in Craven to the Cliffords and by the dissolution of Bolton Priory. The third earl admitted that his financially straitened circumstances did not permit him to retain sufficient keepers nor to maintain adequate fences to confine his red and fallow deer to parks, and, consequently, his herds ravaged the lands of tenants—especially during the winter months, when food sources were in short supply in the upper elevations of Craven. Cumberland described this band of Craven poachers, most of whom came from Beamsley, as persons who lived 'without

[82] Hoyle, 'The First Earl of Cumberland', 66; *DNB, sub* Henry de Clifford, second earl of Cumberland.   [83] PRO STAC 5/C5/11.

[84] *DNB, sub* George Clifford, third earl of Cumberland; R. T. Spence, 'The Cliffords, Earls of Cumberland, 1579–1646: A Study of their Fortunes Based on their Household and Estate Accounts', Ph.D. thesis (London, 1959), 127, 150; Stone, *Crisis of the Aristocracy*, 122.

[85] Hoyle, 'The First Earl of Cumberland', 73–4.   [86] See Ch. 6.4, 6.6.

any honest trade' and supported themselves by hunting in the earl's chases. They sold venison 'in foreign places, both for great sums of money and for corn and grain wherewith they or divers of them maintain themselves and their families'.[87]

Another gang of poachers was led by John Tennant of Bordley in Craven, yeom., whom Cumberland accused of hunting in the chases of Langstrothdale and Littondale. Tennant was a substantial tenant with holdings in the chases of Hawkswick, Owlcote, Littondale, and Langstrothdale. He claimed the right to hunt the deer which bred upon his lands, but Cumberland claimed liberty of warren as well as free chase over Tennant's lands. A kinsman, James Tennant, who was the bailiff of the royal manor of Kettlewell, appears to have been another member of John Tennant's hunting band, together with a number of freehold tenants living in Hawkswick and Owlcote. Cumberland summoned numerous witnesses to Skipton Castle for inter-rogation. He obtained very little evidence, because the witnesses pleaded ignorance and refused to co-operate. Clearly, the men of Craven stood together in their dislike of Cumberland.[88]

In the late 1580s the third earl seldom resided in the West Riding, and his countess was obliged to appeal to the Privy Council for assistance in prosecuting the Craven poachers. The Privy Council wrote to the earl of Huntingdon, the president of the Council in the North, complaining that Sir Thomas Fairfax and other justices made a practice of granting bail to poach-ers as soon as they were clapped in gaol without bothering to examine the poachers regarding their alleged offences.[89]

By 1592 the gentry of Craven and Westmorland, led by Edward Middleton of Middleton Hall, Westmorland, esq., had intervened in the poaching wars and were asserting their right to hunt in the fells on the West Riding–Westmorland border. The third earl would admit of no hunting rights in Craven other than his own, and accused Middleton of proclaiming a 'general hunting' against Cumberland's deer which strayed upon the wastes and moors.[90] In 1595 the 'general hunting' declared against Cumberland had spread to Barden Chase, where Charles Young of Hebden, gent., and the tenants of that neighbourhood recruited professional hunters from Leeds to reinforce their efforts to havoc the earl's deer. An examination of Charles Young revealed that this conspiracy against Cumberland was organized at Appletreewick Fair on St Luke's day (18 October), which suggests that the Yorkes of Gowthwaite may have had a hand in organizing the poaching wars.[91]

Charles Young's band of hunters may also have received encouragement

---

[87] PRO STAC 5/C5/11.   [88] PRO STAC 5/C18/23, C5/11.
[89] *Acts PC, 1589–1590*, xviii. 206–7.   [90] PRO STAC 5/C22/38, C29/8, C6/36.
[91] PRO STAC 5/C58/33, C74/9, C25/20, C22/12; T. D. Whitaker, *The History and Antiquities of the Deanery of Craven in the County of York*, ed. A. W. Morant (3rd edn.; Leeds, 1878), 512–13.

from Sir Stephen Procter, JP, the purchaser of Fountains Abbey. Procter was a fanatical anti-papist who ended up quarrelling with all of his neighbours. When the earl of Cumberland's keepers sought the indictment of Charles Young, his son, his son-in-law, and twenty-one other defendants at the Skipton Sessions, Procter blocked the indictment. Procter stated that his servant, John Bentham of the parish of Horton in Littondale, had hunted by his command, and he boasted that he would maintain Bentham in any action which Cumberland's keepers might wish to bring. With that, the hunters resumed their general hunting of Cumberland's chases and moved their activities closer to Cumberland's principal seat at Skipton Castle when they invaded Skipton and Barden Chases. As the purchaser of Fountains Abbey, Procter claimed liberty of free chase in the chases of Scroop and Carnebrook. He also sought to challenge Cumberland's claim to hegemony in the West Riding by attempting to revive the leet court of the liberty of Fountains and asserting his jurisdiction over fifteen manors, such as Hawkswick, Woodhouse, and Appletreewick, where Cumberland claimed to be the paramount lord.[92] While Cumberland's keepers were trying to protect their master's deer in Craven, another band of deer-stealers across the border in Westmorland took advantage of Cumberland's distraction and made 'continual spoil' in Winfell Park.[93]

During the reigns of James I and Charles I the leadership of the Craven poaching wars passed to Sir John Yorke of Gowthwaite in Nidderdale.[94] The source of the conflict between the third and fourth earls of Cumberland and Sir John Yorke derived from the descent of the manor of Appletreewick, which formerly belonged to the dissolved Priory of Bolton. The Yorkes, who were merchants by origin, had purchased the manor in the reign of Edward VI, when the family was Protestant. In the late Elizabethan period, Sir John began reviving an ancient seigneurial claim to hold a fair at Appletreewick and to exercise liberty of free warren within the manor. The third earl, who also pursued antiquarianism for fiscal purposes, argued that his manor of Woodhouse was the paramount manor to which Appletreewick had been subordinated before the dissolution of Bolton Priory, and he presented evidence that Yorke's ancestors and predecessors had never employed keepers and that the mesne tenants of Appletreewick had always

[92] PRO STAC 5/C25/20, C22/10, C50/18, C7/31, C72/20, all dated 1600–1; see also Manning, *Village Revolts*, 280–2.   [93] PRO STAC 5/C47/31, 28 Jan. 1600.

[94] Although a crypto-Catholic himself, Sir John Yorke was the head of a seigneurial household notorious for its militant Catholicism. He and his wife were prosecuted by Sir Stephen Procter of Fountains Abbey and convicted in a trial in the Court of Star Chamber for allowing a company of Catholic actors to perform an interlude in the great hall of Gowthwaite between the acts of a longer play, which derided the Anglican church (C. H. D. Howard, *Sir John Yorke of Nidderdale, 1565–1634* (1939), 12–17, 22–9; H. Aveling, 'The Catholics of the West Riding of Yorkshire, 1558–1790', *Proceedings of the Leeds Philosophical and Literary Society, Literary and Historical Section*, 10 (1963), 230).

performed suit and paid forester oats, a species of feudal tax, to the bow-bearers of the Forest Court of Skipton, who were Cumberland's ancestors.[95]

Beginning in 1602 and continuing for the next four years, Thomas Yorke, a younger brother of Sir John, recruited a band of fifteen to twenty hunters, which included Jeffrey Wybarre, vicar of Long Preston, and a number of artisans and persons of 'base condition and small estate', and led them on some twenty raids in Skipton, Barden, and Bolton Chases over a period of four years. Some of these men were so poor that they attacked Cumberland's deer armed only with pitchforks.[96] Over the next five years, Francis Clifford, who succeeded as fourth earl of Cumberland in 1605, could cite thirty-eight instances of unlawful hunting by Thomas Yorke and his men, reinforced from time to time by a gang of professional deer-stealers led by Philip Shaw.[97] Earl Francis caused many of the defendants to be examined under oath, but he could not extract an answer from any of the defendants except Sir John Yorke, who insisted that he and his servants killed deer only on his manor of Appletreewick.[98]

From 1610 until 1624 the attacks upon the fourth earl's deer in the chases of Skipton and Barden appear to have intensified. Cumberland complained that Sir John Yorke's brothers, Thomas and Richard, together with nine or ten servants and tenants, spent all of their time hunting his deer. They inhabited alehouses by day and plied their trade by night. At least two more gangs of deer-stealers continued to be active in Cumberland's chases during this period of time. Cumberland claimed that the bands led by Philip Shaw and James Tennant were composed of Yorke's tenants and servants, but Yorke insisted that they were mostly disgruntled tenants of Cumberland.[99]

Despite the many complaints which the fourth earl of Cumberland brought against Sir John Yorke in the Court of Star Chamber, he always encountered difficulty in gathering evidence from the men of Craven, and it appears that he did not succeed in obtaining a conviction until 1616, when Yorke was fined £20.[100] The Caroline Court of Star Chamber took a sterner view of attacks upon aristocratic game reserves and, in 1625, imposed fines of £200 upon Sir John, £50 upon his son John, and £100 upon his servant, Thomas Fenton. The total sum payable was subsequently reduced to £50 and the fine was paid in three instalments between November 1633 and November 1635. The Star Chamber punishments ended the Craven poaching wars, and Sir John died in 1634. However, isolated instances of deer-stealing continued in Cumberland's parks and chases as late as 1641.[101]

---

[95] Whitaker, *History and Antiquities of Craven*, 512–13; PRO STAC 8/102/6.
[96] PRO STAC 8/104/8; see also above, Ch. 7.1.   [97] See above, Ch. 6.4.
[98] PRO STAC 8/102/6.   [99] PRO STAC 8/102/4, 5, 6, 85/19, 20.
[100] Barnes, 'Fines in the High Court of Star Chamber', 187.
[101] Rushworth (ed.), *Historical Collections*, ii. ii, appendix, p. 3; Howard, *Sir John Yorke*, 67 n.; *West Riding Sessions Records*, ed. Lister, ii. 293.

An even more spectacular affront to the dignity of a peer occurred in Lincolnshire early in the seventeenth century. The issues involved included enclosures of common wastes, disputes about hunting franchises, and damage done to crops by stray deer, but the leading cause of the protests, which featured an elaborate skimmington and a general hunting, was the tyrannical behaviour of Henry Fiennes de Clinton, second earl of Lincoln (d. 1616). The bad feeling against Lincoln began as early as the 1570s when, as Lord Clinton, he had launched armed attacks against his neighbours' houses, destroyed their enclosures, made intakes from common wastes, and levied excessive and discriminatory taxes for drainage works in the fens as a commissioner of sewers. The Privy Council had reprimanded Lincoln and removed him from the commission of the peace for a brief time after 1594.[102]

By 1601 the earl of Lincoln was held in such general contempt that one of his enemies, Sir Edward Dymock, was able to stage an elaborate skimmington against the earl at South Kyme, Lincolnshire, in order to revenge himself upon the earl, who had called Dymock 'a mongrel, a cur, a rebel, a peasant of the order of clowns, [an] ale knight'.[103] The skimmington, together with an interlude, or satirical summer play, was part of the May-games which Dymock, who was Lincoln's nephew, sponsored every summer for his tenants. The parts in the interlude were acted by Talboys Dymock, Sir Edward's younger brother, and members of his retinue. The South Kyme May-games lasted through most of the summer, and apparently it was customary for neighbouring villages to exchange entertainments. Talboys Dymock took a dozen or so players to the nearby village of Coningsby on the last Sunday in July 1601 to repay the visit of the Coningsby men a fortnight earlier. Joined by their hosts, they marched through the streets with banners and drums and performed their interlude at each of several alehouses. Spying the hated earl of Lincoln and his servants, they rushed at the rival company with drums beating and banners waving in the intimidating manner of skimmingtons and attempted to frighten the earl's horse. The earl ordered the village constable to arrest Talboys and the drummers, and a scuffle with naked swords ensued. One witness claimed that the procession drummed the earl and his men out of the village towards Tattershall Castle, the earl's seat. Following this incident and another riotous encounter between the retainers of the earl and Sir Edward Dymock, Lincoln complained to the Court of Star Chamber. Talboys retaliated by writing and staging on the last Sunday in August a libellous interlude in the form of the traditional mock funeral for the 'summer lord' of the South Kyme May-games. The interlude, which ridiculed the earl, was performed before an

---

[102] N. J. O'Conor, *Godes Peace and the Queenes: Vicissitudes of a House, 1539–1615* (Cambridge, Mass., 1934), pp. 45–8, 50.
[103] C. Holmes, *Seventeenth-Century Lincolnshire* (Hist. of Lincs., 7; Lincoln, 1980), 102–3.

audience of forty persons, who had also been invited to partake of a venison supper—probably obtained from the earl's deer parks. The Court of Star Chamber fined both the earl of Lincoln and the Dymock brothers for libel and imprisoned them. Sir Edward Dymock's fine was set at £1,000; three lesser defendants were pilloried, whipped, and fined £300 each. The earl remained in prison as late as 1611.[104]

The downfall of the second earl of Lincoln was celebrated by a general hunting in his deer parks. From the beginning of the reign until September 1605, some eighty-three named defendants waged a poaching war against Lincoln and killed 260 of his red and fallow deer and a thousand conies. Four of these defendants were armigerous, including Sir Edward Dymock, Sir Henry Ayscough or Askew, Sir Thomas Standish, and William Skipwith of Utterby, esq.; another twenty-four were gentlemen, including Nicholas Dymock, who acted as captain of the hunters. Like the earls of Cumberland, Lincoln claimed rights of free chase and warren over lands in the possession of tenants and neighbours, but this was disputed by Sir Edward Dymock, Sir Henry Ayscough, and Sir Thomas Standish, who claimed the right to hunt on their own lands. One outraged defendant, Charles Ayscough, gent., when compelled to make answer in the Court of Star Chamber, defiantly told the judges that the earl of Lincoln had illegally enclosed six hundred acres of the common waste of the manor of Tattershall in his red deer park and denied the use-rights thereof to his tenants. Lincoln had also enclosed another six hundred acres of arable lands and common of the manor of Kirkstead, which did not belong to him, within another park, as well as enclosing several highways. Some of the other gentry defendants, at the instigation of Thomas Browne, gent., pleaded that the earl of Lincoln had accused them of hunting at night and in disguise, which offences by a statute of Henry VII were deemed felonies and therefore not examinable in Star Chamber. But many of the defendants, perceiving that the Star Chamber judges meant to punish their offences as a calculated affront to the dignity of an earl, decided to submit themselves and ask for mercy. Sir Thomas Standish was fined £500 in Trinity Term, 1613, and most of the other defendants were fined in lesser amounts.[105]

The animosity between the earl of Lincoln and the Lincolnshire gentry continued, and between 1609 and 1613 the poaching war resumed when the earl's alienated younger son, Sir Henry Fiennes, made common cause with some of the gentry families whose members had suffered punishment

[104] Ibid.; PRO STAC 5/L1/29, L19/11, L34/37, D15/24, D36/27, printed *in extenso* or summarized in O'Conor, *Godes Peace and the Queenes*, 108–26. The dramatic significance of these May-games is discussed in C. L. Barber, *Shakespeare's Festive Comedy: A Study of Dramatic Form and its Relation to Social Custom* (Princeton, NJ, 1959), 36–51.

[105] PRO STAC 8/19/20/21; Barnes, 'Fines in the High Court of Star Chamber', 155.

for involvement in the earlier attacks on Lincoln's parks and chases in 1605. Two of Sir Henry's allies, Stephen Gateward,[106] a tenant of the earl, and William Langhorne, had been defendants in the 1605 Star Chamber prosecutions, and Langhorne had suffered imprisonment in the Fleet Prison. It is possible that Fiennes had animated the earlier attacks on the earl's game reserves, since he possessed the manor of Kirkstead, which the earl had encroached upon in making new imparkments. Most of Fiennes's hunting companions were probably professional poachers brought from afar since they employed stalking horses to kill Lincoln's deer. They also attacked the earl's keepers and mortally wounded one. Fiennes was alleged to have publicly admitted that he killed one of his father's keepers and to have boasted that it would be an easy matter to kneel before King James and obtain a pardon for the same. The Privy Council was still trying to compose the quarrel between the earl and his son on the eve of Lincoln's death in 1616.[107]

The vendetta resumed in 1616, when Thomas, third earl of Lincoln, succeeded upon his father's death. Sir Henry Fiennes held the manor of Kirkstead and a deer park as the heir male of the unhappy marriage between the second earl and Elizabeth, widow of William Norris, the son and heir apparent to Henry, Lord Norris of Rycote. Kirkstead had been left in trust to the use of the second earl until the heir male came of age. The third earl insisted that Sir Henry Fiennes was a bastard and therefore not entitled to the inheritance. He vexed Fiennes and his tenants with costly lawsuits and frequently hunted in Fiennes's deer park. On one occasion, one of Earl Thomas's followers, James Oglethorpe, ambushed Fiennes, struck him with his sword, and called him a 'bastard'. The emnity continued until *c*.1620. The feud ended when the Puritan Theophilus, fourth earl of Lincoln, succeeded.[108]

8.3. *Religious and Cultural Conflict*

Some of the bitterest of conflicts about hunting rights were those which were exacerbated by religious differences. There was a certain amount of truth in the popular perception that Catholic possessers of hunting franchises and well-stocked deer parks lacked the political influence with juries, local magistrates, and crown ministers successfully to prosecute those who raided their game reserves. At the same time, discontented recusant gentry sometimes assuaged their frustration and boredom by joining poaching gangs. Among the victims who might be punished by a skimmington in the form

[106] On Stephen Gateward of *Gateward's Case* (1607), see Manning, *Village Revolts*, 85–6.
[107] PRO STAC 8/91/27; *Acts PC, 1615–1616*, 680–1; See also PRO STAC 8/257/27.
[108] PRO STAC 8/141/7; GEC vii. 694 n.

of a 'hunting' were those who offended community moral standards by not offering hospitality or who failed to relieve the poor.

By the beginning of the seventeenth century, modern sensibilities antagonistic to hunting—often connected with Puritan or Arminian influences—were at work. Sir Hugh Cholmley's recollections of his ancestors, among whom the taste for hunting was pervasive, reveal his revulsion against the deer-hunting culture and the associated habits of violence and prodigality which exposure to these reforming influences could sometimes effect.

The case of Lord Morley and his son-in-law, Lord Monteagle, illustrates the vulnerability of Catholic peers to unlawful hunting. Edward Parker, Lord Morley, was a Catholic peer in an overwhelmingly Puritan area who found himself without friends or allies. Sometime before 1604 he had purchased Hatfield Forest[109] from Robert Rich, third Lord Rich, and maintained his seat at Hallingburne Morley, Essex, near the forest. Although there had been very little poaching in Hatfield Forest when Lord Rich, the largest landowner in the county, owned the forest, Lord Morley was thereafter hard put to defend his deer from his neighbours.[110] In September 1604 Lord Morley caught Sir Henry Colt in the act of coursing a deer with a greyhound. Colt, it seems, had been passing through the forest with kinsmen and servants and stopped for a bit of sport, as gentlemen frequently did when travelling. When Lord Morley reprimanded Colt, the latter answered: 'God's Wounds! What carest thou? I am as good and a better man than thyself, and will maintain these our doings, do thou what thou darest!' Later in the same day, Lord Morley once again discovered Colt and his entourage hunting in the forest. This time, Colt and his cousin, Sir Thomas Colt, and their servants— eight in all—attacked Lord Morley and his servants with drawn swords and wounded Lord Morley. To add further insult to injury, Colt bade Lord Morley, 'Farewell, Goodman Morley!' Lord Morley complained to the Court of Star Chamber that as a 'baron and peer of your highness's realm' the taunts were 'hardly digested' and 'tendeth to the rebuke of the state and the calling of the whole nobility'.[111]

Within a short time the talk in the local alehouses was that Lord Morley could not protect his deer in Hatfield Forest. Organized plundering by gangs of deer-stealers began, and, in September 1605, Morley once again complained to the Court of Star Chamber, because the local constable was afraid to arrest the deer-stealers. The leader of the gang, a particularly menacing man named John Stonden, threatened to kill Morley's keepers and rangers as well as his deer.[112]

---

[109] Hatfield was described as being a forest or chase and a park. It was at least partially enclosed with fences.

[110] *Calendar of Assize Records, Essex Indictments Eliz. I*, ed. Cockburn, nos. 2472, 2474; Emmison, *Elizabethan Life: Disorder*, 238–9.

[111] PRO STAC 5/R16/36, STAC 8/227/15, 16.   [112] PRO STAC 8/227/19.

After Lord Morley's death, his heir, William, fourth Baron Monteagle and eleventh Baron Morley, the peer who warned the government of the Gunpowder Treason, came into conflict with a leading member of the Puritan gentry over title to Hatfield Forest. When Lord Rich sold Hatfield Forest to Lord Morley, Sir Thomas Barrington retained title to one half of the forest, which allowed him to cut wood for Barrington Hall, his seat in Hatfield Broad Oak. Sir Thomas's heir, Sir Francis Barrington, was a contentious and ambitious man who declared his intention to wear Lord Monteagle down with lawsuits to the point where he would have to sell his portion of the forest. A generation earlier, in the 1580s, a similar dispute had arisen between Lord Rich and Sir Thomas Barrington over the title to the hunting, wood, and timber rights. In this case, the dispute was settled amicably— probably because Rich and Barrington's son, Francis, shared the same parliamentary politics and Puritan persuasion.[113] But Sir Francis Barrington did not intend to accommodate the Catholic Lord Monteagle. Barrington incited his tenants to neglect their duty of keeping the fences around Hatfield Forest in repair, and destroyed many of Monteagle's deer when they escaped. He also began imparking his part of the forest and built one-way deer leaps to trap the deer. His servants ambushed Lord Monteagle's rangers when they sought to rechase the deer and locked them up in the county gaol under his authority as a justice of the peace. Unlike his father-in-law, Lord Morley, Lord Monteagle did not live in Essex, but maintained his residence at Starford, Hertfordshire. Barrington was thus able to depict Monteagle, who came to Hatfield Forest only to hunt and to collect his rents and profits from the forest, as a papist and an outsider who neglected his duty of relieving the poor, failed to keep hospitality, and oppressed poor men by taking their commons and troubling them with lawsuits. Barrington also accused Monteagle of robbing the church by collecting impropriated tithes.[114]

Lord Monteagle brought a charge of sedition against Barrington in Star Chamber for creating strife between the king's subjects and a peer of the realm. He also presented evidence that Barrington was himself a harsh and oppressive landlord. Barrington was alleged to have erected illegal enclosures and to have denied Monteagle's tenants their rights to graze their animals and gather fuel in the forest. Monteagle cited the instance of a 90-year-old cottager whom Barrington had indicted on charges of felonious theft for wood-stealing. Knowing that the man was illiterate and could not plead benefit of clergy, Barrington expected that he would be hanged, but the trial jury realized what Barrington was trying to do and reduced the charges to petty theft. The old cottager was instead sentenced to be whipped,

---

[113] PRO STAC 5/R16/36, STAC 8/227/15; *House of Commons, 1558–1603*, ed. Hasler, i. 400, iii. 290; *DNB, sub* William Stanley, 4th Baron Monteagle and 11th Baron Morley (1575–1622).
[114] PRO STAC 8/227/15.

but Barrington bribed the executioner to flog the old man as hard as possible for the total of forty-one lashes. The crowd which witnessed the punishment was outraged by the harsh penalty. The commoners in Hatfield Forest appealed to Lord Monteagle to allow them to tear down Barrington's illegal enclosures. Monteagle granted his permission, but Barrington sent in forty of his servants and followers to beat up the levellers. One of the commoners was killed and twelve were indicted and convicted of riot and fined and imprisoned.[115]

Anthony Browne, first Viscount Montague, and his grandson and heir, Anthony Maria, second Viscount, were Catholic peers whose well-stocked parks in Sussex proved especially vulnerable to deer-stealers. Their Sussex estates included seven deer parks, and those at Battle Abbey and Cowdray enclosed more than 1,750 acres. The two parks at Battle were subjected to frequent raids by local villagers in the 1570s and 1580s. The difficulties encountered in protecting the deer at Battle Abbey may have been one of the reasons why both parks had been disparked by the middle of the seventeenth century.[116]

There existed in the seventeenth century a popular misconception that recusants who were convicted at law and excommunicated by the ecclesiastical courts were powerless to seek legal remedies against poachers. Certainly, it was difficult to persuade juries in Protestant communities to convict poachers who raided the deer parks of Catholic peers and gentry. Between 1596 and 1598 a number of poaching gangs, 'perceiving that the said viscount [Anthony Maria, second Viscount Montague] was under restraint and prison[er] at and by your [Majesty's] commandment', attacked the four deer parks which belonged to the Cowdray estates, plundered the deer, and assaulted Lord Montague's keepers.[117] One band of poachers consisted mostly of Montague's own tenants in the parishes of Fernhurst and Easebourne. They pleaded ignorance and youth and submitted themselves when charged in Star Chamber.[118] Another gang, led by Richard Lee of Herriard, Hampshire, gent., drew its membership from a number of places in Sussex and Surrey. They planned their poaching raids at Midhurst Fair and confessed that their motive for killing Lord Montague's deer was to beat

---

[115] Ibid.

[116] *Acts PC, 1571–1575*, 309; PRO STAC 5/M40/15, M54/24, M10/34; *VCH Sussex*, ix. 107–8.

[117] PRO STAC 8/84/21; Manning, *Village Revolts*, 293. Despite his open avowal of Catholicism, the first Lord Montague had retained a degree of political influence and patronage into the 1580s. In the next decade, he clearly began to feel isolated and slighted. He died in 1592, and his grandson and heir was quite isolated from the governing élite of Sussex (see R. B. Manning, 'Anthony Browne, 1st Viscount Montague: The Influence in County Politics of an Elizabethan Catholic Nobleman', *Sussex Arch. Coll.*, 106 (1968), 103–12; Breight, 'Caressing the Great', 147–66). The second Lord Montague was once again imprisoned following the Gunpowder Plot, but lack of evidence compelled his release in 1606 (Nicholls, *Investigating Gunpowder Plot*, 74).   [118] PRO STAC 5/M15/8, M16/33.

Henry Goring's gang to the kill.[119] Lee's band afterwards celebrated its
victory with a venison supper at Matthew Wilson's house in Petersfield.
Lee said that he was too poor to pay a fine and asked Lord Montague for
mercy.[120]

The attacks on Lord Montague's deer parks in the Easebourne, Midhurst,
and Fernhurst areas resumed in 1609. Several distinct gangs were involved
and included members of families which had participated in the earlier
deer-stealing incidents of the late 1590s. It would appear that some of the
deer-stealers had proclaimed a 'general hunting' against Lord Montague,
and they were now joined by poaching bands from as far away as Haslemere,
Surrey, and Bramshott, Hampshire. Some of these gangs were led by backwoods gentry, of whom Peter Bettsworth of Iping proved to be the boldest
and most impertinent. On one occasion Bettsworth boasted that the testimony of Lord Montague's keepers had failed to persuade a trial jury at the
Chichester Sessions to return a guilty verdict against him; on another, he
freely admitted exercising his greyhounds in Great North Park at Cowdray,
'but whether the said dogs killed any thing or not, he . . . knoweth not'.
Unable to obtain justice locally, Lord Montague's reputation was so discred-
ited that, in 1616, Bettsworth was insolent enough to offer Montague 'conditions of agreement' whereby Bettsworth promised that he would cease
hunting in Montague's parks. It was not until 1618 that the Court of Star
Chamber finally punished Bettsworth. His conviction, after so many years
of unregulated mischief, was probably also connected with a separate prosecution brought against him by the keeper of Alice Holt and Wolmer
Forests in Hampshire.[121] Bettsworth's origins as a yeoman and a deer-stealer
did not prevent him from becoming a member of the county committee and
a justice of the peace during the Interregnum.[122]

If Catholic landowners were particularly vulnerable to poaching attacks
because of their perceived legal disabilities, some of the recusant gentry
were in such desperate financial straits that they probably cared little about
the penalties imposed for unlawful hunting. Recusant gentry deer-stealers
were common enough, and we sometimes encounter ladies who were inciters and abetters of unlawful hunting. But Catherine Gawen affords a
unique example of a recusant lady who actually led and rode with a poaching gang.

Catherine Gawen was the widow of Thomas Gawen, whose family had
held the manor of Norrington in the parish of Alvediston, Wiltshire, since the
fourteenth century. As early as 1592 two-thirds of Thomas Gawen's estate had

---

[119] Sir Henry Goring's poaching gang was still active in 1606, when he served as sheriff of
Sussex and Surrey. In that year Thomas, earl of Arundel and Surrey, accused him of deer-
stealing (PRO STAC 8/45/17).   [120] PRO STAC 5/M12/3, M32/32.
[121] PRO STAC 8/84/21, 22, 23, 143/14; Barnes, 'Fines in the High Court of Star Chamber',
175.
[122] A. Fletcher, *A County Community in Peace and War: Sussex, 1600–1660* (1975), 326,
349.

been sequestered to the crown because of his recusancy. The estate remained sequestered in 1604 at his death and in 1646 when their son Thomas
held the manor. Catherine was twice indicted for uttering scandalous
speeches against the late queen in 1603 and 1605.[123] She had better ex-
pectations of King James, but must have been disillusioned when the second earl of Salisbury, with the king's encouragement, began lawsuits against
the purlieu men of Cranborne Chase in order to expand the boundaries of
the chase.[124]

Catherine Gawen's poaching career appears to have begun in July 1612.
She and John Flower of Anston, Wiltshire, gent., led a band of between ten
and twelve deer-stealers into Tollard Park and Cranborne Chase on numerous occasions during the following months. By October the gang had grown
to between sixteen and twenty persons, who must have been considered
dangerous, for the keepers of Cranborne Chase thought it imprudent to
attempt to apprehend them.[125]

Another example of an attack upon a deer park being employed as a
kind of charivari occurred in Jacobean Lancashire. Robert Hesketh of Rufford
came from an old Lancashire family with strong Catholic associations, but
had conformed and served as a justice of the peace, sheriff, and member
of Parliament. His brothers, Thomas and Richard, were recusants, and Richard
had been executed in 1592. As a magistrate, Hesketh pursued seminary
priests with a vengeance. Considering his family background, it is little
wonder that his Catholic neighbours regarded him as a turncoat. One
neighbour, Thomas Assheton of Croston, esq., who was also a kinsman by
both blood and marriage, devised numerous ways of punishing Hesketh.
Assheton frequently gathered his friends, tenants, and servants together
to hunt in Hesketh's deer park. Hesketh had enclosed a lane which led to
the parish church of Croston, and, when Assheton's wife died in 1612, his
friends and relations decided to hold her funeral in the parish church. The
funeral cortège, one hundred strong and marching with drawn swords,
began by destroying the locked gates which obstructed the path to the
church and attacking two of Hesketh's servants who had been sent to guard
the gates. The mourners re-erected a large wooden cross in the lane where
one had formerly stood for generations, and then proceeded to hold a
Catholic funeral service. Later, Assheton and his friends returned to the
church and destroyed the baptismal font, pulpit, and lectern, and cast the
font into the river which flowed past the church.[126]

One of the most detailed accounts that we possess of the changing attitudes of an English landed family towards the deer-hunting culture is that

---

[123] *VCH Wilts.*, xiii. 11, 16, 41; B. H. Cunnington, 'Search for Arms in Wiltshire in 1612', *Wilts.
Arch. and Nat. Hist. Mag.*, 47 (1937), 637–9.
[124] See Ch. 4.3. [125] PRO STAC 8/11/1.
[126] *House of Commons, 1558–1603*, ed. Hasler, ii. 304–5; PRO STAC 8/180/28. See also
A. Morey, *The Catholic Subjects of Elizabeth I* (1978), 154; J. Bossy, *The English Catholic
Community, 1570–1850* (New York, 1976), 140–1.

provided by Sir Hugh Cholmley (1600–57), which records the fortunes of four generations of the Cholmleys of Roxby and Whitby in the North Riding of Yorkshire from the mid-Tudor period to the end of the Civil Wars. Sir Hugh distinguished himself by fighting on both sides of the first Civil War, and, after making the mistake of switching from the winning side to the losing side, he was afforded the opportunity, during a period of imprisonment, of reflecting upon his ambivalence. Cholmley's autobiography, written in 1656 but not published until 1777, was intended to justify his actions.[127] It also affords a remarkably candid account of his ancestors' attitudes and practices with regard to household servants and retainers, honour and hospitality, duelling and hunting. The Cholmleys were well connected with the peerage in every generation, and their mode of living was in many ways more characteristic of an aristocratic household—a style of living that was regarded with awe by the common people for its 'hawking, hunting, hastiness, mighty power, vain vaunts, trains of horse and servants, riot, mischiefs, bravery, roistering port, or great line'.[128] The attitudes and behaviour of the Cholmleys are further illuminated by their involvement in a notorious dispute in 1600 with Sir Thomas Posthumous Hoby (1566–1640), whose rigidly Puritan demeanour offers a sharp contrast to the roisterous ways of the Cholmleys and their kin.[129]

The founder of the Cholmleys of Roxby and Whitby was Sir Richard Cholmley I (*c.*1516–79). Sir Richard was a soldier, knighted at the Battle of Musselburgh, and had raised his soldiers from amongst his own followers 'in his own country and merely by his own power and interest'.[130] The Cholmleys found impressment by royal commission to be highly distasteful, and Hoby's use of his powers as a commissioner of musters in the 1590s to impress Cholmley tenants was one of the causes of emnity between the Cholmleys and Hoby.[131] Sir Richard purchased lands of the monastery of Whitby, but his principal residence was Roxby, near Pickering Forest, where he 'lived in great port, having a very great family [and] at least fifty or sixty men servants'. When he went to London he was usually attended by between thirty and forty of these undisciplined retainers.[132] There was a

---

[127] *Memoirs of Sir Hugh Cholmley.*

[128] Lawrence Humphrey, *The Nobles, or of Nobilitye* (1563; repr. Amsterdam, 1973), unpaginated [fo. 4ᵛ].

[129] Hoby's notions of correct behaviour presumably derive not only from his religious views, but also from the fact that his father, Sir Thomas Hoby, the English ambassador to the king of France, was the first English translator of Castiglione's *The Courtier.*

[130] *Memoirs of Sir Hugh Cholmley*, 5–8. The Cholmeleys of Brandsby also descend from Sir Richard Cholmley I.

[131] PRO STAC 5/H16/2.

[132] Sir Hugh Cholmley tells the following anecdote about his great-grandfather's servants:

I have been told, by some who knew the truth, that when there had been twenty-four pieces of beef put in a morning into the pot, sometimes not one of them would be left for his own dinner; for, in those times, the idle serving-men were accustomed to have their breakfast,

quarrel between Sir Richard and his brother-in-law, the earl of Westmorland, 'which occasioned continual fighting and scuffles between the earl's men and Sir Richard's when they met whether in London streets or elsewhere'. This, Sir Hugh Cholmley explained, was 'done with less danger of life and bloodshed than in these succeeding ages, because they then fought only with buckler and short sword, and it was counted unmanly to make a thrust'.[133]

Sir Richard's son Sir Henry, known as Harry Cholmley (1556–1616), was 'much given to the pleasure of hunting, and especially with fleet hounds, though I have seldom seen men prosper in their estates that did so'. His grandson Hugh, the memoirist, remarked that these were 'vain, chargeable sports [and] did much increase his expenses'.[134] Sir Henry's household also included a large number of servants, and he was in serious financial trouble by 1600. Although Harry Cholmley was a justice of the peace and outwardly conformed to the Anglican church, his wife Margaret was a recusant and sheltered seminary priests at Whitby. This was another issue which caused conflict between Harry Cholmley and Sir Thomas Posthumous Hoby. By Hoby's own account, his strict enforcement of the penal laws resulted in the conviction of some eighty of Cholmley's tenants, servants, and kindred from the liberty of Whitby Strand. In effect, Hoby had destroyed the Cholmley household, and Harry Cholmley was obliged to discharge most of his servants and retainers—the most 'obstinate' recusants—in order to avoid further legal penalties.[135] Hoby gloated that, through his efforts, Harry and Margaret Cholmley were compelled to go to their parish church, from which they had absented themselves for three years, and to receive communion, which they had never done before.[136] Sir Hugh Cholmley says that his grand-parents converted to Protestantism towards the end of Harry Cholmley's life, but his grandfather never gave up his passion for hunting, and, indeed, died in a hunting accident. He was the forester of Pickering Forest, a Duchy of Lancaster office, and in 1614 the keeper of Pickering Forest and Blandsby Park complained in Star Chamber that he had attempted unsuccessfully to restrain Harry Cholmley and his numerous kin from depleting the king's deer.[137]

Although it must have put a great strain on the family finances, Harry's son, Sir Richard Cholmley II (1580–1632), tried to keep up the family

and with such liberty as they would go into the kitchen, and, striking their daggers into the pot, take out the beef without the cook's leave or privacy; yet he would laugh at this, rather than be displeased, saying, 'Would not the knaves leave me one piece for my own dinner?' (*Memoirs of Sir Hugh Cholmley*, 5–8)

[133] Ibid.   [134] Ibid. 9–11.

[135] By the Act of 1593 (35 Eliz. I, c. 1), the head of a household could be fined £10 per head per month for sheltering convicted recusants.

[136] *House of Commons, 1558–1603*, ed. Hasler, i. 604; PRO STAC 5/H16/2.

[137] *Memoirs of Sir Hugh Cholmley*, 9–11; PRO STAC 8/136/4.

tradition by maintaining a large household. When his cousin Lord Scrope became president of the Council of the North and lord-lieutenant of Yorkshire in 1619, Sir Richard met him at the southern boundary of Yorkshire, 'attended with twenty of his own servants, all well mounted, and in handsome liveries of grey cloth trimmed with silver lace'. Sir Richard was also devoted to hunting—both lawful and unlawful; although he was naturally fair in complexion, his face grew swarthy from 'much using of field sports'.[138] He frequently fought duels, and was fined £3,000 for his involvement in the Essex Revolt. His bride brought him a dowry of £2,000, but it must have been quickly dissipated. 'A few years after, [Cholmley] struck a gentleman in the Star Chamber, the Court sitting, for which he should have lost his hand, but that good friends and money bought him off.'[139]

It was in 1600 that Richard Cholmley II and his friend, William Eure (1579–1646), son and heir of Ralph, third Lord Eure, had their notorious encounter with Sir Thomas Posthumous Hoby. One August morning Cholmley and Eure set out from Roxby to hunt in Pickering Forest. With them were some twenty youthful companions—mostly servants and relatives of the Cholmleys and Eures. They must have reflected upon Hoby's vindictive destruction of the Cholmley household, and decided to visit and spend the night with Hoby at Hackness, which was within Pickering Forest and about nine miles from Roxby.[140] Their visit can only be described as an invasion of the Hoby household—a kind of skimmington intended to humiliate the Hobys. By the laws of hospitality, Hoby was obliged to entertain them and play the good host, but the modes of living and the concepts of hospitality of Hoby and his guests were so different that the encounter was bound to exacerbate the ill feeling between them.[141]

Sir Thomas ate dinner with his guests, but Lady Margaret pleaded illness and remained in her chamber. The guests started drinking healths to Hoby and his wife, which was associated with hunting behaviour—a boisterous demeanour affected when males congregated together before or following a hunt. Hoby declined to join them, drinking 'his ordinary beverage' instead, and asked to be excused after the Eures and Cholmleys began playing cards—despite the well-known prohibition in the Hoby household against gaming. The servants were ordered to go to evening prayer, which was usually conducted in the great chamber, but on this occasion was held in

---

[138] *Memoirs of Sir Hugh Cholmley*, 11–18; PRO STAC 8/136/4.

[139] *Memoirs of Sir Hugh Cholmley*, 11–18.

[140] PRO STAC 5/H16/2, H42/12; DL 1/81/A15; *House of Commons, 1558–1603*, ed. Hasler, ii. 92–4, 323–4.

[141] PRO STAC 5/H16/2. See also the excellent discussions of this incident in the context of changing concepts of hospitality in Heal, *Hospitality in Early Modern England*, 13–14 *et passim*; ead., 'Hospitality and Honor in Early Modern England', *Food and Foodways*, 1 (1987), 321–4.

the great hall. When the servants began singing psalms, William Borne, one of Lord Eure's servants, remained in the hall making rude noises and laughing. At breakfast the next morning, the guests resumed drinking healths with beer and wine and started 'hallooing and shouting' in the great chamber. All of this disturbed Lady Margaret, whose chamber was nearby. Hoby at this time sent a message asking them to engage in some more quiet activity. Sir William Eure, Lord Eure's younger brother, sent word to Lady Hoby, saying that he wished to see her and pay his respects. Lady Hoby, sent back the message that she was not quite ready and would send for him when she was. Later, she stated that she would see Sir William only and not the rest. He was incensed and replied that he cared not for their meat or drink, but had come to see her. Sir William then insulted Hoby by offering to pay for his food and lodging: he would 'set up horns at his gate and begone!' Hearing this, Hoby ordered them all to depart. Instead, the Eures and Cholmley forced their way into Lady Margaret's chamber and tossed one of the Hoby's servants across the room. As one of the guests, George Smith, passed through the screen of the hall into Lady Margaret's chamber, he spied some stag horns on the screen and said that he would have them nailed to Sir Thomas Hoby's head.[142]

Feeling his honour besmirched, Hoby preferred numerous bills of complaint against the Eures and Cholmleys in the Court of Star Chamber. Hoby was awarded £100 damages—to be paid to him publicly. Ultimately, the quarrel was as much about power as honour and religious conformity, and Hoby failed to drive the Eures and the Cholmleys out of political office in Yorkshire. William Eure sat for Scarborough in the Parliament of 1601 while remaining a recusant. Sir Richard Cholmley became deputy-lieutenant of the North Riding when his cousin Lord Scrope became president of the Council in the North and he was also elected to represent Scarborough.[143]

Many poaching wars were basically about land and the use-rights attaching to that land. By calling ancient hunting franchises into question through the issuance of game warrants to courtiers and peers and by trampling upon the rights of purlieu men, James I and Charles I contributed to the survival of the land wars which had been characteristic of the age of bastard feudalism.[144] Land law was complex enough in the sixteenth century, and the fact that liberty of free warren and free chase did not necessarily attach to ownership of land and was not always conveyed by purchase tended to

---

[142] PRO STAC 5/H22/21; *Diary of Lady Margaret Hoby, 1599–1605*, ed. D. M. Meads (1930), 141.

[143] *Memoirs of Sir Hugh Cholmley*, 11–18; *House of Commons, 1558–1603*, ed. Hasler, ii. 93–4, 323–4. Although Lord Eure and Sir Henry Cholmley do not appear to have been present at the incursion into the Hoby household, Hoby named them as the principal defendants in the Star Chamber case because he regarded them as the procurers of the tumult.

[144] Bellamy, *Bastard Feudalism and the Law*, 35–6.

multiply such disputes. The poaching wars or general huntings directed at the earls of Cumberland and Lincoln certainly arose from this problem of ownership and possession and hunting franchises for particular manors and parcels of land becoming divided. This was especially true in the north of England, where mesne tenancies still survived. The tenants and neighbours of the earls of Cumberland and Lincoln were asserting a more unqualified doctrine of private property rights against the claim by these peers that they possessed absolute and exclusive hunting rights when they waged their poaching wars. In the Thames Valley, expansions of royal parks and chases at Richmond, Berkhamstead, Theobalds, and Enfield provoked extensive enclosure riots and poaching by tenants who were deprived of their common rights and also imposed a greater burden of providing poor relief upon those hundreds and parishes which bordered upon the expanded royal game reserves.

Considering the increased number of attacks upon aristocratic game reserves in the reign of James I, it is difficult to avoid the conclusion that this resulted, at least in part, from a decline in the prestige and power of the aristocracy. Before 1603 resentment of aristocratic privileges such as hunting franchises and well-stocked deer parks had manifested itself largely during outbreaks of popular rebellion, such as in 1381, 1549, and 1569, when there was a temporary collapse of order. During the reign of James I, there appears to have been an overall increase in unlawful hunting, frequently led by envious gentry and often focused upon aristocratic game reserves. Aristocratic households were smaller in the early seventeenth century and consequently peers were less able to defend their hunting reserves. Landed magnates agreed with their monarch, James VI and I, that the Game Laws needed to be strengthened, and they turned to the Court of Star Chamber to buttress their social privileges against deer-slayers and libellers. The poaching wars would appear to be a manifestation of that last gasp of bastard feudalism described by Professor Bellamy.[145] With the decline of opportunities for military adventure and service in noble households, many small gentry and yeomanry were set adrift and were more likely to be attracted to poaching gangs.

As Professor Stone has remarked, the attempt of the Tudor monarchs to secure a monopoly on violence was slower and more protracted than is sometimes supposed.[146] This was partly because these monarchs and their early Stuart successors did not really try to put an end to violence, but only to prevent others from resorting to the use of it in private quarrels and disputes with the crown. The kings of England, like the aristocracy and gentry, never seem to have given a thought to the kind of example which they provided to their subjects and inferiors. And yet, there were few more

---

[145] Ibid.   [146] Stone, *Crisis of the Aristocracy*, 107–8.

powerful influences upon popular culture, tastes, and behaviour than the examples set by monarchs and courtly society. With far too few exceptions, they were all immersed in the deer-hunting culture and its symbolic language of violence. Beyond the unavoidable conclusion that blood sports have a brutalizing influence on hunters, the hunting culture perpetuated military values and violent behaviour in times of peace and worked against royal attempts to pacify the English people. That hunting was a rehearsal for war and ought to be reserved for kings and noblemen who were members of a warrior class was an argument that never made much sense as long as all male Englishmen were subjected to a universal military obligation. This was no mere abstract legal principle during the Tudor period when tenants and substantial householders were called upon to serve in the militia and propertyless males were impressed for overseas and foreign campaigns.

Contemporary critics such as Sir John Harington were aware that hunting all too frequently encouraged drunkenness and coarse behaviour rather than promoting martial virtues and military preparedness. This contradiction was especially evident in the example set by James I, who, although more obsessed with hunting than any other British monarch, was certainly no exemplar of the traditional martial and kingly virtues. Moreover, enforcement of the Game Laws and reinforcement of the hunting prerogatives of the crown imposed a heavy burden upon the king's courts—especially the Court of Star Chamber. This had the effect of perverting royal justice, and resulted in the popular belief that James I was more indulgent to murderers than deer-slayers. It also brought the Court of Star Chamber into disrepute.

9

Conclusion: The Persistence of the Deer-Hunting Culture

For the very reason that hunting was a feudal privilege, the wretch who indulged in it by main force, with an audacity and a passion hard to realize, was driven to it less by reason of his poverty than because of the vague delusion that he would to some extent enoble himself.

G. Tarde, *Penal Philosophy*, trans. R. Howell (Boston, 1912; repr. Montclair, NJ, 1968), 332

THE deer-hunting culture was already well established in the thirteenth century, by which time its main characteristics were clearly discernible: hunting was a high-status pastime because it derived from royal favour and feudal privilege and because it exemplified the martial values of a warrior aristocracy. Dining upon venison was an important part of any festive occasion in the great halls of royal palaces and baronial households, and the distribution of venison to retainers and allies and even tenants was associated with royal and aristocratic largesse. Another characteristic had also become evident: a disproportionate number of those who poached the king's deer in defiance of the forest law were of gentry status or higher.[1]

In the early modern period, aristocrats and gentry were much slower to accept the dynastic state and the rule of law than has generally been supposed, and few actions demonstrate this more strikingly than the persistence of unlawful hunting by gentry-led gangs and the habits of violence which accompanied such behaviour. Violence and the readiness to resort to it to defend a code of honour helped to define a person of noble or genteel status and indicates a continuing disposition to actions outside the law and independent of the state.[2] Dr Mervyn James has convincingly demonstrated the survival of this aristocratic culture into late Elizabethan England in a brilliant essay placing the Essex Rebellion of 1601 in context. Dr James calls this the last 'honour revolt' in England and shows how it derived from a cult of honour, a code of martial values, and an emphasis upon aristocratic lineage which reached back to the Middle Ages. This political and military

---

[1] Birrell, 'Who Poached the King's Deer?', 11.
[2] K. B. Neuschel, *Word of Honor: Interpreting Noble Culture in Sixteenth-Century France* (Ithaca, NY, 1989), 65–6; M. E. James, 'English Politics and the Concept of Honour, 1485–1642', in *Society, Politics and Culture: Studies in Early Modern England* (Cambridge, 1986), 308–9.

culture characteristically stood apart from Christian ethics and the concept of the rule of law which characterized a civil society; adherents were dedicated to the profession of arms, were contemptuous of courtiers and lawyers, and freely resorted to duelling, verbal posturing, and, one might add, tumultuous hunting in asserting themselves. Like the second earl of Essex at his state trial for treasonous rebellion, they appealed to the law of nature, which found recognition in the provisions for duelling in the laws of France and other continental countries, but not in the laws of England.[3]

No shame attached to riotous hunting, duelling, and other aristocratic modes of feuding, despite the attempts of crown officials and parliamentary legislation to depict such antics as criminal behaviour. Quite the contrary, unlawful hunting by gentry and noblemen was regarded as admirable and prestigious and was emulated by their plebeian audience. Gabriel Tarde, the nineteenth-century French criminologist, regarded poaching as one of a number of distinctly aristocratic types of crime, along with sacking cities and kidnapping ladies and holding them for ransom.[4] George Rudé has argued that certain kinds of crowd behaviour and of crimes against public order—especially those directed against persons—are attributable to the corrupt example of aristocrats.[5] The Game Laws were enacted in the first place to preserve public order, but enforcement of these laws was always difficult because unlawful hunting and commerce in illicit venison were so widespread among the landed aristocracy and gentry.

The primary justification for prosecuting and punishing deer-stealers before 1603 was that such persons broke the king's peace by their riotous and violent behaviour. But, under James I and Charles I, the Court of Star Chamber gave the appearance of being more concerned with upholding the royal game prerogative and aristocratic hunting privileges than preserving public order. Despite sporadic attempts to prosecute poachers under the Game Act of 1485, which made hunting under certain circumstances felony, deer-stealing and other forms of poaching were invariably punished as misdemeanours. However, as a consequence of the gradual acceptance of theories

---

[3] M. E. James 'At the Crossroads of the Political Culture: The Essex Revolt, 1601', in ibid., 416–17. In a controversial essay, Dr J. S. A. Adamson suggests that, far from disintegrating with the failure of the Essex Revolt, this political and chivalric culture appears to have reasserted itself in the Caroline period when trial by combat was revived along with the Great Council of Peers and an antiquarian obsession with things medieval. The third earl of Essex's proposal to restore the medieval offices of lord high constable and lord high steward, together with his startling offer to engage in a single trial by combat prior to the Battle of Edgehill, are difficult to explain unless one accepts the idea that something of that chivalric culture survived the abortive Essex Revolt ('The Baronial Context of the English Civil War', *Trans. R. Hist. Soc.*, 5th ser., 40 (1990), 104–5).

[4] Tarde, *Penal Philosophy*, 336; cf. also J. S. McClelland, *The Crowd and the Mob from Plato to Canetti* (1989), 63–4.

[5] G. Rudé, *Paris and London in the Eighteenth Century: Studies in Popular Protest* (repr. New York, 1972), pp. 26–8.

of possessive individualism during the seventeenth century, deer came to be regarded as private property rather than wild beasts, because the law began to assume that they existed only in enclosed game reserves.[6]

Increasingly, the Game Laws favoured property owners. Beginning early in the reign of George I, new game legislation treated deer-stealing more strictly. The Game Act of 1719 distinguished deer-stealing from other kinds of poaching by making it a felony punishable by transportation. The Black Act of 1723 made capital felonies of many hunting offences. At first, deer-stealers resorted to blacking to disguise themselves, but after the passage of the Black Act deer-stealing became a more dangerous activity—especially for gentlemen. However, E. P. Thompson insists that deer-stealing declined, not because the risks of blacking were too great, but because, by the middle of the eighteenth century, there were not enough deer remaining in game reserves to make the sport worthwhile.[7]

Although the subject needs more investigation, it would appear that, following the Restoration, the gentry gradually withdrew from deer-stealing and the remaining varieties of poaching became more exclusively plebeian pursuits. As the Game Laws increased the penalties for deer-stealing and associated activities, gentlemen became more aware of the need to respect private property, consolidate their class interests, and adhere to more appropriate standards of behaviour. Landowners were probably reluctant to restock their parks and chases with deer after the Civil War because of the expense involved and the violent behaviour associated with the deer-hunting culture; also, other field sports such as fox-hunting provided plenty of opportunities to cut a figure or break one's neck and were considered a more seemly substitute for deer-hunting. With the development of a permanent standing army, young gentlemen with a taste for adventure could channel their aggressive energies into professional military careers.

Deer-stealing by gentry-led gangs declined in the eighteenth century, but other species of gang poaching continued.[8] Indeed, poaching wars with pitched battles persisted into the Victorian period. When the Game Laws came under attack in the latter part of the eighteenth century, one of the arguments put forward for preserving them was the need to fight the lawlessness which gang-poaching bred. This was another legacy of the deer-hunting culture. In the 1790s, when Britain was at war with revolutionary France, many feared that even a partial repeal of the Game Laws would

---

[6] Munsche, *Gentlemen and Poachers*, 230–1.

[7] 5 Geo, I, c. 28; 9 Geo. I, c. 22; Thompson, *Whigs and Hunters*, 230–1.

[8] Poaching was also a serious problem in the last days of the *ancien régime* in France (cf. Hippolyte Taine, *The Ancient Régime*, trans. John Durand (New York, 1876; repr. 1876; Gloucester, Mass., 1962), 380–1).

open the doors to Jacobinism and social levelling.[9] In actuality, levelling tendencies had long been characteristic of hunting fraternities.

Hunting bands, or gangs as they came to be called in the seventeenth century, were primordial social organizations, but they also imitated the large hunting parties of kings and noblemen. Late-medieval and early modern audiences admired Robin Hood's band of outlaws living in the greenwood, and the widespread taste for organized unlawful deer-hunting as well as feasting upon the forbidden delights of venison surely owes something to the popularity of these gests and ballads. The downward diffusion of these tastes and pastimes also illustrates the influence of aristocratic culture upon popular culture and the function of the gentry and their yeomen servants as a bridge between the two cultures.[10] The claim to gentility was always more widespread than the heralds and the armigerous gentry were pre-pared to allow, and, as many contemporary commentators noted, hunting on either side of the law was a widely-accepted way of asserting one's gentility and gallantry.[11] Thus, unlawful hunting particularly appealed to the small gentry—those of marginal status whose claim to genteel rank was most likely to be questioned.

There is another dimension to hunting fraternities—to use the more neutral term. They also meted out popular justice to those who failed to display neighbourliness and hospitality, to landlords who encroached upon common wastes and woods or who neglected to prevent their deer and rabbits from damaging the crops of tenants and neighbours. One does not have to discover a moral or generous-hearted content in deer-stealing to describe it as a form of popular protest, because personal revenge often plays a large role in popular protest.[12] Such punishments were also handed out by aristocratic owners of game reserves who felt that neighbouring gentry were presumptuous in laying claim to hunting franchises or imparking land where they and their noble ancestors had possessed liberty of free chase. Small gentry were especially assertive in defying the more restrictive hunting qualifications of the Jacobean and Restoration Game Laws, and gentry of all colours keenly resented Jacobean and Caroline courtiers who made extravagant claims to hunting privileges based upon grants of royal game warrants or who attempted to override purlieu rights. Although the

[9] H. Hopkins, *The Long Affray: The Poaching Wars, 1760–1914* (1985), 5–12; J. E. Archer, *By a Flash and a Scare: Incendiarism, Animal Maiming and Poaching in East Anglia, 1815–1870* (Oxford, 1990), ch. 9; M. J. Carter, *Peasants and Poachers: A Study in Rural Disorder in Norfolk* (Woodbridge, Suffolk, 1980), esp. pp. 89–106; C. Kirby, 'The English Game Law System', *American Hist. Rev.*, 38 (1932–3), 247–9; id., 'The Attack on the English Game Laws in the Forties', *Journ. Mod. Hist.*, 4 (1932), 20–1.
[10] See P. R. Coss, 'Aspects of Cultural Diffusion in Medieval England: The Early Romances, Local Society and Robin Hood', *P&P*, no. 108 (Aug. 1985), 42–3, 47, 73, 76.
[11] See Ch. 1.1, Ch. 2.1. [12] As I have already argued in *Village Revolts*, 310–11.

behaviour associated with deer-poaching frequently displayed elements of violence, factionalism, and revenge, it could also, at the same time, be principled and rooted in highly developed concepts of justice and constitutionalism. Unlawful hunting could also be a form of political protest and covert discourse couched in symbolic terms which evaded the legal definitions of sedition and treason. In this vein, deer-stealing and other forms of organized poaching might also be viewed as less confrontational and more controlled alternatives to full-scale rebellion. Such protests did, however, occur within a cultural and social context of martial values and habits of organized violence which must have made the transition to war and the resort to arms more acceptable in 1642.[13]

[13] One can also discover other kinds of evidence for the persistence of martial values through the Tudor and early Stuart periods. Sir John Hale tells us that the number of books and sermons justifying war and preparedness for war increased steadily in England in the years preceding the Civil Wars, and that many of the combatants took up arms with an 'alacrity' which would have been astonishing in the Elizabethan period, when soldiers were recruited only with difficulty. Clergymen—especially Puritan clergymen—easily located biblical texts to justify the idea that war was part of God's plan. In a sermon to the City of Coventry militia in 1622, Samuel Buggs told his audience that they had 'entered . . . one of the two professions which are the only life and lustre of true gentry'. The effect of these sermons by militia chaplains was to 'habituate their auditors to the use of violence in a cause they believed just . . .' (J. R. Hale, 'Incitement to Violence? English Divines on the Theme of War, 1578 to 1631', in *Renaissance War Studies* (1983), 487–9, 502, 505–6; see also James, 'English Politics and the Concept of Honour', 309, 392–413).

Glossary

brach: a type of hound which hunted by scent.

browsewood: tips and small branches of trees cut to provide supplementary fodder for deer or cattle.

buck: a male fallow deer; fallow deer were primarily bred in parks; the buck was less esteemed for hunting than the hart or stag, but its venison was more highly prized.

caltrops: sharpened stakes set in the ground at an angle to impale deer being pursued.

champerty: unlawfully promoting or sustaining a suitor at law in a case where one does not have a proper interest in order to secure a share of the property being disputed.

charivari: see under skimmington.

coppice: a plantation of young trees enclosed with a fence to prevent damage by deer or other browsing animals; the wood from coppices was harvested periodically.

course: to pursue or hunt deer or hare or other game with greyhounds.

drive: a method of hunting whereby a combination of horsemen, men upon foot, and scenting hounds induced a herd of deer to run past a standing or a grove of trees from which archers fired upon the beasts.

expediate: to amputate the toes from two of a dog's paws in order to prevent it from chasing deer or game; also known as 'lawing'.

free chase, liberty of: the right to hunt deer over a specified area which was not necessarily limited to one's own holdings.

free warren, liberty of: the right to hunt deer on one's own land.

hart: the largest animal hunted in England, a male red deer possessing antlers with at least ten tines.

hay or hey: 1. a temporary enclosure in a forest used for confining deer; 2. a woven net used for catching rabbits.

herbage: pasture within a park or forest; the rights to the herbage were often leased.

hunting par force *and at large*: the most formal and ritualistic method of hunting, employed by the royal court and aristocratic hunting parties; the finest hart in the forest was selected, unharboured, and pursued by relays of hounds and the dignitaries of the hunting party upon horseback; during the chase, signals were transmitted by hunting horns; as many hunters as possible assembled for the death, which was followed by the undoing or unmaking of the carcass of the hart.

information: the technical legal term for a bill of complaint filed by the attorney-general in the Court of Star Chamber.

Justice Seat: the supreme court in the judicial system under forest law, presided over by a justice in eyre.

launds or lawns: open clearings in a forest or park provided and maintained for the grazing of deer.

law: as in 'to law a dog'; see under 'expediate'.

lymehound: a type of hound which hunts deer by scent; a bloodhound.

maintenance: promoting or sustaining suits at law in which one does not have a proper interest, or encouraging such litigation for an improper motive; this was one of the great evils associated with bastard feudalism and was punishable in the Court of Star Chamber because it tended to corrupt justice.

parker: a game official charged with the administration of a deer park.

prescription: the title to a right based upon its exercise since time immemorial.

purlieu: areas formerly part of the royal forests, which had been disafforested since the thirteenth century.

purlieu men: freeholders possessing estates worth 40*s*. p.a. within purlieus or disafforested areas once part of the royal forests, who were permitted the limited right to course deer on their own holdings provided they employed only hounds and no other hunting weapons.

quarry: at the ceremonial 'undoing' of a stag or hart, certain parts of the beast were placed upon the hide and fed to the hounds as a reward.

quo warranto: a writ in the common-law courts in which a person was called upon to show by what warrant he held or claimed to exercise an office or a franchise.

rascal deer: smaller deer than harts or stags which were regarded as less suitable quarry for hunting.

ranger: a mounted keeper in a royal forest charged with the duty of rechasing deer from the purlieus back within the boundaries of the forest.

scandalum magnatum: a species of seditious libel consisting of slandering a magnate, i.e. a peer or great officer of state, or publishing or uttering a false rumour which might promote a division between the king and his magnates.

skimmington: a ritual of folk justice in which the culprit, who was accused of violating the customs or moral standards of the local community, was subjected to a punishment in which his person or his effigy was paraded to the accompaniment of 'rough music', provided by the beating of skimmers and other kitchen utensils; the term, by analogy, may be applied to a 'general hunting'.

stag: a male red deer, five years of age.

standing: a wooden platform with a balustrade or other type of enclosure built upon piers from which ladies or elderly courtiers and aristocrats might fire arrows at deer as they were driven past.

Swanimote: a local forest court charged with punishing petty offences against forest law.

toils: woven nets strung upon poles employed for catching deer.

verderers: judicial officers of the forest charged with detecting offences against forest law and certifying the same to justices in eyre of the forest; verderers also punished petty offences.

vert: the trees and undergrowth of a forest which provided cover and browse for the deer; the destruction of the vert constituted a trespass against forest law, which was known as waste and was punishable in the forest courts.

walk: an administrative subdivision of a forest placed in the care of a keeper.

waste (manorial): manorial commons affording use-rights to tenants such as common of pasture or the right to take fuel and timber for repairing the tenants' dwellings and barns.

waste (in forest law): see under vert.

Bibliography

THIS bibliography includes all manuscript collections cited, but only those printed works cited more than once in the footnotes. Consistent with the footnotes and the list of abbreviations, the place of publication of printed books is understood to be London unless otherwise indicated.

I. Manuscript Collections

British Library
  Cotton MSS
  Sloane MSS
Public Record Office
  C 99 (Chancery, Various Forest Proceedings)
  DL 1 (Proceedings, Duchy Court of Lancaster)
  DL 4 (Depositions, Duchy Court of Lancaster)
  DL 5 (Entry Books of Decrees and Orders, Duchy Court of Lancaster)
  E 134 (Exchequer, King's Remembrancer, Depositions)
  E 178 (Special Commissions and Returns in Exchequer)
  SP 12 (State Papers, Domestic, Elizabeth)
  SP 14 (State Papers, Domestic, James I)
  STAC 2 (Court of Star Chamber, Proceedings, Henry VII)
  STAC 3 (Court of Star Chamber, Proceedings, Henry VIII)
  STAC 4 (Court of Star Chamber, Proceedings, Mary I, Philip and Mary)
  STAC 5 (Court of Star Chamber, Proceedings, Elizabeth)
  STAC 7 (Court of Star Chamber, Proceedings, Elizabeth, Addenda)
  STAC 8 (Court of Star Chamber, Proceedings, James I)

II. Printed Sources

Accounts of the Roberts Family of Boarzell, Sussex, c.1568–1582, ed. R. Tittler (Sussex Rec. Soc., 71; Lewes, Sussex, 1977–9).
Acts of the Privy Council of England, ed. J. R. Dasent, 46 vols. (1890–1964).
Anon., *The Institucion of a Gentleman* (1568).
Anon., *The Merry Devill of Edmonton* (1608), in *The Shakespeare Apocrypha*, ed. C. F. Tucker Brooke (Oxford, 1908; repr. 1967).
The Art of Hunting, by William Twici, ed. A. Dryden (Northampton, 1908).
Ascham, Roger, *The Scholemaster* (1570), in *English Works*, ed. W. A. Wright (Cambridge, 1904; repr. 1970).
—— *Toxophilus* (1545), in *English Works*, ed. W. A. Wright (Cambridge, 1904, repr. 1970).

Aubrey's Brief Lives, ed. O. L. Dick (1949; repr. 1950).

Aubrey, John, *Aubrey's Natural History of Wiltshire* (1847; repr. New York, 1969).

The Autobiography of Edward, Lord Herbert of Cherbury, ed. S. L. Lee (1866).

The Autobiography of Sir John Bramston (Camden Soc., os, 32; 1845).

Barber, Fairless, 'The West Riding Sessions Rolls', *Yorks. Arch. Journ.*, 5 (1877–8), 362–405.

Blundell of Crosby, William, *A Cavalier's Notebook*, ed. T. E. Gibson (1880).

The Boke of Saint Albans by Dame Juliana Berner (1586), facsmile edn. by W. Blades (1905).

Boorde, Andrew, *A Dyetary of Helth*, ed. F. J. Furnivall (EETS, extra ser., 10; 1870).

[Breton, Nicholas], *The Court and the Country, or a Brief Discourse Dialogue-wise set down betweene a Courtier and a Countryman* (1618), in *Inedited Tracts*, ed. W. C. Hazlitt (1868; repr. New York, 1968).

Butler, Samuel, *Posthumous Works*, 3 vols. (1715–19).

Caius, John, *Of English Dogges*, trans. Abraham Fleming (1576; repr. 1880).

Calendar of Assize Records, Essex Indictments, Elizabeth I, ed. J. S. Cockburn (1978).

Calendar of Assize Records, Kent Indictments, Elizabeth I, ed. J. S. Cockburn (1979).

Calendar of Assize Records, Sussex Indictments, Elizabeth I, ed. J. S. Cockburn (1975).

Calendar of Assize Records, Sussex Indictments, James I, ed. J. S. Cockburn (1975).

Calendar of the Close Rolls, The Deputy Keeper of the Records (1900–).

Calendar of the Patent Rolls, The Deputy Keeper of the Records (1906–).

Calendar of State Papers, Domestic, 1547–1603, 12 vols. (1856–72).

Calendar of State, Papers, Spanish, Elizabeth, 4 vols. (1892–9).

Castiglione, Count Baldassare, *The Book of the Courtier*, trans. Sir Thomas Hoby (1561; repr. 1900 and New York, 1967).

Chronicon Henrici Knighton, ed. J. R. Lumby, 2 vols. (Rolls Series; 1889, 1895).

Cleland, James, *The Institution of a Young Noble Man*, ed. M. Molyneux, 2 vols. (Oxford, 1607; repr. New York, 1948).

Cockayne, Sir Thomas, *A Short Treatise of Hunting, 1591*, ed. W. R. Halliday (Oxford, 1932).

Coke, Sir Edward, *The Fourth Part of the Institutes of the Laws of England: Concerning the Jurisdiction of the Courts* (5th edn.; 1671).

—— *The Twelfth Part of the Reports* (4th edn.; 1738).

Coke, Roger, 'Detection of the Court and State of England during the last four Reigns', in [Sir Walter Scott (ed.)], *Secret History of the Court of James I*, 2 vols. (Edinburgh, 1811).

The Complete Works of John Lyly, ed. R. W. Bond, 3 vols. (1902; repr. Oxford, 1967).

Descriptive Catalogue of the Charters and Muniments in the Possession of Lord Fitzhardinge at Berkeley Castle, ed. I. H. Jeayes (Bristol, 1892).

Diary of Lady Margaret Hoby, 1599–1605, ed. D. M. Meads (1930).

Dyer, Sir James, *Reports of Cases in the Reigns of Henry VIII, Edward VI, Queen Mary and Queen Elizabeth*, 3 pts. in 3 vols. (1794 edn.).

Early English Meals and Manners, ed. F. J. Furnivall (EETS, os, 32; 1868).

Elyot, Sir Thomas, *The Boke Named the Gouernour*, ed. H. H. S. Croft, 2 vols. (1883; repr. New York, 1967).

Emmison, F. G., *Elizabethan Life: Disorder: Mainly from Essex Sessions and Assize Records* (Chelmsford, 1970).

England as Seen by Foreigners, ed. W. B. Rye (1865; repr. New York, 1967).

The English Courtier and Country-gentleman (1586), in *Inedited Tracts*, ed. W. C. Hazlitt (1868; repr. New York, 1968).

Erasmus, Desiderius, *The Praise of Folly*, trans. John Wilson (1668; repr. New York, 1942).

Foix, Gaston III, comte de, *La Chasse de Gaston Phebus, Comte de Foix*, ed. J. Lavalle (Paris, 1854).

[Gascoigne, George], *The Noble Arte of Venerie or Hunting* (1575; repr. as *The Noble Art* [sic] *of Venerie or Hunting, 1611*; repr. Oxford, 1908).

Gerard, John, *The Autobiography of a Hunted Priest*, trans. P. Caraman (New York, 1955).

Hale, Sir Matthew, *The History of the Common Law of England*, ed. C. M. Gray (1739 edn.; repr. Chicago, 1971).

Hall, Edward, *Hall's Chronicle* (1809; repr. New York, 1965).

Harrison, William, *Description of England* (1587), in Raphael Holinshed, *Holinshed's Chronicles of England, Scotland and Ireland*, ed. Sir H. Ellis, 6 vols. (1897–8).

Hawarde, John, *Les Reportes del Cases in Camera Stellata, 1593–1609*, ed. W. P. Baildon (1894).

Historical Manuscripts Commission, *Laing* (1914).

—— *Salisbury*, 24 vols. (1883–1976).

Humphrey, Lawrence, *The Nobles, or of Nobilitye* (1563; repr. Amsterdam, 1973).

[Hyde], Edward, earl of Clarendon, *The History of the Rebellion and Civil Wars in England*, 6 vols. (Oxford, 1888).

James VI and I, king of England and Scotland, *Basilikon Doron* (1599), in *Political Works of James I*, ed. C. H. McIlwain (Cambridge, Mass., 1918).

John Isham, Mercer and Merchant Adventurer: Two Account Books of a London Merchant in the Reign of Elizabeth I, ed. G. D. Ramsay (Northants. Rec. Soc., 21; Northampton, 1962).

The Journal of Nicholas Assheton, ed. F. R. Raines (Chetham Soc., 14; Manchester, 1848).

Journals of the House of Commons, 117 vols. (1803–63).

Journals of the House of Lords, 119 vols. (1846–87).

Kentish Sources, vi. Crime and Punishment, ed. E. Melling (Maidstone, Kent, 1969).

The Letters of John Chamberlain, ed. N. McClure, 2 vols. (Philadelphia, 1939).

Letters of King James VI & I, ed. G. P. V. Akrigg (Berkeley, Calif., 1984).

Letters and Papers, Foreign and Domestic, of the Reign of Henry VIII, ed. J. S. Brewer *et al.*, 23 vols. in 38 parts (1862–1932).

Leveson-Gower, Granville, 'Note Book of a Surrey Justice', *Surrey Arch. Coll.*, 9 (1888), 161–232.

'The Life of Mr. Arthur Wilson, the Historian . . . Written by Himself', in Francis Peck, *Desiderata Curiosa*, 2 vols. (1732–5), vol. ii.

The Lisle Letters, ed. M. St C. Byrne, 6 vols. (Chicago, 1981).

Lodge, Edmund, *Illustrations of British History*, 3 vols. (1838).

The Loseley Manuscripts, ed. A. J. Kempe (1835).

Lull, Rámon, *The Book of the Ordre of Chivalry*, trans. William Caxton, ed. A. T. P. Byles (EETS 168; 1926; repr. 1971).

Machiavelli, Niccolò, *The Arte of War*, trans. Peter Whitehorne (1560; repr. New York, 1967).

—— *The Prince*, trans. T. G. Bergin (New York, 1947).

Maison Rustique, or the Countrie Farme, trans. Richard Surfleet (1600).

Manwood, John, *A Treatise of the Laws of the Forest* (1615; repr. Amsterdam, 1976).

M[arkham], G[ervase], *Country Contentments, or the Husbandmans Recreations*, in *A Way to Wealth* (1631).

The Master of Game, by Edward Second Duke of York, ed. W. A. and F. Baillie-Grohman (New York, 1909).

Memoirs of Robert Cary, Earl of Monmouth, ed. G. H. Powell (1905).

The Memoirs of Sir Hugh Cholmley (1777; repr. 1870).

Memorandum Book of Richard Cholmeley of Brandsby, 1602–1623 (N. Yorks. Rec. Office, 44; North Allerton, 1988).

Merriman, R. W., 'Extracts from the Records of the Wiltshire Quarter Sessions, 1603–1609', *Wilts. Arch. and Nat. Hist. Mag*, 22 (1885), 1–38.

Middlesex County Records, ed. J. C. Jeaffreson, 6 vols. (Middx. Rec. Soc.; 1886).

Middlesex Sessions Records, ed. W. Le Hardy, 4 vols. (Middx. Rec. Soc.; 1935–41).

Moryson, Fynes, *An Itinerary* (1617), 4 vols. (Glasgow, 1907–8).

Norden, John, *The Surveyors Dialogue* (1607).

Nugae Antiquae, ed. Thomas Park, 2 vols. (1804).

The Parlement of the Three Ages, ed. M. Y. Offord (EETS 246; 1959; repr. 1967).

Peacham, Henry, *The Compleat Gentleman* (1622; repr. Amsterdam, 1968).

Pleadings and Depositions in the Duchy Court of Lancaster, Time of Henry VII and Henry VIII, Edward VI, and Philip and Mary, ed. H. Fishwick (Rec. Soc. Lancs. and Ches., 32, 35, 40; Machester 1896, 1897, 1899).

The Political Works of James I, ed. C. H. McIlwain (Cambridge, Mass., 1918).

Proceedings in Parliament, 1610, ed. E. R. Foster, 2 vols. (New Haven, Conn., 1966).

Records of the County of Wiltshire, Being Extracts from the Quarter Sessions Great Rolls of the Seventeenth Century, ed. B. H. Cunnington (Devizes, 1932).

Reports of Cases in the Courts of Star Chamber and High Commission, ed. S. R. Gardiner (Camden Soc., NS 39; 1886).

The Reports of Sir George Croke, trans. Sir Harbottle Grimston (1657).

The Reports of Sir John Spelman, ed. J. H. Baker, 2 vols. (Selden Soc., 93–4; 1976, 1978).

The Rev. Oliver Heywood, 1630–1702: His Autobiography, Diaries, Anecdote and Event Books, ed. J. H. Turner, 4 vols. (Bingley, Yorks., 1881–5).

A Royalist's Notebook: The Commonplace Book of Sir John Oglander Kt. of Nunwell, ed. F. Banford (1936).

Rushworth, John (ed.), *Historical Collections*, 8 vols. (2nd edn.; 1721–2).

Rymer, Thomas, *Foedera, Conventiones, Literae et Cujuscunque Generis Acta Publica*, 17 vols. (The Hague, 1761).

Select Cases of Trespass from the King's Courts, 1307–1399, ed. M. S. Arnold, 2 vols. (Selden Soc.; 1985–7).

Select Charters and Other Illustrations of English Constitutional History, ed. W. Stubbs (9th edn.; Oxford, 1913).

Select Pleas of the Forest, ed. G. J. Turner (Selden Soc., 13; 1899).

Sessions Rolls, 1581–1698, ed. W. J. Hardy (Hertford County Records, 1; Hertford, 1905).

Sidney Ironworks Accounts, 1541–1573, ed. D. W. Crossley (Camden Soc., 4th ser., 15; 1975).

Smyth of Nibley, John, *The Berkeley Manuscripts*, ed. Sir John Maclean, 3 vols. (Gloucester, 1883–5).

'Staffordshire Suits in the Court of Star Chamber, Temp. Henry VII and Henry VIII', ed. W. K. Boyd, in *Collections for a History of Staffordshire* (William Salt Arch. Soc., NS 1; Stafford, 1907).

'The State of England Anno Dom. 1600 by Thomas Wilson', ed. F. J. Fisher, in *Camden Miscellany XVI* (Camden Soc., 3rd ser., 52; 1936), 1–47.

Statutes of the Realm, 9 vols. (1810–22).

The Stonor Letters, ed. C. L. Kingsford (Camden Soc., 3rd ser., 30; 1919).

Stow, John, *Annales*, ed. Edmund Howes (1631).

Stuart Royal Proclamations, ed. J. F. Larkin and P. L. Hughes, 2 vols. (Oxford, 1973).

Tilley, M. P., *A Collection of the Proverbs in England in the Sixteenth and Seventeenth Centuries* (Ann Arbor, Mich., 1950; repr. 1966).

Tudor Royal Proclamations, ed. P. L. Hughes and J. F. Larkin, 3 vols. (New Haven, Conn., 1964–9).

'Two London Chronicles from the Collections of John Stow', ed. C. L. Kingsford, in *Camden Miscellany XII* (Camden Soc.; 1910), 1–57.

Walton, Isaak, *The Compleat Angler, 1653–1676*, ed. J. Bevan (Oxford, 1983).

[Weldon, Sir Anthony], 'The Court and Character of King James', in [Sir Walter Scott (ed.)], *Secret History of the Court of James the First*, 2 vols. (Edinburgh, 1811).

West Riding Sessions Records, ed. J. Lister, 2 vols. (Yorks. Arch. Soc., Rec. Ser., 3, 54; York, 1888, 1915).

White, Gilbert, *The Natural History of Selborne* (1789; repr. 1965).

The Works of Francis Osborn (9th edn.; 1689).

The Works of Gerard Winstanley, ed. G. H. Sabine (Ithaca, NY, 1941).

III. Printed Secondary Works

Archer, I. W., *The Pursuit of Stability: Social Relations in Elizabethan London* (Cambridge, 1991).

Atkyns, Sir Robert, *The Ancient and Present State of Gloucestershire* (1768).

Aylmer, G. E., *The King's Servants: The Civil Service of Charles I* (1961).

Barnes, T. G., *Somerset, 1625–40: A County's Government during the 'Personal Rule'* (Cambridge, Mass., 1961).

Bellamy, J. G., *Bastard Feudalism and the Law* (Portland, Ore., 1989).

Billacois, F., *The Duel: Its Rise and Fall in Early Modern France*, ed. and trans. Trista Selous (New Haven, Conn., 1990).

Birrell, J., 'Who Poached the King's Deer? A Study in Thirteenth Century Crime', *Midland History*, 7 (1982), 9–25.

Blackmore, H. L. *Hunting Weapons* (New York, 1972).

Blackstone, Sir William, *Commentaries on the Laws of England*, 4 vols. (1765–9; 4th edn., 177; repr. Chicago, 1979).

Blount, Thomas, *Fragmenta Antiquitatis: or Ancient Tenures of Land and Jocular Customs of Manors* (1845).

Brandon, P. F., 'Land, Technology and Water Management in the Tillingbourne Valley, Surrey, 1560–1760', *Southern History*, 6 (1984), 75–103.

Breight, C. C., 'Caressing the Great: Viscount Montague's Entertainment of Elizabeth at Cowdray, 1591', *Sussex Arch. Coll.*, 127 (1989), 147–66.

Brentnall, H. C., 'Venison Trespasses in the Reign of Henry VII', *Wilts. Arch. and Nat. Hist. Mag.*, 53 (1949), 191–212.

Brown, Cornelius, *Lives of Nottinghamshire Worthies* (1882).

Brown, K. M., *Bloodfeud in Scotland, 1573–1625: Violence, Justice and Politics in an Early Modern Society* (Edinburgh, 1986).

Burke, P., *Popular Culture in Early Modern Europe* (New York, 1978).

Burkert, W., *Homo Necans: The Anthropology of Ancient Greek Sacrificial Ritual and Myth*, trans. P. Bing (Berkeley, Calif., 1983).

Cantor, L. M., *The Changing English Countryside, 1400–1700* (1987).

—— and Moore, J. S., 'The Medieval Parks of the Earls of Stafford at Madeley', *North Staffs. Journ. of Field Studies*, 3 (1963), 37–58.

Chafin, William, *A Second Edition of the Anecdotes and History of Cranbourne Chase* (1818).

Chapman, D., and N., *Fallow Deer: Their History, Distribution and Biology* (Lavenham, Suffolk, 1975).

Christianson, P., 'Young John Selden and the Ancient Constitution, ca.1610–18', *Proceedings of the American Philosophical Society*, 128. 4 (1984), 271–315.

Christie, W. D., *A Life of Anthony Ashley Cooper, First Earl of Shaftesbury, 1621–1683*, 2 vols. (1871).

Clay, C. G. A., *Economic Expansion and Social Change, 1500–1700*, 2 vols. (Cambridge, 1984).

Cleere, H., and Crossley, D., *The Iron Industry of the Weald* (Leicester, 1985).

Cliffe, J. T., *The Yorkshire Gentry from the Reformation to the Civil War* (1969).

G[eorge] E[dward] C[ockayne], *The Complete Peerage*, ed. V. Gibbs, 13 vols. (new edn.; 1910–40).

Collin's Peerage of England, ed. Sir Egerton Brydges, 2 vols. (1812).

Colvin, H. M., Ransome, D. R., and Summerson, J. (eds.), *The History of the King's Works*, 6 vols. (1962–83).

Cooke, J. H., 'The Great Berkeley Lawsuit of the 15th and 16th Centuries', *Trans. Bristol and Glos., Arch. Soc.*, 3 (1878–9), 305–24.

Coward, B., *The Stanleys, Lords Stanley and Earls of Derby, 1385–1672: The Origins, Wealth and Power of a Landowning Family* (Chetham Soc., 3rd ser., 30; 1983).

Cox, J. C., *The Royal Forests of England* (1905).

Cummins, J., *The Hound and the Hawk: The Art of Medieval Hunting* (1988).

Dugdale, Sir William, *The Antiquities of Yorkshire*, 2 vols. (1730).

Ellis, W. S. *The Parks and Forests of Sussex* (Lewes, Sussex, 1885).

Erdeswick, Sampson, *A Survey of Staffordshire*, ed. T. Harwood (1844).

Fisher, W. R., *The Forest of Essex* (1887).

Fuller, Thomas, *The Church History of Britain*, 3 vols. (1655; 1873 edn.).

Gilbert, J. M., *Hunting and Hunting Reserves in Medieval Scotland* (Edinburgh, 1979).

Greenblatt, S., *Renaissance Self-Fashioning from More to Shakespeare* (Chicago, 1980).

Greswell, W. H. P., *The Forests and Deer Parks of the County of Somerset* (Taunton, 1905).

Grose, Francis, *Antiquarian Repertory*, 4 vols. (2nd edn.; 1807–9).

Guy, J., *Tudor England* (Oxford, 1990).

Hale, J. R., 'Sixteenth-Century Explanations of War and Violence', in *Renaissance War Studies* (1983), 335–58.

Hammersley, G., 'The Charcoal Iron Industry and its Fuel, 1540–1640', *Econ. Hist. Rev.*, NS 26 (1973), 593–613.

——, 'The Revival of the Forest Laws under Charles I', *History*, 45 (1960), 85–102.

Hanawalt, B. A., 'Men's Games, King's Deer: Poaching in Medieval England', *Journal of Medieval and Renaissance Studies*, 18. 2 (1988), 175–93.

Hands, R., *English Hawking and Hunting in the Boke of St Albans* (Oxford, 1975).

Hay, D., 'Poaching and the Game Laws on Cannock Chase', in D. Hay, P. Linebaugh, J. G. Rule, E. P. Thompson, and C. Winslow (eds.), *Albion's Fatal Tree*, (New York, 1975), 189–253.

Heal, F., *Hospitality in Early Modern England* (Oxford, 1990).

Hilton, R. H., 'The Origins of Robin Hood', in R. H. Hilton (ed.), *Peasants, Knights and Heretics: Studies in Medieval History* (Cambridge, 1976), 221–35.

Hoare, Sir Richard, *The History of Modern Wiltshire*, 5 vols. (1822–43).

Holdsworth, W. S., *A History of English Law*, 13 vols. (1922–52).

Holt, J. C., 'The Assizes of Henry II: The Texts', in D. A. Bullough and R. L. Storey (eds.), *The Study of Medieval Records: Essays in Honour of Kathleen Major* (Oxford, 1971), 85–106.

—— 'The Origins and Audience of the Ballads of Robin Hood', *P&P*, no. 18 (Nov. 1960), 89–110.

Horsfield, T. W., *The History, Antiquities and Topography of the County of Sussex*, 2 vols. (Lewes, Sussex, 1835).

The House of Commons, 1509–1558, ed. S. T. Bindoff, 3 vols. (1982).

The House of Commons, 1558–1603, ed. P. W. Hasler, 3 vols. (1981).

Howard, C. H. D., *Sir John Yorke of Nidderdale, 1565–1634* (1939).

Hoyle, R. W., 'The First Earl of Cumberland: A Reputation Reassessed', *Northern History*, 22 (1986), 63–94.

Hunnisett, R. F., *The Medieval Coroner* (Cambridge, 1961).

Hunter, Joseph, *South Yorkshire: The History and Topography of the Deanery of Doncaster*, 2 vols. (1828).

Hutchins, John, *The History and Antiquities of the County of Dorset*, ed. W. Shipp and J. W. Hodgson, 4 vols. (Westminster, 1861–70).

Ives, E. W., Knecht, R. J., and Scarisbrick, J. J. (eds.), *Wealth and Power in Tudor and Stuart England: Essays Presented to S. T. Bindoff* (1978).

James, M. E., 'English Politics and the Concept of Honour, 1485–1642', in *Society, Politics and Culture: Studies in Early Modern England* (Cambridge, 1986), 308–415.

—— *Family, Lineage and Civil Society: A Study of Society, Politics and Mentality in the Durham Region, 1500–1640* (Oxford, 1974).

Jorgenson, D. A., *Shakespeare's Military World* (Berkeley, Calif., 1956).

Keen, M., *Chivalry* (New Haven, Conn., 1984).

Keen, M., *The Outlaws of Medieval Legend* (rev. edn.; 1979).

—— 'Robin Hood: Peasant or Gentleman?' *P&P*, no. 19 (Apr. 1961), 7–15.

Kiernan, V. G., *The Duel in European History: Honour and the Reign of Aristocracy* (Oxford, 1988).

Kirby, C., and E., 'The Stuart Game Prerogative', *EHR* 46 (1931), 239–54.

Lower, M. A., 'The Trial and Execution of Thomas, Lord Dacre', *Sussex Arch. Coll.*, 19 (1867), 170–9.

MacCaffrey, W. T., 'Talbot and Stanhope: An Episode in Elizabethan Politics', *BIHR* 33 (May 1960), 73–85.

MacCulloch, D., *Suffolk and the Tudors: Politics and Religion in an English County, 1500–1600* (Oxford, 1986).

McIntosh, M. K., *Autonomy and Community: The Royal Manor of Havering, 1200–1500* (Cambridge, 1986).

Manning, R. B., 'Antiquarianism and the Seigneurial Reaction: Sir Robert and Sir Thomas Cotton and their Tenants', *Historical Research*, 63 (Oct. 1990), 277–88.

—— 'The Prosecution of Sir Michael Blount, Lieutenant of the Tower of London, 1595', *BIHR* 57 (1984), 216–24.

—— *Religion and Society in Elizabethan Sussex: A Study of the Enforcement of the Elizabethan Religious Settlement* (Leicester, 1969).

—— *Village Revolts: Social Protest and Popular Disturbances in England, 1509–1640* (Oxford, 1988).

—— 'Violence and Social Conflict in Mid-Tudor Rebellions', *Journal of British Studies*, 16 2 (spring 1977), 18–40.

Mayhew, G., *Tudor Rye* (Falmer, Sussex, 1987).

Munsche, P. B., *Gentlemen and Poachers: The English Game Laws, 1671–1831* (Cambridge, 1981).

Neale, J., *Queen Elizabeth I: A Biography* (1934; repr. New York, 1957).

A New Law Dictionary, comp. Giles Jacob (9th edn.; 1772).

Nichols, John, *The Progresses and Public Processions of Queen Elizabeth*, 3 vols. (1823; repr. New York, 1966).

—— *The Progresses of King James I*, 4 vols. (1828; repr. New York, 1967).

Nichols, M., *Investigating Gunpowder Plot* (Manchester, 1991).

O'Connor, W. R., 'Early Greek Land Warfare as Symbolic Expression', *P&P*, no. 119 (Apr. 1988), 3–29.

O'Conor, N. J., *Godes Peace and the Queenes: Vicissitudes of a House, 1539–1615* (Cambridge, Mass., 1934).

Ortega y Gasset, J., *Meditations on Hunting*, trans. H. B. Westcott (New York; 1972).

Petit-Dutaillis, C., *Studies and Notes Supplementary to Stubbs' Constitutional History*, trans. W. T. Waugh, 3 vols. (Manchester, 1914).

Pocock, J. G. A., *The Ancient Constitution and the Feudal Law: A Study of English Historical Thought in the Seventeenth Century* (2nd edn.; Cambridge, 1987).

Porter, J., 'A Forest in Transition: Bowland, 1500–1650', *Trans. Hist. Soc. Lancs. and Ches.*, 125 (1975), 40–60.

Prouty, C., and R., 'George Gascoigne, *The Noble Arte of Venerie*, and Queen Elizabeth at Kenilworth', in J. G. McManaway, G. E. Dawson, and E. E. Willoughby (eds.), (Washington, 1948), pp. 639–65.

Pugh, R. B., *Imprisonment in Medieval England* (Cambridge, 1970).

Rackham, O., *Ancient Woodland: Its History, Vegetation and Uses in England* (1980).
—— *Trees and Woodlands in the British Landscape* (1976).
Rawle, E. J., *Annals of the Ancient Royal Forest of Exmoor* (Taunton, 1893).
Savage, H. L., 'Hunting in the Middle Ages', *Speculum*, 8 (1933), 30–41.
Scott Thomson, G., *Life in a Noble Household, 1641–1700* (Ann Arbor, Mich., 1959).
Sharp, B., *In Contempt of All Authority: Rural Artisans and Riot in the West of England, 1586–1660* (Berkeley, Calif., 1980).
Sharpe, J. A., *Crime in Early Modern England, 1550–1700* (1984).
Shaw, R. C., *The Royal Forest of Lancaster* (Preston, Lancs., 1956).
Sheail, J., *Rabbits and their History* (Newton Abbot, Devon, 1971).
Shirley, E. P., *Some Account of English Deer Parks* (1867).
[Smart, T. W. W.], *A Chronicle of Cranborne, being an Account of the Ancient Town, Lordship and Chase of Cranborne* (1841).
Somerville, R., *History of the Duchy of Lancaster*, 2 vols. (1953, 1970).
Starkey, D., *The Reign of Henry VIII: Personalities and Politics* (New York, 1986).
Stone, L., *The Crisis of the Aristocracy, 1558–1641* (abridged edn., New York, 1967).
—— *Family and Fortune: Studies in Aristocratic Finance in the Sixteenth and Seventeenth Centuries* (Oxford, 1973).
Stroud's Judicial Dictionary, ed. J. S. James, 5 vols. (4th edn.; 1974).
Strutt, Joseph, *The Sports and Pastimes of the People of England*, ed. J. C. Cox (1903; repr. Detroit, 1968).
Summerson, J., 'The Building of Theobalds, 1564–1585', *Archaeologia*, 97 (1959), 107–26.
Tarde, G., *Penal Philosophy*, trans. R. Howell (Boston, 1912; repr. Montclair, NJ, 1968).
Thiébaux, M., 'The Medieval Chase', *Speculum*, 42 (Apr. 1967), 260–74.
—— *The Stag of Love: The Chase in Medieval Litarature* (Ithaca, NY, 1974).
Thomas, K., *Man and the Natural World: A History of the Modern Sensibility* (New York, 1983).
Thompson, E. P., *Whigs and Hunters: The Origin of the Black Act* (New York, 1975).
Tighe, R. R., and Davis, J. E., *Annals of Windsor*, 2 vols. (1858).
Tittensor, A. M., and R. M., 'The Rabbit Warren at West Dean near Chichester', *Sussex Arch. Coll.*, 123 (1985), 151–85.
Twemlow, F. R., *The Manor of Tyrley* (Collections for a History of Staffordshire, Staffs. Rec. Soc.; Stafford 1948).
Underdown, D., *Revel, Riot and Rebellion: Popular Politics and Culture in England, 1603–1660* (Oxford, 1985).
Victoria History of the Counties of England, ed. W. Page *et al.* (1900–).
Walker, T. E. C., 'The Chase of Hampton Court', *Surrey Arch. Coll.*, 62 (1965), 83–7.
West, M. 'Spenser's Art of War: Chivalric Allegory, Military Technology, and the Elizabethan Mock-Heroic Sensibility', *Renaissance Quarterly* 41. 4 (1988), 654–704.
Whitaker, T. D., *The History and Antiquities of the Deanery of Craven in the County of York*, ed. A. W. Morant (3rd edn.; Leeds, 1878).
White, S. D., *Sir Edward Coke and 'The Grievances of the Commonwealth', 1621–1628* (Chapel Hill, NC, 1979).

Williams, P., *The Council in the Marches of Wales under Elizabeth* (Cardiff, 1958).

Willson, D. H., *King James VI and I* (1963).

Wyndham, H. A., Lord Leconfield, *Petworth Manor in the Seventeenth Century* (1954).

—— *Sutton and Duncton Manors* (1956).

Yates, E. M., *A History of the Landscapes in the Parishes of South Harting and Rogate* (Chichester, 1972).

Youings, J., *Sixteenth-Century England* (Harmondsworth, Middx., 1984).

Young, C. R., *The Royal Forests of Medieval England* (Philadelphia, 1979).

IV. Unpublished Theses and Papers

Barnes, T. G., 'Fines in the High Court of Star Chamber, 1596–1641' (typescript in PRO Round Room).

Brandon, P. F., 'The Common Lands and Wastes of Sussex', Ph.D. thesis (London, 1963).

Spence, R. T., 'The Cliffords, Earls of Cumberland, 1579–1646: A Study of their Fortunes Based on their Household and Estate Accounts', Ph.D. thesis (London, 1959).

Index

Abbott, George, archbishop of Canterbury 204
Abergavenny, the Lords 127
abjuration 71
Act for 'Certainty of Forests' (1641) 208
Acton, Sir Robert 43
Aldbourne Chase 192–3
Alice Holt Forest 67, 162, 224
Alleyn, John 181–2
Amounderness Forest 41, 43
Ampthill, Honour of 150–1
Ancient Constitution 2, 58, 75, 82, 83, 84, 85, 93, 98, 107–8
animal baiting 27, 99, 203
Anne of Denmark, Queen 204
Arundel, Anne, dowager countess of 173
Arundel, Fitzalan earls of 127, 130
Arundel, Philip Howard, 1st earl of 129
Arundell of Wardour, Thomas, 1st Lord 54, 96, 101, 102, 104–5
Ascham, Roger 6
Ashdown Forest 114, 117, 121–2, 175
Assheton, Nicholas 15, 25, 203
assizes 68, 69, 74, 100, 187, 192
Aubrey, John 5, 15
Ayscough or Askew, Charles 219
Ayscough or Askew, Sir Henry 219

Bacon, Sir Francis 42, 151
Bainton, Sir Henry 149, 181, 193
Baker, Sir Thomas 175
Bampton, Hugh 178
Barlow, John 16
Barnwood or Bernewood Forest 67, 98
Barrington, Sir Francis 222–3
Barrington, Sir Thomas 222
Basilikon Doron 24
Baskerville, Thomas 184
bastard feudalism 3, 229–30
Batten, Richard 31, 149, 166
Beaumont, John 211
Bedford, Edward Russell, 3rd earl of 191
Bedford, William Russell, 5th earl of 13
Bellamy, J. G. 230
Berkeley, Anne, Lady 139–40
Berkeley, George, 12th Lord 165
Berkeley, Henry, 11th Lord 10, 12–13, 46, 48, 136–7, 138, 139, 140–1, 142–3, 145, 151, 154, 165, 168, 185, 188

Berkeley, Sir Henry 145–7, 186
Berkeley, Katherine, Lady 13, 139
Berkeley, Sir Maurice I 139–40, 145, 168, 181, 183
Berkeley, Sir Maurice II 147
Berkeley, Sir Richard 26
Berkeley, William, 6th Lord 137
Bettsworth, Peter 224
Black Act of 1723 15, 37, 234
Blackburn, forest of 112
Blackmore Forest 31, 165, 185, 205
Blackstone, Sir William 57, 75, 78, 93
Blount, Sir George 43, 50, 191
Blount, Mountjoy 143–4
Blount, Walter 43
Boke of St Albans 12
Bolton Chase 214
Boorde, Andrew 10, 11, 128
Bowland Forest 15–16, 26, 31, 32, 67, 90, 111–12, 122, 147–8, 193
Brackton, Henry de 75, 76
Braden Forest 89, 163
Bradshaw, Henry 86
Bramston, Sir John 15
Brerton, Sir William 149
Breton, Nicholas 18
Bridewell Palace 199
Bright, Thomas 21–2, 42
Bromley, Sir Edmund 94
Bromley, Sir Henry 44
Browne, Henry 201
Browne, Sir Humphrey 78
Burdets, Thomas 48
Burkert, Walter 36–7
Burleigh, Sir William Cecil, Lord 201–5
Burton, John 97–8
Butler, Samuel 17
Byron, Sir John 50, 93–5

Calton, Sir Francis 176–7
Calton, Josias 177–8
Caltrops 25
Calverly, family of 173–4
Calvert, John 147–8
Canetti, Elias 36
Cannock Chase or Forest 25, 47, 81, 143
Capel, Sir Arthur 173
Capel, Sir Gamaliel 73
Capon, Sir Robert 14

Carew, Sir John 26
Caryll, Sir Edward 130–1
Castelhaven, James Touchet, 3rd earl of 24
Castle Rising Chase 173
Cavendish, Sir Charles 50, 95
Cavendish, William, Lord 51, 153, 175, 188, 191
Chafin, Richard 96–7
Chafin, William 15, 37, 39, 181
Chamber, Richard 10, 72
Chamberlain, John 202–3
Chandos, Gray Brydges, 5th Lord 212
Charles I, King 1, 10, 15, 65, 66, 83, 92, 101, 106, 108, 201–1, 194, 197, 207–9, 229, 233
Charles II, King 24
Charter of the Forest 58–9, 72, 75, 83, 84, 87, 92–3, 100, 107–8
'Chevy Chase' 49
Chippenham Forest 149
   see also Pewsham Forest
Cholmeley, Lady 166
Cholmeley of Brandsby, Richard 10–11, 52, 89, 193
Cholmley of Roxby and Whitby, Sir Hugh 16, 221, 226, 227
Cholmley of Roxby and Whitby, Sir Henry 227
Cholmley of Roxby and Whitby, Margaret 227
Cholmley of Roxby and Whitby, Sir Richard I 122, 226–7
Cholmley of Roxby and Whitby, Sir Richard II 227–9
Chute Forest 67
Clapham, George 157–8, 179
Clarendon, Edward Hyde, 1st earl of 106, 120–1, 187–8
Clarendon, forest and royal park of 30, 174, 177
Cleland, James 7, 24
clergymen 177–8
Clifton, Gervase, Lord 180
Cockayne, Sir Thomas 6, 7
Coke, Sir Edward 75, 77–8, 83, 84, 85, 86, 90, 107–8, 146, 166, 177
Coke, Roger 201
Colt, Sir Henry 221
Colt, Sir Thomas 221
commercial poaching 11, 20, 70, 89, 103, 135, 136, 151–2, 158, 163–8
common wastes 58, 110–11, 114, 116, 130, 152–4, 207
Compton, Henry, Lord 43, 203, 212
Corse Lawn Chase 46, 151
Council in the Marches of Wales 142, 152
Country Contentments 12

Coventry, Sir Thomas 173
Cranbourne Chase 61, 100–8
Craven 52, 179, 213–17
Croft, Sir Herbert 184
Croft, Sir James 210
Cromwell, Thomas 80, 149, 199
Culpeper, Sir Alexander I 174
Culpeper, Sir Alexander II 174–5
Culpeper, Nicholas 175
Cumberland, Francis Clifford, 4th earl of 217, 229
Cumberland, George Clifford, 3rd earl of 164, 214, 215, 229
Cumberland, Henry Clifford, 2nd earl of 157–9, 179, 213, 229
Cumberland, Henry de Clifford, Lord Clifford, 1st earl of 52, 213, 214, 229
Cyvile and Uncyvile Life 197

Dacre of the South, Thomas Fiennes, 9th Lord 16, 79
Danby, Christopher 157
Darrell, family of 14–15
Darrell, Sir Edward 15
Darrell, William 15
Davies, Richard 183
Dean, forest of 67
deer:
   fallow 23, 109, 112, 117, 150, 156, 214
   red 23, 99–100, 109, 112, 117, 125, 150, 214
   roe 23
deer-hunting culture 3, 4–17, 33, 35, 55, 169–70, 171–2, 191–2, 194–5, 225–31, 234–6
deer-park tradition 123–4
Denmark, king of 203
Derby, Edward Stanley, earl of 211
Derby, Stanley earls of 32–2, 112
Derby, William Stanley, earl of 211
Devonshire, William Cavendish, 2nd earl of 42
d'Aubigny, Esmé Stuart, Lord 76
D'Ewes, Sir Simonds 207
disafforestation 113
disparking 110, 115, 126–7, 223
Dormer, Sir John 98
Dorset, Richard Sackville, 2nd earl of 131
Dorset, Thomas Gray, 2nd marquis of 190, 211
Dorset, Thomas Sackville, Lord Buckhurst, 1st earl of 121, 127
dovecotes 9, 76, 133
Downton (also known as) Earldom Chase 176
duelling 4, 5–6, 14, 38, 43, 44, 94–5, 228, 233

Duffield Frith 14
Dymock, Sir Edward 218–19
Dymock, Nicholas 219
Dymock, Talboys 218–19

Edward II, King 14
Edward III, King 14, 63
Edward IV, King 48
Egerton Richard 173–4, 190
Egerton, Sir Rowland 166
Elizabeth I, Queen 3, 8, 9, 27, 29, 30, 31–2, 33, 40, 48–9, 55, 64, 87, 88, 124, 136–7, 143, 200–1, 202, 205
Eltham Palace 199
Elyot, Sir Thomas 6, 7
Enfield Chase 19, 91, 113, 167, 178, 200, 206
English Courtier and Country-gentleman 18
environmental degradation 111, 116–16, 121, 129, 130
Erasmus of Rotterdam 39
Essex, forest of 67, 92–3
Essex, Robert Devereux, 2nd earl of 38, 184, 233
Essex, Robert Devereux, 3rd earl of 8
Eure, Ralph, 3rd Lord 228–9
Eure, Sir William 229
Eure, William 228–9
Exchequer Chamber, Court of 94, 100, 102, 104–5, 108, 137, 138
Exmoor Forest 26, 99–100

Faerie Queene 37
Fairfax, Sir Thomas 215
falconry 7, 12–13, 16, 18, 79, 177, 184–5, 199
Fauconberg, Sir John de 14
Feckenham Forest 28, 44–5
Ferrers, Walter Devereux, Lord 47, 143
festivals, popular 99, 103, 138, 153, 189, 218–20
Fiennes, Sir Henry 25, 219–20
Finch, Sir John 92
Fisher, W. R. 86
fishponds 110, 115, 131–3, 163, 188
Fleetwood of Calwich, William 53–4
Flower, John 225
Foljambe, Godrey I 46, 144
Foljambe, Godrey II 144
Folyot, Sir John 159
forest courts 66–7, 77, 89, 90, 91–3, 94, 98, 106, 156, 208–9, 217
forest law 58, 59, 62–3, 66, 77, 83, 87, 92–3, 116–17
Fortescue, Sir John 88, 89
Foster, Dame Isabel 166

Foulloux, Jacques du 201
Foxe, Sir Edward 43–4
French Revolution 17, 234–5
Frescheville, Sir Peter 46, 144
Frescheville, Peter 144
funerals, Catholic 225
Fyneux, Sir John 77

Galtres Forest 89, 161
Game Act of 1389–90 57, 61
Game Act of 1485 2, 63–4, 69, 70, 77, 219, 233
Game Acts of 1539–40 64, 79, 163 n.
Game Act of 1549–50 64
Game Act of 1580–1 65
Game Act of 1603 60, 85, 163 n., 165, 169
Game Act of 1605 60
Game Act of 1719 234
gamekeepers' warrants 66, 235
Game Laws 2, 4–5, 38, 57–82, 134, 148, 163, 169, 171, 188, 194, 197, 208, 209, 230, 231, 233, 234–5
Garling, Thomas 172–3
Gascoigne, George 40, 200
Gatewood, Stephen 220
Gawen, Katherine 102, 104, 224–5
Gawen, Thomas 102, 104
general huntings 2, 48, 144, 153, 189, 215, 219–21
Gerard John, S. J. 12
Gerard, Thomas, 1st Lord 212–13
Germayne, Sir Ambrose 210
Gifford, Sir Richard 31, 159
Gillingham Forest 97, 180, 183
Goddard, Vincent 192
Goring, Sir Henry 129, 223–4
Greenwich Palace 199
Gresley, Thomas 14
Greville, Sir Fulke 38, 44, 91, 105, 206–7
Grey of Wilton, Arthur, Lord 88, 89
Grey, Lord Leonard 6
Groveley Forest 174

Hale, Sir Matthew 77
Hampton Court Chase 90–1, 120, 200
Hampton Court Palace 165, 199
Harington, Sir John 196, 203, 231
Harrington of Exton, John, Lord 98
Harrison, William 79
Hastings of Braunston, Sir Henry 41–2
Hastings of Woodlands, Henry 13–14
Hatfield Chase, Yorks 42, 149–50, 161
Hatfield Forest, Essex 91–2, 179, 221–3
Hatfield Palace 200, 205
Havering, royal manor of 29, 167, 173, 176–7
Henry III, King 87, 92

Henry V, King 63
Henry VII, King 27, 60, 63, 112, 198
Henry VIII, King 22, 24, 55, 64, 78, 90–1, 111, 124, 125, 189, 198–200
Henry, prince of Wales 26
Herbert of Cherbury, Edward, 1st Lord 16
Hereford, bishop of 212
Hertford, Edward Seymour, earl of 47
High Peak Forest 23, 153–4, 201
Hoby, Lady Margaret 228–9
Hoby, Sir Thomas Posthumus 122, 226, 228–9
Holland, Henry Rich, earl of 92
Holt, J. C. 20, 84
Holte, Sir Thomas 188, 191
hospitality 175, 197, 222, 228–9, 235
Houghton, Sir Richard 147
Howard of Effingham, Anne, dowager lady 189
Hunsdon, Robert Carey, Lord 49
Hunter, Joseph 19–20
hunting bands 17, 25, 36, 37, 40, 42, 160–3
hunting nets or toils 25, 104, 189, 192
hunting, royal 3, 5–6, 9, 11, 124–5, 196–209
hunting seasons 23
Huntingdon, Henry Hastings, 3rd earl of 215
Hutton, Matthew, archbishop of York 202, 205

imparking 110, 111, 124, 126, 205–7, 208
impressment 226, 231
imprisonment 71, 152, 152 n., 165, 181, 192, 193, 219, 220
iron industry 113–5, 126, 130, 142, 142 n., 188
Isham, John 166

James I, King 1, 5, 7, 9, 23, 25, 30, 38, 56, 60, 64, 65–6, 67, 68, 75, 85, 88, 89, 101–2, 106, 108, 112, 148, 162, 166, 194, 196–7, 201–7, 208, 220, 225, 229, 230, 231, 233
James, Mervyn 232
juries, trial 68, 70, 74, 92, 138, 140, 222, 223, 224

Kenilworth Castle 124–5, 138, 200–1
King's Bench, Court of 79, 80, 106, 140, 146, 155
Kingswell, Richard I 178–9
Kingswell, Richard II 178–9
Kingswood Chase 26, 71, 140
Kinnersley, Anthony 135, 193
Kirkby Malzeard, lordship of 52

Lancaster, duchy of 15, 63, 112, 113, 121, 184, 191
Lancaster, Duchy Chamber of 66, 90, 112, 147–8, 193, 197, 204, 205–6, 227
Lancaster, Thomas, earl of 14
Langstrothdale Chase 214–15
Leeke, Francis 144–5, 165, 175–6
legal fees 140
Leicester, Robert Dudley, earl of 48, 69, 124, 136–8, 139, 168, 201
Leigh, Sir Francis 204
Leigh, Sir Peter 45
Leighfield Forest 98
libel 146, 174, 177, 211, 218–20, 225, 229
Lincoln, Henry Fiennes de Clinton, 2nd earl of 218–20, 229
Lincoln, Theophilus Fiennes Clinton, 4th earl of 220, 229
Lincoln, Thomas Fiennes Clinton, 3rd earl of 220
Lisle, Sir Robert Sidney, Viscount 142
Lisle, Thomas Talbot, Viscount 137
Lovell gang 162–3
Lower, Thomas 162
Lucas, Thomas 186–7
Lucy, Sir Thomas 182–3
Lumley, John, 1st Lord 9, 30
Lunsford, Sir Thomas 208

Macclesfield Forest 45
Magna Carta 58, 83, 84, 87, 89, 92, 100, 108
Maison Rustique 25, 27
Malvern Chase 29, 74, 163, 192
Mansell, Sir Robert 184
Manwood, John 84, 88
Markham, Gervase 12, 23, 27, 62
Marven, Sir Edmund 130
Mary I, Queen 87, 137
Mashamshire Chase 157
Matthew, Tobie, archbishop of York 174
Maximillian, Emperor 198
May-games 22, 218–9
Merry Devil of Edmonton 19
Michaelwood Chase 183, 139, 140, 141, 142, 155, 188
Middleton, Edward 215
Midmore, Ellis 133
mills, water 115, 132, 139
Mohun, Sir Reynold 161–2
Molyneux, Richard 211
Montague, Anthony Brown, 1st Viscount 121, 201, 223
Montague, Anthony Maria Brown, 2nd Viscount 68, 121, 223–4
Monteagle, William Stanley, 3rd Lord 46–7, 97, 179, 221–3
Moody, Sir Henry 149

More, Sir John 41
More, Sir Thomas 41
Morley, Edward Parker, 12th Lord 91–2, 179, 221–2
Morley and Monteagle, William Parker, Lord 157
Moryson, Fynes 109, 110
Muggeridge, family of 174
Myerscough Forest 19, 30, 32, 43

Naunton, Sir Robert 38
Needwood Forest 9, 18–19, 31, 32, 112, 113, 184
Neroche Forest 74, 154, 159, 178, 191
New Forest 9, 67, 98, 161
New Hall Palace 199
Noble Arte of Venerie or Hunting 40, 200
Nonsuch Palace 9, 10, 30, 120
Norden, John 29, 132
Norfolk, Thomas Howard, 2nd duke of 10, 72
Norfolk, Thomas Howard, 4th duke of 48, 136, 137, 139
Norris, Francis, Lord 31
Norris, Henry, Lord 220
Norris, William 220
North, Dudley, 3rd Lord 212
Northumberland, Henry Percy, 6th earl of 213
Northumberland, Henry Percy, 9th earl of 114–15
Northumberland, John Dudley, duke of 137
Norton, Sir Richard 164
Nottingham, Charles Howard, 1st earl of 98, 149
Noy, William 80–1

Oatlands, Royal Palace of 24, 199
Oglander, Sir John 9, 203
Osborn, Francis 16, 76, 201

Pakington, Sir John 131
Pareto, Vilfredo 39
Peacham, Henry 6
Pelham, Nicholas 16
Pembroke, Philip Herbert, 4th earl of 17
Pembroke, William Herbert, 1st earl of 145, 180
Pembroke, William Herbert, 3rd earl of 22, 30, 42, 101, 104–5, 145–7, 176
Perrot, Sir John 38
Petit-Dutailis, Charles 35, 84
Petworth, Sussex 114–15, 129
Pewsham Forest 31, 166
Pickering Forest 14, 122, 226, 227–8
Pitt, Sir Edward 43–4
Pitt, William 183–4

poaching gangs 2, 20, 25, 42, 46, 47, 53, 103–4, 136, 139–40, 141, 142, 150–1, 156, 157, 159, 160–3, 165, 168–70, 172, 173, 174, 175–6, 179–80, 181, 183–4, 185, 188–9, 190, 209–20, 221, 223–4, 225, 234–6
poaching wars 2–3, 46, 50, 52, 53, 55, 93–5, 102–6, 139, 141–2, 145–7, 153–4, 159, 168–70, 197, 212–21, 229–30
Pollard, Sir Hugh 26
Pollard, Lewis 79
Popham, Sir John 145
Poyntz, Sir John 132
Poyntz, Sir Nicholas 71, 139–40
prerogative, royal game 1, 75, 82, 88, 107, 197, 208, 233
Procter, Sir Stephen 216
puritanism 222, 228–9

quarter sessions, courts of 67–8, 69, 70, 80, 140, 168, 211, 224

rabbit warrens 9, 30, 59, 70, 109, 110, 115, 124, 128–31, 153, 154–5, 163, 165, 181, 192, 193
Raleigh, Sir Carew 147, 183
rebellions:
    German Peasants' War of 1524–5 17
    Great Revolt of 1381 17, 230
    Gunpowder Plot (1605) 49 n.
    Mid-Tudor (1549) 230
    Oxfordshire (1549) 210
    Pilgrimage of Grace (1536–7) 64, 213
    Suffolk Rising (1569) 210, 230
    Wyatt's 41
recusants, Catholic 89, 102, 105, 130, 157, 174–5, 209, 216, 220–5, 227, 229
Rich, Robert, 3rd Lord 91–2, 221
Richmond, Henry Fitzroy, duke of 80, 201
Rigmaiden, John 193
riots, anti-enclosure 207–8, 235
Robin Hood 15, 17, 20–2, 42, 62–3, 140, 168, 206, 235
Rockingham Forest 28, 67, 86, 89, 98–9
Rowe, Nicholas 182
Russell, George 150
Rutland, Francis Manners, 6th earl of 89, 94

Sackville, family of 121
Sackville, Sir Richard 121, 127
St John of Bletsoe, Oliver, Lord 204
St Leonard's Forest 129
St Lo, William 41
Salcey Forest 67, 87
Salisbury, Sir Robert Cecil, 1st earl of 76, 135, 205–6

Salisbury, William Cecil, 2nd earl of 91, 100–7, 162, 208
Savage, family of 28
Savage, Sir John 28
Savage, John 155
Savernake Forest 14, 47
Saxe-Weimar, duke of 25
Saxton, Christopher 125
scandalum magnatum 211, 218–20, 221
Scroop and Carnebrook Chases 216
Selwood Forest 95–6, 145–7, 165, 181, 183
Selwyn, John 8
seminary priests 12, 225
servants 12, 17, 18, 64, 140, 141–2, 145–7, 150, 151, 158, 161, 167, 171, 176, 178–82, 187, 192, 194, 216–17, 221, 222, 223, 226–9
Shaftesbury, Anthony Ashley Cooper, 1st earl of 13–14
Shakespeare, William 38, 182–3
Shaw, Philip 157, 217
Sherburne, Sir Richard 32–3, 147–8, 179, 193
Sherwood Forest 23, 44, 50, 67, 93–5, 156
Short Treatise on Hunting 7
Shotover Forest 31
Shrewsbury, Francis Talbot, 5th earl of 9
Shrewsbury, George Talbot, 6th earl of 144
Shrewsbury, Gilbert Talbot, 7th earl of 50, 67, 153–4, 210
Sidney, Sir Philip 16, 38, 139
skimmington 2, 157, 218–21, 228–9
Skipton, Barden and Littondale, chases of 158, 215, 216
Skipwith, William 219
Smith of Hill Hall, Sir William the elder 74, 173
Smith of Hill Hall, Sir William the younger 74, 173
Smyth of Nibley, John 10, 12, 46, 48, 138, 139, 141, 142, 155, 168–9, 185
Smyth, Sir John 37
Southwell, Robert, S. J. 12
Stafford, Robert, *alias* 'Friar Tuck' 21, 64
Stainmore Chase 164
Standish, Sir Thomas 219
Stanhope, Philip, Lord 31, 94–5, 155–6, 174
Stanhope, Sir Thomas, Lord 50
Star Chamber, Court of 1–2, 20, 39, 41, 45–6, 56, 58, 59, 61, 65, 66, 68, 69, 70, 73, 77–8, 81–2, 88, 98, 102, 108, 140, 149, 151, 156, 159, 168–9, 174, 175, 184, 185, 192, 194, 196, 197, 208, 209, 211, 212, 217, 218–20, 221, 224, 228, 229, 230, 231, 233
Stillyon, Thomas 175
Stone, Lawrence 209, 230

Stow, John 110
Sussex, Thomas Radcliffe, 3rd earl of 101
Swaine, John 101, 102
Swift, Sir Robert 150
Sydenham, Humphrey 99–100
Sydenham, Roger 99–100
Symmes, Jenkin or John 146–7, 183

Talbot, Sir John 51, 190
Talbot of Bashall, John 52
Talbot-Stanhope feud 50, 95, 144, 175–6
Tarde, Gabriel 232, 233
Tennant, James 215
Tennant, John 215, 217
Theobalds Park, enlargement of 205–7, 208
Theobalds, Royal Palace of 25, 196, 203
Thompson, E. P. 234
Thorneywood Chase 31, 50, 93–5, 155–6
Throckmorton, Sir Clement 166
Throckmorton, Sir Thomas 46, 137, 140, 141–2, 151, 155, 168
Throckmorton, Sir William 151–2
Thynne, Sir John 95–6
Tilgate Forest 129
Tracy, Sir Richard 151–2
trained bands 99, 146
Trenance, Lyttleton 161–2
Tresham, Sir Thomas 186
Tunstall, Cuthbert, bishop of Durham 148
Turville, Sir William 211
Turville, William 190
Twici, William 12
Tyldesley, Thurston 30, 32
Tyrell, George 124
Tyrringham, Sir Thomas 204
Tyrwhitt, William 154

Uglebeard Chase 158
Uvedale, Sir William 143–4

Valor Ecclesiasticus 199
Venerie, La 201
venison 5, 10, 11, 20, 42, 62, 103, 110, 128, 133–4, 135, 150, 153, 158, 160, 161, 163–8, 169, 183, 187–8, 210, 232

Wakefield, manor of 43
Waller, Sir Thomas 19, 175
Waltham Forest 29, 78, 88–9, 108, 167, 173, 176–7, 182
Walton, Isaak 27
Warburton, Sir Peter 76
Warwick, Ambrose Dudley, earl of 49, 69, 137, 168
Warwick, Anne, countess of 141, 168
Warwick Castle 166

Index

Warwick, Robert Rich, earl of 92
Wastnes, George 153, 186
Weald 2, 64, 110–11, 113–16, 201
Weekes, Francis 180–1
Wentworth, Peter 86–7
Whaddon Chase 88, 90, 124
Whichwood Forest 67, 205
White, Gilbert 37, 61
Whittlewood Forest 86, 87
William the Conqueror, King 9
William Rufus 9
Williams, John, bishop of Lincoln 204
Williams, Sir John, Lord 86, 210
Wilson, Arthur 8, 9
Windsor Castle 9, 167, 208–9
Windsor Forest 23, 29, 67, 91, 117–20,
    160–1, 164, 167, 201, 205, 208–9
Winstanley, Gerard 57, 61
Wolmer Forest 67, 178–9, 224

Wolsey, Thomas, Cardinal 198, 199
Woodstock Palace 202
Wortley, Sir Francis, bt. 67–8, 124, 159
Wroughton, family of 14–15
Württemberg, duke of 9
Wybarre or Wibergh, Geoffrey 178, 217
Wyre Forest 52, 191
Wyresdale and Quernmore, forest of 31, 51,
    97, 112, 147–8, 190, 193

Yardley, Edward 53, 176
Yelverton, Sir Henry 75
York, Edward Plantagenet, 2nd duke of 11
York, Sir John 157, 215–7
York, Margaret 177
York Palace or Whitehall 199
Young, Charles 215–6

Zouch, Edward, Lord 204